ORIGINES LITURGICÆ,

OR

ANTIQUITIES

OF

THE ENGLISH RITUAL,

AND

A DISSERTATION ON PRIMITIVE LITURGIES

BY

THE REV. WILLIAM PALMER, M A.

OF WORCESTER COLLEGE, OXFORD

IN TWO VOLUMES.

VOL. I.

THIRD EDITION.

WIPF & STOCK · Eugene, Oregon

Wipf and Stock Publishers
199 W 8th Ave, Suite 3
Eugene, OR 97401

Origines Liturgicae, Or Antiquities
of the English Ritual, Volume 1, Third Edition
And a Dissertation on Primitive Liturgies
By Palmer, William
Softcover ISBN-13: 978-1-6667-3317-4
Hardcover ISBN-13: 978-1-6667-2758-6
eBook ISBN-13: 978-1-6667-2759-3
Publication date 7/29/2021
Previously published by Oxford University Press, 1839

This edition is a scanned facsimile of
the original edition published in 1839.

PREFACE

TO THE FIRST EDITION.

THE Ritual Formularies of the English Church have been illustrated by so many learned Divines, that the reader may justly claim some explanation of the necessity and the nature of the present work.

The valuable writings of LESTRANGE, NICHOLLS, WHEATLY, SHEPHERD, and Bishop MANT, contain excellent commentaries both practical and doctrinal, on the rubrics and prayers of our Ritual; and perhaps scarcely any thing can be added to the information which they have conveyed on these points. But the field of historical and antiquarian discussion is more open. In itself more extensive, it has perhaps been less explored; and its fertility is so great, that had it been consistent with my plan, there would have been no difficulty in very considerably extending these volumes.

Such topics are in fact connected with much that is important; for he who is acquainted with the principles and practice of early times, will best comprehend the purport of our rites. The English Prayer Book was not composed in a few years, nor by a few men: it has descended to us with the improvements and the approbation of many centuries: and they who truly feel the calm and sublime elevation of our hymns and prayers, participate in the spirit of primitive devotion. The great majority of our formularies are actually translated from Latin and Greek rituals, which have been used for at least fourteen or fifteen hundred years in the Christian church: and there is scarcely a portion of our Prayer Book which cannot in some way be traced to ancient offices.

Most of our ritualists have noticed these circumstances; but with the exception of NICHOLLS, who printed the originals of many of our collects from the Sacramentary of Gregory, no one, I believe, has yet published any part of the English Offices in their Original languages.

My own attention was called to this fact, when, in the course of preparation for holy orders, it became my duty to study our Ritual: and while I was endeavouring to ascertain the precise meaning of some expressions, I experienced such difficulties in referring to the originals, as induced me to seek some commentary resembling that which the reader has now before him, and subsequently to resolve, as far as was in my power, to supply the deficiency.

The propriety of such an undertaking does not, I am happy to say, rest on my opinion alone. The late Bishop of Oxford, (DR. LLOYD,) whose authority should have weight on such a subject, was so convinced of its expediency, that he was himself collecting materials for the purpose, which he intended to publish so soon as his avocations should permit[a]. His Lordship's collections were entered on the margin of a folio Prayer Book, in the library given by Dr. Allestree for the use of the Regius Professor of Divinity in this University; and having been kindly permitted to compare them with the results of my own investigations, I have derived from them several valuable observations, which are acknowledged in their proper places.

There is another and still larger body of collections entered on the margin of a Prayer Book in the Bodleian Library, and apparently designed for the same purpose, by Doctor EDWARD BERNARD, Savilian Professor of Astronomy in this University, in the reign of king Charles the Second. I have also very frequently consulted a manuscript Sacramentary of the Anglo-Saxon Church, written about the ninth or tenth century, and given by Leofric bishop of Exeter to his cathedral church before the Norman Conquest. This interesting volume is likewise in the Bodleian Library.

It has been my object, in the following work, to trace the origin and antiquity of our Services, especially of those which have been insufficiently noticed by others; to explain ancient rites and ancient terms; to record the originals of our

[a] I have been informed that his Lordship delivered several private lectures, entirely on this topic, to a class of theological students in this University.

prayers; and to point out the best sources of information on ritual subjects. When I have been unable to ascertain their originals, I have occasionally compared our formularies with those which have been used on similar occasions in other churches. Some of our Offices have been so fully explained and commented on by preceding ritualists, that little ground has been left unoccupied ; and this must in some degree account for the brevity of my remarks on these, compared with what I have said of other Services. The holy Communion has particularly engaged my attention, because it is here that we are to look more especially for analogy with the ancient liturgies.

In the course of these remarks it has been necessary to refer so very frequently to the primitive liturgies, which bear the names of MARK, JAMES, BASIL, CHRYSOSTOM, and other Fathers, that I have been induced to place a Dissertation on Primitive Liturgies at the beginning of the present volume, which may be useful in explaining the authority of documents subsequently referred to, and may contribute to turn the attention of others to these most important and venerable remains.

In conclusion, it becomes my duty gratefully to acknowledge the liberality with which the Delegates of the Oxford University Press have undertaken to publish this work.

CONTENTS

OF

VOL. I.

DISSERTATION ON PRIMITIVE LITURGIES.

INTRODUCTION .... P. 3
Sect. I. LITURGY OF ANTIOCH 15
Sect. II. LITURGY OF CÆSAREA 45
Sect. III. LITURGY OF CONSTANTINOPLE 73
Sect. IV. LITURGY OF ALEXANDRIA 82
Sect. V. LITURGY OF EPHESUS 106
Sect. VI. LITURGY OF ROME 111
Sect. VII. LITURGY OF MILAN 125
Sect. VIII. LITURGY OF AFRICA 134
Sect. IX. LITURGY OF GAUL 143
Sect. X. LITURGY OF SPAIN 166
Sect. XI. LITURGY OF BRITAIN AND IRELAND 176
Additions.—LITURGY OF ARMENIA 190
NESTORIAN LITURGIES 194
INDIAN LITURGIES 196

ANTIQUITIES OF THE ENGLISH RITUAL

Chapter I. Part I. MORNING PRAYER 201
Chapter I. Part II. EVENING PRAYER 252
Chapter II. LITANY 264
Chapter III. COLLECTS, EPISTLES, AND GOSPELS ... 308

A

DISSERTATION

ON

PRIMITIVE LITURGIES.

A

DISSERTATION

ON

PRIMITIVE LITURGIES.

INTRODUCTION.

IN treating of the liturgy, I would be understood to use the term in that restricted sense which it generally bears in the writings of the ancients; as denoting the service used in the celebration of the eucharist. In the eastern churches, that service (though sometimes known by other appellations) has long borne the title of the "divine" or "mystical" liturgy. In the west, the eucharistic office has most commonly been called "missa;" but the term liturgy has also been frequently applied to it.

The study of ancient liturgies is one, which from various circumstances has made but slow progress. It can hardly be said to have commenced until the sixteenth century, when the liturgies of Basil, Chrysostom, James, Mark, and others of eastern origin, were first printed. Before this time, though some writers commented on the offices of their own churches, they were unable to compare various liturgies together, and thence to elicit the truth. At that period, none of the learned men of Europe, even though profoundly versed in general theology, and in the writings of the Fathers, were able to give any satisfactory information relative to these ancient remains, or to form any just or distinct notion of their merits. It was not until the middle of the seventeenth century, that light was first thrown on the Greek liturgies by Goar, in his edition of the Euchologium; and although that work is far from perfect, no one has since enlarged the sphere of its information, or corrected its errors. In this century also, Thomasius published the ancient Roman Sacramentary of Gelasius. Pamelius in the preceding century had edited that of Gregory, which was now illustrated with learned notes by Menard. In the eighteenth century the Roman Sacramentary of Leo was discovered. And not long before, the writings of Gavanti, Bona, Le Brun, Martene, and Muratori gave much information relative to the Roman liturgy. Towards the end of the seventeenth century, the ancient Gallican liturgy was rescued from oblivion by Bona, Thomasius, and Mabillon. In the early part of the eighteenth, Renaudot first gave to the world much satisfactory information relative to the liturgies of Alexandria and Antioch, which had been hitherto almost entirely unknown. Thus it was not until the eighteenth century, that the materials of knowledge were supplied in such abundance, as to enable the student of liturgies to take an extended and unprejudiced view of his subject.

Combined with these circumstances were others, which have much impeded the study of liturgies, and have tended to excite unreasonable prejudices against them. The learned writers of the sixteenth and seventeenth centuries, who in their own provinces of literature remain unequalled, were yet generally destitute of that sort of knowledge which would have constituted them sufficient judges of the merit of liturgies; and hence their opinions were most contradictory on this subject. This circumstance alone was sufficient to impede the study of liturgies; for when the most learned men were divided on the merits of those remains, it seemed an endless labour to investigate the truth.

The controversies of the time also involved this subject in obscurity. Some persons deemed their doctrines supported by the ancient liturgies, and hence thought themselves obliged to contend for their genuineness, and the integrity of their text. Others proved that they contained many things more recent than the time of their reputed authors, remarked with triumph the variations of different manuscripts, and concluded that they were perfectly uncertain, if not altogether spurious. From these causes an opinion prevails amongst a large portion of the learned world, that the ancient liturgies are of little or no value. The following pages are intended to shew, that there are some means of ascertaining the substance and order of Christian liturgies during the primitive ages; and to facilitate the study of those venerable monuments, by directing the reader's attention to such remains, and in such a channel, as seem best calculated to merit his notice, and reward his labours.

It seems to have been often assumed by the learned, that there was originally some one apostolic form of liturgy in the Christian church, to which all the monuments of ancient liturgies, and the notices which the Fathers supply, might be reduced. Were this hypothesis supported by facts, it would be very valuable. But the truth is, there are several different forms of liturgy now in existence, which, as far as we can perceive, have been different from each other from the most remote period. And with regard to the apparent propriety of the Apostles' instituting one liturgy throughout the world, it may be observed, that it is quite sufficient to suppose all liturgies originally agreed, in containing every thing that was necessary for the due celebration of the eucharist; but that they adopted exactly the same order, or received every where the same rites, is a supposition equally unnecessary and groundless.

I have not therefore attempted to reduce all the liturgies, and notices of the Fathers, to one common original; but have rather sought for the original liturgies by a reference to acknowledged facts. The following is the course which I have pursued, in endeavouring to ascertain the nature of the primitive liturgies. Considering that the primitive church was divided into great portions, known by the appellations of Patriarchates, Exarchates[a], or

---

[a] As I shall frequently have occasion to make use of these terms in the following work, I will now briefly explain them to the reader. The primitive church was ruled by bishops, metropolitans, and patriarchs. The bishop of the chief city in each province was entitled metropolitan or primate, and afterwards archbishop, and had a certain jurisdiction over the bishops of that province. He ordained them—received appeals from them in ecclesiastical affairs—presided in provincial synods of bishops—visited the diocese or παροικία of each. See Bingham's Antiquities, &c. book ii. c. 16. The bishop of the metropolis of a civil diocese, which comprised several provinces, was called archbishop, or exarch, and afterwards patriarch, and had much the same sort of jurisdiction over all the metropolitans of that diocese, as each of them had over the bishops of his own province. See Bingham, c. 17. The office of metropolitan is probably as ancient as the apostolic age; that of patriarch is likewise very ancient, though

national churches; and that the supreme bishops in these districts (where there were such bishops) had generally sufficient influence in *latter* ages, to cause their own liturgies to be universally received by their suffragans; I thought it advisable, in the first place, to examine the liturgies of such supreme churches, and inquire whether they appear to be derived from primitive antiquity. If it seem that some other liturgy was used before the existing formulary, I have endeavoured to trace it out. And finally, I have consulted the writings of those Fathers who lived in the immediate neighbourhood, and by means of them endeavoured to ascertain the extent of country through which each liturgy was used, and the antiquity to which we can trace its order and substance. This plan I have followed in all instances, except where there was no supreme church to guide me in the investigation; and I have

we do not find it mentioned by that name till the council of Chalcedon, A D 451. However it certainly existed long before that time, as it seems that the bishop of Alexandria had this sort of jurisdiction in the third century. See Bingham, book ii. c. 16 §. 3. In fact, every bishop, as a successor of the apostles, had a certain degree of influence and authority in the whole church; and they who joined to this, the importance which was derived from the dignity, power, and opulence of the metropolitan or capital cities over which they presided, acquired such a degree of weight and influence, that bishops and metropolitans voluntarily admitted their jurisdiction. The Roman empire about the time of Constantine was divided into thirteen civil dioceses, each of which was ruled by a governor called exarch, vicar of the empire, or prefect. It does not appear that there was a supreme bishop or patriarch in each of these dioceses. The exarchs or patriarchs of the church in the fourth century, were those of Alexandria, Antioch, Cæsarea, Ephesus, Constantinople, Thessalonica, Rome, Milan, and Carthage. To which were added afterwards Jerusalem and Justiniana See Bingham, Antiq book ix. Basnage, Hist. de l'Eglise, tome i.

then had recourse to those remains which appear with reason to represent the original local liturgy.

After a careful examination of the primitive liturgies of the Christian church, it appears to me, that they may all be reduced to four, which have been used in different churches from a period of profound antiquity. The first may be entitled the *great Oriental Liturgy*, as it seems to have prevailed in all the Christian churches from the Euphrates to the Hellespont, and from the Hellespont to the southern extremity of Greece. The second was the *Alexandrian*, which from time immemorial has been the liturgy of Egypt, Abyssinia, and the country extending along the Mediterranean sea towards the west. The third was the *Roman*, which prevailed throughout the whole of Italy, Sicily, and the civil diocese of Africa. The fourth was the *Gallican*, which was used throughout Gaul and Spain, and probably in the exarchate of Ephesus until the fourth century. These four great liturgies appear to have been the parents of all the forms now extant, and indeed of all which we can in any manner discover; and their antiquity was so very remote, their use so extensive in those ages when bishops were most independent, that it seems difficult to place their origin at a lower period than the apostolic age. The liberty which every Christian church plainly had and exercised, in the way of improving its formularies, confirms the antiquity of the four great liturgies; for where this liberty existed, it could have been scarcely any thing else but reverence for the apostolical source from which the original liturgies were derived, that prevented an infinite variety of formularies, and preserved the substantial uniformity which we find to have prevailed in vast districts of the primitive church.

There can be little if any doubt that Christian liturgies were not at first committed to writing, but preserved by memory and practice. However, this did not prevent a substantial uniformity from being continually kept up. Each church might very easily preserve uniformity in its own liturgy; and if all who had originally received the same followed this plan, a general uniformity would be the result. That each church preserved continually the same liturgy is certain. It is impossible to peruse the notices supplied by the Fathers, without perceiving that the baptized Christians were supposed to be familiar with every part of the service; and continual allusions are made to various particulars as well known, which it would be impossible to explain, except by referring to the liturgies still extant. The order of the parts was always preserved, the same rites and ceremonies continually repeated, the same ideas and language without material variation, transmitted from generation to generation. The people always knew the precise points at which they were to repeat their responses, chant their sacred hymn, or join in the well-known prayer. If, then, each church preserved uniformity in its own liturgy, a general substantial uniformity would be found after the lapse of some centuries, in the liturgies of those churches which had originally received the same order. Thus, when we compare the liturgies of the patriarchates or exarchates of Antioch, Cæsarea, and Constantinople, as used in the fourth and fifth centuries, we find a substantial uniformity pervading them all. Those parts which are common to all, are found arranged in the same order in all. The principal rites are identical. They agree in their principal ideas. Every thing, therefore, concurs to prove the original identity of all three. Nearly the same may be said of the liturgies of Rome, Milan, and Africa; and of those of Gaul and Spain. We have therefore the best reasons for affirming, that the catholic church from the beginning has always preserved an uniform order of liturgy. But this uniformity did not exclude improvement and variety. The bishop of each church appears plainly to have possessed the authority of improving his own liturgy by the addition of new ideas and rites: and the exercise of this power, either individually or collectively, accounts for the variations which we find in those liturgies now extant, originally derived from the same model. Nor does it seem that variety of expression, under certain regulations, was excluded at any time by the Christian church. When we examine the remains of the Roman, Italian, Gallican, and Spanish liturgies, we find that they all permitted a variety of expression for every particular feast; always retaining, however, more or less of fixed and permanent matter, and uniformly preserving an identity of order, and the same series of parts. It appears to me that the practice of the western churches during the fifth and fourth centuries, in permitting the use of various "missæ" in the same church, affords room for thinking that something of the same kind had existed from a more remote period. For it does not seem that the composition of new " missæ" for the festivals excited any surprise in those ages, or was viewed as any thing novel in *principle*. Hence I think it probable, that it had been the early custom of many western bishops, to use more or less variety of expression and idea on each particular festival; while they carefully preserved the primitive and well-known order and substance, which had been delivered to them by their predecessors. This sort of variety is still visible in the English liturgy, where different collects and prefaces are used for different festivals, while the main order and substance still remains.

The period when liturgies were first committed to writing is uncertain, and has been the subject of some controversy. Le Brun contends that no liturgy was written till the fifth century; but his arguments seem quite insufficient to prove this, and he is accordingly opposed by Muratori and other eminent ritualists. It seems certain, on the other hand, that the liturgy of the Apostolical Constitutions was written at the end of the third, or beginning of the fourth century; and there is no reason to deny that others may have been written about the same time, or not long after. Whoever compares the account which Cyril, in his fifth mystical Catechesis, gives of the thanksgiving in the liturgy of Jerusalem, with those of St. James's liturgy in Greek and Syriac, will be strongly inclined to think, that St. James's liturgy was already committed to writing in the time of Cyril, or before the middle of the fourth century.

Various obstacles are to be surmounted, before we can form a correct judgment of the value of existing liturgies. As these formularies were in continual use, they necessarily received various additions and changes, to adapt them to the circumstances of successive ages. Some prayers became obsolete, and were omitted. Words and names and prayers were introduced, and acquired importance from the rise of heresy, from civil commotions, or some other cause. These things would induce a rapid and superficial observer to suspect mutilation or corruption, where there were very few difficulties in reality, that could not be made to yield to patient investigation and competent knowledge. The variations of manuscripts afford a ready argument against the text of existing liturgies. Some of these contain a portion of the liturgy, others the whole; some contain rubrics, and others do not; some prescribe the prayers and duties of the deacon and priest, others those of the priest only. In some, peculiar rites are introduced; in others, again, parts of the service are not written down, but left to the memory. All this has arisen merely from the different opinions with regard to *convenience*, which different persons entertained; and is calculated to confirm the antiquity and authenticity of the main body of the liturgy, which is preserved by all manuscripts.

The value of liturgies in affording evidence of the true nature of Christian faith and morality, would be very great, if we could refer unhesitatingly to the monuments in our possession, as exhibiting the text used during the most primitive ages. They must, however, under any circumstances, have a share in the great body of Christian evidence; and where we can shew them to have been used by certain churches, they must be considered as the public formularies of such churches, and therefore more authoritative than the sentiments of an individual.

In proportion as we can trace back their text or their substance into antiquity, their value and importance increase. When their text has been traced to the primitive ages, and we are enabled to bring the sentiments of ancient divines in confirmation of their doctrines, we may receive a satisfaction and confirmation in faith, which cannot perhaps be so fully and completely derived from primitive evidence in any other way. For it was chiefly, if not only, in the mystical liturgy of the eucharist, that the primitive church spoke without reserve of all the sublimities of Christian faith. When the catechumens and infidels, who were permitted to hear the lessons and sermon, had been dismissed, there was no longer any thing to impede the disclosure of those profound truths, which the faith of the ignorant and undisciplined could not yet receive. It was then, that in the fulness of faith and love and confidence, the brethren offered up prayers to God, and saluted one another with the holy kiss. Then the bishop, having prepared the bread and the cup, addressed the people, and exhorted them to " lift up " their hearts," and " give thanks" to their heavenly Father. After which he offered thanksgiving and blessing to God, the Father, Son, and Holy Ghost, for all his goodness and mercy to the human race; and, having consecrated the elements, concluded the thanksgiving and prayers with a doxology, to which all the people answered, Amen. This order varied a little in the different liturgies, but its parts are found in all, as the reader will perceive by the following pages.

All this, however, was only heard and known by the baptized or perfect Christians; for it was a remarkable part of the primitive discipline to conceal from all others the mode of administering the sacraments. The learned Bingham has given a particular account of this in book x. chap. 5. of his Antiquities of the Christian Church; to which I refer the reader for abundant information on the subject. The method of celebrating baptism, confirmation, and the eucharist; the nature and effect of these ordinances; the sublime doctrine of the Trinity; and the Creed and Lord's Prayer; were only communicated to converts about the time of their baptism. Christians were absolutely prohibited from revealing this information to catechumens or infidels; and whenever the early Christian writers speak on such topics, (except when controversy compels them to a different course,) there is usually some reserve in their manner, some reference to the peculiar knowledge of the faithful, and, very frequently, allusions so figurative and remote, as none but a baptized Christian could have understood.

This primitive discipline is sufficient to account for the facts, that very few allusions to the liturgy or eucharistic service, are found in the writings of the Fathers; and that on the more solemn part of consecration, &c. they are almost entirely silent. I would entreat the reader to bear this in mind, if, in perusing the following pages, he should think the passages which I have collected from the Fathers, too few, or too indistinct, to warrant the inferences which I have deduced from them.

SECTION I.

LITURGY OF THE PATRIARCHATE OF ANTIOCH.

THE patriarchate of Antioch originally included that of Jerusalem, and comprised the countries of Judæa, Mesopotamia, Syria, and some provinces of the southern part of Asia Minor[a]. The liturgy which prevailed in these countries merits our particular attention for several reasons. First, because the church of Jerusalem was the mother-church of Christendom, and the faithful first received the title of Christians at Antioch; secondly, because the liturgy used there, appears likewise to have prevailed to a great extent in the adjoining regions; and thirdly, because we have more ancient and numerous notices of this liturgy in the writings of the Fathers, than of any other in existence.

In proceeding to ascertain its nature, our first step is to inquire what liturgies are now used there, and

---

[a] Bingham's Antiq book ix. c. 1. §. 6. c. 2. § 8, 9. The bishop of Jerusalem, though given honorary precedence by the council of Nice, only obtained the jurisdiction of a patriarch in the fifth century, when the council of Chalcedon confirmed this dignity to him, placing under his jurisdiction the three provinces of Palestine, containing about fifty bishoprics, which were abstracted from the patriarchate of Antioch.

whether any of them profess, or appear to be, the original or apostolical liturgy of that country.

The patriarchate of Antioch is chiefly inhabited by the Jacobites or Monophysites, and the Melchites or orthodox. The Monophysites derive their origin from Eutyches, whose errors were condemned by the council of Chalcedon, A. D. 451; they derive their appellation from their doctrine, for they appear to deny the existence of the human nature of Christ, which they affirm to be absorbed in the divinity, and made one with it. They are also called Jacobites from Jacob Baradæus, an eminent leader of this sect in the sixth century. The orthodox (termed Melchites or Royalists by their opponents, from their attachment to the emperors of the east) have always adhered to the profession of the catholic faith, and the communion of the patriarch of Constantinople.

The Monophysites and the orthodox in the patriarchate of Antioch, have long agreed in using liturgies bearing the venerable name of the apostle James; who, according to universal tradition, was the first bishop of Jerusalem. The Monophysites still retain their ancient liturgy. The orthodox have in the course of ages received the liturgies of the Greek or Constantinopolitan church into common use, so that now their ancient liturgy of St. James is only read on one day in the year, namely, the feast day of that Apostle. The Monophysite liturgy of St. James is written in the Syriac language, the orthodox in Greek.

A liturgy of St. James has been used from a very remote period in the churches of the Syrian Monophysites. Barsalibi, archbishop of Amida, a Syrian Monophysite, who lived in the eleventh century,

SECT I.   *Liturgy of Antioch*   17

testified its use in the Syrian church by a commentary which he wrote upon it[b]. According to Abraham Echellensis[c], the Syrians or Monophysites all assert that St. James wrote a liturgy; and this he confirms by the testimony of Joannes Maron, (who lived in the sixth or seventh century[d],) Dionysius bishop of Amida, and Jacobus Edessenus; who affirm that their liturgy had descended to them from the age of the apostles, and that St. James was its author.

A liturgy of St. James has also been used from a remote period by the orthodox of Jerusalem and Syria. In the twelfth century Theodore Balsamon, orthodox patriarch of Antioch, said that the liturgy of St. James was used in Jerusalem and Palestine on the great feast days[e]; though it appears from the context, that the liturgies of Constantinople had by that time come into general use at Antioch. The use of this liturgy in the church of Jerusalem was mentioned about the same time by Marcus, orthodox patriarch of Alexandria, in his questions to Theodore Balsamon. He inquired, whether the

---

[b] Renaudot Liturg. Orient. Collectio tom 11. p 454.
[c] In his Annotations on Hebedjesu de Scriptoribus Chaldaicis p. 135
[d] "Hoc est principium Liturgiæ D. Jacobi Apostoli, quæ omnium liturgiarum antiquissima est, ideoque juxta illius ordinem suas instituerunt cæteri." Joannes Maron cited by Abraham Echellensis not. in Hebedjesu p 138 In speaking of "cæteri," he alluded to the authors of the other liturgies used by the Syrian Monophysites, which are very numerous.
[e] Σημείωσαι ἀπὸ τοῦ παρόντος κανόνος, ὅτι πρῶτος ὁ ἅγιος Ἰάκωβος ὁ ἀδελφόθεος, ὡς πρῶτος ἀρχιερατεύσας τῆς Ἱεροσολυμιτῶν ἐκκλησίας, παρέδωκε τὴν θείαν ἱεροτελεστίαν, ἥτις παρ᾽ ἡμῖν ἀγνοεῖται, παρὰ δὲ τοῖς Ἱεροσολυμίταις καὶ τοῖς Παλαιστιναίοις ἐνεργεῖται ἐν ταῖς μεγάλαις ἑορταῖς Theodor. Balsamon, not. in Can. 32. Concil in Trullo. Bevereg. Pandect tom. i. p 193.

VOL. I.   C

liturgies read in the parts about Alexandria and Jerusalem, and said to have been written by the holy apostles James and Mark, were to be received or not[f]. In the ninth century, the emperor Charles the Bald, in an epistle to the clergy of Ravenna, said, "The liturgy was celebrated before us according to the rite of Jerusalem, whose author was James the Apostle[g]." The most important testimony to the antiquity of an orthodox liturgy of St. James, is contained in the thirty-second canon of the council in Trullo held at Constantinople, A. D. 691. The two hundred and twenty-seven bishops there assembled, commanded that water should be mixed with the wine of the eucharist; according to the ancient custom of the church, which was transgressed by the Armenians. And they fortify this decree by the authority of a written liturgy of St. James. "For James, brother (according to the flesh) " of Christ our God, to whom the throne of the " church of Jerusalem was first committed, and " Basil, archbishop of the church of Cæsarea, whose " fame has extended throughout the whole world, " delivering to us the mysterious liturgy in writing, " have appointed," &c.[h]

[f] Αἱ περὶ τὰ μέρη τῆς Ἀλεξανδρείας, καὶ τῶν Ἱεροσολύμων ἀναγινωσκόμεναι λειτουργίαι, καὶ λεγόμεναι συγγραφῆναι παρὰ τῶν ἁγίων ἀποστόλων Ἰακώβου τοῦ ἀδελφοθέου, καὶ Μάρκου, δεκταί εἰσι τῇ ἁγίᾳ καὶ καθολικῇ ἐκκλησίᾳ, ἢ οὔ, Marcus Alexandrin. cited by Renaudot, Lit. Orient. tom. 1. p. lxxxviii

[g] "Celebrata etiam sunt coram nobis Missarum officia more Hierosolymitano auctore Jacobo apostolo." Carolus Calvus Epist ad Cler. Ravennat.

[h] Καὶ γὰρ καὶ Ἰάκωβος ὁ κατὰ σάρκα Χριστοῦ τοῦ Θεοῦ ἡμῶν ἀδελφὸς, ὃς τῆς Ἱερουσολυμιτῶν ἐκκλησίας πρῶτος τὸν θρόνον ἐνεπιστεύθη, καὶ Βασίλειος ὁ τῆς Καισαρέων ἐκκλησίας ἀρχιεπίσκοπος, οὗ τὸ κλέος κατὰ πᾶσαν τὴν οἰκουμένην διέδραμεν, ἐγγράφως τὴν μυστικὴν ἡμῖν ἱερουργίαν παραδεδω-

It appears, therefore, that the Monophysites and the orthodox of the patriarchates of Antioch and Jerusalem have, from a very remote period, agreed in ascribing their liturgies to St. James the Apostle, who was frequently entitled first bishop of Jerusalem. This fact affords some reason for thinking that they esteemed their liturgies to be very much alike. It is also probable that the Christians of this patriarchate commonly ascribed their liturgy to St. James before the council of Chalcedon, A. D. 451. For a complete separation took place at that time between the orthodox and the Monophysites; thenceforward each side regarded the other as heretical, and accordingly they held no communion. It is highly improbable that either party, under these circumstances, would borrow from the other a title for their liturgy. All must therefore have received this title from their predecessors who lived before the council of Chalcedon.

However, though there is reason to think, that

κότες, τελειοῦν ἐν τῇ θείᾳ λειτουργίᾳ ἐξ ὕδατος καὶ οἴνου τὸ ἱερὸν ποτήριον ἐκδεδώκασιν Canon XXXII. Concil. in Trullo Bevereg. tom. 1. p. 191.

I have not cited the tract ascribed to Proclus, archbishop of Constantinople, who died A. D. 446, and which speaks directly of St. James's liturgy, for strong doubts are entertained of its genuineness by Fabricius, Simon, Leo Allatius, and Le Brun. The latter justly observes, that the name of Chrysostom, applied in this tract to St John of Constantinople, shews that it

could not have been written for at least 300 years after his death. (Expl. de la Messe, III. 380) In fact, had Proclus really written it, it is not credible (considering the interesting nature of its contents) that no notice should have been taken of it by the succeeding ecclesiastical writers. Yet it appears never to have been cited by any writer till the thirteenth or fourteenth century, and the silence of nine hundred years (it must be confessed) throws an additional and serious doubt on the genuineness of this tract.

the Christian churches in the patriarchate of Antioch referred their liturgy to the apostle James before the council of Chalcedon, I am not prepared to contend that they had long done so; much less am I disposed to vindicate the *genuineness* of St. James's liturgy; that is, to maintain that he was either its author or writer. It will appear, however, in the sequel, that I am far from denying the apostolical antiquity of this liturgy in some respects.

Before I proceed to deduce the common origin of the Monophysite and orthodox liturgies of St. James from actual comparison, I must endeavour to establish their texts, and to decide which portions of each may be considered certain, and which uncertain.

The Monophysite liturgy of St. James was first translated from the Syriac into Latin by Renaudot, who published it in the second volume of his valuable work, entitled, "Liturgiarum Orientalium Collectio," and added copious and learned explanatory notes. This liturgy, like all other oriental liturgies, may be divided into two parts. The first part, or Introduction, extends to the beginning of the *Anaphora* or solemn prayer, containing the preface, consecration, &c. and terminates before the priest blesses the people, saying, "The love of God, the grace of "the Son, and the communion of the Holy Spirit, "be with you all[i]." The second part, or *Anaphora*, extends from this benediction to the end of the liturgy. The Introduction is rarely found in the MSS. of Syriac liturgies, and varies very considerably in different MSS. Renaudot has published two forms of it, which agree in very few respects[j]. Nei-

[i] Renaudot, Liturg. Oriental. tom ii p. 30. [j] Ibid pp 1. 12

ther of these is of any antiquity. For there is no mention of the prayers and dismissal of catechumens, energumens, and penitents, in them; yet we know that these rites were formerly used in the liturgy of Antioch, as well as in all the east; and other liturgies still retain some memorials of them.

There is indeed no air of antiquity in the Introduction until we come to the prayer entitled "ante "osculum pacis[k]," which is found in all the copies of St. James's liturgy in Syriac, and which is also cited expressly from it in the very ancient Coptic liturgy of Basil[l]. The text of the liturgy intervening between this prayer and the blessing, beginning, " The love of the Father," &c.[m] already alluded to, may be considered certain, and is probably very old.

The order and text of the Syriac *Anaphora* of St. James, beginning from, " The love of the Fa- " ther," &c. and including the thanksgiving, consecration, and solemn prayers, is perfectly ascertained not only by means of MSS. of various ages, but by ancient commentaries which all accord with it.

I shall now proceed to examine the text of the orthodox liturgy of St. James, which is written in the Greek language. This liturgy was first edited at Rome in A.D. 1526. by Demetrius Ducas[n], and no other copy of the liturgy of St. James in Greek was known to exist until the middle of the eight-

[k] Renaudot, Liturg. Oriental tom. ii p. 29.
[l] Ibid. tom. i. p. 13.
[m] Ibid. tom 11. p. 30
[n] From the edition of Ducas it was copied into the Bibliotheca Patrum It is also found in the Codex Apocryphus Novi Testamenti, tom. iii. by Fabricius; in Assemani's Codex Liturgicus, tom. v. which is the edition to which I shall refer, and the latter part, or Anaphora, translated into English by Dr. Brett in his Collection of Liturgies, p 14

eenth century; when Assemani published another text of St. James's liturgy, from a MS. of the tenth century, and the various readings of a MS. of the twelfth century[o]. These three copies, though they apparently differ frequently in order, yet appear on examination to exhibit very nearly the same text. The variations are generally to be accounted for, by the necessity of writing successively, prayers which were in practice repeated at the same time by different persons; by the introduction of a variety of prayers from other known and respectable sources; and by the adaptation of the prayers and commemorations to the peculiar circumstances of different places and times.

In speaking of these variations, however, I would be understood chiefly to refer to the introduction of this liturgy, namely, to that part which precedes the blessing, beginning " The love of the Lord and " Father," &c. The *Anaphora,* or solemn thanksgiving, consecration, and prayer which follows, is found in the three texts of St. James's Greek Liturgy, without any other difference than a slight variety in the order of the petitions for God's grace, or in the names of those persons who were commemorated in the prayers.

The liturgy of St. James, in the Greek language, has given rise to much controversy, and to great confusion of ideas. Shortly after it was first published, some controversialists of that age employed it to support their doctrines; and while these persons thought themselves obliged to defend the title of this liturgy, and to ascribe its composition to St. James the Apostle, others pronounced it altogether

[o] Assemani Codex Liturgicus, tom. v p. 68. 400.

spurious and modern. Baronius, Bellarmine, Leo Allatius, Bona, and Benedict the fourteenth, have endeavoured to prove that it was actually the production of St. James. Cave, Fabricius, Dorschæus, Basnage, Dupin, and Tillemont, and many others, have rejected it as possessing no legitimate claims to such an antiquity, but exhibiting many signs of interpolation and novelty. Grancolasius, Assemani, and Zaccaria, admit that it contains some things which are not as old as the apostolic age, but yet think that the main structure may be referred to St. James.

A diligent investigation of the subject has led me to conclude that this liturgy, as now extant, is to be regarded as the liturgy of the orthodox of Jerusalem and Palestine, which some time before the tenth century had received several additions and alterations, to adapt it to the formularies of the church of Constantinople.

After the council of Chalcedon, A.D. 451, the orthodox of Antioch and Jerusalem were not many in number; and when the Mahommedans invaded those parts in the seventh century, they protected the Monophysites, while they depressed and persecuted the orthodox. Under these afflicting circumstances, the orthodox Syrians became entirely dependent on the patriarchs of Constantinople, and in consequence the liturgies then used at Constantinople, namely, those of Basil and Chrysostom, were introduced. And by the twelfth century they had come into such general use amongst the orthodox of Syria and Palestine, that no other seem to have been used at Antioch; and even at Jerusalem they appear to have been used on all occasions except the greater feast days, when St. James's liturgy was still employed[q]. These circumstances render it probable that several alterations would have been made in the liturgy of St. James, in order to adapt it to the rites of the Greek church, if any such adaptation were possible.

Let us, then, examine the liturgy of St. James, and see whether there are not evident signs of alterations and adaptations to the Greek rite. We find in this liturgy a hymn resembling οἱ τὰ χερουβὶμ μυστικῶς[r], which last occurs in the liturgies of Constantinople in the same place[s]. This hymn was first introduced into the liturgy of the church of Constantinople in the time of the emperor Justin, in the seventh century[t]; and there is no presumption that it was then derived from the liturgy of any other church. This hymn was therefore peculiar to the Constantinopolitan liturgy, and was introduced into the liturgy of the orthodox of Jerusalem in imitation of it. Certainly this hymn was not known in Syria before the council of Chalcedon, for the Monophysites do not use it. Secondly, the elements are carried to the altar in procession at the same time as in the Constantinopolitan liturgies of Basil and Chrysostom, and the prayer then said, beginning ὁ Θεὸς ὁ Θεὸς ἡμῶν, is taken word for word from Chrysostom's liturgy[u]. Thirdly, the prayer

---

[q] This appears by the evidence of Theodore Balsamon, orthodox patriarch of Antioch, in his reply to the queries of Marcus, patriarch of Alexandria, and by his Annotations on the Thirty-second Canon of the Council in Trullo

[r] Liturgia Jacobi, Assemani, tom. v. p. 16.

[s] Goar, Rituale Græc. p 72 et not. 108. in Chrysost. Liturg.

[t] Ibid. p 131

[u] Liturg Jacobi, Assemani, tom. v p 17 Liturgia Chrysostomi, Goar, p. 63.

SECT. I.   *Liturgy of Antioch*   25

beginning κύριε ὁ Θεὸς ὁ κτίσας, is taken entirely from Basil's liturgy[v], and in one MS. is expressly ascribed to him[w]. Fourthly, the anthem sung before or after the name of the holy virgin in the commemorations[x], is derived from the Constantinopolitan rite, which prescribes such an anthem in this place[y]; and the very anthems of χαῖρε κεχαριτωμένη and ἄξιόν ἐστιν ὡς ἀληθῶς are found in the printed copies and MSS. of Chrysostom's liturgy in the same position[z]. There is no trace in any of the liturgies of the Nestorians, or the Monophysites, of any anthem like these; and as we cannot assign any reason why they should have omitted such an anthem, if they had ever used it, we must conclude that these anthems were not used by the eastern churches before the council of Chalcedon, for otherwise we should have met with them in the liturgies of the Monophysites. When these anthems were first used I cannot precisely say. But it certainly is probable that they were devised at Constantinople, since I find that the orthodox churches of Alexandria and Jerusalem *both* adopted them, and it is more probable that both followed the rite of Constantinople in this respect, than that either originated a custom which was adopted by the church of Constantinople and the other. Fifthly, the anthem ὁ μονογενὴς υἱὸς is sung before the hymn *Tersanctus*, as it is in the Constantinopolitan liturgy[a]. Sixthly, one of

[v] Assemani Cod. Lit tom v. p. 28 Goar, Liturgia Basilii, p. 164.
[w] The Codex Messanensis Assemani, p. 77.
[x] Assemani Cod. Lit tom v p 44, 45. 86.
[y] Liturgia Chrysost Goar, p 78. Basilii, ibid. p. 170
[z] Goar, Rituale Græc. p 78. 103
[a] Liturgia Jacobi, Assemani, p. 6 Goar, Rituale Græc. p. 101

the MSS. published by Assemani contains a prayer taken from Basil's liturgy[b]; and the other manuscript, whose various readings he has given, also includes the same prayer which likewise occurs in the liturgy of Chrysostom[c].

It appears, therefore, that the orthodox of Jerusalem and Palestine did not hesitate to introduce into their own liturgy of St. James several rites and prayers, with or without acknowledgment, from the liturgies of Constantinople. The first MS. of St. James's liturgy, published by Assemani, enables us to determine the text as it was in the tenth century. It was before this time that the alterations or additions which I have described took place. However, besides the prayers and rites which are in this way accounted for, a large number of others remain, (especially in the introduction of St. James's Greek Liturgy,) which we must refer to the orthodox patriarchs of Jerusalem, between the fifth and tenth centuries, as it is impossible to trace them to a more remote antiquity, and they do not appear in the liturgy of any other church.

These remarks will, I trust, be thought sufficient to shew, that the Greek liturgy of St. James, as now extant, is to be regarded as the old liturgy of the Melchites, or orthodox of the church of Jerusalem and the neighbourhood, some time before the tenth century; and that this liturgy had received many additions from the rites of the church of Constantinople before that time.

Having endeavoured to give a clear idea of the view which we are to take of the liturgy of St. James as now extant, I defer for the present any

[b] Assemani, p. 74 Goar, 163   [c] Ibid. p. 402. Goar, 72.

consideration of the question, whether St. James is to be considered as the originator of this liturgy, for this question will more properly be discussed when I have traced the substance of St. James's liturgy to a period antecedent to the council of Chalcedon, A. D. 451.

If it appears that the Monophysites and the orthodox, who held no communion from the period of that council, nevertheless had liturgies which were both ascribed to St. James, and which in order, substance, and expressions, were almost exactly the same; we have reason to think that they were derived from the same original, namely, from the liturgy used by all the Christians of Antioch and Jerusalem before the division.

Let us, then, proceed to compare the Monophysite with the orthodox liturgy of St. James. I have observed that the introduction of the Monophysite liturgy is uncertain as regards its text, and that it bears no marks of antiquity. I have also remarked that the introduction of the orthodox liturgy was interpolated from the Greek rite, and some other source, before the tenth century. Omitting, therefore, any comparison of the *introductions* of these two liturgies, (which originally consisted only in the reading of scripture,) I will compare their *Anaphoræ*, or solemn offices, the text of which is well ascertained, and is generally free from interpolations.

These liturgies begin the *Anaphora* with the benediction, "The love of God, the grace of the "Son, and the communion of the Holy Spirit, be "with you all." Then follow the address, "*Sur-*"*sum corda*," &c. and a preface or thanksgiving:

then the hymn *Tersanctus*, followed by a continuation of thanksgiving; then a commemoration of our Saviour's deeds and words at the last supper, a verbal oblation, and a prayer for the Holy Ghost to sanctify the elements into the sacraments of Christ's body and blood[d]. Whoever compares these parts of the orthodox and Monophysite liturgies together, will be surprised at their minute agreement in sentiments and expressions, when he considers the centuries that have elapsed since the separation of the orthodox and the Monophysites. After this, the solemn prayers for all estates of men and for all things succeed[e]. The order of these prayers is a little different in these two liturgies, but their substance and the words of the petitions generally agree. And it may be remarked, that such prayers as these appear to have been arranged differently in many of the eastern liturgies, being regarded as an accessory part of the liturgy, and admitting of a variety which would have been regarded as unsafe, if it had been introduced into the essential parts of the office. The difference between these prayers, as to expressions, is chiefly caused by a greater fulness and variety of epithet in one than in the other.

After the prayers and commemorations follow a salutation, and a bidding prayer by the deacon[f]. Then a collect introductory to the Lord's Prayer; then the Lord's Prayer and a benediction[g]. After this comes the form of address, τὰ ἅγια τοῖς ἁγίοις, the

[d] Liturgia Jacobi Syriacè Renaudot, tom. ii p. 30—34 Liturgia Jacobi Græcè Assemani, tom. v. p 32—41.

[e] Renaudot, p. 34—38. Assemani, p. 41—48.

[f] Ibid. p. 38, 39. Assemani, p. 48, 49.

[g] Ibid. p 39 40. Assemani, p. 49—52.

bread is broken with some rites which are not probably of any primitive antiquity, and communion takes place [h]. After which come a prayer of thanksgiving, and a benediction of the people [i]. The orthodox liturgy gives these last forms at greater length than the Monophysite.

Whoever compares these venerable monuments will not fail to perceive a great and striking resemblance throughout. He will readily acknowledge their derivation from one common source; and will admit that they furnish sufficient means for ascertaining all the substance, and many of the expressions, which were used in the solemn *Anaphora* of the patriarchates of Antioch and Jerusalem, before the council of Chalcedon, A.D. 451.

I have already remarked, that the title of St. James's liturgy is older than the council of Chalcedon; and we may reasonably infer, that the liturgy which bore this title generally in the fifth century, must have been considered at that time to be very ancient; and therefore must really have been long used in the church. Let us, then, advance another step, and inquire whether the Christian writers of the patriarchate of Antioch enable us to trace back the substance and order of St. James's liturgy to a more remote period. In the early part of the fifth century lived Theodoret, bishop of Cyrus, in the northern part of the patriarchate of Antioch. In a letter to Joannes Œconomus he speaks of the apostolical benediction, " The grace of our Lord Jesus " Christ, and the love of God, and the fellowship of " the Holy Spirit be with you all;" and adds, " this

[h] Ibid. p. 40—42. Assemani, p. 53—58.
[i] Ibid. p. 42. Assemani, p. 60—63.

"is the beginning of the mystical liturgy in all "churchesʲ." When we refer to the Monophysite and orthodox liturgies of St. James, we find both beginning the mystical liturgy, or *Anaphora*, with this very benediction[k].

Shortly before, probably about the end of the fourth century, Jerome, who also lived within the patriarchate of Antioch, said, " Every day the voices " of priests celebrate ὁ μόνος ἀναμάρτητος." This expression is found in the orthodox and Monophysite liturgies of St. James, and it is there appointed to be said by the priest only[l]. In another place he refers to the use of the Lord's Prayer in the liturgy: " Christ taught his apostles to dare to say daily, " with faith, in the (commemorative) sacrifice of that " body, Our Father[m]," &c.

Let us turn to those works of Chrysostom, which were written while he was a presbyter of the church of Antioch. From him, as well as from almost every other writer, we learn that the liturgy commenced with lessons from the Old and New Testaments; which were followed by the

---

ʲ Ἡ χάρις τοῦ κυρίου ἡμῶν κ τ. λ —τοῦτο δὲ ἐν πάσαις ταῖς ἐκκλησίαις τῆς μυστικῆς ἐστι λειτουργίας προοίμιον. Theodoret. Epist. Joanni Œconomo, tom. iii. p. 132. Oper a Sirmond. Paris. 1642.

[k] Liturgia Jacobi Syr. Renaudot, tom. ii. p. 30. Lit Jac. Græc. Assemani, tom. v. p. 32.

[l] " Sacerdotum quotidie ora concelebrant ὁ μόνος ἀναμάρτητος, quod in lingua nostra dicitur : Qui solus est sine peccato. Quæ laus juxta sententiam tuam frustra Deo reputatur, si est communis cum cæteris " Hieronymus, lib. ii. adv. Pelagium. Compare Liturg. Jacobi Syr. Renaudot, p 38. Græc. Assemani, p 47.

[m] " Sic docuit Christus apostolos suos, ut quotidie in corporis illius sacrificio credentes audeant loqui, Pater noster qui es in cœlis," &c. Adv. Pelag. lib iii. c. 15. Compare Renaudot, 39, 40. Assemani, 49—52

exhortations and sermons of the presbyters and bishops[n].

Chrysostom gives the order of the introduction, after the sermon, as follows. He describes the prayers for the energumens, or those afflicted with evil spirits, the catechumens, or those who were preparing to receive the sacrament of baptism, and the penitents[o]. These prayers were made in the form of a litany by the deacon and people; and after each prayer the objects of it were dismissed. Then followed an address, and a prayer of the faithful[p]. This was succeeded by a salutation or kiss of peace[q].

[n] Chrysostomi Hom. vii p. 106. tom. i. edit. Commelin. Hom xviii. p. 226.

[o] Καὶ γὰρ ὑπὲρ τῶν ἐνεργουμένων, ὑπὲρ τῶν ἐν μετανοίᾳ, κοιναὶ καὶ παρὰ τοῦ ἱερέως καὶ παρ' αὐτῶν γίνονται εὐχαί· καὶ πάντες μίαν λέγουσιν εὐχὴν, εὐχὴν τὴν ἐλέου γέμουσαν. Πάλιν ἐπειδὰν εἴρξωμεν τῶν ἱερῶν περιβόλων τοὺς οὐ δυναμένους τῆς ἱερᾶς μετασχεῖν τραπέζης, ἑτέραν δεῖ γενέσθαι εὐχὴν, καὶ πάντες ὁμοίως ἐπ' ἐδάφους κείμεθα καὶ πάντες ὁμοίως ἀνιστάμεθα, ὅταν εἰρήνης πάλιν μεταλαμβάνειν, καὶ μεταδιδόναι δέῃ, πάντες ὁμοίως ἀσπαζόμεθα. Ἐπ' αὐτῶν πάλιν τῶν φρικωδεστάτων μυστηρίων ἐπεύχεται ὁ ἱερεὺς τῷ λαῷ, ἐπεύχεται δὲ ὁ λαὸς τῷ ἱερεῖ. τὸ γὰρ, μετὰ τοῦ πνεύματός σου, οὐδὲν ἄλλο ἐστὶν, ἢ τοῦτο. Τὰ τῆς εὐχαριστίας πάλιν κοινά. Οὐδὲ γὰρ ἐκεῖνος εὐχαριστεῖ μόνος, ἀλλὰ καὶ ὁ λαὸς ἅπας. Πρότερον γὰρ αὐτῶν λαβὼν φωνὴν, εἶτα συντιθεμένων, ὅτι ἀξίως καὶ δικαίως τοῦτο γίνεται, τότε ἄρχεται τῆς εὐχαριστίας. Καὶ τί θαυμάζεις εἴ που μετὰ τοῦ ἱερέως ὁ λαὸς φθέγγεται, ὅπουγε καὶ μετ' αὐτῶν τῶν χερουβὶμ, καὶ τῶν ἄνω δυνάμεων, κοινῇ τοὺς ἱεροὺς ἐκείνους ὕμνους ἀναπέμπει; Chrysostomi Hom. xviii. in Epist. 2. ad Corinth. tom. ix. p. 873. ed. Commelin. Paris. 1609—1617. See Hom xxviii. p. 365. tom. i. same edition. Hom. lxxii. in Matth. p. 624. tom. vii. Hom. vii. in Epist ad Rom p 68. tom. ix Hom. ii. in 2 Ep. ad Cor p. 740. tom. ix.

[p] See the passage quoted in the last note, and this. Καὶ ἡ πρώτη δὲ δέησις ἐλέους γέμει, ὅταν ὑπὲρ τῶν ἐνεργουμένων παρακαλῶμεν. Καὶ ἡ δευτέρα πάλιν ὑπὲρ ἑτέρων τῶν ἐν μετανοίᾳ πολὺ τὸ ἔλεος ἐπιζητοῦσα. καὶ ἡ τρίτη δὲ πάλιν, ὑπὲρ ἡμῶν αὐτῶν. Chrysost. Hom. lxxii. in Matth. p. 624. tom. vii.

[q] Hom. xviii. in Ep. 2. ad Cor. as quoted in last note but one. ἐν τοῖς μυστηρίοις ἀσπαζόμεθα ἀλλήλους. Hom. lxxvii. in Joannem, tom. viii. p. 399.

I now proceed to those passages of Chrysostom which refer to the *Anaphora*, or mystical liturgy. He mentions the benediction of " The grace of our " Lord[r]," &c. the address, " Sursum corda[s]," &c. the solemn thanksgiving ; which he describes in such terms as leave no doubt of its identity with that of the Monophysite and the orthodox liturgies of St. James[t] : the hymn " *Tersanctus*[u]."

[r] Διὰ τοῦτο οὐκ ἀναβαίνοντι μόνον οὐδὲ διαλεγομένῳ πρὸς ὑμᾶς, οὐδὲ εὐχομένῳ ὑπὲρ ὑμῶν, ταύτην ἐπιφθέγγεσθε τὴν ῥῆσιν, ἀλλ᾽ ὅταν παρὰ τὴν ἱερὰν ταύτην ἐστήκῃ τράπεζαν, ὅταν τὴν φρικτὴν ἐκείνην θυσίαν ἀναφέρειν μέλλῃ· ἴσασι γὰρ οἱ μεμυημένοι τὸ λεγόμενον οὐ πρότερον ἅπτεται τῶν προκειμένων, ἕως ἂν ὑμῖν αὐτὸς ἐπεύξηται τὴν παρὰ τοῦ κυρίου χάριν, καὶ ὑμεῖς ἐπιφθέγξησθε αὐτῷ, καὶ τῷ πνεύματί σου Hom. xxxvi. de Pentecost. p 553. tom. v.

[s] Οὐχ ὑπέσχου τῷ ἱερεῖ εἰπόντι, Ἄνω σχῶμεν ἡμῶν τὸν νοῦν καὶ τὰς καρδίας; καὶ εἶπας, ἔχομεν πρὸς τὸν κύριον; Hom. xxxviii de Eucharist p 569 tom. v. Τὰ τῆς εὐχαριστίας πάλιν κοινά. οὐδὲ γὰρ ἐκεῖνος (sacerdos) εὐχαριστεῖ μόνος, ἀλλὰ καὶ ὁ λαὸς ἅπας. πρότερον γὰρ αὐτῶν λαβὼν φωνήν, εἶτα συντιθεμένων, ὅτι ἀξίως καὶ δικαίως τοῦτο γίνεται, τότε ἄρχεται τῆς εὐχαριστίας. καὶ τί θαυμάζεις εἴπου μετὰ τοῦ ἱερέως ὁ λαὸς φθέγγεται ὅπουγε καὶ μετ᾽ αὐτῶν τῶν χερουβὶν, καὶ τῶν ἄνω δυνάμεων, κοινῇ τοὺς ἱεροὺς ἐκείνους ὕμνους ἀναπέμπει, Hom. xviii in 2 Cor. p. 873. tom. ix.

[t] See last quotation, which refers to the part of the thanksgiving immediately before Tersanctus. The following passage refers to the thanksgiving more at large. In speaking of " the cup of blessing," he says, Οὐ γὰρ μικρὸν τὸ εἰρημένον εὐλογίαν γὰρ ὅταν εἴπω, πάντα ἀναπτύσσω τὸν τῆς εὐεργεσίας τοῦ Θεοῦ θησαυρὸν, καὶ τῶν μεγάλων ἐκείνων ἀναμιμνήσκω δωρεῶν. καὶ γὰρ καὶ ἡμεῖς ἐπιλέγοντες τῷ ποτηρίῳ τὰς ἀφάτους εὐεργεσίας τοῦ Θεοῦ, καὶ ὅσων ἀπολελαύκαμεν, οὕτως αὐτὸ προσάγομεν, καὶ κοινωνοῦμεν, εὐχαριστοῦντες, ὅτι τῆς πλάνης ἀπήλλαξε τὸ τῶν ἀνθρώπων γένος, ὅτι μακρὰν ὄντας, ἐγγὺς ἐποίησεν, ὅτι ἐλπίδα μὴ ἔχοντας καὶ ἀθέους ἐν τῷ κόσμῳ, ἀδελφοὺς ἑαυτοῦ κατεσκεύασε καὶ συγκληρονόμους Hom. xxiv. in 1 Cor. p 532. tom. ix

[u] See Hom. xviii in 2 Cor. p. 873. already quoted. Διὰ τοῦτο καὶ ὁ μέγας οὗτος ἀρχιερεὺς (Christus) ἐπειδὰν ἐπὶ τῆς ἁγίας ταύτης ἐστήκῃ τραπέζης, τὴν λογικὴν ἀναφέρων λατρείαν, τὴν ἀναίμακτον προσφέρων θυσίαν, οὐχ᾽ ἁπλῶς ἡμᾶς ἐπὶ τὴν εὐφημίαν ταύτην καλεῖ, ἀλλὰ πρότερον τὰ Χερουβεὶμ εἰπὼν, καὶ τῶν Σεραφεὶμ ἀναμνήσας, οὕτω παρακελεύεται πᾶσιν ἀναπέμψαι τὴν φρικωδεστάτην φωνήν——τὴν διάνοιαν ἡμῶν ἀπὸ τῆς γῆς ἀνασπῶν, καὶ μονονουχὶ βοῶν πρὸς ἕκαστον ἡμῶν, καὶ λέγων, μετὰ τῶν Σεραφεὶμ ᾄδεις, μετὰ τῶν Σεραφεὶμ στῆθι, μετ᾽ ἐκείνων τὰς πτέρυγας πέτασον, μετ᾽

Liturgy of Antioch.

Chrysostom most probably refers to the commemoration of our Saviour's deeds and words at the last supper, as used in the liturgy, when he attributes such great importance to the words of institution of our Lord, which he considers as still chiefly efficacious in the consecration of the eucharist[v]. He often speaks of the eucharist under the title of an unbloody sacrifice, which is quite consistent with the words of verbal oblation in the liturgies of St. James; and in one place he distinctly refers to the invocation of the Holy Spirit[w]. On this part of the liturgy, namely, the words of Christ, the verbal oblation, and the invocation of the Holy Spirit, the Christian writers generally spoke but little, and with caution. It was contrary to the discipline of the church to reveal openly to heathens or heretics the form of consecration, and some other practices and doctrines which were likely to excite opposition or ridicule. With the wisdom of serpents, as well as the harmlessness of doves, the primitive Christians did not give that which was holy unto the dogs, nor cast their pearls before swine; remembering the admonition of Christ, and his salutary caution, "lest they trample them "under their feet, and turn again and rend you."

Chrysostom speaks plainly of the general prayers

ἐκείνων περιίπτασο τὸν θρόνον τὸν βασιλικόν. Serm. vi. in Esaiam. p. 890 tom. iii

[v] Οὐδὲ γὰρ ἄνθρωπός ἐστιν ὁ ποιῶν τὰ προκείμενα γενέσθαι σῶμα καὶ αἷμα Χριστοῦ, ἀλλ' αὐτὸς ὁ σταυρωθεὶς ὑπὲρ ἡμῶν Χριστός· σχῆμα πληρῶν ἕστηκεν ὁ ἱερεὺς τὰ ῥήματα φθεγγόμενος ἐκεῖνα, ἡ δὲ δύναμις καὶ ἡ χάρις τοῦ Θεοῦ ἐστι. τοῦτό μού ἐστι τὸ σῶμα φησί

τοῦτο τὸ ῥῆμα μεταρρυθμίζει τὰ προκείμενα. De Prodit. Judæ, tom. v. p. 463.

[w] Ὅταν ἑστήκῃ πρὸ τῆς τραπέζης ὁ ἱερεὺς, τὰς χεῖρας ἀνατείνων εἰς τὸν οὐρανὸν, καλῶν τὸ Πνεῦμα τὸ Ἅγιον, τοῦ παραγενέσθαι καὶ ἅψασθαι τῶν προκειμένων, πολλὴ ἡσυχία, πολλὴ σιγή. Homil. in Cœmeterii appellat tom. v. p. 486.

which follow, and especially of the commemoration of the living and the dead[x]. He mentions the use of the Lord's Prayer[y], the form τὰ ἅγια τοῖς ἁγίοις[z], the breaking of the bread[a], and the communion. Altogether, it may be said, that there is nothing in the writings of Chrysostom which is inconsistent with the *Anaphora*, as ascertained by a comparison of the orthodox and the Monophysite liturgies of St. James. On the contrary, he confirms its order, substance, and sentiments, in a remarkable manner; and we may therefore say, that the same liturgy (substantially) was used at Antioch in the latter part of the fourth century, as I have shewn to have been used there before the middle of the fifth.

In the same century as Chrysostom, but at an earlier period, lived Ephrem Syrus, deacon of the church of Edessa, beyond the Euphrates, but still within the patriarchate of Antioch. In his discourse "de Sacerdotio," he speaks mystically or ænigmatically of the eucharist, covering his meaning as far as possible from the understandings of those who were not initiated into the Christian religion. However, he plainly refers to the order of the solemn prayer used in the consecration of the eucharist. He speaks of the oblation, then of the prayer of deprecation and repentance to God, then of the invocation of the Holy Spirit to sanctify the gifts, then of the prayer of the priest for all things,

---

[x] Hom. xxi on Acts, tom. viii Hom. xli on 1 Cor. p 702. tom. ix

[y] *Ἂν τοῦτο κατορθώσωμεν, δυνησόμεθα μετὰ καθαρὰς συνειδήσεως καὶ τῇ ἱερᾷ ταύτῃ καὶ φρικτῇ τραπέζῃ προσελθεῖν, καὶ τὰ ῥήματα ἐκεῖνα τὰ τῇ εὐχῇ συνεζευγμένα μετὰ παρρησίας φθέγξασθαι, referring to these words, "forgive us our trespasses as we forgive them" &c. Hom. xxvii. in Genes. p 358. tom. ii.

[z] Hom. vii in Matth. p. 70. tom. vii.

[a] Hom. xxiv. in 1 Cor.

SECT. I. *Liturgy of Antioch.* 35

then of the communion[b]. At the end of the treatise he plainly refers to the latter part of the thanksgiving, and the hymn *Tersanctus*[c]. The allusions are such as would be clearly understood by those who were permitted to be present during the celebration of the eucharist, and by none others; and they confirm remarkably the text of the Syriac liturgy of St. James. He also speaks of the custom of praying or making a commemoration for the departed in the liturgy[d], which agrees with the liturgies of St. James.

Let us now turn our attention towards the writings of Cyril bishop of Jerusalem, whose diocese lay within the patriarchate of Antioch. Cyril probably

[b] He calls the wine mystically " palmes vitis," the bread, " granum frumenti " When these are together with the priesthood, or in the hand of the priest, then "thesauros offert Regi," he offers an oblation to God (Compare Lit. Jacobi Renaudot, p 32 Assemani, p 38.) Then the priest "ante excelsum thronum instanter pro servis orat Dominum, lacrymas et gemitus conservorum deportans, proprioque similiter Domino ferventem deprecationem simul et pœnitentiam offerens, misericordiam et indulgentiam à Rege misericorde postulans (compare Lit. Jac. Ren. p 32, 33 Assemani, p. 38, 39.) ut Spiritus Sanctus pariter descendat, sanctificetque dona in terris proposita. (Compare Lit. Jac Ren. p 33. Assemani, p. 39, 40) Cumque oblata fuerint tremenda mysteria immortalitate plena, prævio sacerdote orationem pro cunctis faciente, (compare Ren p 34, &c. Assemani, p 41, &c) tunc animæ accedentes, per illa tremenda mysteria macularum purificationem accipiunt." Ephraem Syrus de Sacerdotio, tom. 1 p. 1. Oper. Romæ, 1589

[c] " Hujus, inquam, semper memineris vocis, et attende ut possideas thesaurum, animum tranquillum, quo possis spiritaliter in metropolim Hierusalem supernam ascendere, spiritaliaque sacrificia Regi Deo inaccessibili offerre, ubi texantur coronæ immarcessibiles et incorruptibiles, ibique tu coram angelis à Christo coroneris coronâ immortalitatis, ipseque cum supernis illis choris hymnum victoriæ decantes sanctissimæ Trinitati in sæcula sæculorum " Compare Renaudot, Lit Jacobi, tom. 11 p 31. Assemani, tom. v p 33.

[d] See p. 294. tom 111

D 2

wrote the work which we are going to consider about the years 330 or 340. In his fifth mystical catechesis, addressed to those who were recently baptized, he describes the solemn liturgy which was celebrated after the dismissal of catechumens and infidels, with a minuteness which is most satisfactory, and which establishes in a remarkable manner the antiquity of St. James's liturgy.

Cyril begins by speaking of the ceremony of the bishop or priest's washing his hands, as denoting the purity which on this occasion should be in the mind. He then mentions the kiss of peace[e]. These things belong to the introduction of the liturgy; what follows bears on the *Anaphora*. He mentions the form of *Sursum corda*[f], and then most minutely describes the thanksgiving down to the hymn *Tersanctus*[g]. Whoever compares the orthodox and the Monophysite thanksgivings of St. James[h] with this passage of Cyril, will acknowledge that the order, sentiments, and expressions are the same; and will perceive that this portion of the liturgy of St. James can be proved beyond question to be older than the middle of the fourth century, and that it was then used at Antioch and Jerusalem. Cyril does not allude to the words of our Lord, but he plainly refers to the solemn oblation of the gifts[i]. He then proceeds to speak of the invocation and prayer for the Holy Ghost to make the bread and wine the body and blood of Christ[j]. Cyril notices

---

[e] Cyrilli Opera a Milles, p 295.
[f] Ibid. p 296
[g] P 296, 297.
[h] Renaudot, Liturg. Oriental. tom. ii. p. 31. Assemani, Codex Liturg. tom. v. p. 33
[i] εἶτα μετὰ τὸ ἀπαρτισθῆναι τὴν πνευματικὴν θυσίαν, τὴν ἀναίμακτον λατρείαν ἐπὶ τῆς θυσίας ἐκείνης τοῦ ἱλασμοῦ, p. 297
[j] P. 297.

SECT. I.   *Liturgy of Antioch.*   37

next the general prayers for all men and things, the commemoration of the living and dead[k]; and the heads of petitions which he mentions are all found in the corresponding part of the orthodox and the Monophysite liturgies of St. James. His remarks on the Lord's Prayer are next in order[l], and he speaks of the form τὰ ἅγια τοῖς ἁγίοις, and the response of the people[m]; all which occur in the liturgies under consideration. The thirty-third Psalm, " Gustate et videte," was sung while the people received the sacraments[n]. Jerome also testifies that this custom prevailed in Palestine[o]. After communion Cyril says there was a prayer of thanksgiving[p].

All this critically agrees with the order, the substance, and the expressions of the *Anaphora*, which may be deduced from a comparison of the orthodox and the Monophysite liturgies of St. James. And we have already seen the same sort of agreement with the writings of Theodoret, Jerome, Ephrem, and Chrysostom; and these lived at Cyrus, Bethlehem, Edessa, and Antioch, all within the patriarchate of Antioch. This affords strong reason for believing, that a liturgy, substantially the same in every church, prevailed throughout the whole patriarchate of Antioch in the early part of the fourth century.

The next monument of antiquity to which I would refer, as illustrative of the ancient liturgy of

[k] P. 297. Compare Renaudot, p. 33. Assemani, p. 40.
[l] P. 298—300
[m] P. 300.   [n] Ibid
[o] "Quotidie cœlesti pane saturati dicimus, 'gustate et videte.'" Hieronymi lib. ii. in Esai c. 5.
[p] P. 301

the patriarchate of Antioch, is the liturgy of the Apostolical Constitutions. The Apostolical Constitutions are quoted by Epiphanius, archbishop of Salamis, who lived in the fourth century; and they are generally considered by the learned to be older than the council of Nice, A. D. 325, or at least to represent the customs and discipline of the Christian church before that period. The liturgy which bears the name of Clement, bishop of Rome, and which occurs in the eighth book of the Apostolical Constitutions, is certainly a monument of venerable antiquity. I cannot think, however, that it is to be considered as an accurate transcript of the liturgy of any church. In the first place, there is no evidence that it was used any where. Secondly, although from its title we should say that it was the liturgy of the Roman church, it is nevertheless totally unlike the primitive liturgy of that church, while it agrees in substance and order with the liturgies of the east. An author, who affixed to this liturgy a title which could not have been rightly given to it, would not have felt any scruples in altering or improving the liturgy which he published; and indeed he bears witness to the fact of his having made some alteration, by giving the name of a foreign bishop to that liturgy. Had this author simply transcribed the liturgy of Antioch, or of any other eastern church, as used in his time, why should he have given the name of Clement to it, when every one would immediately have detected the impropriety of that appellation? It appears to me, for these reasons, that this liturgy, however ancient it may be, ought not to be regarded as an authentic copy of the liturgy of any church.

Yet, as it agrees more closely with the liturgy of Antioch in the fourth century than with any other I may fairly use it as a confirmation of the antiquity, of that liturgy. In its order, its substance, and many of its expressions, the liturgy of Clement is identical with that of St. James. But the author has evidently permitted his learning and devotion to enrich the common formularies with numerous ideas full of piety and beauty.

We must therefore be content to receive the evidence of the Clementine liturgy in subservience to, and in confirmation of, that liturgy of the patriarchate of Antioch, which I have already traced by authentic documents to the fourth century. According to the Clementine liturgy, the lessons from the Old and New Testament were first read; after which the sermon was delivered[q]. Then follow prayers for the catechumens, energumens, competents, and penitents; and after their successive dismissal, the prayer of the faithful[r], the kiss of peace, and the ablution of hands succeed[s]. The *Anaphora* or *Canon* now begins, with the apostolical benediction of "The grace of our Lord Jesus Christ, " and the love of God[s]," &c. The form *Sursum corda*, &c. follows; and the thanksgiving, in which the author appears to have exerted all his powers to render it worthy of the occasion. However, all the topics of the thanksgiving in St. James's liturgies are introduced, though at great length[t]. After this follows the hymn *Tersanctus*, and a long continuation of thanksgiving in the same strain.

[q] Apost. Const lib. viii. c 5. p. 392. edit. Clerici
[r] Ibid c. 6—11 p 393—398
[s] Cap. 11. p. 398.
[t] C. 12. p 399—402

Then a commemoration of our Saviour's deeds and words at the last supper, a verbal oblation, somewhat different from that of St. James, the invocation of the Holy Ghost, and solemn prayers for all men and things, to which the people answered Amen[u]. After this, there is a prayer of the deacon, and benediction of the faithful. Then the form τὰ ἅγια τοῖς ἁγίος, &c. and the communion[v]. The office terminates with a prayer of thanksgiving, another prayer by the deacon, and a benediction[w]. All this accords remarkably with the liturgy of the patriarchate of Antioch in the fourth century. And we may consider it as a proof, that the order and substance, together with many of the expressions of that liturgy, were in use in the third century.

A remarkable sign of antiquity in the Clementine liturgy is, the omission of the Lord's Prayer between the prayer of the deacon and benediction of the faithful, which precedes the form τὰ ἅγια, &c. It seems that the Lord's Prayer was used in this place, according to the liturgy of Antioch, before the council of Chalcedon. We have seen that Chrysostom and Cyril enable us to trace back this custom to the fourth century. Without doubt, the Lord's Prayer was used in this position all through the patriarchate of Antioch in the early part of the fourth century. Yet it does not occur in this part of the Clementine liturgy. Now it is not credible that the author would have omitted this Prayer, if it had been long used before his time. Yet from the manner and language of Chrysostom and Cyril

[u] C. 12 p. 402—404
[v] C. 13. p. 404, 405.
[w] C 14, 15. p. 405, 406.

we perceive that it must have been used long before *their* time. They both seem to regard this prayer as coeval with the rest of the liturgy; they do not allude to the idea that it had *not* been formerly used in that part of the liturgy. Since, then, the Lord's Prayer was not used, or was but recently used, in the time of the author of the Apostolical Constitutions, and yet appears to have been long used in the time of Cyril and Chrysostom, we must infer that the Apostolical Constitutions were written much before the time of Chrysostom and Cyril. The liturgy of Clement may therefore be justly referred to the end of the third century or beginning of the fourth; and by means of it we can ascertain what parts of the liturgies of St. James may be traced back from the fifth to the third century.

Having shewn that there are strong reasons for believing, that the same liturgy, in point of substance and order, prevailed all through the patriarchate of Antioch in the fourth century, it would seem to follow as a matter of course, that this liturgy had been long prevalent there: certainly, where such a case has been made out, I have a right to infer this, unless something can be brought from the monuments of antiquity which contradicts the inference. We have just perceived a verification of the justice of such a conclusion from the Clementine liturgy, which may be referred to the third century. We are about to receive a proof, that the same order of liturgy had been used in the second century. Justin Martyr was a native of Samaria, and lived within the district which was afterwards known as the patriarchate of Antioch. Justin describes the order of the Christian liturgy in his days; and, as far as it goes, his description agrees exactly with the liturgy of Antioch in after-times. He speaks of the lessons, the sermon, the prayer of the faithful, and the kiss of peace[x]. He mentions the thanksgiving to God, through Christ and the Holy Spirit, for the benefits which he has conferred on us[y]. He appears to speak of the words of our Lord[z]. If he does not refer directly to the verbal oblation of bread and wine, he considers an oblation to be made[a]. The invocation of the Holy Ghost is probably to be inferred from his speaking of the bread and wine being sanctified by the prayer[b].

He mentions prayers made by the priest at this time, besides the prayer of the faithful before the thanksgiving; and he informs us that the people answered Amen at the close of the liturgy[c]. As far as this goes, it gives every reason to say, that the

[x] τῇ τοῦ ἡλίου λεγομένῃ ἡμέρᾳ πάντων κατὰ πόλεις ἢ ἀγροὺς μενόντων ἐπὶ τὸ αὐτὸ συνέλευσις γίνεται, καὶ τὰ ἀπομνημονεύματα τῶν ἀποστόλων, ἢ τὰ συγγράμματα τῶν προφητῶν ἀναγινώσκεται μέχρις ἐγχωρεῖ εἶτα, παυσαμένου τοῦ ἀναγινώσκοντος, ὁ προεστὼς διὰ λόγου τὴν νουθεσίαν καὶ πρόκλησιν τῆς τῶν καλῶν τούτων μιμήσεως ποιεῖται ἔπειτα ἀνιστάμεθα κοινῇ πάντες, καὶ εὐχὰς πέμπομεν Apolog I ed. Thirlby, p. 97.

[y] ἔπειτα προσφέρεται τῷ προεστῶτι τῶν ἀδελφῶν ἄρτος, καὶ ποτήριον ὕδατος καὶ κράματος καὶ οὗτος λαβὼν, αἶνον καὶ δόξαν τῷ πατρὶ τῶν ὅλων, διὰ τοῦ ὀνόματος τοῦ υἱοῦ, καὶ τοῦ πνεύματος τοῦ ἁγίου, ἀναπέμπει· καὶ εὐχαριστίαν ὑπὲρ τοῦ κατηξιῶσθαι τούτων παρ᾽ αὐτοῦ ἐπὶ πολὺ ποιεῖται Ibid. p 96.

[z] τὴν δι᾽ εὐχῆς λόγου τοῦ παρ᾽ αὐτοῦ εὐχαριστηθεῖσαν τροφὴν, κ τ λ. p. 96.

[a] πάντας οὖν οἱ διὰ τοῦ ὀνόματος τούτου θυσίας (αὐτῷ προσφέρουσιν) ἃς παρέδωκεν Ἰησοῦς ὁ Χριστὸς γίνεσθαι, τουτέστιν ἐπὶ τῇ εὐχαριστίᾳ τοῦ ἄρτου καὶ τοῦ ποτηρίου, τὰς ἐν παντὶ τόπῳ τῆς γῆς γινομένας ὑπὸ τῶν Χριστιανῶν, προλαβὼν ὁ Θεὸς μαρτυρεῖ εὐαρέστους ὑπάρχειν αὐτῷ. Justin. Dialog cum Tryph. pars ii. p. 386 ed. Thirlby.

[b] See note [z].

[c] οὗ συντελέσαντος τὰς εὐχὰς καὶ τὴν εὐχαριστίαν, πᾶς ὁ παρὼν λαὸς ἐπευφημεῖ λέγων, Ἀμήν p 96 Apolog. 1.

liturgy of Antioch was substantially the same in the time of Justin, as it was one or two hundred years afterwards.

In conclusion I may remark, that there are satisfactory means of ascertaining the order, substance, and generally the expressions, of the solemn liturgy used all through the patriarchate of Antioch and Jerusalem, before the year 451; that the liturgy thus ascertained, coincides with the notices which the Fathers of that country give concerning their liturgy, during the fifth and fourth centuries; that this liturgy was used in the whole patriarchate of Antioch in the fourth century, with little variety; that it prevailed there in the third century, and even in the second. The liturgy of St. James in Greek and Syriac may therefore be considered to be derived from the most primitive times. And should we say, that the same form in its principal features had existed from the time of the Apostles, I think that we should have good reasons for making the assertion. We cannot, however, rely on the *expressions* of this liturgy as a sure guide to the sentiments of the earliest ages. Unsupported by corroborative testimony, they are of little value beyond the fifth century, and only a certain portion can be corroborated by testimonies of the fourth and third centuries. Nor can we affirm that every part of the *substance* of the liturgy in the fifth century had existed from the beginning; but we may safely say, that whatever parts of the liturgy had existed from the beginning had likewise existed always in the same order relatively to each other; and this order it is, which essentially and mainly constitutes the identity of liturgies.

I have not as yet considered whether the liturgies of Antioch and Jerusalem are properly to be ascribed to St. James. It is obvious, from what has been said, that the text of St. James's liturgies in Syriac and Greek are not to be referred to, as immaculate, and free from the additions and alterations of later ages. With regard to the authorship of St. James, I think there is no sufficient proof for it, while there are many things against it. In fact we cannot trace back the appellation of St. James's liturgy, as given to that of Jerusalem and Antioch, beyond the fifth century. I am persuaded that this appellation began after the time of Basil, exarch of Cæsarea about A.D. 380. He composed, or rather enriched and beautified, the liturgy of his church; and this liturgy, under the name of Basil's liturgy, was soon extensively used in the east. The celebrity of Basil gave lustre to this liturgy, and the church of Jerusalem probably began to affix the name of St. James, first bishop of Jerusalem, to their liturgy, in order that it might not seem inferior to that of their neighbours. The liturgy of Jerusalem being the same as that of Antioch, the title became general throughout the patriarchate of Antioch. Thus, I think, we may account for the origin of this appellation.

SECTION II.

LITURGY OF THE EXARCHATE OF CÆSAREA.

THE exarchate or patriarchate of Cæsarea extended from the Hellespont to the Euphrates; and, with the exception of the proconsular Asia, Phrygia, and some maritime provinces, included the whole territory called Asia Minor[a]. Cæsarea in Cappadocia was the metropolis of this exarchate, which corresponded in extent to the civil diocese of Pontus; and Basil, commonly called "the Great," was consecrated bishop of Cæsarea about A.D. 370. The unanimous voice of antiquity has ascribed to him the composition of a liturgy, and one bearing his name to this day has long been used throughout the whole of Asia Minor.

These facts can be authenticated by sufficient evidence; and I will at once proceed to cite some of the principal authorities which prove the ancient existence and use in the east of a liturgy ascribed to Basil. It must, however, be premised, that from a period antecedent to the council of Chalcedon,

---

[a] Bingham's Antiq. book ii. §. 6. Vita Basilii, p. lxxxiv.
c 17. §. 2. 9, 10 book ix. c. 1 t. iii. ed Benedict. Oper. Basilii.

A.D. 451, the patriarch of Constantinople became possessed of the jurisdiction which had anciently belonged to the exarch of Cæsarea[b]; and that the liturgy of Basil was (probably at an early period) received by the patriarchs of Constantinople, and the churches under their jurisdiction, so that to the present day it is used by those churches.

The emperor Charles the Bald, in the ninth century, wrote thus to the clergy of Ravenna: " The liturgy was celebrated before us according to " the rite of Constantinople, whose author was " Basil[c]." About the year 691, a council of two hundred and twenty-seven eastern bishops, assembled at Constantinople, confirmed one of their decrees thus; " For—and Basil, archbishop of the church " of Cæsarea, whose glory has pervaded the whole " world, delivering to us the mystical liturgy in " writing, appointed," &c.[d] A hundred years before this council, or A. D. 590, Leontius of Byzantium, or Constantinople, in his book against Eutyches and Nestorius, accused Theodore of Mopsuestus thus: "He vainly composed another liturgy, besides " that which was delivered by the Fathers to the " churches, neither regarding that of the Apostles, " nor that of Basil the Great, written in the same " spirit[e]." About the year 520, Peter the deacon

[b] Bingham's Antiq book ii. c. 17. §. 10.

[c] " Celebrata etiam sunt coram nobis missarum officia —more Constantinopolitano, auctore Basilio." Carol. Calv. Imper. Epistola ad clerum Ravennat. v. Bona Rer. Lit. lib. 1. c. 12

[d] Καὶ γὰρ καὶ Ἰάκωβος—καὶ Βασίλειος ὁ τῆς Καισαρείων ἐκκλησίας ἀρχιεπίσκοπος, οὗ τὸ κλέος κατὰ πᾶσαν τὴν οἰκουμένην διέδραμεν, ἐγγράφως τὴν μυστικὴν ἡμῖν ἱερουργίαν παραδεδωκότες, οὕτω κ. τ. λ. Can 32 Concil. Trull. v Beveregii Synops tom i. p 192. edit Oxon. 1672

[e] " Aliam etiam missam effutivit præter illam, quæ a Patribus tradita est ecclesiis; neque reveritus illam Apostolo-

and others wrote to Fulgentius from Rome, whither they had come from the east on an important mission. In their epistle they support some of their arguments by a quotation from the liturgy of Basil: " Wherefore also the blessed Basil, bishop of Cæ-" sarea, in the prayer of the holy altar, which is " used throughout almost all the east, says" &c.[f] Gregory Nazianzen, the intimate friend of Basil, in his oration in praise of Basil testified, that amongst other good works which he performed at Cæsarea was " an order of prayers[g]." Basil himself informs us, that " the customs of divine service which he " had appointed in his monasteries, were consonant " and agreeable to all the churches of God[h]."

These testimonies, combined with the universal tradition of the east, where no person has ever been known to doubt the fact, have induced learned men generally to agree that Basil actually composed a liturgy. The difficulty, however, generally expressed, is this. That from the variety of text exhibited by several liturgies which bear the name of Basil, it is impossible to ascertain the correct text of the liturgy as it was composed by him[i].

rum, nec illam magni Basilii, in eodem spiritu conscriptam." Leontius Byzant adv. Nestor. et Eutych. lib iii. c. 18. Bibl. Patrum.

[f] " Hinc etiam beatus Basilius, Cæsariensis episcopus, in oratione sacri altaris, quam pæne universus frequentat oriens, inter cætera, inquit," &c. Petrus Diaconus de Incarnat. et Gratia D. N. J C. cap. 8. inter Fulgentii Opera

[g] Εὐχῶν διατάξεις, εὐκοσμίαι τοῦ βήματος Gregor Nazianz Orat. 20 tom 1 p. 340. ed. Billii Paris 1630.

[h] Πρὸς δὲ τὸ ἐπὶ ταῖς ψαλμῳδίαις ἔγκλημα—ἐκεῖνο εἰπεῖν ἔχω, ὅτι τὰ νῦν κεκρατηκότα ἔθη, πάσαις ταῖς τοῦ Θεοῦ ἐκκλησίαις, συνῳδά ἐστι καὶ σύμφωνα. Basil. Magni Epist. 207. tom. iii. ed. Benedict.

[i] Cave, Hist. Literar. Dupin. Bona, R Liturg. lib. i. c. 9. §. 2. Garnier, Opera Basilii Præfat tom. ii. p. lxxxv.

On comparing the printed editions of liturgies in different languages, bearing the name of Basil, so much difference, indeed, is to be found between them, that persons little versed in ritual matters may easily be perplexed. The difference, however, between these various texts, as they are printed, appears to such persons greater than it really is. For instance, the learned Cave, following many other erudite critics, declares, that "the copies of "Basil's liturgy are more short and more pure in "proportion to their antiquity: as clearly appears "from the liturgy which Andreas Masius translated "from the Syriac language[j]." Here the learned Cave, with Masius, Rivetus, Bona, and others, were led astray, by not knowing that every Syrian liturgy is to be joined to an introduction, which is common to the numerous liturgies of the Syrian Monophysites, but which is rarely found in MSS. and then generally united to the liturgy of St. James. So that the liturgy translated by Masius only contained the Anaphora, or latter part of the liturgy, as it is performed. And if we complete the Syrian text of Basil's liturgy, by adding this introductory part, it will appear perhaps longer, instead of shorter, than any other text of Basil's liturgy[k].

It is a fact, however, that on critically comparing the various texts of Basil's liturgy together, such considerable differences are found, as cannot be accounted for merely by the common variety of readings in ancient works, nor by the inaccuracy of translators, but must be referred to design. These

[j] Cave, Historia Literaria, tom. i.
Renaudot, Liturg. Orient. Collectio, tom i. p. 172. tom. ii. p 563.

various texts may be reduced to three. First, the Constantinopolitan; which has been used from time immemorial throughout the patriarchate of Constantinople, and in the country and language of Basil. Secondly, the Alexandrian; which has also been for a long time used in the patriarchate of Alexandria, and is found in three languages, the Coptic, the Greek, and the Arabic. Thirdly, the Syrian; which is only extant in the Syriac language.

The Constantinopolitan text will first be examined on its intrinsic merits, and afterwards it will be compared with the Alexandrian. To ascertain the correct text of the Constantinopolitan recension or copy of Basil's liturgy, does not seem so difficult as some persons imagine. It is true, that no two MSS. are found perfectly alike. But the difference arises either from the common inaccuracy of transcribers, the variety of rubrics, (which in fact do not appear in the most ancient MSS) or the introduction of certain formulæ or rites, which are easily distinguished by an experienced eye. The real text of the liturgy seems never to have been mutilated, but is found without any substantial variation in every manuscript. Some of these MSS. are of great antiquity, and yet in all it appears that the same rites, the same order, the same words are found. Montfaucon, the most profound antiquary of his own, or perhaps any age, says that he saw in the Barberini library at Rome a MS. of Basil's liturgy in Greek uncial characters, above 1000 (1120) years old[1]; and which consequently was written about the time of the council in Trullo, A.D. 691. This council of two hundred and twenty-seven eastern

[1] Montfaucon, Diarium Italicum, p 210.

bishops cited Basil's liturgy as a written document for the purpose of proving that water, according to the ancient custom of the church, should be mixed with the wine of the eucharist[m]. And if we turn to the MSS. of Basil's liturgy, according to the Constantinopolitan church; we find them all saying, "Likewise taking the cup of the fruit of the vine, "*having mixed it*[n]," &c.

About the year 520, Peter the deacon and his companions, who had come from the east to Rome on a mission of importance, wrote to Fulgentius and other African bishops on the nature of Christ, and the necessity of divine grace; and in support of the latter doctrine quoted from the liturgy of Basil, which they said was then used by almost the whole east. Their words are as follows: "Hinc "etiam beatus Basilius, Cæsariensis episcopus, in "oratione sacri altaris, quam pæne universus fre- "quentat oriens, inter cætera; 'Dona,' inquit, 'Do- "mine, virtutem et tutamentum, malos, quæsumus, "bonos facito, bonos in bonitate conserva, omnia "enim potes, nec est qui contradicat tibi, cum enim "volueris salvas, et nullus resistit voluntati tuæ.' "Ecce quam breviter, quamque distincte doctor "egregius olim huic controversiæ finem ponit, "docens per hanc precem, non a seipsis, sed a Deo, "malos homines bonos fieri, nec sua virtute, sed "divinæ gratiæ adjutorio, in ipsa bonitate perseve- "rare[o]."

---

[m] Concil. in Trullo, Canon 32.

[n] Ὁμοίως δὲ τὸ ποτήριον ἐκ τοῦ γεννήματος τῆς ἀμπέλου λαβὼν, κεράσας. Liturgia Basilii, Goar

Rituale Græc. p. 168.

[o] Petrus Diacon de Incarnat. et Gratia D. N. J. C. c 8. Inter Fulgentii Opera.

Critics have long remarked with confidence, that the words cited by Peter the deacon are not to be found any where in the liturgies ascribed to Basil[p]. From whence they have concluded, that these liturgies have been greatly interpolated or mutilated since the time of Basil. Renaudot was the first to remark, that it is not necessary to suppose that Peter quoted these words from one part of Basil's liturgy, but that he may have selected and united passages which occur in different places[q]. He also remarked, that the most important words which Peter afterwards refers to, are actually found in the liturgy of Basil according to the church of Constantinople; videlicet, "Malos quæsumus bonos facito, "bonos in bonitate conserva." But he has left the affair involved in some obscurity, by not assigning any sufficient reason why the remainder of the quotation cannot also be traced. However, the Constantinopolitan text of Basil's liturgy supplies the originals of two other parts of this celebrated quotation, as I proceed to shew. "Dona, Domine, vir- "tutem et tutamentum"—Φρούρησον, ἐνδυνάμωσον[r]. "Malos, quæsumus, bonos facito, bonos in bonitate "conserva"—τοὺς ἀγαθοὺς ἐν τῇ ἀγαθότητί σου διατήρησον, τοὺς πονηροὺς ἀγαθοὺς ποίησον ἐν τῇ χρηστότητί "σου[s]. Omnia enim potes"—σὺ γὰρ εἶ ὁ ἐνεργῶν τὰ πάντα ἐν πᾶσι[t].

Thus far the quotation accords with the existing text of Basil's liturgy. But it must be confessed,

[p] Garnier, tom. ii. Oper Basilii, præfat. p. lxxxv Cave, Hist Literar Dupin, Eccles. Hist cent 4
[q] Renaudot, Liturg Orient Coll. tom i p. xxxviii.
[r] Goar, Rituale Græcum, p 174
[s] Ibid. p 171.
[t] Ibid. p. 162.

that the latter part of the quotation, namely, "Nec "est qui contradicat tibi, cum enim volueris salvas, "et nullus resistit voluntati tuæ," is not to be found in any liturgy bearing the name of Basil. Several reasons, however, may be assigned for this. First the copy of Basil's liturgy referred to by Peter the deacon may have contained some prayer or rite introduced by the bishop of some particular church, in which the passage may have occurred, and yet would not be found in the great body of MSS. Secondly, this passage may have occurred in the prayers which were made over the penitents, which have long ceased to exist in Basil's liturgy; and yet we know from the nineteenth canon of the council of Laodicea, commented on by Theodore Balsamon, and from many other sources, that some prayers of the kind were formerly universal in the east. But, thirdly, I cannot help suspecting that this passage did not occur in the liturgy, and that some person may have introduced it here to suit his own purpose. It has been remarked to me by a learned friend, that the passage in question contains "a manifest allusion to Rom. ix. 15—19. and that "these words do not *necessarily* convey the doctrine "of particular election;" yet I do not think it probable that any person who did not hold this doctrine, and that of irresistible grace, would have placed the above passage prominently before the minds of the people by introducing it into the liturgy. The words of St. Paul need explanation, and would be more properly commented upon in a sermon than introduced into a prayer.

At the first glance, the doctrines of irresistible grace and particular election seem to be conveyed in those words, "cum enim volueris salvas, et "nullus resistit voluntati tuæ;" and, taken with the remainder of the quotation made by Peter, they would induce us to think that Basil held those doctrines. This, however, was not the fact. Basil asserted the freedom of the human will, and believed that God desired the salvation of all men[u]. We do not find sentiments like those which Peter apparently attributes to him, either in those liturgies which bear the name of Basil, or indeed in any Oriental liturgy that I have read. Considering, then, that such expressions as occur in the quotation, would probably have been used in the liturgy only by one who held the doctrines of Augustine, and that Basil did not hold those doctrines; I think there is reason to suspect that the above expressions did not occur in Basil's liturgy, but have been introduced by some persons who wished to claim his authority in favour of the doctrines alluded to. We may therefore conclude, that the first half of the quotation made by Peter the deacon is found in the Constantinopolitan text of Basil's liturgy; and that the remainder is probably an interpolation, or, at all events, affords no reason to think that the text has been mutilated. It may perhaps be necessary to remark, that when it is said by Peter in the conclusion, "docens per "hanc *precem*;" we are not to infer that the quotation he has made formed *one* collect of the original liturgy; but that the liturgy itself, which the

---

[u] See the passages quoted by bishop Tomline from this Father in the fifth chapter of his "Refutation of Calvinism;" especially those from vol. i. p. 127. 197. vol. ii p. 78.

Fathers often called *precem* or εὐχὴν[v], contained these words.

Considering the Constantinopolitan text alone, therefore, I think there is no reason to dispute the *prima facie* evidence for its genuineness, which arises from its having been from time immemorial used in the country and language of Basil himself, without any dispute or suspicion ever having arisen on the subject in that part of the church. This text is found alike in all MSS. of whatever age or country that represent the Constantinopolitan liturgy of Basil. The interpolations and modern additions are easily detected, the variations are naturally accounted for. If some parts are doubtful, the greater part is not so. We find it substantiated by a council of two hundred and twenty-seven eastern bishops, three hundred years after the time of Basil, bishops who lived in the same country, spoke the same language, and ruled the same churches as Basil himself. We receive additional conviction from the quotations of Peter the deacon, who lived little more than a hundred years after the time of Basil. We also know that the Christians, for some time after the death of Basil, alluded but little in their writings to the mode of celebrating the eucharist, being prevented by the law of secrecy; and, therefore, we have altogether as much evidence for the genuineness of the text, as could have been expected from ancient

[v] Ὁ μὲν ἱεράρχης εὐχὴν ἱερὰν ἐπὶ τοῦ θείου θυσιαστηρίου τελέσας. Dionys Areop. de Eccl Hierarchia, c 3 p 283 tom 1 edit. Cordern. " Quapropter et ipsius *canonica precis* textum direximus subter adjectum, quem (Deo propitio) ex apostolica traditione suscepimus" Vigil Rom in Epistola ad Profuturum Bracarensem "Orationem Dominicam idcirco mox post *precem* dicimus" Gregorii Magni. Epist. 64 lib. vii.

writers. Considering all this, I see no sort of reason to doubt that the Constantinopolitan is the genuine text of Basil's liturgy. Certain parts may afford just grounds for discussion, but of the remainder, I think, there can be no just doubt. Supposing, then, that this was the only text in existence, we should have no great difficulty in ascertaining the true text of Basil's liturgy.

It must not be concealed, however, that another text exists. This is the Alexandrian or Egyptian, which can be well ascertained by ancient MSS. and by a comparison of ancient versions in different languages. The Alexandrian liturgy of Basil is found in the Coptic[w], Greek[x], and Arabic[y] languages, and these versions concur in establishing one text. The text thus ascertained is different from that of Constantinople, and the variation is so marked, that it cannot have proceeded merely from the inaccuracy of transcribers or translators, or any other ordinary cause. It is true, indeed, that the latter part of this text, or the Anaphora of the liturgy, agrees in order and main substance with the corresponding part of the Constantinopolitan text; so that (though differing materially in expressions and ideas) they are plainly and indisputably derived from the same original form. But the introduction or preparatory part[z], and the expressions and ideas, are in many respects very dissimilar.

[w] Translated into Latin by Renaudot, Liturg. Orient. tom. i. p. 1.

[x] E codice regio. Renaudot, Lit. Oriental. tom. 1. p. 57.

[y] Translated indifferently into Latin by Victor Schialach, a Maronite Syrian, published at Augusta Vindelicor. A D. 1604, and copied into the Bibliotheca Patrum. It is of no value now, since Renaudot has translated the Coptic, of which it was a version.

[z] Renaudot, tom. 1. p. 1—13.

To ascertain the antiquity of this Egyptian text requires some trouble. The Coptic version is no doubt very old, for Coptic has not for many centuries been spoken in Egypt, at least not such Coptic as that of the liturgy of Basil; and there is no reason to doubt that this liturgy in Coptic is as old as the Mahommedan invasion of Egypt about A. D. 640, and perhaps even more ancient. The Arabic version cannot have been made till some time after the Arabs conquered Egypt in the seventh century. The Alexandrian text in Greek is probably very old. There is even reason for thinking that it is older than the separation of the orthodox and Monophysites at the council of Chalcedon, A. D. 451. It does not commemorate any of those persons who lived after the council of Chalcedon, and were accounted to be saints by the Monophysites only, whose names occur abundantly in the Coptic and Arabic versions. It is also probable that the Coptic, and its version the Arabic, were derived from a Greek original; for in both, certain expressions are retained in Greek, chiefly the directions of the deacon to the people. These are of such a simple and ordinary description, being in fact directions to the people to "pray," or "look towards the east," or "stand up," or bow their heads[a], that no reason can be assigned for their use in Greek, except we suppose the liturgy in early times to have been performed in that language, and the people to have been made particularly well acquainted with these directions of the deacon, which it was thought in-

---

[a] προσεύξασθε, Renaudot, p. 2. στάθητε, p. 13. εἰς ἀνατολὰς βλέπετε, ibid. οἱ καθήμενοι ἀνά- στητε, ibid. τὰς κεφαλὰς ὑμῶν τῷ Θεῷ κλίνατε, p. 21, &c. &c.

expedient to alter when the liturgy was translated into Coptic.

If we look for testimonies amongst ecclesiastical writers as to the ancient use of Basil's liturgy in Egypt, we shall not find them of the same antiquity as those which demonstrate the use of this liturgy in the patriarchate of Constantinople and the east. The oldest testimony which Renaudot, the most diligent investigator of this subject, has brought forward, is that of Severus Aschmoniensis, an Egyptian bishop of the Monophysites, who lived in the tenth century, and who speaks of Basil as the author of a liturgy[b]. There is an abundance of evidence after his time without doubt. But there is an allusion to the use of Basil's liturgy in Egypt (as it seems to me) which is of importance, as coming from a remote country, and a writer who evidently gave the common tradition of his age, rather than any inventions of his own. This is the anonymous Irish writer of about the year 700, published by Spelman from a MS. in the Cottonian library[c], which was considered by Spelman, Abp. Usher[d], Dr. O'Conor[e], and other critics, to be above eleven hundred years old. This writer, having spoken of the "cursus," or offices of St. Mark, (founder of the patriarchal see of Alexandria,) adds these words: "*After Mark*, Gregory Nazianzen, whom Jerome "affirms to be his master, and St. Basil, brother of "the same St. Gregory; Anthony, Paul, Macarius, "or John, and Malchus, chanted according to the "order of the Fathers[f]." I know not how to

[b] Renaudot, Liturg. tom. i. p. 170.
[c] Concilia, tom. i. p. 176.
[d] Britt. Eccl. Antiq. p. 185.
[e] Rer Hibern. Scriptores, tom. i. p cxxxii.
[f] "Beatus Hieronymus adfirmat ipsum cursum qui dicitur

account for this writer's classing Gregory Nazianzen and Basil amongst those persons who chanted *after Mark,* or used his offices or liturgy, except by supposing that the liturgies of Gregory Nazianzen and Basil were then used in Egypt, as they are to this day by the Egyptian Monophysites. What else could have induced him to class Gregory and Basil, who lived in the north of Asia Minor, amongst those who used the Alexandrian offices which were derived from St. Mark ; and to include their names in a list of Egyptian worthies? There can be little doubt also that this writer meant to allude to liturgies used by the orthodox Egyptians. For he would hardly have alluded to the offices or liturgy (two things that he appears to confound[g]) of the heterodox, in the same manner in which he spoke of the offices or "cursus" of St. Mark, which he describes as being not only the original source of Gregory's and Basil's, but of that which was used in his own country. Indeed catholics in those ages did not busy themselves in investigating the ecclesiastical rites and liturgies of the Monophysites. This writer must therefore have alluded to liturgies

præsente tempore Scottorum, beatus Marcus decantavit, et post ipsum Gregorius Nanzenzenus, quem Hieronymus suum magistrum esse adfirmat. Et beatus Basilius frater ipsius sancti Gregorii, Antonius, Paulus, Macharius vel Joannes, et Malchus, secundum ordinem Patrum decantaverunt." Spelman, Concilia, tom. i. p. 177. This writer appears to forget that it was not Gregory Nazianzen, but Gregory Nyssene, who was Basil's brother. That the word "ipsius" here is meant to express identity, I judge from its position, and its use in the context

[g] Mabillon has remarked already, that this author appears to confound the *cursus*, or offices for the canonical hours with the liturgy or office for the communion ; as he speaks of the hymn "Gloria in excelsis," the "Tersanctus," &c as if they occurred in the "cursus," while we know that they were used at the communion by the western churches.

of Gregory and Basil used by the orthodox Egyptians. And in this case there is every probability that the liturgy of Basil was used in Egypt before the year 451. For after that time the orthodox and heterodox anathematized each other, and held no sort of communion. Whatever they had in common, therefore, they must have derived from a period antecedent to the year 451. Now it seems that they both used Basil's liturgy.

It is highly probable, then, that the Egyptian or Alexandrian text of Basil's liturgy (with the exception of a few late additions, which are discerned without difficulty) is older than the council of Chalcedon, A.D. 451. And here the difficulty occurs with fresh force. How are we to account for the difference between the Constantinopolitan text of Basil's liturgy, and the Alexandrian text which seems to claim so great an antiquity? Which is the true text? Or is neither true? Did the text of Basil suffer some great alterations in both patriarchates within a short period after his time? Or did this alteration take place only in one? To this last question I am prepared to reply in the affirmative. There is good reason to maintain, that the liturgy of Basil underwent designed alterations when it was introduced into the patriarchate of Alexandria, and that it was suited, as far as was convenient, to the Egyptian or Alexandrian liturgy which had previously been used.

First, it appears probable that the introduction, or preparatory portion of the ancient Egyptian liturgy, was substituted for the corresponding part of Basil's liturgy. The Alexandrian text of Basil's liturgy, as it stands, consists of two parts. The introduction, and the Anaphora or solemn prayer of consecration[h], &c. This introduction is common to all the Alexandrian or Egyptian liturgies of the Monophysites, and to the Ethiopic[i], which appears to have been a rite distinct from, and independent of the Alexandrian, even from the time of Athanasius[j]. It was also formerly used in the orthodox Alexandrian liturgy of St. Mark, where distinct traces of it are to be found[k]. This introduction, therefore, (at least the chief parts and general design of it,) seems older than the council of Chalcedon, A.D. 451, since it was common to the orthodox and Monophysites, and may probably have been nearly the same in the time of Athanasius, A.D. 330. If so, Basil's liturgy was adapted to the old Egyptian introduction: and this idea is rendered probable by the subsequent practice of almost the whole east in after-ages. For the universal custom seems to have been, to retain always the ancient introduction, and to admit variety only in the Anaphora or canon[l].

Secondly, the directions of the deacon in this liturgy of Basil are inserted in places and in language peculiar to the ancient Alexandrian rites, as may easily be seen by collating the Coptic, Ethiopic, and orthodox (i.e. St. Mark's) liturgies with those of the Syrian, Greek, and western churches[m].

[h] Renaudot, Liturg. tom. i. p. 1—13—25.
[i] Ibid. p. 500—513.
[j] See section iv. of this Dissertation.
[k] Renaudot, tom. i. p. 131—144. See section iv. for observations on St. Mark's liturgy.
[l] The Syrian Monophysites for nearly forty liturgies have only one introduction The Copts have only one for their three liturgies. The Ethiopians only one for twelve liturgies Renaudot, tom. i. p. 172.
[m] οἱ καθήμενοι ἀνάστητε Renaudot, tom. i. p. 13. 28. 45 153 516. προσχῶμεν vel "Respondete," p. 65. 29 101. 516, &c. referred to by Cyril Alexandrinus, and others. See sect. iv. of this Dissertation.

Thirdly, a prayer of absolution or benediction is introduced at the close[n], which is plainly derived from the old Egyptian rite, nothing like it appearing any where else. Fourthly, the benediction beginning, "The grace of our Lord," &c. which appears to have prevailed all through the east about the time of Basil[o], but which seems not to have been used by the Egyptian church[p], is omitted. Fifthly, the Egyptian text of Basil's liturgy[q] is shorter than the Constantinopolitan[r] in the exact places where the ancient Egyptian liturgy was shorter than others; for instance, in the thanksgiving[s].

It may therefore be considered certain, that the rule of strict conformity to the order and substance of Basil's liturgy was not adhered to by those who introduced it into use in the patriarchate of Alexandria. And if this be the case, the alterations which were made to adapt it to the Egyptian customs may have extended to all the points in which the Alexandrian text differs from the Constantinopolitan. Now, if we bear in mind that there is sufficient evidence that the Constantinopolitan text is genuine, if it be considered alone; and if it appears that the

---

[n] Renaudot, tom. i. p. 22. 36. 80. 519.

[o] Theodoret, Epist. ad Joan. Œcon. tom. iii. p. 132. ed. Sirmond. 1642. cited in section i. of this Dissertation.

[p] Renaudot, Liturg. Cyrilli, p. 40; Marci, p. 144; Canon. Æthiop p. 513

[q] Renaudot, tom i p. 13 64.

[r] Goar, Rituale Græc. p. 165 —168.

[s] Renaudot, Liturg. Cyrilli, p. 46. Marci, p. 153, 154. Canon. Æthiop. p. 516. In the liturgy of Mark we find the thanksgiving at greater length, in imitation of the Greek rite to which it was approximating, (see sect. iv.) Compare with these thanksgivings Chrysost. Liturg. Goar, p. 75, 76. Renaudot, Liturg. Jacobi, tom. ii. p 31. Assemani, Liturg Jacobi, tom. v. Codex Liturgicus, p. 133—135, &c.

Alexandrian text differs from it in such a way, that there must have been designed alterations in one or both of these texts: if there be no sort of tradition or reason to think that the Constantinopolitan text has been designedly altered; and, on the other hand, there be reason to think that the Alexandrian has been altered to suit the ancient Egyptian rites: under these circumstances, I think, there can be no reasonable doubt, that the Alexandrian is not to be regarded as the authentic text of Basil's liturgy, but that the Constantinopolitan is. This, it must be repeated, is what we should have expected from the *prima facie* view of the case. We should have expected, that the text which from time immemorial had been used in the country, the language, the church of Basil, without any doubt or suspicion of its genuineness, would be in fact the most genuine text. And it is this text which I have endeavoured to establish.

A difficulty, however, occurs here. How could the liturgy of Basil, if it was thus altered in Egypt, be called the liturgy of Basil any longer? I reply, that it might justly continue to be called so; for it still remained *substantially* the same liturgy. And the great oriental rite or form of liturgy which was thus for the first time naturalized in Egypt, was immediately derived from the edition of it written and improved by Basil. It was natural too, that the name of a Father, so renowned in the Christian church, should be retained to give dignity and acceptance to the new rite.

To account for the introduction of this liturgy into Egypt is not difficult. Basil, celebrated in all churches for his zeal for the orthodox faith, was, no doubt, particularly famous in Egypt for being the great founder of the monastic institute in Pontus and the neighbouring provinces. The monastic rule, whether of Anachorites or Cœnobites, prevailed sooner and more extensively in Egypt than perhaps any where else. And it was here, and in Syria, that Basil learned the discipline which, on his return, he established in Pontus[t]. It is not wonderful, therefore, that his liturgy should have been gladly received in Egypt. It is, of course, quite uncertain at what exact date this took place, or who was the author of the alterations that were made in Basil's liturgy. But perhaps we should not be much astray if we fixed on Cyril, patriarch of Alexandria, in the early part of the fifth century; who is said by the Monophysites of Egypt to have perfected the liturgy of St.Mark, or the ancient Alexandrian liturgy[u], and whose liturgy, still extant amongst them, is evidently the ancient rite of the church of Alexandria, probably corrected and improved by him[v]. If Cyril effected an improvement in the liturgy of St. Mark, he might well have done the same for the liturgy of Basil. And his remaining works shew him to have been a man well qualified for the task.

The Syriac text of Basil's liturgy was the third text which I mentioned at the beginning of this sec-

[t] Vita Basilii, tom. iii. Oper. edit. Benedict. c. 3 §. 4. &c. p. xlv.

[u] " Secunda (Liturgia) quam Egyptii consueverunt usurpare tantum per Quadragesimale jejunium, et mensem Cohiac, est Liturgia Marci quam *perfecit* Cyrillus." Abulbircat, cited by Renaudot, tom. i p. 171

[v] See section iv. of this Dissertation.

tion. It appears to be rarely used by the Syrians, for MSS. of it are very scarce. However, Renaudot saw one very ancient MS. of it. Masius translated this Syriac liturgy of Basil into Latin[w]. On comparing this version with the Constantinopolitan text of Basil's liturgy, I find that, so far from being a different text, it is generally a literal translation, and only varies from the Greek to introduce a few ill-placed interpolations, which any one may detect at a glance; or else to insert prayers and rites literally taken from, or digested according to, the Syriac liturgy of St. James, and all the other liturgies of the Syrian Monophysites. In fact, this Syriac text of Basil's liturgy affords a very strong confirmation of the genuineness of the Constantinopolitan text; and it cannot for an instant claim the authority of an original text.

I may therefore conclude, that the Constantinopolitan contains the authentic text of Basil's liturgy. And it were much to be desired that we had a critical edition of it, drawn from ancient MSS. and corrected by the accounts of ecclesiastical writers.

Having inquired into the best means of ascertaining the text of Basil's liturgy, let it be our next care to examine briefly the order and substance of the authentic text. The early part of the introduction, up to the dismissal of the catechumens, certainly comprised the reading of Scripture and the bishop's or presbyter's sermon; after which, without doubt, there were prayers for the catechumens, energumens, and penitents, who were successively

---

[w] His version is found at p 548 tom ii Renaudot, Liturg. Oriental. Coll.

SECT. II.   *Liturgy of Cæsarea.*   65

dismissed. Various rites and prayers are introduced into this part of Basil's liturgy by modern, and even by old MSS., which may reasonably give rise to discussion as to the probability that they were used in the time of Basil. The hymn *Trisagios,* Ἅγιος ὁ Θεὸς, ἅγιος ἰσχυρὸς, ἅγιος ἀθάνατος, ἐλέησον ἡμᾶς, was introduced into the liturgy in the time of the emperor Theodosius the younger, some time after the death of Basil[x]. The prayer of *Trisagios* must therefore be more recent than the time of Basil. Omitting, however, any further discussion on this introductory part, which would be of little importance, and would take up too much space, let us consider the part which follows the dismissal of those that have no right to communicate.

First, there are three prayers; the two former called "prayers of the faithful," εὐχαὶ πιστῶν[y], the third entitled εὐχὴ προσκομιδῆς[z] (an intermediate prayer[a] having been inserted considerably after the time of Basil). Then comes the apostolical kiss of peace[b]. The Constantinopolitan Creed, which follows[c], was inserted after the time of Basil. Here the Anaphora, Prosphora, or solemn prayer begins with the benediction of "The grace of our Lord[d]," &c. Then *Sursum corda,* &c. The preface or thanks-

---

[x] Goar, Rituale Græc. not. 80. in Liturg. Chrysostomi, p. 126. This must not be confounded with the hymn *Tersanctus,* beginning, "Holy, Holy, Holy," &c. which was never used at any time, or in any office, except in the solemn thanksgiving preceding consecration. On the other hand, the hymn *Trisagios* was never used in that thanksgiving. This rule will enable the reader to correct me if I should at any time seem to use the two terms indifferently.

[y] Goar, p 162, 163.
[z] Ibid. p. 164.
[a] P. 163.
[b] P. 165.
[c] Ibid.
[d] Ibid.

VOL. I.   F

giving[e]. The hymn **Tersanctus**, sung by all the people[f]. A continuation of thanksgiving[g]. A commemoration of our Saviour's deeds and words at the last supper[h]. The verbal oblation to God of his own creatures of bread and wine[i]. The invocation of the Holy Ghost to make the elements the body and blood of Christ[j]. Then follow long prayers for the church, for all men, and all things[k], the Lord's Prayer[l], the benediction of the people by the bishop or priest[m], the breaking of the bread, the form τὰ ἅγια τοῖς ἁγίοις, or "holy things for the holy[n]," the communion of clergy and laity, and the thanksgiving after communion[o].

This, then, was the form which prevailed at Cæsarea in Cappadocia during the latter part of the fourth century. And this was the form which was received with such approbation by the catholic churches of the east, that in little more than an hundred years Peter the deacon testified that almost the whole east used it. This was the form which soon prevailed throughout the whole exarchate of Cæsarea, and the patriarchate of Constantinople, where it has remained in use ever since. This was the form which was received by all the patriarchate of Antioch, translated into Coptic, revised by the patriarchs of Alexandria, and admitted into their church, used alike by orthodox and heretics. At this day, after the lapse of near fifteen hundred

[e] P. 165, 166
[f] P. 166
[g] P. 166—168
[h] P. 168
[i] τὰ σὰ ἐκ τῶν σῶν σοι προσφέροντες, p 168
[j] P. 169. Omit the interpolated words of the deacon according to ancient MSS.
[k] P 170—174
[l] Goar, p. 174.
[m] Ibid.
[n] P 175.
[o] Ibid

years, the liturgy of Basil prevails without any substantial variety from the northern shore of Russia to the extremities of Abyssinia, and from the Adriatic and Baltic seas, to the furthest coast of Asia. In one respect this liturgy must be considered as the most valuable that we possess. We can trace back the words and expressions of the greater portion to about the year 370 or 380. This is not the case with any other liturgy. The expressions of all other liturgies we cannot certainly trace, *in general*, beyond the fifth century. It is true we can often ascertain satisfactorily the expressions used at that date, and we may have no reason to deny that the same words were used long before. We can also trace their substance, and order, and some of their expressions, with certainty to a far greater antiquity. But we have not only the same sort of means for inferring and tracing the antiquity of the order and substance of the liturgy of Cæsarea in primitive times, but can actually ascertain the expressions used there about the year 380.

It may fairly be inquired here, how far we are to extend the office of Basil in composing this liturgy. There is no reason to think that it extended further than to enrich the ancient formularies of Cæsarea, by the addition of new fervour and sublimity to their devotion, and of beauty and correctness to their diction. Those that presided over the church in primitive times had the power of improving and enriching its formularies, provided the main substance was still preserved. Of the exercise of this power we probably have an instance in the liturgy of Basil. For while there are good reasons for affirming that he made no alteration in the main order and substance of the Cæsarean liturgy, it would hardly have borne his name had he merely put in writing the liturgy previously used at Cæsarea. No monument of antiquity, as far as I am aware, gives us any direct information as to the part which Basil took in composing the liturgy which bears his name. But we know from his own writings, that "the customs of psalmody," or divine service at the canonical hours, which he had appointed in his monasteries, were "consonant and "agreeable to all the churches of God[p]." And we may thence conclude, that as nothing apparently was introduced into his liturgy merely for the sake of novelty, it bore a great resemblance to that which had previously been used at Cæsarea. We are also aware, that the same order and substance which are visible in Basil's liturgy were used long before his time in the patriarchate of Antioch[q], and in the countries of Europe which afterwards became a portion of the patriarchate of Constantinople[r]. And it will presently appear that, according to the Fathers, the same order and substance was extensively prevalent in the exarchate of Cæsarea also before the time of Basil.

The law of secrecy, which was so rigidly adhered to in the Christian church for many ages, and which especially forbade any discovery of the rites of the eucharist[s], was in no part of the church more strictly obeyed than in the exarchate of Cæsarea. The effect of this caution is, that we have very few

[p] See Basil. Epist 207. tom. iii. Oper. edit. Benedictin. cited near the beginning of this section.

[q] See the first Section of this Dissertation.

[r] Section III. of this Dissertation.

[s] Bingham's Antiquities, book x. c. 5. §. 8.

notices amongst the Fathers of that exarchate relative to the liturgy.

Of the doctrines of the eucharist there are indeed abundant testimonies in these authors; but of the rites with which it was administered there is a very sparing and cautious mention. However, as far as this goes, it proves that the same liturgy (as to order and substance) prevailed in Cappadocia before the time of Basil as afterwards. Basil himself, in a book written about A.D. 374, speaks of the prayer of consecration in the liturgy in terms which seem to imply that the same order and substance had been long and generally used. He says, that in the prayer of consecration the church "was not content "merely with those things which the Apostle or "the Gospel commemorated, but that many things "were said before and after, as having great efficacy "in the mystery[t]." This accords perfectly with the liturgy of Basil, where the thanksgiving precedes the things commemorated by the Apostle Paul and the Gospels, and the invocation of the Holy Ghost follows them; all which were held by the church to have great efficacy in the mystery or sacrament[u]. It is remarkable that a verbal coincidence is found between these expressions of Basil's and his liturgy[v].

[t] Τὰ τῆς ἐπικλήσεως ῥήματα, ἐπὶ τῇ ἀναδείξει τοῦ ἄρτου τῆς εὐχαριστίας καὶ τοῦ ποτηρίου τῆς εὐλογίας, τίς τῶν ἁγίων ἐγγράφως ἡμῖν καταλέλοιπεν; οὐ γὰρ δὴ τούτοις ἀρκούμεθα ἃν ὁ Ἀπόστολος ἢ τὸ Εὐαγγέλιον ἐπεμνήσθη, ἀλλὰ καὶ προλέγομεν καὶ ἐπιλέγομεν ἕτερα ὡς μεγάλην ἔχοντα πρὸς τὸ μυστήριον τὴν ἰσχὺν, ἐκ τῆς ἀγράφου διδασκαλίας παραλαβόντες. Basil.

de Spiritu Sancto, c. 27. p. 55. tom. iii. Oper. ed. Bened.

[u] Bingham's Antiq. book xv. c. 3. §. 11. Albertinus de Eucharistia, lib. i c. 6

[v] δεόμεθα καί σε παρακαλοῦμεν, Goar, p. 169. καὶ ἀναδεῖξαι τὸν μὲν ἄρτον ταῦτον, ποίησον αὐτὸ, κ. τ. λ.———τὸ δὲ ποτήριον τοῦτο, αὐτὸ τὸ τίμιον αἷμα, κ. τ. λ. Ibid

Gregory, bishop of Nyssa in Cappadocia, and brother of Basil, speaks of the exclusion of catechumens before the mysteries. He afterwards alludes to the thanksgiving of the liturgy, including the mention of seraphim with six wings, and the hymn (*Tersanctus*) sung by Christians *with* them[w]. In Basil's liturgy we find the preface or thanksgiving making mention of seraphim with six wings; with whom the congregation are encouraged and supposed to join in singing *Tersanctus*. Gregory Nyssene elsewhere argues in support of the divine μυσταγωγία, or liturgy, that the oblation of our gifts, or εὐχαὶ, (things devoted or vowed to God,) should take place before we pray to God for his benefits[x]. This accords exactly with the order and substance of Basil's liturgy, where the verbal oblation of the gifts of bread and wine takes place before the solemn prayers[y]. We may observe that Gregory

[w] "Me tui pudet, quod cum consenueris, *adhuc ejiciaris cum catechumenis*, tanquam insipiens puellus, et qui arcana non potest celare, cum dicendum sit mysterium. Unire populo mystico, et arcanos disce sermones. Eloquere nobiscum illa quæ *sex alas habentia seraphim, cum* perfectis Christianis dicunt *hymnos canentia*. Desidera *cibum* qui confirmat animam, gusta *potum* qui cor exhilarat, ama mysterium quod eo modo qui non cadit sub aspectum, veteres transmittit ad juventutem" Gregorii Nyss Opera, Paris. 1615. tom. i. p 957 Compare Goar, Liturg Basil, p 162 166. 168. 170, &c.

[x] In speaking of our Saviour's words, ὅταν προσεύχησθε, he says, ἔξεστι δὲ δι' αὐτῶν τῶν τῆς προσευχῆς λόγων τὴν θείαν μυσταγωγίαν κατανοῆσαι, then afterwards, εὐχὴ μὲν ἐστὶ, καθὼς εἴρηται, χαριστήριος δωροφορίας ἐπαγγελία. ἡ δὲ προσευχὴ τὴν μετὰ τὴν ἐκπλήρωσιν τῆς ἐπαγγελίας τῷ Θεῷ γινομένην πρόσοδον διερμηνεύει διδάσκει οὖν ἡμᾶς ὁ λόγος, μὴ πρότερον αἰτεῖσθαί τι παρὰ τοῦ Θεοῦ, πρὶν αὐτῷ τι τῶν κεχαρισμένων δωροφορῆσαι. εὔξασθαι γὰρ χρὴ πρότερον, εἶτα προσεύξασθαι. Gregor Nyss. de Orat. Dominica Orat. 2. tom. 1 p 724 See also the context.

[y] Goar, Lit. Basil p 168 170, &c.

Nyssene speaks of the same order which we now perceive in Basil's liturgy, as the established and well-known order of those churches, which it could scarcely have *then* been, had it been first introduced by Basil.

Gregory Nazianzen preserves a cautious silence on the rites of the eucharist; he only speaks of bishops as priests who offer unbloody sacrifices to God[z], which is explained by the liturgy of Basil[a]. But there is a convincing proof that the order of Basil's liturgy is much older than his time, in the fact, that, in the early part of the fourth century, Armenia received the *same order* from the church of Cæsarea. This will be shewn in an Appendix to the Dissertation.

If we compare the liturgy of Cæsarea improved by Basil with that used at Antioch and Jerusalem in the fourth century, we shall find the order and substance of both exactly the same. This identity will be seen by comparing together the accounts which I have given of the Anaphoræ of both. It may well furnish an object of interesting inquiry, *how* a substantial uniformity of liturgy could have been caused in such a great tract of country at so early a period; more especially, when we reflect that the bishops had the power of making improvements in their liturgies, and that in fact almost all the monuments of this liturgy exhibit circumstantial varieties. In the fourth century no œcumenical bishop had yet been created. Antioch and Cæsarea

---

[z] Ὢ θυσίας πέμποντες ἀναιμάκτους ἱερῆες. Gregor Naz. tom. ii. p. 81 Θεῷ δὲ δῶρον, θυσίαι καθάρσιαι, ibid p. 201.

[a] τὰ σὰ ἐκ τῶν σῶν σοι προσφέροντες, Goar, Rit. Græc. Lit. Bas p. 168.

were subject to independent patriarchs. I know not how we are to account for this uniformity of liturgy in any other manner, than by supposing it to have prevailed from the beginning. In fact, we find vivid traces of this liturgy, as used at Antioch, in the second century[b]. The liturgy of Cæsarea may have subsisted as long. In the fourth century the same form appears to have been long used all through the patriarchate of Cæsarea. This (besides being inferred from the Fathers of that patriarchate) is to be presumed from the simple fact, that Basil's liturgy was immediately and silently received into use by all the churches of that patriarchate.

The Greek or Constantinopolitan text of Basil's liturgy is found in Goar's "Rituale Græcorum[c]." The text, however, which he has printed is modern. To confirm and ascertain it, we must refer with much trouble to the various readings of MSS. which he has placed at the conclusion of the liturgy. It were to be desired, that some critic versed in ritual studies would give us an edition of Basil's liturgy, drawn from the oldest MS., with various readings at the foot of the page. None of the rubrics are found in the oldest MSS., and it would perhaps be better to explain the rites which they describe in notes, so as not to encumber the text with interpolations. Goar's notes on the liturgy of Basil are few; but as the liturgy of Chrysostom is substantially the same as Basil's, the notes of Goar on the former liturgy may be consulted with satisfaction by those who wish to understand the rites of the latter.

[b] See section I. of this Dissertation, p. 41, 42   [c] P. 158 &c.

SECTION III.

LITURGY OF THE PATRIARCHATE OF CONSTANTINOPLE.

THE church of Byzantium, originally subject to the metropolitan of Heraclea, in the Thracian civil diocese, was elevated to dignity and power by means of Constantine the Great, who transferred the seat of empire from old Rome to that city, which thenceforth bore the name of Constantinople, or New Rome. The second general council, held at Constantinople A.D. 381, raised the bishop of that church to a dignity and precedence second only to the bishop of Old Rome; and he acquired jurisdiction over the entire civil diocese of Thrace, which comprised a large portion of European Turkey. Ere long the patriarch of Constantinople extended his authority over the ancient exarchates or patriarchates of Ephesus and Cæsarea, which were formally placed under his jurisdiction by the council of Chalcedon, A.D. 451[a]. And the whole of Greece also became subject to him.

Besides the liturgy of Basil which I have noticed in the last section, the churches subject to the

[a] Bingham's Antiq. book ii. c. 17. § 10; book ix c. 4 §. 2.

patriarch of Constantinople have from a remote period used another liturgy, which bears the name of Chrysostom. It must be confessed, that the records of antiquity do not furnish us with many allusions to this appellation of the Constantinopolitan liturgy. A tract ascribed to Proclus, patriarch of Constantinople in the early part of the fifth century, certainly speaks of the liturgy of Chrysostom. But this tract is apparently spurious, since it does not seem to have been referred to before the thirteenth century; and yet, (as I have observed above, p. 19) its contents are of so interesting a nature, that it must have been noticed before that time, had it been long in existence. It also seems to me that the author of this tract refers to the liturgy of St. James as we *now* see it, with the voluminous additions made by the orthodox of Jerusalem subsequently to the council of Chalcedon, A. D. 451; for he describes the liturgies of Basil and Chrysostom as being much shorter than those of James. And hence I conclude that this author lived considerably after the time of Proclus, for there is not the slightest presumption from any other source that the liturgy of James in the time of Proclus was longer than that of Basil; on the contrary, I am of opinion that it was rather shorter: and a large portion of James's liturgy, as now extant, was certainly added at a period much later than the age of Proclus. Theodore Balsamon speaks of the liturgy of Chrysostom[a], and Leo Thuscus translated it into Latin for Rainaltus de Monte Catano, about

---

[a] Theodor. Balsamon. Respons. ad Marcum Alexandrinum ap. Leunclavii Jus Græco-Rom. lib. v.

A. D. 1180[b]. I have not seen a work of Grancolas, who is said to have collected in it several testimonies to the antiquity of the appellation of this liturgy[c]. But however interesting it might be to prove that Chrysostom had improved or corrected the Constantinopolitan liturgy, we should remember that a public formulary of this kind is of more importance as exhibiting the sentiments of the church, than as containing those of an individual Father; and since we are, at all events, certain that this liturgy has from time immemorial been the peculiar liturgy of the church of Constantinople, we need not perplex ourselves in inquiring whether Chrysostom had any share in its correction or improvement. We should also reflect, that if we cannot ascribe this text to Chrysostom, it may perhaps be much older than his time. Learned men have represented the text of Chrysostom's liturgy as very corrupt and uncertain. Cave observes, that of many editions you find scarcely any which do not differ immensely from each other. Montfaucon remarks, that the text which he copies from Saville's edition, and that given by Morell, differ "toto cœlo." Saville asks, " What have the version of Erasmus and the edition " of Morell in common ?" Hales of Eton puts the same question, and he also notices several prayers and forms which could not have been so ancient as the time of Chrysostom. In addition, he extracts from the genuine works of Chrysostom several prayers for catechumens, energumens, &c. which, as

[b] This version is found in the "Liturgiæ sive Missæ Sanctorum," &c. by F. Claudius de Sainctes, Antwerp, 1560.

[c] Johannes Grancolas, "Les anciennes Liturgies," &c. Paris, 1697. referred to by Zaccaria Bibliotheca Ritualis, tom i. p. 13.

that Father affirms, were used in the liturgy, but are not found in that bearing his name. And he remarks, that all these things make the liturgy in question apocryphal and doubtful[d].

After examining carefully the various editions of Chrysostom's liturgy, I must respectfully but decidedly differ from these learned critics. It is true, that the introductory part of this liturgy has at various times received many additions, and that the rubrics and directions vary in different MSS. But this is of little or no consequence. We know that in primitive times the introduction contained lessons, psalms, a sermon, and prayers for catechumens and penitents, who were all dismissed before the prayer of the faithful. All this we find in the liturgy of Chrysostom, except prayers for penitents, which have been omitted in all liturgies, owing to the extinction of the ancient penitential discipline. But passing over this introductory part, which never contained any of the more important or solemn rites in primitive times, let us turn to the prayers of the faithful which follow, and to the whole mystical liturgy up to the thanksgiving after communion[e]. And I will venture to affirm, from an actual comparison of the different editions of Chrysostom's liturgy, and the various readings of MSS. given by Goar, that the text can be satisfactorily ascertained.

---

[d] See Cave, Historia Literaria, tom. i. p. 305, &c. Montfaucon, Oper. Chrysostomi, tom. xii. p. 775.

[e] See Liturg Chrysostomi ap Goar, Rituale Græc. p. 70—84. Compare with this the readings of the Barberini MS. above nine hundred years old, which Goar has published, p. 99, &c. Goar's edition of Chrysostom's liturgy, with notes, should be studied by any one who wishes to understand the liturgical rites of the Greek church.

It is true, that there are verbal differences, arising from the inaccuracy of transcribers; that the older MSS. contain no rubrics, and the new contain many; that some churches have even invented and introduced prayers and rites which others have not; that some MSS. contain only the prayers for the use of the priest, and others, those of the priest, deacon, and people. But such varieties as these only confirm the antiquity of the text used by the officiating minister, which is preserved in all without any corruption or mutilation. The edition of Morell is taken from a more modern MS. than that of Erasmus, and therefore it contains more rubrics, and a few other recent additions. But this is the only difference. The main body of the liturgy is exactly the same in both, the rites identical, the ancient prayers word for word the same[f]. As to the objection of Hales, that certain forms and prayers at the beginning and end of this liturgy were more recent than the time of Chrysostom, it may be remarked, that these forms and prayers are not found in the more ancient MSS. of Chrysostom's liturgy. We have therefore no right to charge the text with them, and accuse the whole of novelty. With regard to the other argument of Hales, that certain prayers are not found in this liturgy which were used in the liturgy in the time of Chrysostom; I have only to observe, that Montfaucon and other able critics have determined that the works in which these occur were written at Antioch before Chrysostom went to Constantinople, and therefore

---

[f] The liturgy of Chrysostom, with a version said to have been made by Erasmus, was published at Paris, 1537. 8vo. The edition of Morell was published at Paris, 1560.

they bear no relation to the liturgy of Constantinople. In conclusion, I must repeat my opinion, that the text of Chrysostom's liturgy can be satisfactorily ascertained.

It would be unnecessary repetition to detail the order of the part of Chrysostom's liturgy which follows the dismissal of the catechumens, for it is identical with that of Basil, to which I must refer the reader[g]. The difference between this part of the liturgies of Basil and Chrysostom is caused by greater fulness of idea in one than in the other, but by nothing else.

Since the liturgy of Chrysostom professes by its name to be the peculiar liturgy of the church of Constantinople, and since it has been used there and in the surrounding churches from time immemorial, we may naturally expect that some notices relative to its order and substance may be found amongst the writings of the Fathers who lived in that vicinity. It is remarkable, that scarcely any writers of eminence lived in the neighbourhood of Constantinople or in Greece for the first five or six centuries. However, we shall find in the few works which were written during this period, and in these districts, some allusions which establish the antiquity of the order and substance of Chrysostom's liturgy. Severianus, bishop of Gabala, to whom Chrysostom intrusted the care of the church of Constantinople during his own absence, is said by critics to have preached in that city a homily on the parable of the prodigal son, which appears among Chrysostom's works. In this homily he speaks in an ornamental

[g] See the last section

and figurative style of several parts of the liturgy. He notices successively the proclamation of the deacons to the catechumens, &c. to depart out of the church, the hymn *Tersanctus*, and the Lord's Prayer, said at the altar[h]. Chrysostom himself, in works written after his elevation to the patriarchal chair of Constantinople, speaks of the form *Sursum corda*, &c.[i] of the hymn *Tersanctus*[j], of the prayers or oblation for the church, &c.[k] and of the form *Sancta sanctis*[l]. However few these notices may be, yet as they agree with the substance and order of Chrysostom's liturgy, and as no opposing testimonies seem to exist, we may regard them as sufficient to prove that the same order and substance of liturgy prevailed in the fourth century at Constantinople, as in subsequent ages. I would not be understood to affirm positively that the whole text is so ancient, nor that all the rites ascend to that century, because there is reasonable ground for doubt with regard to certain parts; but I think we may justly consider the main substance and order to be as old as the fourth century. If such a form of liturgy was used at Constantinople in the fourth century, it is very probable that it may have been used also in the neighbouring churches. In fact, we find that all the churches of Thrace, Macedonia, and Greece, have from time immemorial used this very liturgy of Chrysostom. Had these churches ever used a dif-

---

[h] See tom. vi. Oper. Chrysost. p. 375. 377. edit. Front. Ducæi vel Commelini

[i] Hom. xxii. in Epistolam ad Hebræos, p. 1898. tom. x

[j] Hom. xiv in Hebr p. 1852.

tom. x. Hom. xxiv. in Act. Apost. tom. viii. p. 627.

[k] Hom. xxi. in Act. Apost. tom viii. p 606.

[l] Hom. xvii. in Hebr. p. 1872 tom. x.

ferent species of formulary, they would not have relinquished it without leaving some sign or vestige of their original liturgy, some tradition that a different formulary had once been used, or some trace of difficulty or opposition in the reception of a new rite. The liturgy of Constantinople, however, seems to have been received by all as a thing neither strange nor new; but, on the contrary, as representing that rite which they and their predecessors had received in long succession from the most primitive times.

I will now close this section with some few remarks on what may be justly called the *great oriental liturgy*. In the first section I have shewn that a certain form of liturgy prevailed in the fourth century from Arabia to Cappadocia, and from the Mediterranean sea to the other side of the Euphrates; and that this form could be traced nearly up to the apostolical age. In the second section we have seen, that the same form of liturgy prevailed in the fourth century through the greater part of Asia Minor, where it had existed from time immemorial. In the present section we have learned, that the same form of liturgy was used in Thrace in the fourth century; and that it seems to have existed there, and in Macedonia and Greece, from time immemorial.

When I reflect on the vast extent of these countries, the independence of the churches which existed there, the power which each bishop had of improving the liturgy of his church, the circumstantial varieties which we find between the liturgies of these churches, and yet the substantial identity of all; it seems to me difficult, if not impossible, to account for this identity and uniformity in any other manner, than by supposing that the Apostles themselves had originated the oriental liturgy, and communicated it to all those churches at their very foundation. The uniformity between these liturgies, as extant in the fourth or fifth century, is such as bespeaks a common origin. Their diversity is such as to prove the *remoteness* of the period at which they were originated. To what remote period can we refer as exhibiting a perfect general uniformity of liturgy, except to the apostolic age? Let us remember also, that existing documents of the second century enable us to trace this liturgy to that period; and that in the time of Justin Martyr (to whose writings I allude) the Christian church was only removed by one link from the Apostles themselves.

SECTION IV

LITURGY OF THE PATRIARCHATE OF ALEXANDRIA.

THE patriarchal see of Alexandria, founded by the holy evangelist Mark[a], has for eleven hundred years been in the possession of the sect of Jacobites, or Monophysites. This sect was originated by Eutyches in the fifth century; and as almost all the Copts, or native Egyptians, speedily embraced his doctrines, the see of Alexandria was soon occupied by Monophysite patriarchs: and although, through the favour of the eastern emperors, the orthodox were generally in possession of that see, the Monophysites preserved an unbroken succession of bishops amongst themselves[b], until, in the seventh century, the Mahommedans conquered Egypt from the eastern emperors, and, being received with open arms by the Monophysites, placed their patriarch in possession of the churches at Alexandria and throughout Egypt[c]. From that period to the present, the Monophysites have held possession of all

---

[a] Euseb Hist. Eccl. lib. ii c. 16 et 24.
[b] Renaudot, Hist. Patriarch Alexand. p. 120, &c.
[c] Renaudot, Liturg. Oriental. Coll. tom. i. p. lxxxii

the churches of Egypt; and the orthodox, or Melchites, have been at all times a small and unimportant section of the community.

The Egyptian Monophysites use three liturgies, written in the ancient Coptic language, which prevailed in Egypt before, and about the time of, the Mahommedan invasion. These liturgies they ascribe to Basil, (as we have seen in the second section of this Dissertation,) to Gregory Nazianzen, called Theologus, and to Cyril, patriarch of Alexandria[d].

It appears probable, that they were not originally written in Coptic, but in Greek. This idea is supported by the occurrence of several Greek phrases in the Coptic liturgies as now extant. These phrases are of such a simple and ordinary nature, being directions to the people to "stand up," "bow their "heads," &c.[e] that it is impossible to assign any adequate reason for their use in a foreign language, except by supposing that the liturgy was originally in Greek, and that the people were made particularly well acquainted with these formulæ, which it was therefore thought inexpedient to alter. The same supposition is confirmed by the knowledge we have that Greek was commonly spoken at Alexandria and in the neighbourhood, when the gospel was first preached in Egypt, and that the Egyptian Fathers generally wrote in Greek; and it is rendered still more probable by the existence of very ancient Greek MSS., which appear to be copies of the ori-

---

[d] They use Basil's liturgy on all fast days, Cyril's in Lent and the month Cohiac, and Gregory's on feast days. Renaudot, tom. i p. 171.

[e] As στάθητε, Renaudot, tom i. p. 13. εἰς ἀνατολὰς βλέπετε, ibid. οἱ καθημένοι ἀνάστητε, ibid. τὰς κεφαλὰς ὑμῶν τῷ Θεῷ κλίνατε, p 21, &c.

ginals from which the Coptic version was made[f]. It is very probable, however, if not certain, that the Coptic language, though not employed in divine service in Lower Egypt, was used in Upper Egypt from the time that Christianity penetrated there. It appears that Antony, the great founder of the monastic institute in Egypt, did not understand Greek; neither did many of his most celebrated disciples. Many who lived in the monasteries of Nitria and Scetis, and the Tabennesiotæ in the furthest part of the province, and the ascetics of Antony's rule in the deserts near the Read sea, only understood the Coptic language, and yet they spent days and nights in psalmody and reading the scriptures. We also find the subscriptions of Egyptian bishops to the councils of Ephesus and Chalcedon in Coptic, because they were unacquainted with Greek. How could all these have performed the liturgy and offices of the church, unless the Coptic had been used in divine service in many parts of Egypt[g]?

It is difficult, if not impossible, to assign the period when the Greek language was completely relinquished by the Copts in the celebration of their liturgy. Renaudot is inclined to ascribe the substitution of the Coptic for the Greek, to Benjamin, patriarch of the Monophysites, who was placed in possession of the see of Alexandria by the Mahommedans[h].

That the primitive rite of the church of Alexan-

---

[f] Renaudot, tom 1 p cv &c. and p 57

[g] "Quomodo igitur sacra fecissent, officiaque celebrassent, nisi publicus multis in locis linguæ vulgaris usus in sacris fuisset?" Renaudot, tom. 1. p. 205, 206

[h] Tom. i. p lxxxii.

dria is to be found amongst the liturgies used by the Egyptian Monophysites, will appear probable, when we consider the scrupulous care with which they seem to have preserved ancient customs. In fact, when the division took place at the council of Chalcedon, A.D. 451, the Monophysites adhered to all ecclesiastical traditions which did not interfere with their own peculiar doctrines, with as much care as the orthodox themselves.

As the Monophysite liturgies, however, differ from each other, it becomes a question, *which* is to be considered as the best representative of the ancient Alexandrian rite. And here it would seem at the first glance, that the liturgy of Cyril, which bears the name of a patriarch of Alexandria, is more likely to represent the Alexandrian rite, than those of Basil and Gregory Nazianzen, who were bishops of cities in Cappadocia. A further light is thrown on this by an actual inspection of the three liturgies. For while Basil's and Gregory's liturgies appear to be (as they profess) derived from the rite used in Cappadocia and the adjoining countries; the liturgy of Cyril stands distinguished from them all in many remarkable particulars.

These arguments, intended to shew the probability of Cyril's liturgy being the ancient Alexandrian rite, are supported by the tradition of the Egyptians themselves. Abulbircat calls Cyril's liturgy, " the liturgy of Mark, which Cyril perfected[1]," and this must mean the liturgy of the church of Alexandria founded by St. Mark. In the sixteenth century an ancient monument was published, which gives

---

[1] "Secunda—est liturgia Marci, quam perfecit Cyrillus." Abulbircat cited by Renaudot, tom i. p. 171.

force to this tradition. A manuscript of the tenth or eleventh century, written in Greek, was discovered amongst other MSS. of rarity and value in a remote monastery of Calabria, inhabited by the oriental monks of St. Basil. This MS. bears the title of St. Mark's liturgy[k], was evidently intended for the use of the Alexandrian church[l], and is perhaps the only liturgy, except the Ethiopian general canon, which resembles the Coptic liturgy of Cyril in the order of its parts.

The difference between St. Mark's liturgy and that of Cyril Alexandrinus, occurs chiefly in the introductory part. In the Anaphora there is very little difference: and it will appear in the sequel, that the variations in the liturgy of St. Mark are chiefly to be attributed to the dependence of the orthodox, (who used it,) upon the church of Constantinople. But on comparing Cyril's and Mark's

[k] St. Mark's liturgy was first published at Paris, A D 1583, edited by Johan. à S Andrea. It is found in the Bibliotheca Patrum, in Assemani's Codex Liturgicus, tom. vii. in Fabricius's Codex Apocryph. Nov. Testamenti, tom iii. and in Renaudot's Liturg. Orient. Collectio, tom i p. 131. to which last I refer in this section.

[l] In this liturgy there are prayers that the waters of the river (Nile) may be raised to their just measure, p 148, St. Mark is commemorated as the person who shewed to them the way of salvation, p. 149; and there are prayers for the holy and blessed pope, i e. the patriarch of Alexandria, p 151

Dionysius, bishop of Alexandria, in the third century, speaks of his predecessor *pope* Heraclas, παρὰ τοῦ μακαρίου πάπα ἡμῶν Ἡρακλᾶ παρέλαβον Dionys. Alexandr. ap. Euseb Hist. lib vii c. 7 And from that time to the present, the patriarchs of Alexandria have always been called Pope, a title which the Monophysites as well as orthodox apply to their respective patriarchs. But, indeed, this title was at first common to all bishops; thus Cyprian, bishop of Carthage, was addressed by the Roman clergy as "*Papa* Cyprianus." See abundance of examples and proofs in Bingham's Antiquities, book ii. c. 2. § 7.

liturgies together, their resemblance is found to be most striking; and it is impossible to deny that they have proceeded from one common source, namely, the ancient liturgy of the Egyptian church before the council of Chalcedon, A. D. 451. For here we have two liturgies agreeing in substance and order, both professing by their titles to be derived from the rites of the Egyptian church; both differing in order from the liturgies of all other churches in the east and west; and used by two bodies of men in Egypt, who have held no communion with each other since the council of Chalcedon.

The existence and use of the liturgy of St. Mark amongst the orthodox of Egypt is proved by the testimony of Mark, orthodox patriarch of Alexandria in the twelfth century, in his Questions to Theodore Balsamon, patriarch of Antioch. He inquired "whether the liturgies read in the parts " of Alexandria and Jerusalem, and said to have " been written by James ὁ ἀδελφόθεος, and by Mark, " are to be received by the holy catholic church, " or no[m]."

Theodore Balsamon himself says, in his Commentary on the Thirty-second Canon of the Council in Trullo, that the liturgy of St. Mark was for the most part used by the church of Alexandria[n]. It is true, that he mistakes it for the liturgy of James, as appears by the context. But his testimony establishes

[m] αἱ περὶ τὰ μέρη τῆς Ἀλεξανδρείας, καὶ τῶν Ἱεροσολύμων ἀναγινωσκόμεναι λειτουργίαι, καὶ λεγόμεναι συγγραφῆναι παρὰ τῶν ἁγίων ἀποστόλων Ἰακώβου τοῦ ἀδελφοθέου, καὶ Μάρκου, δεκταί εἰσι τῇ ἁγίᾳ καὶ καθολικῇ ἐκκλησίᾳ ἢ οὔ, Leunclav. Jus Gr. Rom. L. V.

[n] οἱ δὲ Ἀλεξανδρεῖς λέγουσιν εἶναι (scilicet, liturgiam) καὶ τοῦ ἁγίου Μάρκου ᾗ καὶ χρῶνται ὡς τὰ πολλά. Balsamon in Can 32. Concil Trull. Bevereg. Concil. tom. 1. p. 193.

the fact, that St. Mark's liturgy was used in the twelfth century by the orthodox of Alexandria, though he was not acquainted with the nature of that liturgy.

The use of this liturgy by the orthodox of Alexandria may be traced further back, I think, by the testimony of the ancient writer of the seventh or eighth century already alluded to. "St. Jerome," he says, "affirms that St. Mark chanted the course " (or liturgy, as appears by his preceding remarks) " which is now called the Irish course; and after " him Gregory Nazianzen, whom Jerome affirms to " be his master, St. Basil, brother of the same St. " Gregory, Antony, Paul, Macarius or John, and " Malchus chanted according to the order of the " Fathers[o]." Here this author appears plainly to me to refer to the Egyptian liturgies bearing the name of Gregory Nazianzen and Basil, as I have remarked elsewhere. Now though he speaks of two of the liturgies used by the Monophysites of Egypt, he does not speak of Cyril's, which is the third: but he speaks of St. Mark as being the first institutor of the Egyptian rites. And this seems plainly to refer to the custom of the orthodox Alexandrians, who did not give their liturgy the name of Cyril, (though it was the same as Cyril's Coptic liturgy,) but of St. Mark; preferring the name of its first institutor to that of Cyril, who, according to the

---

[o] "Beatus Hieronymus adfirmat, ipsum cursum qui dicitur præsente tempore Scottorum, beatus Marcus decantavit, et post ipsum Gregorius Nanzenzenus, quem Hieronymus suum magistrum esse adfirmat. Et beatus Basilius frater ipsius sancti Gregorii, Antonius, Paulus, Macharius vel Joannes, et Malchus, secundum ordinem Patrum decantaverunt." Spelman. Concilia, tom. 1. p 177

Monophysites, "perfected the liturgy of Mark." We may perhaps regard this testimony as sufficient to shew, that a liturgy of the orthodox of Alexandria was called by the name of St. Mark in the seventh century, as we know it was in the twelfth.

Now this appellation in itself is a proof that the orthodox Egyptians thought the liturgy to which they gave it, the original liturgy of Alexandria. And the circumstance of the Monophysites calling one of their liturgies by the name of Cyril is a proof that they esteemed it to have been the liturgy of Alexandria. And, as I said before, Mark's and Cyril's liturgies differ from all other liturgies in the world, except the Ethiopic, but agree with each other.

The liturgy of the Ethiopians adds strength to these arguments. Ethiopia was converted to Christianity by Frumentius about A.D. 330, and he was ordained bishop of Ethiopia by the blessed pope Athanasius, bishop of Alexandria[p]. At the schism in the Alexandrian patriarchate in the time of Dioscorus, and the council of Chalcedon, the Ethiopians followed the example of the Copts, and adhered to the Monophysite patriarch. Of course the origin of the Ethiopic liturgy is to be traced to Alexandria, from whence were derived their Christianity and their ecclesiastical orders. We should expect, then, to find a conformity between the most ancient Ethiopian liturgy and the Alexandrian rite. And the most ancient Ethiopic liturgy agrees exactly in

[p] Socrates, Hist. lib. 1. c. 19. Sozomen lib ii. c 24 Theodoret. lib. i. c. 23. Ludolf. Hist Ethiop. lib iii. c 2

order and substance with the liturgies of Cyril and Mark, and with no others[q].

This Ethiopic liturgy appears plainly to be an independent rite; that is, although it received some additions from the Alexandrian rite in the fifth or sixth centuries, yet it did not receive all the additions that were made to the Alexandrian liturgy. And if so, it is highly improbable that its original order and substance were transposed or relinquished. For had such a transposition or alteration taken place, in order to suit the Alexandrian liturgy, then, surely, parts of that liturgy which were very celebrated and very excellent, would not have been omitted, as we find they are[r]. Now, if, on the hy-

---

[q] I assume that the general canon (as it is called) of the Ethiopians is their oldest liturgy, because it does not appear to bear the name of any apostle or saint, and yet is more used and regarded than any of the others, though they have the names of apostles and famous saints. And the presumption from this is, that they esteem it to be their principal and most ancient liturgy. It occurs in Renaudot, t. i. p. 499, &c.

[r] First, in the Ethiopic liturgy the address, "Lift up your hearts," &c. does not occur, as Cassander has observed before me, see his Liturgic. p. 27 This form and the responses which follow are certainly wanting in the Ethiopic liturgy. Yet they are most ancient and most celebrated in the Christian church; and in the fifth century were used, not only at Alexandria, but in all other churches, except that of Ethiopia Cyprian speaks of these words, and Augustine said, "Every day throughout the whole world the human race reply, that they lift up their hearts unto the Lord." De Ver. Relig. Chrysostom testifies the use of these forms at Antioch; Cyril at Jerusalem; Cæsarius and Eligius in Gaul; finally, in all liturgies, except the Ethiopian, the same words are to be found. Secondly, the Lord's Prayer does not follow the prayer of consecration in the Ethiopic liturgy. Yet in the fifth century Augustine said, "quam totam petitionem (scil. sanctificationis) ferè omnis ecclesia Dominicâ oratione concludit." Epist. 149. Benedict.

SECT. IV.   *Liturgy of Alexandria.*   91

pothesis of Renaudot, Basil's liturgy had been the original liturgy of Alexandria, then the same order as Basil's would have originally prevailed in Ethiopia, and then (since the Ethiopian liturgy does not agree with the liturgy of Basil, but with those of Cyril and Mark) they *must* have altered the substance and order of their ancient liturgy. But if the liturgy of the Ethiopians suffered so material an alteration in order and substance, how highly improbable is it, that they would have omitted to introduce some of the best portions of the liturgies which it was altered to suit[s].

If, then, it has appeared that there are strong objections to thinking that the Ethiopian liturgy originally exhibited a different order from what it does now, (although it may have received many additions and interpolations in the course of ages,) if this has appeared, then we must consider it as a proof that the liturgies of Mark and Cyril are, as they profess and appear to be, derived from the ancient Alexandrian rite which prevailed in the time of Athanasius. For these liturgies agree in order and substance with the Ethiopian general canon, which appears to have been an independent rite from its origin, and to have been derived from Alexandria in the time of Athanasius, A.D. 330.

Much controversy has been excited by the liturgy

edit. num. 16 And without doubt the liturgies prove, that in the fifth century, not only the Egyptian, but every other church, used the Lord's Prayer at the end of the prayer of consecration or *canon*. Many Fathers also of the fourth and third centuries mention this, amongst whom Chrysostom, Cyril of Jerusalem, Optatus, and Cyprian, are well known

[s] See Liturg Cyrilli Renaudot, p 46 50, Marci, 144. 159. Compare Liturg. Æthiop. Renaudot, p 513. 518

of St. Mark. Some persons have thought it genuine, or that it was actually composed by St. Mark[t]; others have proved that it contains many things which could not have been used in the time of that Evangelist; from whence they infer that it is to be regarded as an imposture[u]. Controversies, however, on this subject can produce no satisfactory results, from the absence of any sufficient evidence. To prove that St. Mark wrote a liturgy is impossible. It is equally impossible to prove that he did not do so. The objections that have been made to this liturgy only prove that the *whole* of it is not as old as the apostolic age. But the only really important question, relative to the origin of this liturgy, which admits of a satisfactory decision, is, whether we are to regard it as the ancient liturgy of the church of Alexandria. And if I have succeeded in establishing an affirmative reply to this question, we may be enabled to account for this liturgy obtaining the title of "St. Mark's;" for it was the liturgy used by St. Mark's church, and was derived from the instructions which he had first given to that church. In my opinion, this appellation of "St. " Mark's liturgy" began about the end of the fourth or beginning of the fifth century, after Basil had composed his liturgy, which appears to have been the first liturgy that bore the name of any man. Other churches then gave their liturgies the names of their founders. And so the Alexandrians and Egyptians gave theirs the name of "St. Mark's;"

[t] Zaccaria, Biblioth. Ritual tom. 1. p. 10 Sirletus in Epist. ad Joh. à S Andrea, &c.
[u] Dorschæus, Mysaria Mys-sæ, p. 225; Le Nourry, App. ad Bibl. Patrum, p. 57. Paris. 1694; Cave, Hist Literar.; Bona, Rer. Lit. lib. i. c. 8, &c

and they of Jerusalem and Antioch called theirs "St. James's." And early in the fifth century it appears that Cyril, patriarch of Alexandria, perfected and improved the liturgy of Mark, from whence this improved liturgy came to be called by the Monophysites, "St. Cyril's;" and by the orthodox, "St. Mark's."

With regard to the liturgy of the Melchites, or orthodox of Alexandria, now known as "St. Mark's "liturgy," I may be permitted to make a few remarks, which will tend to account for the differences that exist between it and the Monophysite Coptic liturgy of Cyril. The liturgy of St. Mark, therefore, is to be regarded as a liturgy used by the orthodox Egyptians after the council of Chalcedon, A.D. 451, altered and arranged by them to suit the liturgies of Constantinople. Renaudot has not taken this view of St. Mark's liturgy; but I think it tends to explain several things which he has remarked without accounting for[v]. The orthodox of Egypt, after the invasion of the Mahommedans, were a small and persecuted party. For a hundred years they had no patriarch, they could hold no public assemblies, and their clergy were ordained either at Constantinople or Cæsarea. Being thus entirely dependent on the patriarch of Constantinople, it is not unnatural to suppose that they adapted their rites as much as possible to the Constantinopolitan. And we find ultimately, that they actually received the liturgies of that church to the exclusion of their own. Let us, then, examine the liturgy which they used after this state of depression, and before

---

[v] See his Notes on St Mark's Liturgy, tom. 1. p. 353, &c.

they received the Constantinopolitan liturgies, and ascertain whether there are any traces of an approximation to the Greek rite[w].

First the ancient prayers of absolution[x] and incense appear to have been amalgamated and formed into the prayer called the "prayer of Introit[y]," to correspond with the Greek prayer of the same title[z], while no such title occurs in the Coptic or Ethiopic liturgies. Secondly, the prayer after St. Paul's Epistles[a] seems to have given way to a "prayer of "Trisagios[b]," to correspond with a similar prayer in the Greek[c], while nothing of the kind occurs in the Coptic and Ethiopic. Thirdly, the Gospel is preceded by an offering of incense[d] with the same words as are used in the Greek rite[e], while no such words are prescribed in the Coptic and Ethiopic liturgies. Fourthly, the Cherubic hymn, of which there is no mention in the Coptic or Ethiopic rites, is appointed to be sung[f] at the same place as in the Greek[g]. Fifthly, the kiss of peace precedes the

---

[w] In this comparison it must be remembered, that the liturgy of Cyril must be affixed to the general introduction of the Egyptian liturgy, which is placed before the liturgy of Basil, from p. 1. to p. 13. Renaudot, tom. 1.

[x] Renaudot, p. 3 5
[y] Ibid p. 135
[z] Goar, Rituale Græc p 67
εὐχὴ τῆς εἰσόδου τοῦ ἁγίου εὐαγγελίου.
[a] Renaudot, p. 6.
[b] Ibid p. 136.
[c] Goar, Rituale Græc. p. 68.
εὐχὴ τοῦ τρισαγίου
[d] Renaudot, p. 137
[e] Goar, Rituale Græc p 69.

[f] Renaudot, p. 141 Renaudot has not sufficiently explained the rubric which here occurs in the liturgy of Mark, and is as follows. καὶ ψάλλουσιν οἱ Χερουβὶμ μυστικῶς. This, he says, means that they are to repeat a prayer beginning οἱ Χερουβὶμ, κ. τ. λ But in truth it plainly refers to the Greek cherubic hymn, which was introduced precisely into this part of the Greek liturgy in the time of the emperor Justin, (see Goar, not 108. in Liturg Chrysost.) and which begins οἱ τὰ Χερουβὶμ μυστικῶς εἰκονίζοντες, &c. Goar, p. 106
[g] Goar, p. 72

Creed[h], as in the Greek liturgies[i], while in the Coptic and Ethiopic it follows the Creed[j]. Sixthly, the prayer of Prothesis, which had probably occurred at first in the beginning of the liturgy, was placed close to the Creed, like the Greek[k]. This position of the prayer of Prothesis has been remarked by Renaudot, who seems at a loss to account for this disturbance of the order of the liturgy. Seventhly, in the general prayers, before the commemoration of the Virgin Mary, the anthem Χαῖρε κεχαριτωμένη is introduced[l]. Now there is no such anthem in the Coptic and Ethiopic liturgies, and yet it is incredible, that if it had ever been in these, it would have been afterwards omitted. We must therefore look for some foreign authority for the introduction of this anthem into St. Mark's liturgy. And we find it in the Greek or Constantinopolitan liturgy, where there is always an anthem of the kind in this place[m], and in the ancient MS. of Crypta Ferrata this very anthem is prescribed both in Basil's and Chrysostom's liturgies[n].

I have no doubt that other persons may discover more instances of changes made by the orthodox Alexandrians to adapt their liturgy to the Constantinopolitan rite[o]. Thus much, however, may suffice to shew, that in places where it varies from the

[h] P. 143 Renaudot
[i] Goar, p. 75.
[j] Renaudot, p. 12. 512, 513. tom. i.
[k] Ibid. p. 143 Compare p. 3. and Goar, Rit. Græc p. 74, 75.
[l] Renaudot, p. 149.
[m] Goar, p. 78

[n] Ibid p 103. 178.
[o] These will probably be easily traced in the Anaphora, which seems to have been modelled in many respects after the language and manner of the Constantinopolitan liturgies of Basil and Chrysostom.

Coptic liturgy of Cyril, and the Ethiopic general canon, the liturgy of Mark is not to be esteemed the rule by which we are to judge of the ancient Alexandrian rites: though in these very places it often throws great light on the Coptic and Ethiopic liturgies, and affords strong confirmation of their antiquity. So little remains of the history of the orthodox Alexandrians, that it is impossible to determine exactly the time when these alterations were introduced. It must certainly have occurred before the twelfth century, because the MS. of St. Mark's liturgy is as old as that time. Very probably it took place about the eighth century, when the orthodox had again patriarchs of their own, some of whom might have adapted their liturgy to the rites which had been gradually introduced by priests ordained in Constantinople during a century of persecution and depression. And considering the small number of the orthodox in Egypt, the persecutions which they suffered, and their subsequent adoption of the liturgies used at Constantinople, it may be regarded as wonderful that any monument of their ancient liturgy has survived.

Before I state the order and substance of the ancient Alexandrian liturgy, it may be advisable to correct the mistakes of Renaudot as to the monuments which most authentically represent it. Renaudot states that the Anaphoræ of the Coptic liturgy of Basil, and of St. Mark's, have "*the same* "*order*, prayers agreeing in the same meaning, "similar rites, but a great variety in the expres-"sions[p]." It is strange that a man of such learn-

---

[p] " Superest pars secunda in qua major omnino Marci et Basilii liturgiarum diversitas. Est quidem non in illis modo

ing and diligence should have made such a mistake; but a simple inspection is enough to refute him. The order is perfectly different. Renaudot indeed remarks elsewhere, that these Anaphoræ of Basil and Mark *do not agree*[q], from whence he infers, that St. Mark's was not the common canon of the old Alexandrian rite, but belonged to some particular church. And the proof which he brings for Basil's liturgy having been the canon of the Alexandrian church (at least after the conquest of Egypt by the Mahommedans) is, that it accords with the Ethiopic general canon, which is nothing but "a liberal ver-"sion of Basil's Coptic liturgy[r]." It is scarcely necessary to refute this, because all that it attempts to prove is, that Basil's liturgy was chiefly used by the Copts *after* the Mahommedan invasion. But the important question is, what liturgy was used during the time of the Christian emperors; which question is not touched by the result of Renaudot's argument. However, the proof which he brings,

---

sed in omnibus antiquis aliis cujuscumque linguæ, *idem ordo*, orationes in eandem sententiam convenientes, ritus similes, sed insignis ex verborum varietate diversitas." Tom. 1 p. xciv

[q] "Secunda pars——non est eadem, neque convenit nisi eâ quam diximus generali conformitate rituum et sententiarum, cum prima et præcipua Coptica, quæ est Basilii. Ex eâ igitur ratione illam (Marci) qualis Græcè edita est, non esse canonem, ut uno verbo vocare possumus, communem veteris Alexandrini ritus intelligimus, sed *singularem*," &c p. xcvi.

[r] "Fieri enim facile potuit ut ex magno illo ecclesiarum numero quæ Alexandrino patriarchæ suberant, nonnullæ eadem (Marci) frequentius uterentur, quamvis major earum pars Basilianâ——uti soleret, saltem à capta à Mahumedanis Ægypto Ita enim rem se habere demonstrat Æthiopum——disciplina Canon enim generalis Æthiopum qui communem liturgiæ formam continet, Basilianæ Liturgiæ Copticæ quædam liberior versio est," p xcvi

that Basil's liturgy was chiefly used by the Copts after the Mahommedan invasion, is invalid. For the Ethiopic general canon is not (as he says) a liberal version of Basil's liturgy, but accords with Cyril's and Mark's, as any one may see by an actual comparison.

Let us, then, proceed to examine the chief features of the ancient Alexandrian rite, as depicted in the liturgies of Mark and Cyril, supported by the Ethiopic general canon; omitting, however, any notice of that part of the introduction which preceded the dismissal of the catechumens, because in the most primitive times there was little else contained in it besides the reading of lessons and the sermon.

After the dismissal of the catechumens and some prayers of the faithful[s], the priest and people saluted each other thus, "Peace be with you;" "And with thy spirit[t]." Then followed the apostolical kiss of peace. The deacon proclaimed στῶμεν καλῶς[u], and the form of "Sursum corda," &c. followed[v]. Then began the eucharistia or thanksgiving, in which the great peculiarity of the Egyptian rite becomes immediately visible. All the solemn prayers for men and things, the commemorations of the living and the dead, are inserted in this place[w], after the form "Sursum corda." Then the thanksgiving being resumed again, as it proceeds, the deacon successively commands those who are sitting, to "arise[x]," and "look towards the east[y]." The thanks-

[s] Renaudot, tom. i. p. 10—12. 139, 140 511—513
[t] P. 12 60. 141.
[u] 64. 98.
[v] P. 40. 144.
[w] P. 41—45. 146—153. 514—516.
[x] P. 45. 153. 516.
[y] P. 46. 153. 516.

giving continues, and the priest mentions the " ten " thousand thousand angels and archangels who " stand ministering to God[z]," and the two seraphim with six wings, with two of which they veil their faces, " on account of the divinity of God invisible " and incomprehensible by the mind[a]." With these beings the people praise God, saying the hymn *Tersanctus*[b]. The priest implores God to bless with the Holy Spirit the sacrifice and gifts of bread and wine placed before him[c]. Then follow the commemoration of our Lord's deeds and words at the last supper[d], a verbal commemoration of his death, resurrection[e], &c. the offering of the gifts which God has given us[f], a prayer of humble deprecation[g], and the invocation or prayer to God to send the Holy Ghost, and make the bread and cup the body and blood of Christ, that they may be efficacious for obtaining spiritual benefits for those who are to partake of them[h]. Then follow the breaking of the bread[i], the Lord's Prayer[j], a benediction[k], and the form τὰ ἅγια τοῖς ἁγίοις. Then the communion of clergy and laity, which is succeeded by a thanksgiving.

[z] P. 46. 154 516
[a] P. 46.
[b] P. 46. 154. 516.
[c] P 46 155 It is not found in the Æthiopic, and perhaps did not originally occur in this part of the Alexandrian liturgy
[d] P. 46, 47 155. 517.
[e] P. 47. 156 517
[f] P. 47 157. 517
[g] P. 47, 48. This does not occur in St. Mark's or the Æthiopic liturgy, and is therefore of doubtful antiquity

[h] P 49 158 517
[i] P. 49 518 Mark's liturgy defers the breaking of bread till after the Lord's Prayer, in imitation of the Greek rite Compare Goar, Rit. Græc. p. 80, 81
[j] P. 50. 159.
[k] P. 22. 519 In the liturgy of St Mark it is omitted, to suit the Greek rite, and another benediction more like the Greek is introduced

It will be observed, that the difference between this liturgy and the great oriental liturgy of Antioch, Cæsarea, and Constantinople, already described, is in the *order* of the parts. The general and solemn prayers for men and things occurred in the middle of the Egyptian eucharistia or thanksgiving, and before the hymn *Tersanctus*. In the oriental liturgy the general prayers are deferred till after the end of the benediction of the gifts. Another peculiarity in this rite was the directions of the deacon to the people during the course of the thanksgiving, to "arise," "look towards " the east," and "attend," or "sing" the hymn *Tersanctus*. Of this there is nothing to be found in any other rite.

Let us now compare this liturgy with the writings of the Fathers of the Alexandrian patriarchate, amongst whom the law of secrecy was so carefully attended to, that we have very few memorials of the Egyptian rites amongst them. The dismissal of catechumens is mentioned by Cyril of Alexandria[1], and is alluded to by almost every Egyptian father. Cyril also quotes a passage in the prayer of the faithful[m]. He also refers to the salutation of "Peace

---

[1] Ὁ κατηχούμενος—καὶ τοῖς τελείοις συναναθεὶς τὴν αἴνεσιν, τῶν ἔτι μυστικωτέρων ἀποφοιτᾷ, καὶ θυσίας εἴργεται τῆς ἐπὶ Χριστῷ. Cyril. Alex. de Adorat in Spir et Veritat. lib xii. p. 445. tom. i. Paris. 1638.

[m] Δεδιδάγμεθα δὲ καὶ λέγειν ἐν προσευχαῖς· Κύριε ὁ Θεὸς ἡμῶν εἰρήνην δὸς ἡμῖν, πάντα γὰρ ἀπέδωκας ἡμῖν. Cyril. Alex. Epist. ad Joan. Antioch. tom. v pars ii.

p 105 Epistolarum In the Greek text of the Alexandrian prayer of the faithful we find these words, Βασιλεὺς τῆς εἰρήνης τὴν σὴν εἰρήνην δὸς ἡμῖν, πάντα γὰρ ἀπέδωκας ἡμῖν Renaudot, tom. 1. p 59. In the Coptic we find the same, "O Rex pacis, da nobis pacem tuam, qui omnia dedisti nobis," p. 10. In the Æthiopic the same words occur, p. 511

"be with you," and the reply, and the kiss of peace[n], which are likewise mentioned by Isidore of Pelusium[o], and Origen[p]. The form of στῶμεν καλῶς is apparently referred to by Cyril Alexandrinus[q]. The eucharistia or thanksgiving is mentioned by Dionysius, bishop of Alexandria[r], and Origen[s]. Athanasius speaks of the prayer for the emperor[t]. The commemoration of the departed is mentioned by the Egyptian bishops in their epistle to Anatolius, bishop of Constantinople[u], by John Cas-

[n] Speaking of our Saviour's saying, εἰρήνη ὑμῖν, he says, τοιγάρ τοι καὶ ἐν ταῖς ἁγίαις μάλιστα συνόδοις, ἤτοι συνάξεσι, παρ' αὐτὰς τοῦ μυστηρίου τὰς ἀρχὰς τοῦτο δὲ ἡμεῖς ἀλλήλοις φαμέν. Cyril. Alex. com. in Joh. c. 20. lib. xii. tom. iv. p. 1093 Paris 1638.

[o] "Pacem Sacerdos ex cathedræ fastigio ecclesiæ pronunciat, Dominum scilicet imitans cathedram assumentem, cum pacem suam discipulis relinqueret et daret. Illud autem quod a plebe responditur, 'Et cum spiritu tuo,' hanc habet sententiam," &c. Isidor. Pelus. Epistol lib. i ep. 122. p. 38. edit. Paris. 1638

[p] In Ruffinus's translation of Origen's Commentary on the Epistle to the Romans, we find mention made of the *osculum;* but Ruffinus has evidently used *post* instead of *ante,* in order to suit the liturgy of Italy. "Ex hoc sermone ('salutate invicem in osculo sancto') aliisque nonnullis similibus, mos ecclesiis traditus est ut *post* (lege, *ante*) orationes osculo se invicem suscipiant fratres." Origen. lib x. in Rom. xvi. 16.

tom. iv. ed. Bened. p. 683.

[q] Speaking of the deacon's office, he says, ἢ οὐκ αὐτοὶ προστάττουσι διακεκραγότες ἐν ἐκκλησίαις—ἐν κόσμῳ μὲν ἑστάναι, Ador. in Spir et Verit. p 454. tom. i lib xiii.

[r] Dionysius objected to rebaptizing a certain man thus, εὐχαριστίας γὰρ ἐπακούσαντα, καὶ συνεπιφθεγξάμενον τὸ 'Αμὴν, καὶ τραπέζῃ παραστάντα, καὶ χεῖρας εἰς ὑποδοχὴν τῆς ἁγίας τροφῆς προτείναντα· καὶ ταύτην καταδεξάμενον, καὶ τοῦ σώματος καὶ τοῦ αἵματος τοῦ Κυρίου ἡμῶν Ἰησοῦ Χριστοῦ μετασχόντα ἱκανῷ χρόνῳ, οὐκ ἂν ἐξ ὑπαρχῆς ἀνασκευάζειν ἔτι τολμήσαιμι. Dionys. Alex. ad Xystum Rom. ap. Euseb. lib vii c. 9.

[s] Ἡμεῖς δὲ τῷ τοῦ παντὸς δημιουργῷ εὐχαριστοῦντες, καὶ τοὺς μετ' εὐχαριστίας καὶ εὐχῆς τῆς ἐπὶ τοῖς δοθεῖσι προσαγομένοις ἄρτους ἐσθίομεν. Orig. adv. Cels. lib. viii. tom. i. p. 766.

[t] Σὺ δὲ θεοφιλέστατε βασιλεῦ, ποῦ τοὺς λαοὺς ἂν ἤθελες ἐκτεῖναι τὰς χεῖρας καὶ εὔξασθαι περὶ σοῦ, Athanas Apol. ad Imp. Constant cap. 16. p 304. tom. 1 ed. Paris. 1698

[u] "Etiam in venerabili dip-

sian[v], and by Origen, who appears to quote from the liturgy, and his quotations are accordant in meaning and substance with the prayers in the Egyptian liturgies[w].

The deacon's proclamation to "arise" is probably alluded to by Cyril[x]. The part of the preface or thanksgiving which speaks of "ten thousand thou-"sand angels," &c. is perhaps referred to by Origen[y];

tycho, in quo piæ memoriæ transitum ad cœlos habentium episcopum vocabula continentur, quæ tempore sanctorum mysteriorum secundum sanctas regulas religuntur, posuit et Dioscori nomen." Epist. Ægypt Episcop ad Anatol Constant cited in Cassian's Works, p. 333.

[v] "Quamobrem—vix a presbytero abbati Paphnutio potuit obtineri ut non inter Biothanatos (i e suicidos) reputatus, etiam memoria et oblatione pausantium judicaretur indignus" Cass. Collat 2. c. 2. p. 332 Oper. Atrebat. 1628

[w] Πολλάκις ἐν ταῖς εὐχαῖς λέγομεν, Θεὲ παντόκρατορ τὴν μερίδα ἡμῖν μετὰ τῶν προφητῶν δός. τὴν μερίδα ἡμῖν μετὰ τῶν ἀποστόλων τοῦ Χριστοῦ σοῦ δὸς, ἵνα εὑρεθῶμεν καὶ μετ' αὐτοῦ τοῦ Χριστοῦ. He immediately afterwards amends the expression thus, δός μοι μερίδα μετὰ τῶν προφητῶν—δός μοι μερίδα μετὰ τῶν ἀποστόλων. Orig. Hom. xiv. in Jeremiam (olim xi.) p. 217, 218. tom. iii. ed. Benedict. In the liturgy of Mark we find, Κύριε Θεὲ πάτερ παντοκράτορ, p. 144, and having spoken of πατριαρχῶν, προφητῶν, ἀποστόλων, &c. the liturgy proceeds thus, δὸς ἡμῖν μερίδα καὶ κλῆρον ἐχεῖν μετὰ πάντων τῶν ἁγίων σου, p 150 Renaudot. See nearly the same in the liturgy of Cyril, p 40—42 probably a little altered and added to after the time of Augustine, who first objected to the primitive custom of praying for the martyrs and saints. Another petition is found in the Alexandrian liturgy, which agrees in sense with Origen's quotation at p. 6 of Basil's Coptic liturgy. See Renaudot, tom. i.

[x] ἣ οὐκ αὐτοὶ προστάττουσι διακεκραγότες ἐν ἐκκλησίαις—διανιστᾶσιν εἰς προσευχάς; Cyril Alex. de Ador. in Spir. et Verit. lib. xiii. p. 454 tom 1

[y] Having spoken of the oblations made to the true God and not to dæmons, he adds, εἰ δὲ καὶ πλῆθος ποθοῦμεν ὧν φιλανθρώπων τυγχάνειν θέλομεν, μανθάνομεν ὅτι χίλιαι χιλιάδες παρειστήκεισαν αὐτῷ, καὶ μυρίαι μυριάδες ἐλειτούργουν αὐτῷ· αἵτινες, ὡς συγγενεῖς καὶ φίλους τοὺς μιμουμένους τὴν εἰς Θεὸν αὐτῶν εὐσέβειαν ὁρῶντες, &c. See the whole context. Orig adv Celsum, lib. viii p. 766. tom. 1. ed. Benedict.

SECT. IV. *Liturgy of Alexandria* 103

at least, the idea was familiar to him in connection with this part of the liturgy. The part of the thanksgiving which speaks of the cherubim covering their faces with their wings on account of the nature of God, is perhaps alluded to by Cyril Alexandrinus[z], and this mystical explanation is given by other Egyptian Fathers. The deacon's proclamation to "sing" the hymn *Tersanctus* seems peculiar to the Egyptian liturgy, and we find an allusion to it in the writings of Cyril[a]; in the same place he seems to notice the hymn *Tersanctus*, which is also alluded to by Origen[b]. The oblation is spoken of by Cyril[c], Athanasius[d], and Origen[e]. Theophilus of Alexandria[f], Isidore of Pelusium[g], and perhaps

[z] Σύμβολον δὲ τὸ, ταῖς πτέρυξι κατακαλύπτειν τὰ Σεραφεὶμ τό τε πρόσωπον καὶ τοὺς πόδας, πέτασθαι δὲ ταῖς δυσὶν, τοῦ μὴ δύνασθαί τινας ἢ ἀρχὴν ἢ τέλος ὁρᾶν ἐννοιῶν ἢ λόγων τῶν περὶ Θεοῦ y ril. Alex. Com. in Esaiam, lib 1. orat 4 p 103. tom. ii.

[a] The deacon's office he says is to proclaim ποτὲ μὲν, ὑμνολογεῖν ὅτι προσήκει λαοῖς. De Ador. in Spir. et Ver. p. 454. tom. i. This seems to refer to the forms προσχῶμεν or "Respondete" Renaudot, tom i. p. 65, 29, 101, 516. The hymn alluded to by Cyril was probably the hymn *Tersanctus*.

[b] Probably alluded to in the words τοὺς μιμουμένους cited above, from lib. viii. adv. Celsum. For Christians *imitated* the angels in singing the hymn *Tersanctus*.

[c] ὁ κατηχούμενος—θυσίας εἴργεται τῆς ἐπὶ Χριστῷ See note[1], page 100

[d] ἢ πῶς οἷόν τε ἦν προσφορὰν προκεῖσθαι, ἔνδον ὄντων τῶν κατηχουμένων, εἰ γὰρ ἔνδον ἦσαν οἱ κατηχούμενοι, οὔπω ἦν ὁ καιρὸς τῆς προσφορᾶς. Athanas. Apol. cont. Arian p. 148 tom i. ed. Benedict.

[e] καὶ τοὺς μετ' εὐχαριστίας καὶ εὐχῆς τῆς ἐπὶ τοῖς δοθεῖσι προσαγομένους ἄρτους ἐσθίομεν, σῶμα γενομένους διὰ τὴν εὐχὴν ἅγιόν τι καὶ ἁγιάζον τοὺς μετὰ ὑγιοῦς προθέσεως αὐτῷ χρωμένους Adv. Celsum, lib. viii. p 766. tom. i.

[f] Speaking of Origen he accuses him thus: "Non recogitat panem Dominicum quo Salvatoris corpus ostenditur, et quem frangimus in sanctificationem nostri, et sacrum calicem, quæ in mensa ecclesiæ, et utique in anima sunt, per invocationem et adventum Sancti Spiritus sanctificari." Theoph. Alex. Liber Paschal I

[g] μὴ ὕβριζε τὴν θείαν λειτουργίαν, μὴ ἀτίμαζε τὴν τῶν καρπῶν

Origen[h], refer to the invocation of the Holy Ghost. The concluding *Amen* of the people is mentioned by Athanasius[i], and Dionysius of Alexandria[j], as the breaking of the bread is by Theophilus Alexandrinus[k] and others.

I have not the slightest doubt that a more minute examination of the Egyptian Fathers than I have been able to make, would discover many additional proofs and coincidences. What has been done will perhaps shew, that there is a sufficient confirmation of the general order of the Egyptian liturgy already described, from the writings of the Egyptian Fathers. I have myself observed some other things, which might give confirmation to what has been said. But as they arise chiefly from a conformity of expression and idea on many topics between the Egyptian Fathers and liturgies, the discussion would be too long.

I have, then, shewn that a certain form of liturgy prevailed throughout the patriarchate of Alexandria in the fifth century, from a comparison of the liturgies used by two bodies of men who have held no communion since that time. I have compared the liturgy thus ascertained with the writings of the Egyptian Fathers of the fifth, fourth, and third centuries; and so far as I can discover from thence, the same order appears to have prevailed from the ear-

---

εὐλογίαν—ἀλλὰ μεμνημένος ὡς αἷμα Χριστοῦ τὴν τούτου ἀπαρχὴν τὸ θεῖον ἐργάζεται πνεῦμα, οὕτως αὐτῷ κέχρησο Lib. i Epist. 313.

[h] When he says, σῶμα γενομένους διὰ τὴν εὐχήν Lib viii adv Cels cited above

[i] τί ἐὰν τοσούτων λαῶν συνελθόντων μία γένηται φωνὴ, λεγόντων τῷ Θεῷ τὸ 'Αμήν, Apolog. ad Imper Constant. c. 16. p. 305. tom. 1

[j] In the passage quoted in note [r], page 101.

[k] In the passage quoted above in note [f], p. 103. from the Lib Pasch. I

liest period. I have also remarked, that the Ethiopians have probably had the same liturgy, *as to order*, since the fourth century, when they derived it from Alexandria; and I find that order agreeing with the Alexandrian of the fifth century, already ascertained. In conclusion, then, we can ascertain with considerable certainty the words and expressions of the Alexandrian liturgy before the council of Chalcedon, A.D. 451; and we can trace back its substance and order to a period of far greater antiquity. In fact, there is nothing unreasonable in supposing that the main order and substance of the Alexandrian liturgy, as used in the fifth century, may have been as old as the apostolic age, and derived originally from the instructions and appointment of the blessed Evangelist Mark.

The liturgies of Cyril and Mark are found at p. 38 and 131 of the first volume of Renaudot's Collection of Oriental Liturgies. The reader, however, should remember, that he must prefix the Introduction, which extends from page 1 to page 12 of the same volume, in order to complete Cyril's liturgy. The notes of Renaudot on Cyril's and Mark's liturgies are useful. But the chief explanations of Egyptian rites (chiefly those of the Monophysites in latter times) are found in his notes on Basil's liturgy in the same volume. The Ethiopian liturgy with notes is found at the end of the volume.

SECTION V.

LITURGY OF THE EXARCHATE OF EPHESUS.

THE ancient exarchate or patriarchate of Ephesus extended over the provinces of Hellespontus, Phrygia, Asia, Lycaonia, Pamphylia, and the maritime territory included within that line. The exarch of Ephesus, who had been previously an independent patriarch, became subject to the jurisdiction of the patriarch of Constantinople about the time of Chrysostom; and the fourth general council, held at Chalcedon, A.D. 451, confirmed this arrangement. However, the bishop of Ephesus, as well as the bishop of Cæsarea, (who was in the same circumstances,) retained the name and some of the authority of an exarch in succeeding ages; and in general councils they have always sat and subscribed immediately after the patriarchs.

The whole exarchate of Ephesus has for a length of time received the Constantinopolitan liturgies of Basil and Chrysostom; but I think there is some reason to affirm that the order which is represented by these liturgies, has not always prevailed in that exarchate. A celebrated council held at Laodicea in Phrygia some time in the fourth century, was attended by the bishops of Asia and Phrygia, that is, of the exarchate of Ephesus. The nineteenth canon of this council has long been celebrated for the minute directions which it gives for the celebration of the liturgy; being in fact almost the only canon made during several centuries, that appears to regulate the order of divine service. Such a canon could not have been made without some cause; and I see none more probable than this; that a different order of liturgy had previously been used, which it was then thought expedient to alter.

It seems to me that this canon appoints an order similar to that which is now used in those churches, namely, that of the liturgies of Basil and Chrysostom. First, it directs a homily of the bishop. This is well known to have been customary in those liturgies at all times. Secondly, the prayer of catechumens. This is preserved by the above liturgies[a]. Thirdly, the prayer of penitents. This was formerly used according to Joannes Zonaras[b]; but the extinction of the penitential discipline rendered it useless, and therefore it has been omitted. Fourthly, *three* prayers of the faithful; the first said in silence, the two others, διὰ προσφωνήσεως. There are certainly three prayers in this part of Basil's and Chrysostom's liturgies[c]; but the difficulty is, that the two former only are entitled "Prayers of the "Faithful." However, I think it not improbable,

---

[a] Liturgia Chrysostomi, Goar, p. 70 Basilii id. p. 161.

[b] In his Commentary on the nineteenth canon of the council of Laodicea. Vid. Beveregii Pandect. tom. i p. 461.

[c] I say *three*, because the prayer of the cherubic hymn is not so ancient as the rest. For according to Cedrenus, this hymn was not used till the time of the Emperor Justin. Goar, p. 131. not 101. in Chrysost. Liturg.

either that the third prayer may have altered its title to "a Prayer of Oblation;" or else that it may have been more recent than the council of Laodicea, and the silent prayer formerly said before the existing "Prayers of the Faithful," may in process of time have become obsolete, as happened in the western liturgies[d]. And in either case we have the number of prayers mentioned by the council of Laodicea. Fifthly, this canon appointed the kiss of peace to be given, and the oblation or liturgy to be celebrated; which accords with the order of the liturgies of Basil and Chrysostom.

It seems to me, therefore, that the council of Laodicea established within the patriarchate of Ephesus the same order of liturgy which now prevails there: and if so, we may suspect that an order different from that of the liturgies of Basil and Chrysostom formerly prevailed; and further, that it differed from them chiefly in that part which intervened between the sermon and the beginning of the oblation or thanksgiving, because it is only this part of the liturgy that is regulated by the canon which we are considering.

In the ninth section of this Dissertation the reader will see, that there are several reasons for thinking the ancient Gallican liturgy had been originally derived from that of the exarchate of Ephesus, or of the churches of Asia and Phrygia. Perhaps by examining the order of this Gallican liturgy, we may find some clue to guide us through the

---

[d] Bingham shews that silent prayers were used in the east and west Book xv. chapter i. section 1. This subject is noticed in section 7. of this Dissertation in speaking of the collect of the Milan liturgy called "super sindonem."

intricacies of this subject. It seems to me that the liturgy referred to, differed from those of Basil and Chrysostom exactly in that part which is so carefully regulated by the council of Laodicea. *First*, we have no account of any prayers made after the sermon for catechumens and penitents, during the earliest ages of the Gallican and Spanish churches, who used the same liturgy. They are not mentioned by Gregory of Tours, by Isidore of Seville, nor by any of the authors referred to by Mabillon, in his treatise on the Gallican liturgy. It is true that Martene understands the author of the tract which he has published, and which is referred to Germanus bishop of Paris, to speak of prayers for catechumens[e]. But I confess, that in perusing the passage to which he alludes, I am unable to see that the author of the tract does more than refer to prayers for catechumens, as an ancient custom of the church, which he seems to describe as a thing not then practised, and which he does not affirm to have been used in the *Gallican* church. Supposing, however, that these prayers for catechumens were used in Gaul, of which we have no sort of authentic evidence, they might very probably have been imported from the east about the same time as the *Trisagios*, which is prescribed in that tract, and which was first introduced into the eastern liturgy in the fifth century[f]. *Secondly*, we have no account of any prayer or prayers "of the faithful," in

---

[e] See Martene, Thesaurus Anecdotorum, tom. v. p 94.

[f] See Martene ut supra p. 91, and Goar, Rituale Græcum, p 126. not. 80. in Liturg. Chrys The hymn *Trisagios* mentioned here, must not be confounded with the seraphic hymn, or *Tersanctus*, which occurs in the course of the solemn thanksgiving, before the consecration.

the Gallican liturgy. But instead of this, the elements were placed on the altar, and the diptychs, containing the names of the living and dead, recited; after which the priest made a prayer. The kiss of peace and oblation succeeded, as in the liturgies of Basil and Chrysostom.

It seems, therefore, that the Gallican liturgy differed from those just mentioned, exactly in that part which is regulated by the canon of Laodicea[g]. And since we should be able to account for that canon, by supposing that a liturgy like the ancient Gallican, prevailed in Asia and Phrygia before the council of Laodicea; and further, since we have independent reasons for thinking that the Gallican liturgy was derived in the second century from that of Asia and Phrygia; it seems to me highly probable that a liturgy which resembled the ancient Gallican prevailed in the exarchate of Ephesus until the fourth century, when it was altered by the council of Laodicea, in order to make it conformable to the great oriental rite, which has been used there ever since.

[g] It may be objected that I remark in the ninth section, that there was another difference between the Gallican and oriental liturgies, namely, that the Gallican did not contain the long prayers for all estates of men, and for all things, which in the oriental occurred after the consecration. But there is no sort of improbability in the idea, that the churches of Asia and Phrygia may have received such prayers into that part of the liturgy *before* the council of Laodicea, in which case their "*oblation*" or canon would have exactly agreed with that of the oriental liturgy, and the council of Laodicea would only have had to direct the "*oblation*," or canon, to follow the kiss of peace, as it actually did.

SECTION VI.

LITURGY OF THE PATRIARCHATE OF ROME.

It has been much debated among learned men, whether the Roman liturgy can justly claim any considerable antiquity. Some have referred its composition to Gregory the First, commonly called "the "Great," patriarch of Rome, A. D. 590. Others think it impossible at this day to ascertain the text, even as it stood in the time of that prelate[a]. This subject has been confused, by mistaking for each other two very different things, the missal and the liturgy. The Roman *missal* (formerly called Sacramentary, or book of sacraments) was a large volume containing a number of missæ or offices for particular days, which were to be added, in the proper place, to the canon in which the more solemn prayers and the consecration were contained. By the Roman *liturgy* I understand the canon which did not vary, and the number and order of the prayers which were to be added from the missal.

[a] Dupin, Hist. Ecc. cent vi. tom. v. p. 102. Brett's Collection of Liturgies, p. 333, &c.

The various readings of manuscript sacramentaries are supposed to render it impossible to determine the text as it stood in the time of Gregory; but on examining these difficulties, it will be found that they do not prevent us from ascertaining the liturgy: for all the variations, interpolations, and uncertainties of these MSS. relate to the individual missæ. In these I readily admit that a great variation, both of words and sentiments, may be found; and it is therefore a matter of some difficulty to decide which of the missæ are as old as the time of Gregory. Such doubts and difficulties, however, do not extend to the number and order of the prayers in each missa, nor to the canon. On the contrary, we find in all, the same number of prayers, arranged in the same order, and designated by the same titles. The canon, or invariable part, preserves the same text in all MSS. The only difference that occurs is the introduction of some short prayer, or of the name of some person to be commemorated: but such interpolations are very rare, and when found are easily detected; and in no case is the canon itself either mutilated or altered. We can therefore ascertain both the invariable and the variable parts of the Roman liturgy. This agreement of MSS. in one common order and text derives strength from a consideration of the different ages and countries in which they were written. Manuscripts of Italy, of England, Germany, and Gaul, whether written at the same period or not, all furnish the same order of prayers and canon. To this evidence we may add the writings of various liturgical commentators in the eighth, ninth, and tenth centuries; which, though composed in different countries, all concur in establishing the same facts as the manuscripts.

It appears, then, that there is no difficulty in ascertaining what the Roman liturgy was in the time of Gregory the Great. It may however be inquired, whether Gregory is to be considered the author of that liturgy. To answer this question, we must have recourse to ancient history. We are there informed with minuteness of the amount of Gregory's alterations and improvements. He collected, arranged, improved, abbreviated the collects of the individual missæ[b]. He inserted a short passage (which is known) into the canon[c]. And he joined the Lord's Prayer to the canon[d], from which it had previously been separated by the breaking of the bread. All this amounts to positive proof that Gregory was the reviser and improver, not the author of the Roman liturgy.

An attempt has been made to prove that the Roman liturgy was composed between the time of Vigilius and Gregory[e]. The former, who lived fifty years before the latter, speaking of the canon, said,

---

[b] "Gelasianum codicem de missarum solemniis, multa subtrahens, pauca convertens, nonnulla vero superadjiciens—in *unius libri* volumine coarctavit." Joannes Diaconus in Vita Gregorii Magni.

[c] "Sed et in ipsa missarum celebratione tria verba maximæ perfectionis plena superadjecit: 'Diesque nostros in tua pace disponas, atque ab æterna damnatione nos eripi, et in electorum tuorum jubeas grege numerari.'" Ven. Bedæ Hist. Eccles. lib ii c. 1. Compare Menard. Sacramentar. Gregorii p. 2.

[d] "Orationem vero Dominicam *mox* post precem dicimus, quia mos apostolorum fuit, ut ad ipsam solummodo orationem oblationis hostiam consecrarent." Gregorii Mag. Epist. ad Joannem Syracusan. Epist. xii. lib. ix. edit. Benedict. (olim 64.)

[e] Brett's Collection of Liturgies, part ii. p. 331.

" that they had received it from apostolical tradi-
" tion[f]." Gregory spoke of the canon extant in his
time, as having been composed by a scholastic, or
learned man[g]. It is argued, that if the canon in
Vigilius's time had been received from apostolical
tradition, and if that in Gregory's time had been
composed by a scholastic, the canons of Vigilius
and Gregory must have been different, and the
latter must have been written since the time of
Vigilius.

I reply, first, that Gregory and Vigilius may very
well have spoken of the same canon; for even if a
scholastic had composed the canon, yet he might be
supposed to have received its order, and substance,
and principal expressions, from apostolical tradition;
and therefore the canon so composed might be said
to have come from apostolical tradition. It has been
answered, "that this is no proof that the scholastic
" lived before Vigilius[h]." It certainly is not; but
on the other hand, there is no proof from what Gregory says, that the scholastic lived *after* Vigilius.
Gregory does not hint when he lived. The scholastic
may have lived five hundred years before Gregory
or five only, as far as his testimony goes. But that
the author of the Roman canon did not live within
fifty years before Gregory the Great, may be considered certain from the silence of all antiquity on the
subject. While ancient writers speak repeatedly of
the care of Gregory, and of many of his predecessors,

---

[f] " Quapropter et ipsius canonicæ precis textum direximus subteradjectum, quem (Deo propitio) ex apostolica traditione suscepimus." Vigil. Romanens. Epist. ad Eucherium vel Profuturum Episcopum Bracarens.

[g] Gregor. Magnus, lib. vii. epist. 64.

[h] Brett, ut supra, p. 332.

in regulating the Roman liturgy, they never speak of any author of that liturgy, who lived between the time of Vigilius and Gregory. To this argument may be added the improbability, that a form which Vigilius declared to have been derived from apostolic tradition, should in the course of a few years be exchanged for another, composed by a scholastic, whose name and character have been ever since unknown. These arguments, and the total absence of all proof to the contrary, impel me to the conclusion, that the Roman liturgy was substantially the same in the days of Vigilius, as it was when Gregory was raised to the patriarchal chair of Rome.

Vigilius, patriarch of Rome, wrote in A.D. 538 an Epistle to Profuturus, bishop of Braga in Spain, in which he says, that they had received the text of the canon from apostolical tradition. He also speaks of the various prayers which were used along with this canon, which he calls "capitula" and "preces." "In these," he says, "they made commemoration of "the holy solemnity, or of those saints whose nati-"vities they celebrated." The whole description which Vigilius gives, coincides accurately with the Roman liturgy in subsequent times[1]. The canon

---

[1] "Ordinem quoque precum in celebritate missarum nullo nos tempore, nulla festivitate significamus habere diversum, sed semper eodem tenore oblata Deo munera consecrare. Quoties vero Paschalis, aut Ascensionis Domini, vel Pentecostes et Epiphaniæ, sanctorumque Dei fuerit agenda festivitas, singula capitula diebus apta subjungimus, quibus commemorationem sanctæ solennitatis, aut eorum facimus, quorum natalitia celebramus. Cætera vero ordine consueto prosequimur. Quapropter et ipsius canonicæ precis textum direximus subteradjectum, quem (Deo propitio) ex apostolica traditione suscepimus. Et ut charitas vestra cognoscat, quibus locis aliqua festivitatibus apta connectes, Paschalis diei

and order of prayers were therefore esteemed very ancient in the time of Vigilius, A.D. 538; and the correctness of this opinion is in fact supported by the testimonies of various writers. Symmachus, bishop of Rome before Vigilius, is said by Walafridus to have appointed the hymn *Gloria in excelsis* to be sung on Sundays and the nativities of the saints, before the liturgy[j]. Here is nothing of a newly composed office or canon. It is related that Gelasius, patriarch of Rome A.D. 492, performed a work somewhat similar to that of Gregory the Great. He ordained prayers or collects, and prefaces composed with caution[k]; and these he arranged in a sacramentary, which in subsequent ages commonly bore his name[l]. Gelasius, however, did not alter the canon, or order of prayers. We do not read of any such alteration being made by him. Modern times have brought to light an ancient sacramentary[m], which is with good reason considered by learned men to represent the Roman sacramentary as regu-

preces similiter adjecimus." Vigil Romanens. Epist. ad Profuturum Bracarens.

[j] Walafridus Strabo, de Reb Eccl. c. 22.

[k] " Fecit sacramentorum præfationes et orationes cauto sermone." Anastasius, Bibliothecar. in Vita Gelasii.

[l] In a list of books belonging to the abbey of S. Richerius, A.D. 731, the following passage occurs: "De libris sacrarii, qui ministerio altaris deserviunt, Missales Gregoriani tres; Missalis Gregorianus et Gelasianus modernis temporibus ab Albino ordinatus; Missales Gelasiani xix." Lib. iii. c. 3. Chronic. Abbat. Centulens. sive S. Richerii apud Dacherii Spicileg. tom. iv

[m] The sacramentary of Gelasius was first published from a manuscript of great antiquity in the queen of Sweden's library, by Thomasius, in his work entitled " Codices Sacramentorum," &c. Romæ, 1680. Muratori in his "Liturgia Romana vetus," &c. tom. i. ed. Venetiis 1748, reprinted this sacramentary, as did Assemani in his " Codex Liturgicus," tom. iv. Its authenticity is acknowledged by Mabillon, Muratori, Cave, and other eminent critics.

lated by Gelasius[n]. It contains several books, as his appears to have done. A comparison of it with any ancient copy of Gregory's sacramentary will shew alterations in the latter, exactly corresponding with those which Gregory is said to have made in Gelasius's sacramentary. This ancient manuscript appears to have been written in or after the time of Gregory the Great in some remote province, and therefore it contains a few things which were added to the Roman liturgy after the time of Gelasius; but it represents the order of prayers and canon generally as they were in the time of Gelasius, and that order and canon are the same as those which were used in the time of Gregory, one hundred years afterwards.

The Roman liturgy is therefore as old as the time of Gelasius A.D. 492, and there is neither proof nor presumption that he was its author, though doubtless he composed many collects, and a considerable part of the sacramentary. In fact, a manuscript sacramentary is in existence, which is supposed by learned men to have been written before the time of Gelasius[o], and evidently refers to the same order and canon as that used in his time. By Muratori it is referred to the time of Felix, patriarch of Rome,

[n] Cave, Historia Liturg. tom i. p. 464. Thomasius, Codices sacramentorum. Muratori, de Reb. Liturg. Dissertat. Liturg. Rom. tom i. p. 51, &c.

[o] This sacramentary was first published by Blanchinius in the fourth volume of Anastasius Bibliothecarius, under the title of the Sacramentary of Pope Leo It was copied from a MS. in the library of the Chapter of Verona, written 1000 (1100) years ago. Muratori has given a learned dissertation on this sacramentary in the first volume of his Liturgia Rom. vet in which also he has reprinted the Leonian sacramentary See also for an account of the controversies relative to this document Zaccaria Bibliotheca Ritualis lib. i. c. 3. p. 41, &c.

A. D. 483; but it is more generally known by the appellation of the Leonian sacramentary. Leo the Great, bishop of Rome in the time of the council of Chalcedon, A.D. 451, is said to have added to the canon certain words which are specified[p], and hence we may infer that the remainder of the canon was in existence before his time. Critics discover in the writings of this bishop many passages which seem to have been transcribed almost verbatim into the sacramentary, and they also detect in several parts of that book a style, which, as they affirm, bears internal evidence of the authorship of Leo[q]. It is certainly by no means improbable that he may have written several missæ. The fifth century was remarkable for the number of persons who composed missæ in the west, and Leo may very well have been amongst the number. Some time before Leo, Innocentius, bishop of Rome, speaks of the Roman rites in his time as having descended from St. Peter the Apostle; and there is no sort of reason to think that they differed materially from those used in the time of Gelasius at the end of the same century[r]. We find from his directions to Decentius, bishop of Eugubium, that the kiss of peace was then, as in after-times, given *after* the canon, according to the

[p] "Sanctum sacrificium," "immaculatam hostiam." Anastas Biblioth. in Vita Leonis. Walafrid. Strabo, de Reb. Eccles. c. 22. Compare Menard. Sacramentar Gregorii, p. 3.

[q] See Muratori Liturg Rom. vet. tom. i. p. 19, &c

[r] "Si instituta ecclesiastica, ut sunt a beatis apostolis tradita, integra vellent servare Domini sacerdotes, nulla diversitas, nulla varietas in ipsis ordinibus et consecrationibus haberetur—quis enim nesciat, aut non advertat, id quod a principe apostolorum Petro Romanæ ecclesiæ traditum est," &c. Innocent. Epist. ad Decentium Eugub. Labbe, Concil. tom. ii. p. 1245.

Roman rite[s]. It appears also, that the names of those who offered were recited after their oblations had been commended to the acceptance of God in the *canon*[t], as we find to have been the case afterwards at Rome; and not *before* the canon, as in the Gallican and Spanish liturgies. As far then as the testimony of Innocentius goes, it proves the substantial conformity of the Roman rite at the beginning of the fifth century with that at the end of the same century.

The deficiency of more ancient evidence, at least of any generally known, forbids me to penetrate further into the darkness of antiquity. I leave to those who are more interested in the subject, the task of investigating minutely the writings of those Fathers who lived in Italy and Sicily, and whose works may be supposed to throw light on the ancient Roman liturgy. Suffice it to say, that this liturgy was substantially the same in the time of Gelasius as it was in that of Gregory, that it appears to have been the same in the time of Innocentius at the beginning of the fifth century, and was esteemed at that time, and in the subsequent age, to be of apostolical antiquity.

[s] "Pacem ergo asseris ante confecta mysteria quosdam populis imperare, vel sibi inter sacerdotes tradere, cum post omnia, quæ aperire non debeo, pax sit necessario indicenda," &c Ibid p. 1246 Compare Menard Sacr. Gregor. p. 4.

[t] "De nominibus vero recitandis, antequam preces sacerdos faciat, atque eorum oblationes, quorum nomina recitanda sunt, sua oratione commendet, quam superfluum sit et ipse pro tua prudentia recognoscis—prius ergo oblationes sunt commendandæ, ac tunc eorum nomina, quorum sunt oblationes, edicenda, ut inter sacra mysteria nominentur, non inter alia quæ ante præmittimus, ut ipsis mysteriis viam futuris precibus aperiamus." Ibid. p 1246. See Menard, Sacr. Gregor. p. 377. Bona, Rer. Liturg. lib. ii. c. 16. §. 6. p. 473, &c.

But though we are left at the end of the four first centuries by Innocentius, the earliest Roman writer who has been quoted as alluding to the liturgy, we may, perhaps, by looking in another direction, acquire some further information on the subject. The period at which Christianity penetrated into Africa is uncertain; but it is very likely that the first missionaries may have come from Rome, as being the nearest apostolical church, and abounding in every thing which could assist such an enterprise. It is probable, for the same reasons, that the first bishops of Africa may have been ordained at Rome. These circumstances would induce us to conjecture, that the African liturgy was originally the same as the Roman; and in fact it appears, from an investigation of the few notices relative to the liturgy which are extant in the writings of the African Fathers, that the Roman and the African liturgies were alike[u]. If we consider the independence of the African churches in the time of Cyprian, A. D. 250, and therefore the improbability that they should have received their liturgy from the church of Rome, unless it had been brought by their first bishops; and if we reflect that these bishops must have been ordained long before the time of Cyprian and Tertullian, we may perhaps see some reason for tracing back the general order and substance of the ancient Roman liturgy, as used in the time of Gregory the Great, to the second century. Another proof of the antiquity of the same liturgy is derivable from the liturgy of Milan, commonly called the Ambrosian. Various circumstances prove the great

[u] See section viii. of this Dissertation.

antiquity of the latter formulary, and its diversity from the Roman, at least since the time of Gregory the Great, but probably from the fifth century. Yet the Milan liturgy is evidently derived originally from the Roman[v], and as the bishop of Milan possessed the authority of patriarch or exarch over the Italic diocese, and was not ordained by the patriarch of Rome, but perfectly independent of him, there seems no more probable way of accounting for the use of the Roman liturgy during the primitive ages in the Italic diocese, or all the north of Italy, than by supposing that it was introduced by the first bishops, who were probably ordained at Rome. Combining these circumstances together, there seems nothing unreasonable in thinking that the Roman liturgy, as used in the time of Gregory the Great, may have existed from a period of the most remote antiquity; and perhaps there are nearly as good reasons for referring its original composition to the apostolic age, as there are in the case of the great oriental liturgy, which I have noticed in the three first sections of this Dissertation. That several particular words and expressions and prayers were of a more recent date, is indeed apparent. We are well aware that the primitive liturgies were not committed to writing at first, but to memory; and thus, of course, many variations would be introduced; yet the principal substance and order might still be preserved; and it is only for the antiquity of the main order that I contend, not for that of every individual part.

Let us, then, examine briefly the order of this ancient liturgy, omitting those parts which appear

[v] See section vii.

from competent evidence to have been introduced after, or not very long before, the time of Gregory the Great. It began at first with a collect, and lessons from scripture, amongst which a psalm was read or sung, until early in the fifth century an anthem or psalm was appointed to precede them[w]. Then followed the sermon, the dismissal of catechumens, and silent prayers made by the priest and people[x]; after which, the oblations of the people, consisting chiefly of bread and wine, were received while the offertory was sung. The elements being selected from these, and placed on the altar, the priest read the collect called "secreta," or "super

[w] The preparations, Psalm *Judica, Confiteor*, &c preceding the anthem called *Introitus* in the Roman liturgy of modern times, are little older than the eleventh century. The *Introit* was appointed by Cœlestine, bishop of Rome, A. D 423. " Hic——constituit ut Psalmi David 150 ante sacrificium psallerentur antiphonatim ex omnibus, quod antea non fiebat, sed tantum Epistolæ beati Pauli recitabantur, et sanctum Evangelium." Vita Cœlestini e libro Pontificali. Labbe, Concilia, tom. ii. p 1610. Compare Missale Romanum, ordo Missæ, p. 187, 188. The *Kyrie eleeson* had been introduced from the East into the Roman church before the year 529, when it is mentioned by Concil. ii. Vasens. canon 3. Gregory the Great, Ep ad Jo Syracus. Ep. xii. lib. ix edit Benedict, says that they repeated it at Rome differently from the Greeks, namely, by saying *Christe eleeson* as often as they said *Kyrie eleeson* Comp Miss. Rom. p. 188 The *Gloria in excelsis* was appointed to be sung by Symmachus, bishop of Rome, in the sixth century. Walafrid. c. 22. The collect appears in the sacramentaries of Leo and Gelasius, and is mentioned by the fourth council of Carthage, A. D 416. After this came on certain occasions the Prophet, and always the Epistle, Psalm called *Gradual*, and Gospel. See Bona, Rer. Lit. lib. ii. c. vi. vii

[x] Of the secret prayer a relic remains in the Roman missal, where the priest, immediately before the anthem called *Offertory*, says, " Oremus." Miss. Rom. p. 190. This custom is mentioned by several ancient ritualists, as Amalarius, lib iii. c. 19. p 415. The priest recited an *apologia*, or confession, privately in this place; see Menard, Sacr. Gregorii, p 242. et notæ, p. 322.

"oblata[y]," and then began the preface or thanksgiving, with the form "Sursum corda," &c.; at the close of which the people chanted the hymn "Tersanctus[z]." The canon now commenced with commending the people's gifts and offerings to the acceptance of God, and prayers for the king and the bishop, with a commemoration of the living, and especially of those who had offered liberally[a]. This was succeeded by a prayer, that the oblation of bread and wine might "be made to us the body and "blood of Jesus Christ our Lord God." The commemoration of our Saviour's deeds and words in celebrating the eucharist followed[b]. After which came an oblation of the sacraments, as a sacrifice of bread and wine, and a petition that they might be presented by the angels on the altar in heaven. Then followed a commemoration of the departed faithful, and prayer for communion with them[c]. The canon being now completed, the bread was broken, and divided into portions for distribution, and then the Lord's Prayer was recited[d]. After which, the clergy and people interchanged a kiss of peace, and all communicated, and the priest concluded the office with a short prayer. This we may certainly affirm to have been the order and substance of the Roman liturgy in the fifth century,

[y] The oblation intervening in the modern Roman missal, beginning "Suscipe," &c. and the "Lavabo," &c. are much more recent than the time of Gregory. See Miss. Rom. 190, 191.

[z] See Menard, Sacr. Gregor p. 1.

[a] See Menard, Sacr. Gregor. p. 2.

[b] Ibid. p. 2
[c] Ibid. p. 3.
[d] This ancient order of the Roman liturgy is still visible in the liturgy of Milan Since the time of Gregory the Great, the Lord's Prayer has been joined immediately to the Roman canon, and the bread is broken afterwards.

and it will be difficult to adduce any reason for thinking, that the same had not prevailed for a very great length of time before.

I am not aware that any one has yet attempted to give a correct edition of Gregory's sacramentary, on the principle of comparing manuscripts of various countries. It seems to me that such a course would afford the best prospect of attaining a correct text. Much, at all events, might thus be fixed, though a portion would still remain uncertain. English manuscripts particularly should be collated with Italian, because Gregory's sacramentary was sooner used in England than in any other country beyond the Roman patriarchate. German manuscripts should come next, and the Gallican sacramentaries, used before the Roman rite was introduced, would furnish some illustrations. With regard to the ancient Roman liturgy, or the order of prayers and canon, there is neither doubt nor difficulty, as I have already shewn.

The Roman liturgy was illustrated with much learning by John Bona, presbyter cardinal of the Roman church[e]; and the works of Menard[f], Gavanti[g], Martene[h], and Le Brun[i], may be consulted by those who wish to acquire further information on the subject.

---

[e] In his work, entitled Rerum Liturgicarum libri duo Paris. 1672.

[f] Divi Gregorii Liber Sacramentorum, Paris. 1642

[g] Commentaria in Rubricas Missalis et Breviarii Romani cum notis Merati. Augustæ Vindel. 1763.

[h] De Antiquis Ecclesiæ Ritibus libri iv. Rothomag. 1725.

[i] Explication de la Messe, &c.

SECTION VII.

LITURGY OF THE EXARCHATE OF MILAN.

THE liturgy of the church of Milan bearing the venerable name of Ambrose, archbishop of Milan, and primate or exarch of the Italic diocese in the fourth century, has long been celebrated. Several attempts have been made at different times to introduce the Roman liturgy in its place, but the attachment of the clergy and people of Milan to their ancient rites has prevailed against the zeal of rash and prejudiced innovators. The Ambrosian liturgy certainly differs in several respects from that of Rome; but it will be seen, in the sequel, that this difference was originally less than might at first sight appear.

The earliest ecclesiastical writer who has been cited as speaking of the Ambrosian rite is Walafridus Strabo, who died A.D. 849, and who wrote thus: "Ambrose, bishop of Milan, appointed for his " own church, and for the rest of Liguria, the ar- " rangements of the liturgy and other offices, which " are preserved even to this day in the church of

"Milan[a]." An anonymous Irish writer, of about the year 700, speaks of Ambrose as the author of some offices[b], in which he may perhaps allude to the liturgy.

The Ambrosian liturgy, that is, the order of variable prayers, and the text of the canon, can be ascertained by means of ancient MSS., of which two, still extant at Milan, are as old as the ninth or tenth century[c]. The testimony of Walafridus, and the tradition of the church of Milan, at a distance of four hundred years after the death of Ambrose, are not sufficient proofs that he composed missæ for the use of his church; but it is by no means improbable that he may have done so; and this would partly account for the sacramentary, or collection of missæ used at Milan being called by his name; although the substance of the canon and the order of the variable prayers are probably much more ancient than his time.

The first thing to be remarked of this liturgy is, that it has been different from the Roman ever since the time of Gregory the Great, A. D. 594. This patriarch probably first placed the Lord's Prayer immediately after the Roman canon[d], or before the breaking of bread. The Milan liturgy, which agrees in almost every other respect with the ancient Roman, differs from it in placing the breaking of bread between the canon and the Lord's Prayer[e], as was the case at Rome until the time of

[a] Walafridus Strabo, de Reb. Eccl. c 22.
[b] Spelman, Concilia, tom. 1. p. 177.
[c] Muratori, Liturg. Rom. vet. tom. i. p. 130, &c
[d] Epist. xii. ad Jo. Syracus. lib. ix. edit. Benedict.
[e] Miss. Ambros. ap. Pamelii Liturgic. tom. i. p. 303, 304. Bona, Rer. Lit. lib. i. cap. x. §. 2.

Gregory. The Milan liturgy is therefore more ancient than the time of Gregory the Great.

Another difference between the liturgy of Milan and the Roman, seems to carry back the former to a period of much greater antiquity. In the ancient canon of Milan it appears that the second oblation of the elements, which occurs in the Roman canon after the words of institution, is wanting. Two MSS. of the ninth or tenth century, the oldest monuments of the Milan rite now existing, concur in excluding the second oblation from the canon[f]. This seems to me a proof that the Milan liturgy has been distinct from the Roman, at least since the fifth century, as it appears that this oblation is extant in the sacramentary of Gelasius; and Leo is said to have added some words to it[g]. With these two exceptions, we shall find that the liturgy of Milan was essentially the same as the Roman in the time of Gregory the Great.

On examination, the liturgy of Milan is found to consist of the following parts, omitting those which have been introduced into it since the time of Gregory.

The anthem called "Ingressa[h]"—"Kyrie eleëson[i]" —"Gloria in excelsis"—the Collect—the Prophet[j]—

[f] Muratori, Liturg. Rom. vet. p. 133. tom i.

[g] See sect vi note P, p 118.

[h] Missale Ambros. A. D. 1522. fol. 127. Pamelii Liturg. tom i. p. 293 Bona, p. 66. All the preceding matter in the Ambrosian liturgy is modern.

[i] "Kyrie eleeson" is only repeated in this place during Lent. See Miss. Ambros. fol. 60. 66; Bona, p 67.

[j] "Audistis filii librum Job hodie legi qui solemni munere est decursus et tempore." Ambros. Epist. xx. ad Marcellinam. "Hæc de prophetica lectione libata sint : Evangelii quoque lectio quid habeat consideremus." Epist. xlii. ad Marcellin.

the Psalm[k]—Epistle[l]—Alleluia—Gospel and Sermon[m]—Prayer "Super sindonem"—oblations of the people[n]—Prayer "Super oblata"—Preface and Canon, which agrees in almost every respect with the Roman canon of the fifth century, except in omitting the second oblation[o]—breaking of bread—Lord's Prayer—kiss of peace—communion—prayer " Post communionem."

[k] " Quantum laboratur in ecclesia ut fiat silentium cum lectiones leguntur. Si unus loquatur, obstrepunt universi · cum psalmus legitur ipse sibi est effector silentii Omnes loquuntur, et nullus obstrepit." Ambros. Præfat. in Psal. i. p. 741. tom i. ed. Benedict

[l] " Factum est ut illâ Dominicâ, prophetica lectione jam lectâ, ante altarium staret qui lectionem B. Pauli proferret." Greg Turon de Mir. S. Martini, lib. i. c. 5

[m] " Post lectiones atque tractatum dimissis catechumenis," &c. Ambr. Ep xx. ad Marcell.

[n] " Cum autem tempus advenisset quo dona sacræ mensæ erant offerenda," &c. Theod. lib v. c. xvii

[o] The prayer for kings is thus referred to by Ambrose. " Itaque peto ut patienter sermonem meum audias. Nam si indignus sum, qui a te audiar, indignus sum, qui pro te offeram, cui tua vota, cui tuas committas preces." Ambrosius, Epistola ad Imp. Theodosium xv. p. 946. tom. ii. He also speaks in several places of the words of our Redeemer used in the consecration of the elements. " Si tantum valuit humana benedictio, ut naturam converteret, quid dicimus de ipsa consecratione divina, ubi verba ipsa Domini Salvatoris operantur? nam sacramentum istud quod accipis Christi sermone conficitur——ipse clamat Dominus Jesus, *Hoc est corpus meum* Ante benedictionem verborum cœlestium alia species nominatur, post consecrationem corpus Christi significatur." Lib. de Myster cap. 9. " Hunc panem dedit (Christus) Apostolis ut dividerent populo credentium, hodieque dat nobis eum, quem ipse quotidie sacerdos consecrat suis verbis." De Benedict Patriarch cap ix. Although Ambrose and Gaudentius of Brescia repeatedly speak of the figurative, mystical, and commemorative sacrifice, I do not see that they refer to any express or verbal oblation in the liturgy. The second oblation mentioned in the text occurs in the recent editions of the Milan liturgy, but this and other things have been gradually introduced from the Roman rite.

Let us now compare this with the Roman liturgy about the time of Gregory the Great. The "In-gressa" is the same as the Roman "Introitus," introduced before the time of Gregory. The "Kyrie eleëson" was used with a litany, as it formerly was in the Roman and other western churches, up to the ninth century, according to Goar and Bona[p]. The "Gloria in excelsis," and the collect, had been used in the Roman liturgy before the time of Gregory. The Prophet and Psalm were only more frequently used at Milan than Rome. The Epistle, Alleluia, and Gospel, all occurred in the Roman rite. The prayer, "Super sindonem" is the chief difficulty to be explained[q] : but in fact there was anciently such a prayer in the Roman liturgy. Here occurred the Apology, or Confession of the priest, which he repeated in silence, while the people also prayed in secret; and then the offertory anthem was sung, while the oblations of the people were received. And of this a vestige still remains in the Roman rite; for the Gospel (or Creed when it is said) being ended, the priest says, *Oremus*, " Let us pray," which was mentioned by Amalarius in the ninth century ; but no prayer, whether in secret or aloud, follows this exhortation, which is immediately succeeded by the offertory anthem[r]. This custom of secret prayer became obsolete at Rome from no form being appointed for the purpose. In Milan, however, the ancient prayers at this part of the liturgy have survived, having been embodied in regular collects, which were inserted in every missa.

[p] Bona, Rer. Liturg. p. 337.
[q] Pamel. tom. i. p. 297. Bona, lib. i. c. x. §. 2. p. 66.
[r] See this subject noticed in the latter part of the preceding section, note [x], p. 122.

The form of oblation which occurs in the Ambrosian missal after the reception of the people's oblations[s] is probably a recent thing; the ancient oblation took place in the canon, where it still remains. The prayer "Super oblata," corresponds to the "se-"creta" of the Roman liturgy in the fifth century. The preface and canon I have already noticed. The ablution of the priest's hands occurs nearly about the middle of the Milan canon; in the Roman liturgy it occurs before the beginning of the preface: but this ceremony was probably introduced into the western churches after the time of Gregory, since it is not mentioned by Isidore Hispalensis, nor, I believe, by any western writer before the ninth century, when Amalarius and Fortunatus alluded to it[t]. When introduced, it was used in different parts of the Roman and Ambrosian liturgies. I have already remarked on the position of the breaking of bread, and the Lord's Prayer, as proving the antiquity of this rite. The kiss of peace occurred in the same place as it did in the ancient Roman and African liturgies, which differed in this respect from all the other liturgies of the east and west.

It appears, then, that the Milan liturgy agreed substantially with the Roman up to the time of Gregory the Great, so as to afford unequivocal signs of a common original. There are several minor differences between the Milan liturgy and the Roman of later times; such as the repetition in the former of "Kyrie eleëson" in various places, the sing-

---

[s] Miss Ambros. fol. 127. Pamel. p. 297

[t] Amalar. lib. i. c. 19. p. 416 Fortunatus in vita S. Marcelli Ep. Parisiensis ap. Surium cal. Novembr. See Gerbert.Liturg.Aleman.tom.i. p. 330.

ing of an anthem before and after the Gospel, &c.; but these things, though they render the Milan rite different from the Roman, are of no great consequence, and they must be attributed to the archbishops of Milan. Considering the evident signs of a common origin exhibited by the liturgies of Rome and Milan, and the independence of the early bishops of Milan, who had patriarchal authority over the Italic diocese[u], it is not improbable that the order and main substance of the liturgy of Milan were derived from Rome, when the Christian church was first planted in the north of Italy.

It seems that the church of Milan adopted most of the improvements and additions gradually made in the Roman liturgy up to the time of Gregory. During the same period several peculiarities of small moment were probably introduced by the bishops of Milan also. In the time of Gregory, the church of Milan did not adopt the chief alteration made by him, which alteration in fact we know was objected to by other churches, as, for instance, by the Sicilians. From that time (if not previously) the liturgy of Milan began to be considered a peculiar rite; and as the Romans gave their sacramentary the names of Gelasius and Gregory, so the Milanese gave theirs the name of Ambrose; who, in fact, may have composed some parts of it. After the time of Gregory, the Milan liturgy doubtless received several additions, such as the oblation after the offertory, the

---

[u] This is satisfactorily proved by Basnage, Histoire de l'Eglise, livre vii. chap. i; who shews that Ambrose had, and exercised, patriarchal jurisdiction over the seven provinces of the Italic civil diocese, and that the bishops of Milan were not ordained by the bishops of Rome, nor under their jurisdiction.

ablution of hands, the Nicene Creed, and latterly the second oblation in the canon. The church of Milan has, however, preserved many most ancient rites, not only in the liturgy, but in various parts of the ritual and offices. The ancient Italic version of the Psalter, used in the west before the time of Jerome, is still retained in use by this church. The same version is also found in all the Prophets, Epistles, and Gospels read in the Milan liturgy[v].

No one has yet attempted to furnish an authentic edition of the ancient sacramentary of Milan from a collation of MSS.; but the documents which have been published establish satisfactorily the order of the variable prayers, and the text of the canon, which is all we need in examining the liturgy.

Joseph Vicecomes, doctor of theology at Milan, attempted to trace back the Ambrosian or Milan liturgy to the apostolic age. He ascribes its origin to St. Barnabas, who, he says, first preached the Gospel at Milan[w]; but this theory is altogether destitute of proof. He observes also, most incorrectly, that the liturgy of Milan scarcely agrees in any respect with those of other nations, or with the Roman[x]. Bona makes some observations on the liturgy of Milan, but does not attempt to explain its original derivation[y]. What I have said in this section may perhaps tend in some degree to the elucidation of the liturgy of Milan, which has not yet

---

[v] Bona, Rer. Lit. lib. i. c. x. p. 67.
[w] De Missæ Ritibus, lib. i. c. xi. xii. Milan, 1615.
[x] "Nec fere quicquam in eo reperies, quod cum aliarum gentium ordinibus nedum cum Romano conveniat." Cap. xii. p 171.
[y] Rer Lit. lib. i. c. 10.

(as far as I know) been attempted. Before I conclude, I must notice the liturgy of the church of Aquileia, which was the principal church in the provinces of Venetia and Istria in the north of Italy, but in early times was subject to the archbishop of Milan. This church and others adjoining, as Forum Julii, had formerly peculiar rites, which were supplanted by the modern Roman about A. D. 1596. There are MSS. of this liturgy of various ages in existence; one is of the eleventh century[z], and apparently is the same as the ancient Roman liturgy. In fact, it seems that the same liturgy prevailed throughout the whole of Italy and Sicily during the primitive ages. There is no record of any material difference between the rites of these churches.

[z] For further information on this subject, see Zaccaria Biblioth. Ritualis, tom. i. p. 65, &c.

SECTION VIII.

LITURGY OF AFRICA.

I NOW enter on the consideration of the rites used by the churches of Africa, the civil diocese of which comprised the provinces of Africa Proconsularis, Byzacium, Numidia, Tripolis, and the two Mauritanias[a]. These churches, once conspicuous in the Christian world, adorned with the piety and learning of illustrious Fathers, and ruled by nearly five hundred bishops, have long ceased to exist. Weakened by unhappy schisms, they were unable to bear up against the tide of Mahommedan infidelity, which in the seventh and eighth centuries threatened to overwhelm the world. No monument of the African liturgy remains: we must be content, therefore, to seek for its relics amongst the writings of those Fathers who lived in Africa.

In perusing many works relating to the primitive liturgy and offices of the Roman church, it has appeared to me, that the most valuable allusions to

---

[a] Bingham, book ix. c. 2. §. 5

Roman customs are almost always found in the writings of African Fathers; and it is remarkable that they profess in those places to describe the rites of their own churches, and not those of the Roman. I have thence been inclined to conjecture that the African rites were generally the same as the Roman; and in fact there is no sort of difficulty in supposing that Christianity and religious rites came from Rome to Africa. The geographical position of Africa, separated by deserts from Egypt and the East, renders it more probable that Christianity should have come from the apostolical church of Rome than from any other quarter. Spain and Gaul were probably not converted to Christianity before Africa, therefore it is not likely that they sent missionaries to that country.

The Roman liturgy differed from those of Antioch, Cæsarea, Constantinople, Alexandria, and all the East, and from those of Gaul and Spain in the West, in directing the kiss of peace to be given after the consecration was finished. The only liturgy now remaining which agrees in this respect with the Roman, is that of Milan, which was evidently derived originally from it. The ancient African also agreed with the Roman from the earliest period, in placing the kiss of peace after consecration, as we learn from Tertullian[b] and Augustine[c]. This

---

[b] "Habita oratione cum fratribus, subtrahunt osculum pacis quod est signaculum orationis.—Quale sacrificium est a quo sine pace receditur." Lib. de Orat. c. xiv. p. 134, 135. ed. Rigalt. Paris. 1664.

[c] "Ecce ubi est peracta sanctificatio dicimus orationem Dominicam quam accepistis et reddidistis. Post ipsam dicitur *Pax vobiscum,* et osculant se Christiani in osculo sancto." August. Serm. 227. in die Paschæ, p. 974. tom. v. oper. Benedict.

similarity in so remarkable a point, renders it highly probable that we may find further signs of conformity between these two liturgies; and if it should appear that all the accounts we have of the African liturgy, harmonize with the opinion that it was originally the same as the Roman, we may fairly conclude that such an opinion is correct.

Augustine says, that about his time the custom of singing anthems from the Book of Psalms before the liturgy began at Carthage[d]. We find that Cœlestine bishop of Rome, about the same time, adopted a similar rule at Rome[e]. The reading of Scripture then commenced. Augustine sometimes speaks of the first lesson being taken from the Prophets, and followed by the Epistle[f]. In other places he refers to the Epistle as the first lesson[g]. In like manner we find that at certain seasons the Epistle was preceded by a lesson from the Prophets, in the Roman church[h]. After the Prophet (when it was read), and the Epistle, came a Psalm[i], which corresponds with the Roman Gradual, and to which there is no other exact parallel in any of the eastern or western rites.

---

[d] "Hilarius quidam—nescio unde adversus Dei ministros, ut fieri assolet irritatus, morem qui tunc esse apud Carthaginem cœperat, ut hymni ad altare dicerentur de psalmorum libro, sive ante oblationem, sive cum distribueretur populo quod fuisset oblatum, maledica reprehensione ubicumque poterat lacerabat." August. Retractat lib. ii. c. 11

[e] See note w, section vi. p 122.

[f] "In omnibus lectionibus quas recitatas audivimus si animadvertit caritas vestra, primam lectionem Isaiæ prophetæ —deinde adscendit apostolica lectio," &c. Serm. xlv. p. 218. tom. v.

[g] "Primam lectionem audivimus Apostoli—deinde cantavimus psalmum—post hæc Evangelica lectio." Serm clxxvi. p. 839. tom. v.

[h] Vide Lectionar. vel Comitem Pamel. Liturg. tom. ii. p. 1, &c.

[i] See note g in this page.

SECT. VIII.   *Liturgy of Africa.*   137

After the Psalm, the Gospel was read, and the bishop preached [k]. Then the catechumens were dismissed [l], and the oblations of the faithful were received [m]. Cyprian and Augustine speak of the beginning of the preface, *Sursum corda,* "Lift up your hearts [n];" to which the latter adds the form, "Gratias aga- "mus Domino Deo nostro [o];" and both speak of the thanksgiving or preface, which is also referred to by Tertullian [p]. The singing of the hymn *Tersanctus* is alluded to by Tertullian [q]. All these things perfectly agree with the ancient Roman liturgy. Optatus speaks of a verbal oblation made for the church, which very nearly agrees with that of the Roman church [r]. Tertullian says that they

[k] This is manifest from almost all the sermons of Augustine, which profess to have been delivered immediately after the reading of Scripture.

[l] "Post sermonem missa fit catechumenis manebunt fideles, venietur ad locum orationis." Augustin. Serm xlix. de Temp. p 275. tom. v.

[m] "Locuples et dives es, et Dominicum celebrare te credis, quæ corbanam omnino non respicis, quæ in Dominicum sine sacrificio venis, quæ partem de sacrificio quod pauper obtulit sumis." Cypr. de Oper. et Eleemos. p. 203. ed. Fell.

[n] "Ideo et sacerdos ante orationem, præfatione præmissa parat fratrum mentes dicendo: *Sursum corda:* ut dum respondet plebs, *Habemus ad Dominum:* admoneatur nihil aliud se, quam Dominum, cogitare debere." Cypr. de Orat. Dom. p. 152. Aug. de Don. Persev.

c. 13 p. 839 tom x.

[o] Aug. de Don. Persev. c. cit.

[p] Cypr. de Orat. Dom. ut supra. Aug. de Don. Persev. c. cit. Tertullian. lib. i. adv. Marcionem, c. xxiii. p. 377. "Super alienum panem alii Deo gratiarum actionibus fungitur."

[q] "Cur illa angelorum circumstantia non cessant dicere, *Sanctus, Sanctus, Sanctus.* Proinde igitur et nos angelorum, si meminerimus, candidati jam hinc cœlestem illam in Deum vocem, et officium futuræ claritatis ediscimus." Tertull. de Orat. c. iii. p. 130.

[r] "Quis dubitet, vos illud legitimum in Sacramentorum mysterio præterire non posse? Offerre vos Deo dicitis pro Ecclesia quæ una est: hoc ipsum mendacii pars est, unam te vocare, de qua feceris duas. Et offerre vos dicitis pro una ecclesia, quæ sit in toto terrarum orbe diffusa." Optat. contra

sacrificed or offered for the emperor[s], which is also consistent with the Roman liturgy. Cyprian speaks of the commemoration of the living[t]. Augustine seems to refer to prayers and an oblation before consecration[u]; and Optatus and Fulgentius speak of an invocation of the Holy Spirit to perform the sanctification of the elements[v]. This is almost the only point in which any material difference can be pointed out between the Roman and the African liturgies. The former never contained such an in-

Parmen. lib. ii. p. 45. Paris. 1679. Compare Gregor. Sacr. a Menard. p. 2

[s] "Itaque et sacrificamus pro salute imperatoris sed Deo nostro et ipsius sed quomodo præcepit Deus, prece pura." Tertull. ad Scapulam, p. 69. c. 2 Compare Greg. Sacr. p. 2.

[t] "Ad communionem admittuntur, et offertur nomen eorum." Cypr. Epist xvi. p. 37. et Epist. lxii. p. 147. Compare Greg. Sacr. Menard. p 2 Martene, de Antiq Eccl Rit. lib 1. c. 4. art. 8. p. 400, &c.

[u] Speaking of the words of the apostle, 1 Tim ii. 1. "Eligo in his verbis hoc intelligere quod omnis vel fere omnis frequentat Ecclesia, ut *precationes* (*obsecrationes*) accipiamus dictas, quas facimus in celebratione Sacramentorum, antequam illud, quod est in Domini mensa, incipiat benedici; *orationes* cum benedicitur et sanctificatur, et ad distribuendum comminuitur, quam totam petitionem fere omnis Ecclesia Dominica oratione concludit" —This he explains from the scriptural use of the word προσευχή; proceeding thus— " si usitatius ut dixi, in Scripturis *votum* appellatur εὐχὴ, excepto nomine generali *orationis*, ea proprie intelligenda oratio quam facimus ad votum, id est πρὸς εὐχήν. Voventur autem omnia quæ offeruntur Deo, maxime sancti altaris oblatio—*ideo in hujus sanctificationis præparatione existimo Apostolum jussisse proprie fieri* προσευχὰς *id est, orationes,*— hoc est enim ad votum quod usitatius in Scripturis nuncupatur εὐχή." Aug. Epist. cxlix p. 509 tom. ii. Compare Greg. Sacr. Menard. p. 2.

[v] " Quid est enim tam sacrilegum, quam altaria Dei (in quibus vota populi et membra Christi portata sunt: quo Deus omnipotens invocatus sit, quo postulatus descendit Spiritus Sanctus," &c. Optat. cont. Parmen lib. vi. p. 111. See also Fulgent. lib. ii. qu. 2. ad Monimum, and contra Fabian. Excerpta a Sirmondo, p. 36. 39.

vocation. But the African church may very well have introduced this form in imitation of the oriental liturgies, in which it had been extant from a most remote period. I have not found any distinct allusion to the words of our Saviour[w]. The verbal commemoration of Christ's passion and death is spoken of by Cyprian and Fulgentius[x]. The commemoration of the departed saints is mentioned by Augustine, Cyprian, and Tertullian[y]; as is also the termination "in sæcula sæculorum," and the response of the people, Amen, by Tertullian[z]. We also read, in Augustine, of the breaking of the bread or body for distribution[a], and of a benediction of the people, to which the canons of the African church refer, as " an imposition of hands[b];" and Optatus alludes to the absolution of penitents sometimes given at this time[c]. The Lord's Prayer then followed, and is

[w] The tract De Cœna Dom. which alludes to them, and is ascribed to Cyprian, is spurious; as is "Sermo 28. de Verbis Domini," 84 in Appendix of Augustine's works, tom 5.

[x] " Passionis ejus mentionem in sacrificiis omnibus facimus —quotiescunque ergo calicem in commemorationem Domini et passionis offerimus," &c. Cypr. Ep. lxiii. ad Cæcil. p. 156. " Cum tempore sacrificii commemorationem mortis ejus faciamus." Fulgent. cont. Fabian. Excerpta a Sirmond. p. 36.

[y] Aug. de Sanct Virginitat. c. 45; de Civ. Dei, lib. xxi. c. 10. Cypr. Ep. xii p. 27. xxix. p. 77. Tertull. de Coron. Militis, p. 102; de Monogamia, p. 531 A; de Exhort. Cast. p. 523 D.

[z] Tertull. de Spectaculis, c. 25. p. 83

[a] See Epist. cxlix. cited in note [u], p. 138.

[b] "*Interpellationes* autem— fiunt cum populus benedicitur. Tunc enim antistites velut advocati susceptos suos per manus impositionem misericordissimæ offerunt potestati." Epist. cxlix. p. 509. tom. ii. Concil. African. A.D. 424, canon lxx. Labbe, tom. ii. p. 1662. Codex Canon. Eccl. Afr A. D. 390. canon ciii. ib. p. 1117.

[c] " Etenim inter vicina momenta, dum manus imponitis, et delicta donatis, mox ad altare conversi, Dominicam orationem prætermittere non potestis." Optatus, lib. ii. p. 52.

spoken of by Augustine, Optatus, and Cyprian[d]. The salutation of peace, "Pax vobis," and the holy kiss, are alluded to by Augustine, Optatus, and Tertullian[e]. Augustine speaks of the anthem sung during communion[f], and of the thanksgiving, "post communionem[g]."

This is perhaps almost all we can know about the African liturgy, and, as far as it goes, it agrees perfectly with the ancient Roman, except in the single instance of the invocation of the Holy Spirit, which was probably introduced from the east, or from Gaul and Spain. Some passages from the African Fathers have been cited, which may be imagined to refer to a liturgy different from the Roman. Thus, for instance, Tertullian and other Fathers speak of prayers for the emperor and his court[h], &c.; Augustine, of prayers for infidels, catechumens[i], &c. which do not appear in the ancient

[d] Augustini Epist. cxlix. ad Paulin. p. 509. tom. ii. quoted above, in note [u], p. 138. The following passage is also valuable. "Ideo cum dicitur, *Sursum cor;* respondetis, *Habemus ad Dominum*—ideo sequitur episcopus vel presbyter qui offert, et dicit cum responderit populus, *Habemus ad Dominum sursum cor: gratias agamus Domino Deo nostro*—et vos adtestamini, *dignum et justum est* dicentes. Deinde post sanctificationem sacrificii Dei—ecce ubi est peracta sanctificatio dicimus orationem Dominicam—Post ipsam dicitur *Pax vobiscum;* et osculantur se Christiani in osculo sancto." August. 227. in die Paschæ p. 974. tom. v. See Optatus Milev. lib. ii. adv Parmen. cited above in note [c]. Cypr. de Orat. Dom. p. 146.

[e] For testimony of Augustine, see last note, and note [c], p. 135. "Et non potuistis prætermittere quod legitimum est. Utique dixistis *Pax vobiscum*—salutas de pace, qui non amas." Optat. Milev. lib iii. p. 79. Tertull. de Orat. cited in note [b], p. 135.

[f] Retractat. lib. ii c. 11.

[g] "Quibus peractis, et participato sancto Sacramento, gratiarum actio cuncta concludit." Epist. cxlix. ad Paulin. p. 509. tom. ii.

[h] Tertull. in Apolog. p. 31 A. Arnob. adv. Gentes, lib. iv. sub finem.

[i] August. Epist. ccxvii. ad Vitalem, p. 799. tom. ii.

Roman canon. But in fact we have no proof that these prayers were used in the African canon; they may have occupied the place of the Roman collect before the lessons; and even if they did occur in the canon, it would not have constituted any material difference between the Roman and African rites, for we often find that such small additions were made in ancient liturgies, the main substance and order still remaining identical[j]. I am altogether satisfied that the African liturgy agreed in very many points with the primitive Roman, and that no material difference can be shewn between them. If this were the proper place for doing so, and if I did not fear to enlarge this dissertation too much, it would be easy to trace this conformity of the Roman and African rites through the offices of Baptism, Matrimony, &c. and to bring a large body of

[j] Victorinus Afer, lib i. adversus Arianos, cites the following passage from the African liturgy: "Sicuti et in oblatione dicitur, munda tibi populum circumvitalem, æmulatorem bonorum operum, circa tuam substantiam venientem." Fulgentius, in his remarks on 1 Cor. xi. 23 amongst the Excerpta published by Sirmond. p. 36, says, "Cum tempore sacrificii commemorationem mortis ejus faciamus, charitatem nobis tribui per adventum sancti Spiritus postulamus: hoc suppliciter exorantes ut per ipsam charitatem, qua pro nobis Christus crucifigi dignatus est, nos quoque gratia sancti Spiritus accepta, mundum crucifixum habere, et mundo crucifigi possimus: imitantesque Domini nostri mortem, sicut Christus quod mortuus est peccato, mortuus est semel, quod autem vivit, vivit Deo, etiam nos in novitate vitæ ambulemus, et munere charitatis accepto, moriamur peccato, et vivamus Deo." p. 39. "Hoc autem quod petimus, id est, ut in Patre et Filio unum simus, per unitatem gratiæ spiritualiter accipimus." This plainly shews that the African canon contained petitions which did not exist in the Roman, but it does not prove that they were originally different. The invocation of the Holy Spirit was derived from Gaul, Spain, or the East, by the African church. The petition for unity was no doubt introduced, in consequence of the schisms so prevalent in Africa.

evidence to prove the original derivation of the African rites from those of the Roman church.

When we reflect on the patriarchal jurisdiction of the archbishop of Carthage, the resolute independence of the African churches in the third and following centuries, and their rejection of the pretended jurisdiction of the patriarch of Rome[k], we shall find it difficult to account for the identity of the African and Roman rites in any other manner, than by supposing that the first bishops of Africa were ordained at Rome, and carried thence the liturgy and ritual, which in after-ages prevailed in Africa. It is unknown at what period the church was founded in Africa; but as Tertullian was presbyter of Carthage at the end of the second century, as the acts of the martyrdom of Perpetua and Felicitas speak of Optatus as bishop of Carthage about the year 200, and Agrippinus bishop of Carthage is said to have assembled a council of many bishops about A.D. 215; it seems probable that the church of Africa was founded some time not remote from the middle of the second century, or about the same time as the church of Gaul.

[k] See these points proved by Basnage, Hist. de l'Eglise, liv. iv. ch. 1.

SECTION IX.

LITURGY OF GAUL.

IT has been long known that the ancient liturgy of Gaul differed from that of Rome, though the precise nature of the difference was unknown, until Bona and Thomasius discovered and published some ancient monuments of the Gallican liturgy[a]. To the learned Mabillon we are indebted for a valuable commentary and observations on these remains[b]; and at a later period, Martene published an ancient treatise on the Gallican liturgy, professing to have been written by Germanus, bishop of Paris, in the sixth century, which materially elucidates this subject[c].

Mabillon traces the composition of the Gallican liturgy principally to three authors; Musæus, presbyter of Marseilles; Sidonius, bishop of Auvergne; and Hilary, bishop of Poictiers. Had this learned writer said "missal," instead of "liturgy," it would

---

[a] Bona, Rer. Lit lib. i. c. 12. Thomasius, Codices Sacramentorum 900 annis vetustiores. Rom. 1680.

[b] De Liturgia Gallicana. Paris. 1685.

[c] Martene, Thesaurus Anecdotorum, tom. v. p. 85, &c.

probably have been more correct; for we must in the present instance, as before, distinguish between these two things. Musæus, who died after the middle of the fifth century, is said by Gennadius to have composed for Eustasius, bishop of Marseilles, an excellent and considerable book of sacraments, with lessons, psalms, and forms of supplicating God, and attesting (*contestandi*) his beneficence[d]. This word *contestandi* is referred by Mabillon to the ancient Gallican custom of calling the preface, which begins *Vere dignum* &c., by the name of *contestatio*, a term which we find applied to it in ancient MSS. of the Gallican liturgy[e]. Sidonius, bishop of Auvergne, who died A. D. 494, also composed a book of Sacraments; and Gregory of Tours, in the sixth century, wrote a preface to it[f]. Hilary bishop of Poictiers, who died A. D. 368, is said by Jerome to have composed a book of hymns, and another of mysteries, that is, of sacraments[g].

Such seem to have been the authors of the Gallican missal, which contained the liturgy adapted to the various feast days. This liturgy at the close of the sixth century was different from the Roman, as appears by the interrogations of Augustine, first archbishop of Canterbury, to Gregory, patriarch of Rome. He asks, "why the customs of churches " are different, when their faith is the same, and one " custom of liturgy prevails in the church of Rome, " another in those of Gaul[h]?" Abbas Hilduinus, in

[d] Gennad de Vir illustr c. 81.
[e] Mabillon, Lit. Gall. p. 28.
[f] Gregor. Turonens. Hist. Franc. lib. ii. c 22.
[g] Hieron. de Scriptor. c. 100.

[h] "Cum una sit fides, sunt ecclesiarum diversæ consuetudines, et altera consuetudo missarum in sancta Romana ecclesia, atque altera in Gal-

his Epistle to Louis the Pious, prefixed to the Areopagitica, speaks of ancient MSS. then extant, containing the old Gallican rite, which had prevailed from the first reception of the Christian faith in Gaul, until the Roman was introduced[i]. The Roman rites were introduced in place of the ancient Gallican, in the time of the emperor Charlemagne. A beginning had been made with the Roman chanting and psalmody, which king Pepin introduced into the Gallican church; as Paul, bishop of Rome, intimates, in the epistle which, with the Roman books of anthems and responses, he sent to that prince. Pepin also sent young men to Rome, for instruction in chanting[j]. Thus the Roman chant and psalmody were introduced, which was very displeasing to the members of many churches[k], who had not the same political attachment and obligations to the Roman patriarch as their king. Afterwards Charlemagne, son of Pepin, who was also politically indebted to the bishop of Rome, obtained from pope Hadrian the sacramentary of Gregory, or the ancient Roman sacramentary, improved and revised by that bishop; and subsequently he ordained, by an imperial edict, that every priest should celebrate the liturgy in the Roman manner[l]. This exer-

---

liarum tenetur." Bed. Hist. Eccl. lib. i. c. 27.

[i] "Cui adstipulari videntur antiquissimi et nimia pene vetustate consumpti, missales libri, continentes missæ ordinem more Gallico, qui ab initio receptæ fidei, usu in hac occidentali plaga est habitus, usque quo tenorem, quo nunc utitur, Romanum susceperit." Hilduin. Areopagit. apud Su-

rium, Octob. 9.

[j] Mabillon, Lit. Gall. p. 16. Carol. Mag. adv. Imag. lib. 1. c. 6.

[k] Carol. Magn. adv. Imagines, lib. i. c. 6 "Plures ecclesiæ quæ quondam apostolicæ sedis traditionem in psallendo suscipere recusabant, nunc eam cum omni diligentia amplectantur." p. 54 ed. 1549.

[l] Mabill. Lit. Gall. p. 17.

tion of royal power was probably very disagreeable to many of the churches of Gaul; and we find, in fact, that not very long after, in the time of the emperor Charles the Bald, there seems to have been some question whether the ancient rite was not to be resumed again[m]. However, the liturgy that was introduced being orthodox, and there being no valid ground of objection to it in itself, the churches of Gaul obeyed the decree of Charlemagne, and gave their sanction to it. Thus the ancient Gallican liturgy was exchanged for the Roman; "whether," as Mabillon says, "it was effected by the Roman "pontiffs, who took every care within their power to "bring all other churches to an accordance with the "Roman; or whether it was done by Charlemagne, "to please them[n]." And being once effected, the power of the Roman see, which now became very great, prevented any restitution of the ancient rite.

From the time of Charlemagne, all the sacramentaries were taken from the Roman order; and so effectually was the ancient liturgy abolished, that Charles the Bald, grandson of Charlemagne, appears to have seen the peculiar rites of the Gallican church for the first time celebrated by priests from Toledo in Spain, where the same liturgy as the

[m] " Usque ad tempora abavi nostri Pipini, Gallicanæ ecclesiæ aliter quam Romana vel Mediolanensis ecclesia divina celebrabant officia, sicut vidimus et audivimus ab iis, qui ex partibus Toletanæ ecclesiæ ad nos venientes, secundum morem ipsius ecclesiæ coram nobis sacra officia celebrarunt. Celebrata etiam sunt coram nobis missarum officia more Hierosolymitano, auctore Jacobo apostolo; et more Constantinopolitano, auctore Basilio· *sed nos sequendam ducimus* Romanam ecclesiam in missarum celebratione." Carol. Calv. Imper. Epist. ad Cler. Ravennatens.

[n] Mabill. Lit. Gall. p. 16.

Gallican was still used. This ancient liturgy afterwards fell into obscurity; and until the time of Bona, who found a MS. of it, the opinions of learned men as to its nature were various and uncertain.

I have thus presented the substance of Mabillon's investigations relative to the antiquity of the Gallican missal, and added whatever remarks seemed to me calculated to illustrate the subject. The result of the whole may be briefly stated as follows; that at the end of the eighth century there was a liturgy used in the churches of Gaul so universally, as to be called the Gallican liturgy, or rite; and so anciently, as to be esteemed coeval with the introduction of Christianity into that country. We are not to suppose, when we are informed that Musæus, Sidonius, and Hilary *composed* books of sacraments, missæ, or mysteries, that they effected any alteration in the liturgy of Gaul. In ecclesiastical writings such expressions imply nothing more than the composition of a variety of collects and prayers for the various feast days, to be used on those days instead of the ordinary portions of the liturgy which corresponded to them. Thus we find that Gregory the Great is said to have *composed* a book of sacraments; but this is explained to mean nothing more than the composition of new collects instead of old ones, or the alteration and abbreviation of those previously extant. There is therefore no sort of proof that Musæus, Sidonius, or Hilary made any alteration in the Gallican liturgy extant before their time; but it is utterly improbable, if not impossible, that they should have done so. If these persons had each composed a different liturgy, three liturgies would have been used in Gaul; but we find, that in the following ages there was only one rite prevalent there, which was esteemed very ancient[o]; and that too without any intimation then, or in later times, that a different liturgy had formerly prevailed in any part of Gaul. Besides this, we have no reason to think that the persons above named had such influence as to cause their own liturgy to be universally received by the Gallican church. And, finally, if any liturgy composed by an individual in the fourth or fifth century had been adopted by the whole Gallican church, we should assuredly have found the name of the author affixed to the Gallican liturgy; but of this we find no sort of trace in the monuments of that church. We may therefore conclude, that the main order and substance of the liturgy was not altered by any of these authors, but remained substantially the same in the fifth century, as it had been before the time of Hilary of Poictiers.

If then it appears probable that the same rite had been used all through Gaul from time immemorial, and if no decree of any council, no authority of any patriarch or prince, can be cited to explain this general conformity, we must look to the only remaining cause by which it could have been produced, namely, to the derivation of all the Gallican churches and liturgies from some one source. That

---

[o] " Advenit dies Dominicus, et ecce rex cum his qui ab hoc sacerdote communioni abesse jussi fuerunt, ecclesiam est ingressus. Lectis igitur lectionibus, quas *canon sanxit antiquus,* oblatis muneribus super altare Dei," &c. Gregor. Turon. cap. 17. de Vit. Patrum

" Altera consuetudo missarum in s. Rom. eccl. atque *altera* in Galliarum tenetur." Beda, lib. i c. 27. *Interrogatio Augustini ad Gregor. Magnum.* " Missales libri continentes missæ ordinem *more Gallico.*" Hilduin. Abb. Areopagitica. ap. Surium, Oct. 9.

source could not have been the church of Rome, or the church of Milan; for the Gallican rites differed materially from theirs: but the church of Lyons may well claim the Gallican liturgy as her own.

If it should be true that Lyons was the first Christian church of Gaul, and that she sent misionaries through a large portion of that country long before any missionaries from Rome came there; it will appear certain that her influence must have been extensively diffused through Gaul, which would render it probable that any missionaries from Rome would conform themselves to her liturgy. I proceed to shew, in the *first* place, that Lyons was the first Christian church in Gaul. The question which has been debated with vehemence by French divines, as to whether there were any sees in France, founded by the Apostles, seems to me capable of an easy termination. No authority on this subject can be so powerful as that of Irenæus, who lived in Gaul, and was separated by only one link from the Apostles themselves. Now in his work against heresies, amongst other arguments against the Valentinians, who had obtained a footing even in Gaul, he refers to the doctrines or traditions of the churches founded by the Apostles; such as Rome, Smyrna, and Ephesus; as a sufficient means of proving the falsehood of the Valentinian doctrines[p]. If there had been any apostolical churches in Gaul, at Lyons, Arles, Vienne, or Paris, as has been alleged, Irenæus would not have referred the Valentinians *only* to Rome, and the eastern apostolical churches, but would have directed them to the nearest repositories of apostolical

[p] Irenæus adv. Hæres. lib. iii. c. 3.

tradition. His subject required him to mention any such churches in Gaul, had they been in existence; and yet neither he nor Tertullian, who shortly after used a similar argument[q], ever alluded to any apostolical church in Gaul. If no Gallican church be of apostolical antiquity, there is no difficulty in proving Lyons the oldest church in Gaul. It is universally admitted that Lyons was founded at least in the age after the apostolic. Pothinus, bishop of Lyons, died in prison A. D. 177, at upwards of ninety years of age. Irenæus, a disciple of Polycarp, bishop of Smyrna, succeeded; and Eusebius, in little more than a hundred years after his time, says that he was bishop of the churches of Gaul[r]. This expression implies at least that he was Metropolitan of Gaul, but it more probably means that he was the only bishop in Gaul. This last interpretation is supported by eminent divines, and confirmed by the silence of all authentic history, with regard to the existence of any other bishop in Gaul at that time, or even long after. The two ecclesiastical historians, Sulpitius Severus and Gregory of Tours, who both lived in Gaul, the former in the fourth, the latter in the sixth century, confirm this opinion. Sulpitius speaks of the martyrdoms of Lyons, A. D. 177, as being the first martyrdoms seen in Gaul; "for," he adds, "the religion of God was received *late* be-" yond the Alps[s]." Gregory of Tours mentions no

[q] Tertull. de Præscript adv. Hæreticos, c. 36.

[r] φέρεται δ' εἰσέτι νῦν—γραφὴ —τῶν κατὰ Γαλλίαν δὲ παροικιῶν ἃς Εἰρηναῖος ἐπεσκόπει. Euseb. Hist Eccl. lib. v. c 23.

[s] "Sub Aurelio deinde Antonini filio, persecutio quinta agitata. Ac tum primum inter Gallias martyria visa, *serius* trans Alpes Dei religione suscepta." Sulp. Sever. Hist. Sacr. lib. ii. c. 32.

SECT. IX.   *Liturgy of Gaul.*   151

bishop of Gaul, as living before the time of Pothinus, bishop of Lyons, and places the foundation of all the principal sees of Gaul a hundred years after that period[t]. The authentic acts of the martyrdom of Saturninus, mention that on his arrival at Toulouse, (about the year 250, or not long after,) only a few churches had risen in some cities by the devotion of a few Christians[u]. If Christian churches were rare in Gaul in the third century, they must have been still more so in the second; and in fact, Lyons is the only see which can shew an unquestionable succession from the second century. "We " wish," says the learned Tillemont, " that we could " shew from history, that there were really several " bishops in Gaul, but we find nothing on which we " can depend in this affair with any certainty[v]." Lyons may therefore justly be considered the oldest Christian church in Gaul. *Secondly,* it appears that the church of Lyons very early sent missionaries to convert the pagan nations of Gaul. It seems probable that Benignus, Andochius, Thyrsus, and Felix, disciples of Polycarp, preached the Gospel at Marseilles, Lyons, Langres, Saulieu, and Dijon[w]. At Autun they converted Symphorian, who suffered martyrdom in the reign of Aurelius, about A.D. 180, according to Ruinart[x]. It appears that Irenæus, at a later period, instructed several disciples to preach the Gospel in Gaul; amongst whom

[t] Gregor Turonens. Hist. Franc lib. i c 28, 29.
[u] Passio S. Saturnini ap. Ruinart. Acta Martyrum sincera, p. 130. edit. Amsterdam. 1713
[v] Tillemont, Hist. Eccl. tom. iii. part 1. p. 455. edit. Brussels, 1699
[w] Tillemont, Hist. Eccl tom. iii. part 1 p. 63, &c Ruinart. Acta Martyrum, p 79, 80.
[x] Ruinart. p. 80.

were Ferreolus a presbyter, Ferrution a deacon, Felix a presbyter, Fortunatus and Achilles deacons. The two first were sent to preach the Gospel at Bezançon, and the three last, at Valence in Dauphiné. It is probable that they converted a large number of the inhabitants of these towns, and suffered martyrdom A. D. 211 or 212 [y]. The church of Lyons, therefore, from her foundation, sent missionaries into various parts of Gaul to the north, south, and west; and their labours extended over a space of three or four hundred miles in length. Without doubt, the piety and knowledge of Irenæus gave a new vigour to the Gallican church. He himself says, that in his time there were churches among the Celts, and in Germany [z]. Tertullian, a few years after, says, that divers nations of the Gauls were submitted to Jesus Christ [a], yet there is no reason to think that what was done there, had been effected by any but by the disciples of the church of Lyons. Whatever churches, then, were founded during the second and early part of the third century in Gaul, seem to have received their ministry and ecclesiastical rites from Lyons. Thus room was left for a gradual extension of the liturgy of Lyons through a large part of France; and under these circumstances we may reasonably suppose, that the missionaries who appear to have come from Rome to Gaul about the middle of the third century or not long after [b], did not insist on introducing the Roman rite, but acquiesced in the

---

[y] Tillemont, tom. iii. part 1 p. 163, &c.
[z] Adv. Hæres. lib. i. c. 3. See Tillemont, tom. iv. part 3. p. 987.
[a] Tertull. in Jud. c vii p. 189. ed. Rigalt. Paris. 1674
[b] Gregor. Turonens. Hist lib. i. c. 28. lib x. c. 31. Liber de Gloria Confessorum, c 30.

ancient liturgy and rites of the Gallican church. That they did so, we can have little or no doubt; for how otherwise can we account for all the churches of Gaul in two centuries afterwards[c] cordially agreeing in one form of liturgy, and that form quite different from the Roman? If these missionaries had introduced the Roman liturgy, we should assuredly have found that some great disputes on the subject of the liturgy occurred in Gaul about the third or fourth century. There would have been a tradition in Gaul, that at some remote period the liturgy was in some places altered, the Roman abolished, and the Gallican introduced; but there is no trace of any such tradition. If then these missionaries received the liturgy of Gaul, and if it has appeared probable that the liturgy they received was no other than that which was used at Lyons; we see that the church of Lyons may well be regarded as the source from which the ancient Gallican liturgy was derived.

It may next be inquired, Whence did the church of Lyons derive her liturgy? To trace the liturgy of this church is to trace her origin. In the present instance, there is but little difficulty in the task. It is admitted by all the learned, and supported by irresistible evidence, that the church of Lyons was founded by missionaries from Asia. Irenæus, bishop of Lyons, was a disciple of Polycarp of Smyrna. Several missionaries of the church of Lyons and the neighbourhood are also said in memorials of authority to have been disciples of Polycarp[d]. Po-

---

[c] I think the expression of Gregory of Tours, above quoted, *antiquus canon*, implies as much. If the Gallican canon, or rule of liturgy, was *ancient* in the sixth century, when Gregory wrote, we may carry it back at least to the *fifth* century, which was the second after the arrival of the Roman missionaries.

[d] Ruinart. Acta Mart. p. 80

thinus, the predecessor of Irenæus, seems to have come from the east; and several of the early members of the church testify by their names an eastern origin[e]. Accordingly when the great persecution took place in A. D. 177, and their bishop, with many other Christians, suffered martyrdom, the church of Vienne and Lyons wrote an account of their sufferings to the churches of Asia and Phrygia, and to no others.

It was therefore from Asia that the church of Lyons derived her ecclesiastical traditions; and there can be no doubt that they of Asia received their traditions from St. John the beloved disciple. It appears from authentic history, that St. John exercised a diligent superintendence over the churches of Asia and Phrygia[f]; and hence probably, in conjunction with the civil rank of Ephesus, arose the authority of the bishop of that city, who sat in the chair of John, and exercised patriarchal or metropolitical jurisdiction over the churches of Asia, Phrygia, and other adjoining provinces. We need not wonder, then, that the churches of Asia contended sharply in the second century for that custom of observing Easter, which had been delivered to them from ancient times[g]. United to the natural unwillingness to change ancient customs, which men have generally felt, was the reverence with which they thought of their apostolical ruler St. John, and of the holy men who had been his disciples and followers. Polycrates, bishop of Ephesus, in his Epistle to Victor of Rome, and the Roman church, says, that "John, who rested on the

[e] Lib. v. cap 1. Hist. Eccl Eusebii, v. not. Valesii in loc.
[f] Euseb. Hist. Eccl. lib. iii.
[c] 1 lib. iii. c. 23.
[g] Euseb. Hist. Eccl. lib. v. c. 24.

"bosom of the Lord, who was a priest, and wore
"the *petalon*, who was a martyr and teacher, and fell
"asleep at Ephesus; Polycarp, bishop of Smyrna;
"Thraseas, bishop of Eumenia; Sagaris, bishop of
"Laodicea; the blessed Papirius; Melito, bishop
"of Sardis; all kept the feast of Easter on the
"fourteenth day[h]." It is plain, from all these things, that the churches of Asia received their ecclesiastical customs and liturgy from St. John, rather than from any other of the Apostles.

Under these circumstances, it would appear probable that the ancient Gallican liturgy and rites were originally derived from St. John; and some testimonies may be found which will confirm this idea. In the seventh century the churches of Britain and Ireland differed from the Roman and other western churches in the celebration of Easter. This difference was caused by the adoption of different paschal cycles. In the celebrated conference on this subject, held at Strenaeshalch in Britain, between Colman and Wilfrid, Colman defended the British and Irish rule, saying, that they derived it by tradition from St. John. Wilfrid very justly replied, that they did not derive this tradition from St. John, for they did not, like him, keep the feast on the fourteenth day of the first month, without any regard to the day of the week on which it fell[1]. It might appear from this, that Colman had knowingly stated an untruth: but Aldhelm, abbas Meldensis, afterwards bishop of Sherborn, about the end of the same century, enables us to redeem the character of Colman from this charge. It appears

[h] Euseb. Hist. Eccl. lib. v. c. 24.   [1] Beda, Hist. Eccl. lib. iii. c. 25.

from him, that the British and Irish derived their paschal cycle from that of Severus Sulpitius, a monk of Gaul[j], and it is this tradition which the Irish and British ascribed to St. John. The simple reason, then, for Colman's reference to St. John was, that the ancient Gallican customs were esteemed to be derived from that Apostle.

The cycle of Sulpitius might have been introduced into Ireland by Patrick, who conversed with the holy Martin, bishop of Tours: and amongst the disciples of the latter was Sulpitius, and also Germanus, the principal instructor of Patrick[k]. The same Germanus may have introduced the cycle of Sulpitius into the British church, when at the request of the British clergy, and by direction of the council of Arles, he came, A. D. 429 and 447, with Lupus and Severus, to oppose the Pelagian heresy in Britain[l].

However this may appear, we are certain that the tradition of the Irish, and probably of the British churches was, that St. John actually originated the Gallican rites. The ancient Irish author, whose tract was published by Spelman, is by all critics allowed to have written not later than the beginning of the eighth century. He affirms it

---

[j] Aldhelmi Epistola ad Geruntium, &c. apud Bonifacii Mogunt. Ep. num. 44. "Porro isti (Britanni) secundum decennem novennemque Anatolio computatum, aut potius juxta Sulpicii Severi regulam, qui 84 annorum cursum descripsit, 14 lunæ cum Judæis paschale sacramentum celebrant." On the subject of the paschal controversy, between the Britons and Romans, see Appendix ad Bed. Hist. Eccl. a Smith, Num. ix. O'Conor, Rer. Hibernicar. tom. i. Prolegomena, p. 2. pag. cxix.

[k] O'Conor, Rer. Hibern. Scriptores, p. lxxxii xci. ciii. See also Usser. Brit. Eccl. Antiq. c. xvii. p. 482.

[l] Usserii Antiq. c. xi. xii.

positively thus: " John the Evangelist first chanted " the Gallican *course*," (i. e. offices or liturgy, which, as Mabillon observes, this author seems to confound together,) " then afterwards the blessed Polycarp, " disciple of St. John; then afterwards, thirdly, Ire- " næus, who was bishop of Lyons in Gaul, chanted " the same *course* in Gaul[m]." This author distinguishes the Gallican course from the Roman, St. Mark's, the Irish and British, the Oriental, the Ambrosian, and that of Benedict the abbot. In the next section it will be seen that there are reasons for thinking that the Spanish liturgy must have been originally derived from the Gallican in the third century; and combining this proof of the antiquity of the Gallican liturgy with the tradition of the ancient British and Irish churches above noticed; remembering the testimony of Hilduinus Abbas, that the same liturgy had prevailed from the first introduction of Christianity into Gaul; and reflecting that Lyons, the first church in Gaul, derived her liturgy from the churches ruled by St. John, that there is no trace or tradition of any other liturgy having prevailed in Gaul in primitive times, that this ancient liturgy differed from the Roman, the Alexandrian, and the oriental; it appears altogether probable that the Gallican liturgy was derived originally from the instructions given by St. John to the churches of Asia and Phrygia, and therefore that we may invest it with the dignity of an apostolical liturgy. In treating of the liturgy of Ephesus in the fifth section of this Dissertation, I have remarked, that although the great oriental liturgy has long been used in the churches of Asia

[m] Spelman, Concilia, tom i. p. 176.

and Phrygia, yet there are reasons for thinking that up to the fourth century a different form was used there; and on consulting the remains of the Gallican liturgy, I have shewn that it is very likely that the council of Laodicea, held in Phrygia in the fourth century, introduced the great oriental liturgy in place of another which resembled the ancient Gallican. If this be so, we may feel almost certain that the Gallican liturgy was derived from a period of apostolical antiquity.

Having examined the origin and history of the Gallican liturgy, I may now proceed to state its order and substance, according to the monuments which still remain. As to the very words of this liturgy during the primitive ages, or indeed at any time, we need not attempt to seek for them. The Gallican missals admitted of more variety in the method of performing divine service than any other. The number and order of the lessons and prayers, the main substance and tendency of some of them, the words commemorating our Redeemer's deeds and words at the institution, the hymn *Tersanctus*, the Lord's Prayer, and a few minor particulars, seem to have been all that was fixed.

Germanus informs us, that the liturgy began with an anthem followed by *Gloria Patri*[n], after which the deacon proclaimed silence, and a mutual saluta-

[n] Germanus de Missa, Martene, Thesaur. Anecdotorum, tom. v. p 91. "Dum sanctam ingrederentur basilicam, hanc antiphonam ex improviso primicerius qui erat imposuit," &c Gregor. Turon. Hist lib ii. c. 37. "Et ecce chorus psallentium qui ingressus basilicam, postquam dicta gloria Trinitati, psallentii modulatio conquievit," Greg. Turon. Gloria Martyrum, lib. i. c 34. See Le Brun, tom iii. p 250. Le Brun has given the best and fullest exposition of the Gallican liturgy that I have seen. He has corrected several slight errors into which Mabillon and others have fallen

tion having passed between the priest and people, the hymn *Trisagios*, in imitation of the Greek rite, was sung, and was followed by *Kyrie eleëson*[o], and the song of Zacharias the prophet beginning *Benedictus*[p], after which the priest read a collect, entitled *Post prophetiam* in the Gallican missals. The office so far, though ancient, cannot be traced to the most primitive ages of the Gallican church, as doubtless the liturgy originally began with the lessons from holy Scripture, which I now proceed to consider.

A lesson from the prophets or Old Testament was first read[q], then one from the Epistles[r], which was succeeded by the hymn of the three children, *Benedicite*[s], and the holy Gospel[t]. In latter times the book of the Gospels was carried in procession to the pulpit by the deacon, who was accompanied by seven men bearing lighted tapers, and the choir

---

[c] Germanus, p. 91. Concil ii. Vasens. can. 3.

[p] Germanus. p. 92. "Fratres vero consacerdotesque qui aderant, locum Palladio episcopo ad agenda festa præbuerunt, quo incipiente Prophetiam," &c Gregor. Turon. lib. viii. c. 7.

[q] Germanus, p. 92. " Hæc ergo mensa unde cibus vitæ spiritalis accipitur——cum vel præscripta legis vel prophetarum voces ab Ecclesiæ viris ad revelationem divini consilii tractantur." Hilarius Pictav Tractat in lxvii. Ps. p. 225 edit Benedict. "Est et mensa lectionum Dominicarum in qua spiritalis doctrinæ cibo alimur." Idem, p. 428.

[r] Germanus, p. 92.

[s] Germanus, p 92 "Jubet Rex ut Diaconum nostrum, qui ante diem ad missas psalmum responsorium dixerat, canere juberem." Greg Turon. lib viii c 3

[t] Germanus, p. 93. Gregor. Turon lib. viii cap. 4. Cæsarius, Hom. 80. numbered 281. in the Appendix of the Sermons of Augustine, tom. v. p. 468. "Lectiones sive Propheticas, sive Apostolicas, sive Evangelicas etiam in domibus vestris, aut ipsi legere, aut alios legentes audire potestis: consecrationem vero corporis vel sanguinis Domini non alibi nisi in domo Dei," &c. See also Concil. iii. Lugd. tom. iv p. 1585.

sung anthems before and after the Gospel[u]. After the Gospel was ended, the priest or bishop preached[v], and the deacon made prayers for the people[w], (probably in imitation of the Greek liturgies, where a litany of the kind occurs after the Gospel[x],) and the priest recited a collect, *Post precem*[y]. Then the deacon proclaimed to the catechumens to depart[z], but whether any previous prayers were made for *them* seems doubtful. Germanus speaks of its being an ancient custom of the church to pray for catechumens in this place, but his words do not absolutely prove that there were particular prayers for them in the Gallican church, and no other author refers to the custom, as far as I am aware. The catechumens, and those under penitential discipline, having been dismissed[a], silence was again enjoined, and an address to the people on the subject of the day, and entitled *Præfatio*, was recited by the priest[b], who then repeated another prayer[c]. The oblations of the people were next received[d], while the choir sang an offertory anthem, termed *sonum* by Germanus. The elements were placed on the holy table, and covered with a large and close veil

[u] Germanus, p. 93. Greg. Tur. lib. viii. c. 4.
[v] Germanus, p. 93, 94. Hilarius Pictav. Tract. in lxvii Ps cited above. Andoeni vita S. Eligii, c. 22. Cypriani vita S. Cæsarii Arelat. c. ii. 19.
[w] Germanus, p. 94.
[x] Goar, Rituale Græc. p. 69.
[y] Germanus, p. 94. "Usque ad orationem plebis quæ post Evangelia legeretur. "Concil. iii. Lugd. Conc. tom iv. p 1585. See Le Brun, tom. iii. p. 249 254.
[z] Germanus, p. 94.
[a] Germanus, p. 94. Gregor. Turon. Vitæ Pat. c. 17.
[b] Le Brun, tom. iii. p. 255.
[c] Le Brun, ibid. This prayer was sometimes entitled, "Collectio ante Nomina."
[d] Germanus, p. 94. Concil. Matisconens. ii. can. 4. A. D. 585.

SECT. IX. *Liturgy of Gaul.* 161

or pall[e], and in latter times the priest here invoked the blessing of God on the gifts[f]. Then the tablets called *diptychs,* containing the names of the living and departed saints, were recited, and the priest made a collect "post nomina[g]." Then followed the salutation and kiss of peace; after which the priest read the collect, "ad pacem[h]." The mystical liturgy now commenced, corresponding to the Eastern "prosphora," or "anaphora," and the Roman *preface* and *canon.* It began with the form " Sursum corda[i]," &c. and then followed the preface or thanksgiving, called "contestatio," or "immo- " latio[j]," in which God's benefits to the human race were variously commemorated; and at the proper place the people all joined in singing the hymn *Tersanctus*[k]. The thanksgiving then con-

---

[e] Gregor. Turon Historia Franc. lib. vii. c. 22. Germanus, p. 95.
[f] Le Brun, tom. iii p. 257
[g] Germanus, p. 95. Miss Gothic. ap. Mabillon de Liturg. Gall. p. 188. 191, &c Le Brun, tom iii p 257, 258. Innocentius of Rome, in the fifth century, in his Epistle to Decentius of Eugubium, reproved this position of the prayers.
[h] Germanus, p 95. Miss Goth. p. 188. 191, &c
[i] " *Sursum corda* ideo sacerdos habere admonet, ut nulla cogitatio terrena maneat in pectoribus nostris in hora sacræ oblationis," &c. Germanus, p. 96. " Cum enim maxima pars populi—recitatis lectionibus exeunt de ecclesia, cui dicturus est sacerdos *Sursum corda?*" Cæsarii Hom. 80.

August. Oper. tom. v. Append. p 469.
[j] Miss. Gothic ap Mabillon, Lit. Gall. p. 188. 191, &c. " Cum nos rite sacrosancta solemnia celebrando, *Contestationem* de sancti Domini virtutibus narraremus." Gregor. Turon. lib. ii de Mirac. S. Mart. c. 14 Hilary of Poictiers seems nearly to transcribe a portion of the thanksgiving. Hilar. Pictav lib iii. de Trinitate, p 811 edit. Benedict. " Hanc oblationem Ecclesia sola puram offert Fabricatori, offerens ei cum *gratiarum* actione ex creatura ejus—quomodo autem constabit eis eum panem in quo *gratiæ actæ sint,*" &c. Irenæus adv. Hæres. lib. iv. c. 18. al. 34.
[k] Miss. Goth. Mabillon, 189. &c " At ubi expedita contestatione omnis populus *sanctus*

tinued in the form called "post sanctus[1]," which terminated with the commemoration of our Saviour's deeds and words at the institution of this sacrament[m]. Afterwards the priest recited a collect, entitled "post mysterium," or "post secreta," probably because the above commemoration was not committed to writing, on account of its being esteemed to have great efficacy in the consecration. The collect, "post mysterium," often contained a verbal oblation of the bread and wine, and an invocation of God to send his Holy Spirit to sanctify them into the sacraments of Christ's body and blood[n]. After this the bread was broken[o], and the Lord's Prayer repeated by the priest and people, being introduced and concluded with appropriate prayers, made by the priest alone[p]. The priest or bishop

in laudem Domini proclamavit," &c. Gregor. Turon. lib. ii. de Mirac S Mart. c. 14. "In omnibus missis—semper Sanctus S. S eo ordine quo ad missas publicas dicitur dici debeat." Concil ii Vasens. can 3. "Consistens quis extra ecclesiam—spectet celebres hymnorum sonitus." Hilar Pictav. p. 174. edit. Benedict Cæsarii Hom. 80. Append. S. August. tom. v. p. 469

[1] Miss. Gothicum, Mabillon, de Liturgia Gallicana, p. 189, &c.

[m] Ibid.

[n] Ibid. p. 228. 230. 285. 296. 300.

[o] Germanus, p. 96. "Verum ubi explicitis verbis sacris, confracto Dominici corporis sacramento, et ipse sumpsit, et aliis distribuit ad edendum," Gregor. Turon. lib. i. de Gloria Martyrum, c 87. It appears that the bread was broken before the Lord's Prayer was said, for the prayer generally called "post secreta," is sometimes in the Gothic Missal termed "collectio ad *panis fractionem.*" Mabillon, p 251.

[p] Miss. Goth. Mabillon, p. 189, &c. Germanus, p. 96. "Quadam die Dominica cum reliquo populo stabat. Factum est autem cum Dominica oratio diceretur, hæc aperto ore cœpit sanctam orationem cum reliquis decantare." Gregor. Turon. de Mirac. S. Mart. lib ii. c. 30. "Audiat orantis populi consistens quis extra ecclesiam vocem." Hilar. Pictav. Tract. in lxv. Ps. p. 174. edit. Bened. Cæsarii Hom. 80. in Append. August. Oper. tom. v. p. 469. edit Bened. Hom. 81 pag. 471.

then blessed the people, to which they answered, Amen[q]. Communion afterwards took place, during which a psalm or anthem was sung[r]. The priest repeated a collect of thanksgiving[s], and the service terminated.

It is obvious that this liturgy was an independent rite, and that it cannot be said to have been derived from the oriental, the Alexandrian, or the Roman forms. However, it came nearer to the oriental form than to either of the others. The chief difference between the Gallican and oriental liturgies consisted in this, that the prayers for the living and departed members of the church, occurred *after* the thanksgiving and consecration in the oriental liturgy; while in the Gallican they *preceded* the salutation of peace and thanksgiving. There is another difference which has been already noticed, namely, that the Gallican had not the three prayers of the faithful, which seem to have been introduced into the oriental liturgy about the early part of the fourth century.

With regard to the form of consecration, some difficulty occurs. The more sacred part of this form, which contains our Lord's words, is not written in any of the Gallican missals: however, we may not unreasonably suppose that it accorded with the corresponding portion of the Spanish or Mos-

---

[q] Germanus, p. 96. Miss. Gothic. 189, &c. Cæsarii Hom. 80, 81. tom. v. Append. Oper. S. August. p. 469, 470.

[r] Aureliani Regula in fine. The response of the communicants, *Amen*, is probably referred to by Hilary of Poictiers: "Inter divinorum quoque sacramentorum officia, responsionem devotæ confessionis accipiat," p. 174. edit. Bened. Though he may allude in this place to the general response made at the end of the benediction.

[s] Miss. Goth. Mabillon, p. 190. 193, &c.

arabic liturgy. But a greater difficulty occurs with regard to the portion of the Gallican liturgy which immediately followed our Saviour's words. The collect called "post secreta" sometimes contains, like the oriental rite, a verbal oblation of the gifts to God, and an invocation of God to send his holy Spirit, and make the elements the mystical body and blood of Christ. In other missæ, however, one or both of these forms are wanting. That the more solemn part of the liturgy in the Gallican church contained some such invocation, in addition to the thanksgiving and words of institution, is, I think, to be derived from the words of Irenæus: "The "bread which is of the earth, having received the "invocation of God, is no longer common bread, but "the eucharist[t]." This invocation seems to imply more than a thanksgiving, it is such a "calling "upon" God as is supposed to be "received" by the bread. What can we more naturally understand by this expression, than the invocation which is found in all the oriental and Alexandrian liturgies, "that "God will send his holy Spirit to consecrate the bread "and wine?" This form has always been called the "invocation" by the oriental churches, as Grabe shews from the writings of Cyril of Jerusalem, and Basil[u]; and many of the oriental liturgies give it the same appellation[v]. It seems also, that the Spanish or Mosarabic liturgy, which was the same as the Gallican, contained some invocation of this

[t] Ὡς γὰρ ἀπὸ γῆς ἄρτος προσλαμβανόμενος τὴν ἐπίκλησιν τοῦ Θεοῦ, οὐκέτι κοινὸς ἄρτος ἐστὶν, ἀλλ' εὐχαριστία Iren. adv. Hæres. lib. iv. c. 18. al. 34.

[u] See Irenæi Oper. a Grabe, p. 400. not. 1.

[v] Renaudot, Liturg. Orient. tom i. Lit. Basil. p. 16. Cyril. 48. p. 238, &c.; tom ii. p. 33. 88, &c.

kind; for Isidore Hispalensis says, that the "sixth "prayer" of the liturgy, which corresponded with the Gallican "post secreta," "was the confirmation of "the sacrament, that the oblation which is offered to "God, *being sanctified by the Holy Spirit*, may be "confirmed as the sacrament of the body and blood[w]." I think, therefore, that there are reasons enough to warrant us in holding the opinion, that the liturgy of the Gallican church originally contained always some invocation or prayer to God for the sanctification of the elements; an invocation which we actually find in several of the ancient Gallican "missæ."

[w] "Porro sexta exhinc succedit, confirmatio sacramenti, ut oblatio quæ Deo offertur, sanctificata per Spiritum Sanctum, corporis et sanguinis (sacramentum) confirmetur." Isidori Hispal. de Eccl. Officiis lib. 1. c 15.

SECTION X.

LITURGY OF SPAIN

As the abolition of the ancient Gallican liturgy, and the substitution of the Roman in its place, was effected by the emperor Charlemagne; so likewise, in about three centuries afterwards, the churches of Spain were obliged by the authority of the Spanish monarchs, who were influenced by the Roman patriarch, to relinquish their ancient liturgy, and receive in its place the Roman. The Spanish liturgy was abolished in Arragon about A.D. 1060, in the reign of Ramiro the First[a]; but it was not for some time after relinquished in Navarre, Castille, and Leon. Gregory the Seventh of Rome wrote to Alphonso the Sixth, king of Castille and Leon, and to Sancho the Fourth, king of Navarre, A.D. 1074[b], and made the greatest exertions to have the ancient liturgy abolished in Spain; giving as his reason, that it contained certain things contrary to the catholic faith[c]. This charge was most erroneous, and

---

[a] Pinii Tract. de Lit. Mosarab. tom. i. Oper. Thomasii, a Blanchinio c. 6 §. 1. N⁰. 220, 221. §. 2. N⁰. 230. 232, 233.
[b] Pinius, ibid. p. xlvi.
[c] Ibid. p. xlvii.

was only intended to throw obloquy on the Spanish liturgy; for only a very short time before, A.D. 1064, three bishops, deputed by all the prelates of Spain, had attended the council of Mantua, and presented the Spanish or Mosarabic missal for the inspection of that council, and of Alexander the Third of Rome; by whom it was approved, and declared orthodox[d]. Roderic Ximenes, archbishop of Toledo, relates that the clergy and people of all Spain were in disturbance, at being compelled by the king Alphonso and the Roman legate to receive the Gallican office[e]; that is, the Roman, which had now been long used in Gaul, and was probably most familiarly known in Spain by the title of Gallican. However, the king at last succeeded in his design, (which had been chiefly instigated by the queen Constantia,) by threatening death and confiscation to all who opposed it; and then, according to Roderic, while all wept and lamented, it became a proverb, that " quo " volunt reges vadunt leges[f]." From this time the Mosarabic or Spanish liturgy became almost extinct, until, in the beginning of the sixteenth century, cardinal Ximenes endowed a college and chapel in

[d] Ibid. p. xliii.

[e] "Quia Ricardus legatus se gerebat in aliquibus minus caute—fuit ab Urbano summo pontifice revocatus; verum ante revocationem *clerus et populus totius Hispaniæ* turbatur, eo quod Gallicanum officium suscipere a legato et principe cogebantur." Roderic Toletan. de Reb. Hist. lib. vi. c. 26.

[f] "Sed rex cum esset magnanimus, et suæ voluntatis pertinax executor, nec miraculo territus, nec supplicatione suasus, voluit inclinari; sed mortis supplicia et direptionem minitans resistentibus, præcepit ut Gallicanum officium in omnibus regni sui finibus servaretur. Et tunc cunctis flentibus et dolentibus, inolevit proverbium: 'Quo volunt reges vadunt leges.'" Ibid.

Toledo, for the celebration of that ancient rite[g]; and this is now perhaps the only place in Spain where the primitive liturgy of that country and of Gaul is in some degree preserved.

On examining the Mosarabic liturgy, it appears to have agreed almost exactly with the ancient Gallican rite[h]. Much confusion has been caused by not distinguishing between the Spanish liturgy and missal. The liturgy may be old, though many " missæ " may be modern; nay, all the prayers now existing in the missal may be modern, and yet the liturgy be most ancient. The number and order of the parts is that which gives us the characters of the liturgy; and on examining the remains of the ancient Spanish missal, we find that the liturgy accorded in these respects with the early Gallican. This uniformity is recognised in the Epistle of the emperor Charles the Bald to the clergy of Ravenna, in which he intimates that priests who came to him from Toledo in Spain had performed in his presence the ancient liturgy of the Gallican church, which had been abolished by his ancestor Charlemagne[1]. This shews that in the ninth century the Spanish and the ancient Gallican liturgies were considered to have been the same. The Spanish liturgy was therefore different from the Roman in the ninth century. And it is plain also that this difference had existed since the sixth century; for Isidore, bishop of Seville, describes the liturgy so minutely,

[g] Pinius ut supra, cap. viii.
[h] Lesleus, in his preface to the Mosarabic missal, sect v. traces the conformity of the Gallican and Mosarabic missals; and, section vi refutes the arguments of those who deny that conformity.
[1] See this passage cited in sect 9. note [m], p. 146.

as to leave no doubt that it was the same as that afterwards used in Spain, and very different from the Roman[j]. And Vigilius of Rome, about A.D. 538, writing to Profuturus, bishop of Braga in Spain, on the subject of the liturgy, informed him, as if he had been ignorant on the subject, that at Rome they were always accustomed to consecrate the elements after the same tenor, or in the same words; and that on each feast day they made commemoration of the subject of that day, by subjoining certain collects, &c.: and, finally, that he might receive full information on the subject, he transcribed for Profuturus the Roman canon, and the collects &c. for Easter[k]. All this shews that the Roman liturgy was at that time not well known in Spain; and we may observe, with regard to the above passage, that it not only shews that the Roman liturgy was not used in Spain A.D. 538, but contains a sort of tacit allusion to the ancient Roman and Spanish modes of celebrating the liturgy. For when it is said by Vigilius, that they always consecrated in the same manner, and when he adds the canonical prayer to his letter, we see a distinct reference to the Roman custom of always using the same canon, and only admitting variety in the prefaces, collects, &c. While, on the other hand, we know that the Spanish and Gallican churches varied the canon, as well as the prefaces and collects, for almost every festival; which seems evidently to be alluded to.

If then it appears that in the sixth century the Spanish churches had their liturgy distinct from the

[j] Isidor. Hispalens. de Eccl. Offic. lib. 1. c. 11—15. [k] Cited above in note[l] of section 6 p. 115.

Roman, we are justified in thinking that they had used the same from a period of remote antiquity. There was no supreme power over them, which was likely to have introduced this liturgy at a recent period. The patriarchs of Rome had no right to introduce any liturgy into the Spanish church; and even supposing that they had, would they have introduced one entirely different from their own[1]? Nor have we any reason to think that the oriental liturgy was brought from Constantinople by the Goths, when they invaded Spain, as Pinius would contend[m]. For there is no reason to suppose that the bishops of Spain would have relinquished their original liturgy, to adopt another which was introduced by the barbarian invaders of their country; nor is there, as far as I am aware, any proof that the Goths who invaded Spain had received Christianity and a liturgy in the east; and, finally, the liturgy of Spain does not seem to have been derived from the oriental formularies, but to have accorded with the Gallican. Neither have we any reason to think that the rites of the Gallican church were imposed on that of Spain; or that the latter adopted the rites of the former, at any period approaching towards the sixth century. We have no trace in history or tradition of such an approximation. And, in fact, Isidore of Seville, in the sixth century, attributed the origin of the Spanish liturgy to St. Peter[n]; which shews that he considered it of the

---

[1] Lesleus, Præfat. Missal Mosarab sect. x proves at length that the Roman was not the original liturgy of Spain.

[m] Pinius, ut supra, cap. ii. §. 1.

[n] "Ordo autem missæ vel orationum, quibus oblata Deo sacrificia consecrantur, primum

most remote antiquity, and had little idea of its having been derived from the Gallican.

It is however apparent that this liturgy must have been derived from the Gallican at a most remote period, simply from combining the fact of the substantial identity of both, with their circumstantial variation, and the ancient independence of the two churches. If we regard the geographical position of the two countries, we perceive that Gaul was more likely to receive the Christian faith at an early period than Spain; and, in fact, we have more ancient accounts of churches and bishops in the former than in the latter country. It is true that St. Paul is said by many ecclesiastical writers to have visited Spain; that an inscription (of questionable authenticity however) records the persecutions inflicted on Christians in that country in the time of Nero; that Irenæus, Tertullian, and Cyprian, speak of Christians in Spain: but it seems that religion was for some time only in an infant state there. The earliest mention of Spanish bishops occurs in the writings of Cyprian[o], nearly a hundred years after the time of Pothinus, bishop of Lyons. The first Spanish martyr of whom we have any authentic account, is Fructuosus of Tarragona, who suffered in the time of Decius, about A. D. 259[p]. If we take probability for our guide, in the absence of certainty, we may say, that the chief missionaries came from Gaul to Spain, and with the ecclesiastical orders introduced the liturgy of their own

a Sancto Petro est institutus, cujus celebrationem uno eodemque modo universus peragit orbis." Isidor. Hisp de Eccl. Off lib. i. c. 15

[o] Cyprian. Epist. lxvii. edit. Fell. p. 170.

[p] Ruinart, Acta Martyrum, p. 219.

church: and in this point of view, we must assign a very great antiquity to the Gallican and Spanish liturgy, since it could scarcely have been brought from Gaul to Spain later than the beginning of the third century. Of course, in saying this, I would not be understood to affirm, that we can ascertain the words of the Spanish or Gallican liturgy at such a remote period. It has happened, in fact, from the custom of these churches, in varying almost every part of the liturgy for each feast, that we can scarcely do more than determine the general substance and order of that liturgy at any time.

The Spanish or Mosarabic liturgy was minutely described by Isidore Hispalensis in the sixth century; and his description coincides perfectly with those monuments of it which still remain. During the middle ages, and in the time of cardinal Ximenes, the Mosarabic liturgy received an addition of several rites, which are now used in it[q]; but others are plainly derived from the church of Constantinople, which is another proof of the independence of the Spanish liturgy both of the Roman and Gallican; and affords an additional confirmation of the ancient existence of this rite, which was already so long established, before the contentions of the eastern and western churches, in the ninth and preceding centuries, as to have borrowed from the former several improvements. The Mosarabic missal published by cardinal Ximenes, A. D. 1500, is now very scarce. It was republished by Lesleus at Rome A. D. 1755, with learned annotations, which amply

[q] Lesleus, Præfat Missalis Mosarab. sect. vii shews what portions of the Mosarabic liturgy and missal were added in the time of Ximenes, and during the middle ages.

SECT. X. *Liturgy of Spain.* 173

merit a perusal. Martene, in his valuable work, "De Antiquis Ecclesiæ Ritibus," lib. i. c. 4. n°. 12, has printed so much of the Mosarabic missal as is sufficient to give a satisfactory view of its nature. Isidore of Seville, Leander, and other Spanish bishops, are said to have composed this missal, which is probably a very correct statement, since we may very well attribute to them many, or even all, of the distinct "missæ," which make up that volume. But the original model and substance of the liturgy, as I have said, was apparently derived from the Gallican church, by which it had been probably received from the churches of Asia and Phrygia.

The Mosarabic liturgy began with an anthem and responsory[r], and a collect[s], which were succeeded by a lesson from the Prophets or Old Testament[t]; another anthem[u], or, on certain days, the Song of the Three Children[v]; the Epistle[w], Gospel, and Alleluia chanted with a verse[x]. Of course the

[r] Martene, tom i. p. 457. This is probably alluded to by Isidore, de Eccl. Off., who speaks of anthems and responsories in lib i c. 7 and 8, just before he alludes to collects and lessons.

[s] Martene, p. 457. Observe that the termination of most prayers in the Mosarabic liturgy is separated from the body of the prayer, and seems altogether formed like those of the Greek rite. See Goar, Rit. Græc. Liturg. Chrysost. et Basil. Isidore probably refers to the collect in cap. 9. lib. i.

[t] Martene, p 457. Isidor. lib. i. c. 10.

[u] Martene, p 457.

[v] Idem, p. 458. Concil. Tolet. iv. can. iv "Hymnum quoque trium puerorum—hoc sanctum concilium instituit, ut per omnes ecclesias Hispaniæ vel Galliæ (Narbonensis) in omnium missarum solemnitate—decantetur."

[w] Martene, p. 458.

[x] Idem. Concil. Toletan. (anno 633.) iv. can. 12. "In quibusdam Hispaniarum ecclesiis Laudes post Apostolum decantantur, priusquam Evangelium prædicetur, dum canones præcipiunt, post Apostolum non Laudes sed Evangelium annuntiari," &c. Bona shews that the "Laudes" here

sermon occurred anciently in this place. Then the catechumens being dismissed, the oblations of the faithful were received, and in the meantime the choir sung an offertory anthem[y]. The elements being placed on the table, the preface, resembling the address to the people at the beginning of the Gallican liturgy, was read[z]. Then followed a prayer commending the prayers and oblations to the acceptance of God[a]; the names of the living and departed were read, and prayer made for them[b]; a collect was recited before the kiss of peace[c]. Then

---

means the "Alleluia," &c. after the Gospel. Rer. Lit. lib. ii. c. 6. No. 4 Isidore speaks of the "Laudes," or "Alleluia," in this place; and after remarking, that in Africa it was only sung on Sundays, and between Easter and Pentecost, adds these words; "Verum apud nos, secundum *antiquam Hispaniarum traditionem*, præter dies jejuniorum vel quadragesimæ, omni tempore canitur Alleluia." c. 13

[y] The offertory anthem is called "Sacrificium." Martene, p. 459 Isidore, Hispal. c. 14, speaks of it. The oblation at p. 458. of Martene is modern. The confession or apology, p. 459, beginning "Accedam ad te," is probably ancient.

[z] Martene, p. 459 This preface is peculiar to the Gallican and Spanish liturgies. What may be the antiquity of the preface it is impossible to conjecture, but I do not think it so ancient as many other parts of the liturgy. Isidore mentions it, c. 15. "Prima earumdem (orationum) oratio admonitionis est erga populum, ut excitentur ad exorandum Deum."

[a] This we take on the authority of Isidore, c 15: "Secunda invocationis ad Deum est, ut elementa suscipiat, preces fidelium, oblationemque eorum." The prayer in Martene, p. 460, does not particularly allude to the above subjects, but in the time of Isidore it seems generally to have done so. It is preceded by a sort of hymn, *Trisagios*, and a short bidding prayer, which seem plainly to be formed after the Greek model.

[b] Martene, p. 460. Isidor. c. 15 "Tertia autem effunditur pro offerentibus, sive pro defunctis fidelibus, ut per idem sacrificium veniam consequantur."

[c] Martene, p. 460. Isidor. c. 15 "Quarta post hæc infertur pro osculo pacis, ut charitate omnes reconciliati invicem, digni sacramento corporis et sanguinis Christi consocientur," &c.

SECT. X.   *Liturgy of Spain.*   175

began the more solemn part of the office with the form "Sursum corda[d]," &c.; which was succeeded by the thanksgiving called *illatio*[e]; the hymn *Tersanctus*[f]; a continuation of thanksgiving; a petition for the sanctification of the elements; the words of institution[g]; a prayer for the confirmation of the oblation, by means of the Holy Ghost, as the sacrament of Christ's body and blood[h]; the Constantinopolitan Creed[i]; the breaking of bread[j]; and Lord's Prayer[k]. The priest blessed the people, who answered, Amen[l], and communion took place, while the choir sang *Gustate et videte*, "O taste and see "how gracious[m]," &c. Then the priest recited a prayer of thanksgiving, and the assembly was dismissed[n].

[d] Martene, p 461

[e] Idem, p. 461, 462 Isidor. c. 15. "Quinta infertur illatio in sanctificatione oblationis, in qua etiam ad Dei laudem terrestrium creatura, virtutumque cœlestium universitas provocatur, et 'Osanna in excelsis' cantatur—." The *illatio* seems to be considered by Isidore as including *the words of institution*, from his connecting the sanctification with it.

[f] Martene, p 462. Isidore, quoted in last note.

[g] Martene, p. 462, probably referred to by Isidore as before.

[h] "Porro sexta exhinc succedit confirmatio sacramenti, ut oblatio quæ Deo offertur, sanctificata per Spiritum Sanctum, corporis et sanguinis (sacramentum) confirmetur." Isidor c. 15. See Martene, p. 462. Cardinal Bona attests the fact, that the Mosarabic missal still contains this invocation: "Ritus enim Mosarabicus — post consecrationem brevem ponit orationem quæ *post pridie*, sive *post secreta* inscribitur: et in ea sacerdos precatur, ut descendat Spiritus Sanctus, et dona benedicat atque sanctificet" Rer. Lit. lib. ii. c. 13. N⁰ 5.

[i] Martene, p. 464. Isidor. c. 16. Concil. Toletan iii. can. 2.

[j] Martene, p. 464.

[k] Idem. Isidor. c. 15. Concil. Tolet. iv. can. 9.

[l] Martene, p. 465. Isidor c. 17.

[m] Martene, p. 465.

[n] Idem, p. 466.

SECTION XI.

LITURGY OF BRITAIN AND IRELAND.

THE early history of the British church is obscure; and although we learn from Tertullian and Origen, that Christianity had extended thither by the third century, it is not easy to fix the period at which regular churches were formed. Leaving the discussion of this and similar topics in the hands of those learned persons who have already considered the subject, we are at least certain, that the British church in the fourth century was ruled by bishops, who attended the councils of Arles, Sardica, and Ariminum. Could we hold any decided opinion as to the quarter whence these prelates or their predecessors originally derived their orders, we might form some conjecture on the nature of the primitive British liturgy; but it were much to be wished, that we might be relieved from the necessity of doing this, by the discovery of some MS. containing British rites. It is by no means impossible that some such monument may yet be discovered, as the British churches did not for a long time submit to the authority of the Saxon archbishops.

Archbishop Usher, who is followed by bishop Stillingfleet, and many other writers, says, that we read in an anonymous book on the origin of ecclesiastical offices, written nine hundred (eleven hundred) years ago, that Germanus and Lupus introduced the "ordinem cursus Gallorum," or Gallican liturgy, into Britain[a]. After carefully examining the tract referred to by the archbishop, I profess myself unable to perceive that any such assertion is made. It appears to me even, that this anonymous Irish author, if he alludes at all to the British liturgy, must be understood to say that it was *different* from the ancient Gallican. He says that John the Evangelist first chanted the Gallican course or liturgy: but the course of the Scoti, or Irish, he traces to S. Mark. The latter course, according to him, was brought to Gaul by Cassian, and being received in the monastery of Lerins, was used by Germanus and Lupus, who preached in Britain and Ireland, and constituted a bishop named Patrick archbishop in those countries[b]. It seems then, that this author considered the Gallican and Irish courses different; and if we were to understand him to allude to the rites of the British church, when he says that Patrick was constituted archbishop in Britain and Ireland, and *there* chanted the same course[c] which he had learned from Germanus and Lupus, we should only learn that the British rites agreed with the Irish, and therefore differed from those of Gaul.

[a] Usserii Britannicar Eccl. Antiq. c. xi. p. 185. ed Lond. 1687. Stillingfleet, Origines Britann c. iv. p. 216. ed Lond. 1685.

[b] Vid. Spelman, Concilia, tom. i. p. 176, 177. Lond. 1639.

[c] Ibid. p. 177.

But, in truth, I do not see that the anonymous author in that place necessarily refers to the British liturgy; and there are some circumstances which induce me to think that he does not. It seems probable that the Irish liturgy, from the time of Patrick, A. D. 432, did not differ very much from the ancient Roman, but that the British did. I shall presently give my reasons for thinking the ancient Roman and Irish not very unlike. That the Roman and British differed greatly, is proved by the words of Augustine, first archbishop of Canterbury, as given by Bede. He addressed the British bishops in the following terms: "In many respects you act "in a manner contrary to our customs, and indeed "to those of the universal church: and yet if you "will obey me in these three things; to celebrate "Easter at the proper time; to perform the office "of baptism, in which we are born again to God, "according to the custom of the holy Roman and "apostolical church; and with us to preach the "word of God to the English nation; we will tole- "rate all your *other customs*, though *contrary to* "*our own*[d]." In these last words it seems to me, that there is enough to warrant our holding the opinion, that the Roman and British liturgies were "contrary," or different. Another proof that the British liturgy differed from the Irish after the time

[d] "Dicebat autem eis, quia in multis quidem nostræ consuetudini, immo universalis Ecclesiæ, contraria geritis: et tamen si in tribus his mihi obtemperare vultis; ut Pascha suo tempore celebretis; ut ministerium baptizandi, quo Deo renascimur, juxta morem sanctæ Romanæ et Apostolicæ Ecclesiæ compleatis; et genti Anglorum una nobiscum verbum Domini prædicetis: cætera quæ agitis, quamvis moribus nostris contraria, æquanimiter cuncta tolerabimus." Bed. Histor. Eccles. lib. ii. c. 2.

of Patrick, (and therefore probably from the Roman, as we shall see hereafter,) is afforded by the very ancient catalogue of the saints of Ireland, probably written in the seventh century, and published by archbishop Usher. This document informs us that for some time after Patrick, the Irish had only one liturgy, but that then a second was introduced by the bishop David, and Gildas and Cadoc, Britons; and from that time different liturgies were used by the saints of Ireland[e]. David, Gildas, and Cadoc, lived in the sixth century; and, if we give credit to this ancient writer, it appears that the British and Irish liturgies were different up to that period. Assuming then, for the present, that the Irish liturgy from the time of Patrick was nearly the same as the Roman, we are led to the conclusion, that the British differed from the Roman, which is in fact almost expressly affirmed by Augustine.

But what then could the ancient British liturgy have been? In reply to this question I would remark, that we have no trace or record of more than two primitive liturgies in the west. These were the Roman and the Gallican. The latter was used in Gaul and Spain, from a period of remote antiquity. If the British clergy originally derived their orders from the nearest Christian province, namely, from Gaul, they would also probably use the Gallican liturgy; and if this was the case, the British liturgy in subsequent ages would have been different from the Roman and the Irish, as we have seen that it was. I do not mean to enter on a consideration of the time when Christianity penetrated into Britain.

[e] Usserii Britan. Eccles Antiq. c. xviii. p 473, 474.

There may have been Christians in this country in the apostolic age, or shortly after. Britain, though so much more remote from the great scene of apostolic preaching than Gaul, may possibly have received some rays from the Gospel before that country. It is even not impossible that Eleutherius of Rome may have written to Lucius, a British chief, or that Bran, the father of Caractacus, may have received Christianity at Rome during the lifetime of the apostles, and converted some of his fellow-countrymen on his return to Britain. All this may or may not be true; but I do not see that there is any proof, or strong presumption, that the British bishops originally derived their orders from Rome. It is infinitely more probable that they were ordained in Gaul. When there is no sort of authentic history or tradition, that the first British bishops were consecrated at Rome, we are at once led to the conclusion that the simple natural course was adopted, and that the bishops of Gaul (the nearest province) ordained the first bishops of the British church. Certainly there is nothing in the ecclesiastical history of the two countries to oppose such an idea. We do not read of bishops in Britain before there were any in Gaul; on the contrary, while we know that the church of Lyons was ruled by bishops in the second century, we hear of no British bishops until early in the fourth. I do not say that regular churches may not have existed in this country from a much more remote period; but the simple fact is, that there are much more ancient accounts of the apostolical succession of orders in Gaul than in Britain. I do not see any thing therefore to oppose the idea, that the British bishops were first ordained in Gaul; and if so, they probably received the Gallican liturgy, which being different from the Roman, and the Irish after the time of Patrick, would exactly meet the few notices which antiquity supplies, as to the nature of the liturgy used in Britain.

The liturgy of Ireland during the first ages was probably the same as that used in Britain, because it is likely that any presbyters who may have come to the former country were sent thither by the British church. Christianity had certainly penetrated into Ireland long before the time of Patrick; though this holy bishop, from his arduous and successful labours in that island, merited and received the title of "Apostle of the Irish;" and as there seems to be no authentic account of the original source from whence Christianity had come to Ireland, the mere geographical position of that country, in relation to its sister island, would induce us to think that the former must have received religion and ecclesiastical rites from the latter.

In the time of Patrick, however, a great change took place in the state of Christianity in Ireland. Religion spread into all parts, many bishoprics were founded, and the church arose from a state of infancy, and assumed that regular and apostolical form which has continued ever since. No monument of the ancient Irish liturgy was known to exist, until Dr. O'Conor, a few years ago, published an account of one which is in the duke of Buckingham's library at Stowe[f]. The writing of this MS. according to the specimen of it given by

---

[f] Dr. O'Conor's remarks on this manuscript occur in his Appendix to vol. i. of the Catalogue of MSS. in Stowe library, A D. 1819.

Dr. O'Conor, in the second volume of his " Rerum " Hibernicarum Scriptores," does not seem to me to be of very great antiquity; and if I may be permitted to conjecture its age from that of other MSS., I should say it was written about the tenth or eleventh century, and probably not very long before the year 1064, between which and the year 1026, Dr. O'Conor says, the very curious inscribed case covering the MS. must have been formed[g]. But we should remember, that although not written before the tenth or eleventh century, it may at that time have been copied from a more ancient MS., which was probably the fact.

This missal is in several ways proved to have belonged to the Irish church. First, it contains rubrics in the Irish language[h]; secondly, it contains a number of names of Irish saints and worthies[i]; thirdly, it makes a commemoration in the prayers *omnium quoque Scotorum*[j], " and of all the Irish," (the Irish being always called Scoti, until the eleventh or twelfth century). Besides this, it accords with the few traces of the Irish liturgy which we can find amongst ancient writers. In the synod of Matiscon in Gaul, A. D. 624, Agrestius objected against Columbanus, an Irish monk, abbot of Bobio in Italy, that he used a number of collects in celebrating the liturgy. On the other hand, Eustasius, a friend of Columbanus, defended this custom[k]. On

[g] O'Conor, Appendix, p. 35, &c.
[h] P. 47.
[i] P. 49.
[j] P. 48.
[k] " At ille (Agrestius) prorupit dicens, se scire Columbanum a cæterorum more desciscere, et ipsa missarum solemnia multiplicatione orationum vel collectarum celebrare." See the whole context, and the re-

referring to Dr. O'Conor's description of the MS. missal, we find it actually does contain several collects before the epistle[1], contrary to the practice of most of the western churches.

The anonymous Irish writer on the Origin of Ecclesiastical Offices, quoted by Usher, and referred to above, speaks of S. Mark's having appointed all the people to sing *Gloria in excelsis, Tersanctus,* and the Lord's Prayer[m]; and as he refers the origin of the Irish liturgy (however erroneously) to S. Mark, these forms must have been used in it. When we turn to Dr. O'Conor's description of the MS. missal, it seems that all these forms occur there. It is remarkable that the Nicene Creed, in this MS., does not contain the addition *Filioque,* which was generally received by the western churches before the end of the ninth century; neither does it include the article of the descent of our Saviour into hell[n].

This ancient liturgy begins with an anthem, followed by litanies, and the hymn *Gloria in excelsis*[o]; after which are several collects or "prayers, for the "priest, the people, the universal church, the peace "and prosperity of princes and kingdoms, for the "distributors of alms[p]," &c. The Epistle, Gospel, and Creed, follow next in order[q]. The remainder

---

ply of Eustasius, who was abbot of Luxovium, in the Life of S. Eustasius, Acta SS. Benedictin sæculum ii. p. 120.

[1] P. 43. of O'Conor's Appendix.

[m] "Sed beatus Marcus Evangelista—totam Ægyptum et Italiam taliter prædicavit sicut unam ecclesiam, ut omnes *sanctus,* vel *Gloria in excelsis Deo,* vel *orationem Dominicam* et *Amen,* universi tam viri quam fœminæ decantarent." Tract. de Cant. et cursibus Eccl. Spelman. Concilia, tom 1. p. 177.

[n] O'Conor, p. 45 47
[o] P. 41—43.
[p] Ibid.
[q] P 44, 45

of the office, including the canon, seems to accord pretty nearly with the ancient Roman, omitting "all festivals and prayers that have been added to "it since the tenth century." The prayers which follow the offertory in the Roman missal are wanting in the Irish; the prayer *Deus qui humanæ substantiæ*, the *Lavabo*, and prayer *Suscipe S. Trinitas*, are omitted. The bread and wine are not offered separately, but simultaneously[r]. The festivals to be commemorated in the preface or thanksgiving "are placed in the Irish missal in the following or-"der: 1. Nativity; 2. Circumcision; 3. Epiphany; "4. *Natale calicis Domini* (or Lent); 5. Easter; "6. *In clausula Paschæ* (Low-Sunday, the octave "of Easter-day); 7. Ascension; 8. Pentecost. For "these festivals there is but one common preface, "nor is there any distinction, save the inserting in "that preface the name of each festival as it occurs "in the calendar[s]." The canon contains several variations from the ancient Roman of no great consequence. The words following, *Hanc igitur*, contain a petition that the people may be delivered from idolatry; and remind us of the various prayers which occur in the sacramentary of Gelasius at this part of the service[t]. The *Memento* for the departed contains a long list of Irish worthies, the latest of whom, according to Dr. O'Conor, "died before the "middle of the seventh century[u]." The chief peculiarity of this formulary is, that they are invoked after the manner of western litanies, *Ora pro nobis*. Dr. O'Conor remarks in general of this liturgy, that

[r] P. 46, 47
[s] P. 47.
[t] See Bona, Rer Liturgic lib ii. c. 12. num. 4.
[u] O'Conor, p. 49.

"all the improvements which have been made in the Roman missal since the days of Berno, A. D. 1012, and which were universally adopted in Ireland at the synod of Kells, in 1152, are wanting in this; and therefore this must be considered as the missal which was in use in Ireland before that time, probably from the days of Columban. It is in fact one of the most valuable monuments that has escaped the ravages of the tenth century[v]."

I agree with the Doctor in thinking this a valuable and curious record; and that it affords us a clue in our inquiries relative to the ancient Irish liturgy. It is the only document in existence which can be referred to the liturgy of Ireland, before the jurisdiction of the Roman patriarch was established in that country. It seems, however, that this liturgy accorded very nearly with the ancient Roman; and it would in fact be probable, antecedently to a knowledge of this fact, that the Irish used the Roman liturgy from the time of Patrick; for it seems that Palladius and Patrick were successively ordained bishops of the Scoti, or Irish, by Cœlestine patriarch of Rome, A. D. 431 and 432[w]; and it is natural to imagine, that they brought the Roman liturgy into Ireland. However, the Irish also received the ancient British liturgy in the following century, as I have already observed; and it seems that in later times there were great varieties in the mode of celebrating divine worship in Ireland, which were mentioned by Gillebert bishop of Limerick A. D. 1090[x], and which appear to have been removed by

[v] P 49.
[w] Usser. Britan. Eccl. Antiq. c 16, 17.
[x] In his book *de Usu Ecclesiastico*, which was written "ut diversi et schismatici illi

the synod of Kells, A. D. 1152, when the Roman rites were established.

With regard to the liturgy of the Saxon church in England, there are no such difficulties as those which attend the British and Irish. There can be no doubt that Augustine and his companions, who preached the Gospel in some part of the heptarchy, at the end of the sixth and beginning of the seventh centuries, carried with them the sacramentary of Gregory, patriarch of Rome, by whom they had been sent to this country. In fact, the liturgical books of the Anglo-Saxon church in subsequent times were nothing else but transcripts of that sacramentary[y]. As, however, each bishop had the power of making some improvements in the liturgy of his church, in process of time different customs arose, and several became so established as to receive the names of their respective churches. Thus gradually the "Uses" or customs of York, Sarum, Hereford, Bangor, Lincoln, Aberdeen, &c. came to be distinguished from each other.

The missals and other ritual books of York and Hereford have been printed; but I have inquired in vain for the names of the bishops who originated the few peculiarities which they contain. Their rubrics are sometimes less definite than those of the Sarum "Use," and they contain some few offices in commemoration of departed prelates and saints, which are not found in other missals, &c. The "Use" or custom of Sarum derives its origin from Osmund, bishop of

---

ordines, quibus Hibernia pene tota delusa est, uni catholico et Romano cedant officio." Usser. Vet. Epist. Hibernicar. Sylloge, p. 77.

[y] For instance, the missal of Leofric bishop of Exeter, in the Bodleian Library.

that see in A. D. 1078, and chancellor of England. We are informed by Simeon of Durham, that about the year 1083 king William the Conqueror appointed Thurstan, a Norman, abbot of Glastonbury. Thurstan, despising the ancient Gregorian chanting, which had been used in England since the sixth century, attempted to introduce in its place a modern style of chanting invented by William of Fescamp, a Norman. The monks resisted the innovations of their abbot, and a scene of violence and bloodshed ensued, which was terminated by the king's sending back Thurstan to Normandy[z]. This circumstance may very probably have turned the attention of Osmund to the regulation of the ritual of his church. We are informed that he built a new cathedral; collected together clergy, distinguished as well for learning as for a knowledge of chanting; and composed a book for the regulation of ecclesiastical offices, which was entitled the "Custom" book. The substance of this was probably incorporated into the missal and other ritual books of Sarum, and ere long almost the whole of England, Wales, and Ireland adopted it[a]. When the archbishop of Canterbury celebrated the liturgy in the presence of the bishops of his province, the bishop of Salisbury

[z] Simeon Dunelmensis in an. 1083, p. 212. X. Scriptores. Joannes Bromton, p. 978. ibid.

[a] Successit Osmundus regis cancellarius, XXIV annis sedens. Hic ecclesiam novam apud Saresberiam ædificavit, et clericos insignes tam literis quam cantu aggregavit, ita ut ipse episcopus libros scribere, illuminare, et ligare non fastidiret. Hic composuit librum ordinalem ecclesiastici officii quem *Consuetudinarium* vocant, quo fere tota nunc Anglia, Wallia, et Hibernia utitur." Chronicon Joannis Bromton, X. Scriptores, p. 976. Knyghton de Eventibus Angliæ, lib. ii. c 3. p. 2351, X. Scriptores. It is said that the Sarum Use was adopted in some part of France, and even in Portugal.

(probably in consequence of the general adoption of the "Use" of Sarum) acted as *precentor* of the college of bishops, a title which he still retains. The churches of Lincoln and Bangor also had peculiar "Uses;" but I am not aware that any of their books have been printed. A MS. pontifical, containing the rites and ceremonies performed by the bishop, still (I believe) remains in the church of Bangor; it is said to have belonged to Anianus, who occupied that see in the thirteenth century. The church of Aberdeen in Scotland had its own rites; but whether there was any peculiarity in the missal I know not, as it has never been published. The breviary of Aberdeen, according to Zaccaria, was printed in A. D. 1609[b], (qu. 1509?) Independently of these rites of particular churches, the monastic societies of England had many different rituals, which, however, all agreed substantially, having all been derived from the sacramentary of Gregory. The Benedictine, Carthusian, Cistertian, and other orders had peculiar missals. Schultingius nearly transcribes a very ancient sacramentary belonging to the Benedictines of England[c]; bishop Barlow, in his MS. notes on the Roman missal, speaks of a missal belonging to the monastery of Evesham[d]; and Zaccaria mentions a MS. missal of Oxford, written in the thirteenth or fourteenth century, which is in the library of the canons of S. Salvator at Bologna[e]. This last must probably

---

[b] Zaccaria, Bibliotheca Ritualis, tom i. p 131

[c] Schultingius, Biblioth. Eccles tom. iii pars 2. p. 145—202.

[d] MS notes opposite the title-page of Missale Romanum, Antwerp. 1619. A. 5. 7 Th. Bodleian Library.

[e] Biblioth Rit tom. i p. 64.

be referred to some of the monastic societies, who had formerly houses in Oxford; as the bishopric or church of Oxford was not founded till the sixteenth century.

It may be remarked in general of all these missals and rituals, that they differed very little; the sacramentary of Gregory was used every where, with various small additions. However, the rites of the churches throughout the British empire were not by any means uniform at the middle of the sixteenth century, and needed various corrections; and therefore the Metropolitan of Canterbury, and other bishops and doctors of the holy catholic church, at the request and desire of king Edward the Sixth, revised the ritual books; and having examined the oriental liturgies, and the notices which the orthodox fathers supply, they edited the English ritual, containing the common prayer and administration of all the sacraments and rites of the church. And the reader will perceive by the following work, that although our liturgy and other offices were corrected and improved, chiefly after the example of the ancient Gallican, Spanish, Alexandrian, and Oriental, yet the greater portion of our prayers have been continually retained and used by the church of England for more than twelve hundred years.

APPENDIX.

LITURGY OF ARMENIA.

(See page 70.)

THE liturgy of the Armenians affords a very strong presumption, that the order and substance of Basil's liturgy prevailed in the exarchate of Cæsarea long before his time. Armenia, an extensive country to the east of Cappadocia, had in part received Christianity before the time of the emperor Maximin, A. D. 235; (see Euseb. lib. ix. c. 8;) but the greater portion of the Armenians were converted by Gregory, surnamed the Illuminator, about the beginning of the fourth century. Gregory had been instructed at Cæsarea in Cappadocia, and was consecrated a bishop by Leontius, archbishop of that city. Armenia soon became entirely Christian, and was included in the exarchate of Cæsarea. Basil ordained many bishops in Armenia; and for a considerable time the principal bishops of that country were always ordained by the exarchs of Cæsarea. See Basil, Epist. 99, 120, &c. Blondel, de la Primauté, p. 656, &c. Tillemont, tom. ix. p. 187, &c. In the sixth century the Armenians adopted the Monophysite errors from Jacobus Baradæus, (Nicephorus, lib. xviii. c. 53,) and separated from the catholic church about A. D. 551; and from this period, at least, their principal bishop, who resided at Etzmiazim, assumed patriarchal authority amongst them, and took the title of *Catholic* of Armenia.

The Armenians have only one liturgy, which is written in the ancient Armenian language, and has been used by them from time immemorial. It was first published by Le Brun, in the fifth volume of his " Explication de la Messe," &c. from a Latin translation made by M. Pidou de S. Olon, a Romish bishop, who had spent many years in the east, and was well acquainted with the Armenian language and customs. The MS. from which M. Pidou translated, only contained that part of the liturgy which was repeated by the priest; the remainder, including the parts recited by the deacon and choir, were supplied from the Armenian missal, printed by the Propaganda at Rome, A. D. 1677, and from the memory of the translator. The sources from which this translation has been compiled are, therefore, not always such as to command implicit reliance; but we may at least depend on the authenticity of the part translated from the Armenian MS., which is amply sufficient for my present purpose.

This liturgy has, like most others, received many additions in the course of ages; some apparently from the Jacobites of Syria, some from the Constantinopolitan offices, and others are peculiar to itself. There are several prayers extracted from the liturgy of Chrysostom, and actually ascribed to him. These were probably introduced at some time when the Armenians made a temporary reunion with the catholic church, which Photius says was the case in his time. (See Baronius, an. 863. p. 250, 251.) I will briefly notice the main order of the Armenian liturgy, omitting those parts which cannot be traced to primitive antiquity. All the introductory matter contained in articles 9, 10, 11, and 12, p. 70—138, must be omitted, as the liturgy originally began with lessons. The *Trisagion* mentioned in art. 13, p. 140, was introduced into the eastern liturgies in the fifth century. In article 14, p. 154, &c. we first meet with the really primitive part of the Armenian liturgy, which begins with a Psalm, and lessons from the Prophets, Epistles, and Gospels. There are no prayers for catechumens, penitents, &c. these having become obsolete; but the dismissal of those classes still remains, art. 15, p. 173. In article 16, p. 194, &c., the ancient anaphora begins; and I would now refer the reader to the description of the liturgy of Basil, which I have given at p. 65, 66, in order that he may compare it with what follows. The Armenian liturgy directs the " kiss of " peace," p. 194 ; the benediction of "The grace of our " Lord," &c. p.196; "Sursum corda," &c. p. 197; the thanksgiving, p. 198, 199; the hymn *Tersanctus*, sung by all, p. 200 ; a continuation of thanksgiving, p. 201, 202 ; a commemoration of our Saviour's deeds and words at the last supper, p. 202, 203; a verbal oblation to God of his own creatures, p. 205 ; an invocation of the Holy Ghost, to make the elements the body and blood of Christ, p. 207, 208; prayers for the church, for all men, and all things, p. 286, &c.; the Lord's Prayer and benediction of the people, p. 310, &c.; the form "Sancta sanctis," p. 313; breaking of the bread, p. 322; the communion, p. 328; the thanksgiving after communion, p. 351.

The whole groundwork and order of the Armenian liturgy, therefore, coincides with the Cæsarean, as used in the time of Basil; and as there is no sort of proof or presumption that the Armenians have ever changed the order of their liturgy, (though they have added much to it, and taken away some things,) it affords a strong presumption, that the order of Basil's liturgy was used at Cæsarea at the beginning of the fourth century, when the Armenians derived their liturgy from that church through the instrumentality of Gregory the Illuminator.

NESTORIAN LITURGIES.

THE Nestorian sect derives its appellation from Nestorius, a presbyter of Antioch, who was created patriarch of Constantinople A. D. 428, and for his errors with regard to the union of the divine and human nature in Jesus Christ, was deposed and excommunicated by the general council of Ephesus, A.D. 431. Nestorius, however, had many followers in Syria, and through the influence of Alexander of Hierapolis, Ibas of Edessa, but above all, by means of the celebrated academy of Edessa, his tenets spread rapidly in the East. His disciples received the protection of the king of Persia when they were expelled from the dominions of the eastern emperors, and their bishops were placed in possession of all the sees in Mesopotamia, and the other territories of that prince. The Nestorians, thus firmly established in the fifth century, have frequently been called Chaldean Christians. Their catholic or patriarch resided at Seleucia, and subsequently at Bagdad, and Mosul; and in the following centuries they sent missionaries to India and China, whose exertions were attended with considerable success. See Mosheim's Eccl. History, century 5; Le Brun, Explication de la Messe, tom. vi. p. 369, &c.

The Nestorian liturgies are three in number; the first is called "the liturgy of the Apostles, com-" posed by S. Adæus, and S. Maris;" the second, "the liturgy of Theodorus;" and the third, that of "Nestorius." They are written in the ancient Syriac language, and were published by Renaudot, in the second volume of his Oriental Liturgies.

Renaudot thinks it probable, that the rites of the Nestorians are those of the Christians of Mesopotamia, before Nestorianism infected those churches, tom. ii. p. 599. The first of the Nestorian liturgies certainly, from its title, professes to be the apostolical liturgy of Mesopotamia; for, according to the universal tradition of the East, Thaddæus, or Adæus, otherwise called Lebbæus, and Jude, a disciple of our Lord, preached the Gospel at Edessa, and throughout Mesopotamia. See Eusebius, Hist. Eccl. lib. i. c. 13; lib. ii. c. 1. Renaudot. Liturg. Oriental. Coll. tom. ii. p. 567. Ephrem Syri Testamentum, p. 401. tom. ii. Oper. edit. Assemani. Assemani Bibliotheca Orientalis, tom. iii. pars ii. p. 4,

&c. I cannot, however, concur in the opinion, that the Nestorians preserved the original liturgy of Mesopotamia; because Ephrem Syrus, who lived at Edessa (the very centre of apostolical preaching) considerably before the rise of Nestorianism, gives an account of the liturgy, which is totally at variance with all the Nestorian liturgies. The three Nestorian liturgies concur in placing the general prayers for all men *before* the invocation of the Holy Ghost; see Renaudot, p. 590, &c. 592; 620, 621; 630. 633; while the ancient liturgy of Edessa, as described by Ephrem Syrus, (see the quotation in note [b], p. 35,) placed the general prayers *after* the invocation of the Holy Ghost.

With regard to the other two liturgies, ascribed to Theodore of Mopsuestia and Nestorius, little need be said. They seem to have few claims to primitive antiquity. Leontius of Byzantium, A.D. 590, it is true, refers to the existence of a liturgy of Theodore, (see note [e], p. 46,) but this does not prove the genuineness of that liturgy; and in fact it seems improbable that either Theodore or Nestorius composed the formularies which bear their names, as a different order seems to have prevailed in their churches, and all the adjoining countries; and the documents under consideration are evidently more recent than the Nestorian "liturgy of the Apostles," resembling it very much in the order of their parts, and yet composed in a florid and verbose style, far removed from the simplicity of primitive liturgies.

LITURGY OF INDIA.

CHRISTIANITY appears to have penetrated to India at an early period, as the name of a bishop of the church in "Persia and India" occurs amongst the acts of the general council of Nice, A.D. 325. (Gelasii Hist. Syn. Niceni, pars ii. c. 35. Labbe, Concilia, tom. ii. p. 267.) Cosmas, who, about the year 547, wrote a treatise on Christian topography, states that in Taprobana or Ceylon, and Male or Malabar, there were Christian churches; and in Calliana or Calinapore, a bishop who was ordained in Persia. The Nestorians must by this time have been established in India, as they had for nearly a century been in possession of the churches in Persia; and, of course, the bishops of India ordained by Nestorian prelates were themselves Nestorian. The liturgy of the Christians of Malabar, or St. Thomas, has not come down to us free from interpolations and alterations. Menezes, who in the sixteenth century was appointed archbishop of Goa by the Portuguese, some time after their discovery of India, took care to reform the Nestorian liturgy of Malabar. (See an account of his alterations in Le Brun, Cérémonies de la Messe, &c. tome vi. p. 451, &c.) This liturgy was translated from Syriac into Latin, and is found in the Bibliotheca Patrum. Le Brun has endeavoured to restore it, as extant before the time or Menezes, (tom. vi. p. 468, &c.) When the dominion of the Portuguese in India was shaken by the Dutch and a portion of the native Christians in Malabar recovered their independence in the latter part of the seventeenth century, they received bishops from the Jacobite patriarchs of Antioch, and have ever since continued in the Jacobite communion. Of course they use the liturgy of St. James in Syriac, of which I have already spoken, section i. p. 16. 20, &c. and probably other liturgies of the Jacobites, many of which have been printed by Renaudot in the second volume of his Oriental Liturgies.

ANTIQUITIES

OF THE

ENGLISH RITUAL.

ANTIQUITIES

OF THE

ENGLISH RITUAL.

CHAPTER I.—PART I.

THE MORNING PRAYER.

INTRODUCTION.

BEFORE I enter on the consideration of those particular formularies which the church of England has appointed for morning and evening prayers, it will be advisable, as an elucidation of what is to follow, to consider most briefly the original of the canonical hours of prayer, or of those seasons of every day which were appointed for the worship of God, the services which were anciently performed at those hours, and the books in which the services were contained.

FIRST, let us consider the antiquity of the hours of prayer. To direct our attention to that which more immediately concerns the church of England, I will only treat upon those hours of prayer which were formerly received in that and other western churches. They were seven in number. Matins, the first, third, sixth, and ninth hours, vespers, and compline. Matins were divided into two parts, which were originally distinct offices and hours; namely, the nocturn, and matin lauds.

The *nocturns* or vigils were derived from the earliest periods of Christianity. We learn from Pliny, as well as from Justin Martyr, Tertullian, and various writers of the three first centuries, that the Christians in those times of persecution held their assemblies in the night, in order to avoid detection. On these occasions they celebrated the memory of Christ's death in the holy mysteries. When persecution had intermitted and finally ceased, although the Christians were able to celebrate all their rites, and did administer the sacrament in the day-time, yet a custom which had commenced from necessity was retained from devotion and choice; and nocturnal assemblies for the worship of God in psalmody and reading still continued[a]. The monastic orders, who in the fourth century arose under Pachomius, Anthony, Basil, and others, in Egypt, Pontus, and Syria, tended to preserve this custom of nocturnal vigils: and in the following centuries we find from the testimony of Cassian, Augustine, Sidonius, Apollinaris, Sozomen[b], &c. that the same custom remained in most parts of the East and West. In the sixth century Benedict, the great founder of monastic societies in the West, prescribed the same in his Rule[c]; and doubtless the nocturnal assemblies were common about that time, especially in monasteries[d].

[a] Bingham, Antiquities, &c book xiii. ch. 10. §. 11, &c. Bona, de Divin Psalmodia, c 1. §. 3. N° 3. § 4. N°. 2, 3.

[b] Bingham, book xiii. c 10.

§. 12. Bona, Div. Psalmodia, cap i. 4. N°. 5.

[c] Regula Benedicti, c. 8, 9, 10, &c.

[d] Regula Columbani, c 7

The *lauds,* or more properly *matin lauds,* followed next after the nocturns[e], and were supposed to begin with day-break. We find allusions in the writings of Cyprian, and all the subsequent Fathers, to the morning as an hour of prayer[f]: but whether there was in the third century any assembly of the church for the purpose of public morning worship, I cannot determine. However, about the end of the third, or beginning of the fourth century, there was public worship at this hour, as we learn from the Apostolical Constitutions, where we have the order of the service[g].

In later times, when the discipline of the clergy and of monastic societies relaxed, the custom of rising in the night for the purpose of celebrating public worship became obsolete in most places; so that the nocturnal service was joined in practice to the matin lauds, and both were repeated at the same time early in the morning. Hence the united office obtained the name of *matins;* and afterwards this name was applied more especially to the nocturns, while the ancient matins were distinguished by the name of *lauds*.

Prime, or the first hour, followed lauds. This was first appointed as an hour of prayer in the Monastery of Bethlehem, about the time of Cassian, or the beginning of the fifth century[h].

De Cursu. B. Isidorus Hispal. de Eccl. Off c. 22. Bona, Div Psalmodia, c. 1. §. 4. N°. 6.

[e] See the *nocturns,* called Matutini, for first Sunday in Advent. Breviarium Sarisb. pars hyemalis, fol. 2. p 1, &c , fol. 5. p. 1. *Lauds,* fol. 5 p. 1.

[f] Cyprianus de Oratione Dominica. V. Bona, Div. Psalm. c i. §. 4. N° 3, &c. Francolinus de Tempore Hor. Canon. c. 12, &c.

[g] Apost Const. l. viii. c 38

[h] Cassian. de Institut Cœnob. lib iii. c. 4. Bingham, Antiquities, lib xiii. c. 9. §. 10

The *third, sixth,* and *ninth* hours of prayer, are spoken of by the early Fathers of the second and third centuries; but it does not appear that there was any particular service or assembly at those hours until the fifth century, when the monasteries of Mesopotamia and Palestine introduced public worship adapted to them[1].

Vespers, or evensong, is mentioned by the most ancient Fathers[j], and it is probable that the custom of holding an assembly for public worship at this time is of the most primitive antiquity. Certainly in the fourth century, and perhaps in the third, there was public evening service in the eastern churches, as we learn from the Apostolical Constitutions[k]: and Cassian, in the beginning of the fifth century, appears to refer the evening and nocturnal assemblies of the Egyptians to the time of St. Mark the Evangelist[l].

Compline, or completorium, was the last service of the day. This hour of prayer was first appointed by the celebrated abbot Benedict in the sixth century[m].

The church of England, at the revision of our offices in the reign of Edward the Sixth, only prescribed public worship in the morning and the evening; and in making this regulation she was perfectly justified: for though it is the duty of Christians to pray continually, yet the precise times and seasons of prayer, termed canonical hours, do not rest on any divine command; nor have they

---

[1] Bingham, book xiii. c. 9 §. 8, &c. Bona, c i § 4.

[j] Tertullian. Liber de Jejuniis, p. 549, &c. Concil. Laodicen. can. 18.

[k] Apost. Const. l. viii. c 36.

[l] Cassian. Institut. Cœnob. lib. ii. c 5.

[m] Bona, de Div. Psalmodia, c. xi.

ever been pronounced binding on all churches by any general council: neither has there been any uniformity in the practice of the Christian church in this respect. Besides this, the churches of the Alexandrian patriarchate, which were founded by the holy evangelist Mark, only appointed two public assemblies in the day; and no more were customary, even in the monasteries of Egypt, the rest of the day being left for private and voluntary prayer and meditation. Thus also the church of England left her clergy and people to follow in private the injunction of the Apostle, to "pray without ceasing;" for, as John Cassian observes, a voluntary gift of praise and prayer is even more acceptable to God than those duties which are compelled by the canons[n]: and certainly the church of England did not intend that her children should offer the sacrifice of praise and thanksgiving only in the morning and evening when she appointed those seasons for *public* worship. Indeed, we find that a book of private devotion, containing offices for six several hours of prayer, including Compline, and entitled the "Orarium," was published by royal authority A. D. 1560, from which Dr. Cosins, bishop of Durham, chiefly derived his "Collection of Private "Devotion," &c. The Primer, which was a translation of the "Orarium," contained psalms, hymns in verse, and lessons for six hours of prayer; viz. matins, lauds, prime, third, sixth, and ninth hours, and the evening[o].

[n] Cassian. Institut. Cœnob. lib. iii. c. 2. "Gratius est voluntarium munus, quam functiones quæ canonica compulsione redduntur· pro hoc quoque David gloriosius aliquid exultante, cum dicit. *Voluntarie sacrificabo tibi* et *Voluntaria oris mei beneplacita sint tibi, Domine.*"

[o] See the "Orarium seu libellus precationum per Re-

SECONDLY, I proceed to consider the service which was originally appointed for the hours of prayer, or canonical hours, as they were sometimes called.

As the nocturnal assemblies were first held for the purpose of administering the eucharist, so when that sacrament was celebrated at another time, the nocturnal service still retained the psalmody and reading of scripture, which was always the commencement of the liturgy or eucharist. In different churches different customs of reading and singing prevailed. In one place the psalms were read, in another they were sung, in another they were expounded; here they were very numerous, there very few: sometimes they were separated by lessons, sometimes by prayers: in different places they were read or sung without intermission, and were followed by one or by many lessons. Psalmody, generally without lessons, formed the substance of the services for the other hours of prayer. In the English and many other western churches, these services generally terminated with prayers, which were longest at Prime and Vespers.

The office of Matins, or Morning Prayer, according to the church of England, is a judicious abridgment of her ancient services for Matins, Lauds, and Prime; and the office of Evensong, or Evening Prayer, in like manner, is an abridgment of the ancient service for Vespers and Compline. Both these offices have however received several improvements,

giam Majestatem Latinè æditus." 1560, Londini, Wilhelmi Seres, &c. "The Primer" appeared in the same year, and was afterwards reprinted under the following title · "The Primer and Catechisme, set forth at large, wyth many godly Praiers necessarie for all faithfull Christians to reade." London, Willyam Seres. Anno 1566.

in imitation of the ancient discipline of the churches of Egypt, Gaul, and Spain, as will appear in the sequel.

THIRDLY, I will briefly notice the books in which the offices for the canonical hours, according to the western church, were formerly contained.

The *Psalter* of David was used in two Latin versions. First the Roman, which was in fact the ancient Italic slightly corrected by Jerome; and was in primitive times used by all the western churches. Secondly, the Gallican, which was a correct version made by Jerome from the Septuagint, and from being first received into public use in Gaul (towards the end of the sixth century) was called Gallican. This version was used in the English church immediately after it was received in Gaul, and is nearly the same which, in an English translation, we still use. The Gallican Psalter in the end completely supplanted the Roman all over Europe, except at Milan, and in one or two other places.

The Psalter used in the celebration of divine service generally contained, at the end, several hymns taken from the Old and New Testament, such as Benedictus, &c. and the Te Deum, and Athanasian Creed, all of which were appointed for the service of the canonical hours[p].

The *Bible* contained the lessons of Scripture, which were not formerly selected and placed in a distinct volume, but were read at the nocturns from the Bible itself.

---

[p] For much information on this subject, see Dr. Waterland's History of the Athanasian Creed, ch. iv. p 59, &c ed. Cambridge, 1724. See also Zaccaria, Bibliotheca Ritualis, lib i c. 4 art 3. p. 96, &c. tom. i

The *Antiphonarium* contained the anthems and responsories, which were sung in the course of divine service.

The *Hymnarium* comprised the hymns in verse, which from the time of Ambrose were chanted in the canonical hours.

The *Collectarium* included the collects to be said at the end of the services, and the *capitula* or short lessons, which were also sometimes recited in the offices.

The *Homilarium, Passionarium,* and *Martyrologium,* contained the comments of the Fathers on the Gospel of the day, and the account of the martyrdom of the saints for each distinct festival[q].

About the eleventh century, the *Breviary* was formed out of all these books; the lessons, anthems, responsories, hymns, &c. for the different days of the year, being all placed in the same volume with the Psalter, Prayers[r], &c.: and in latter times the Breviary was divided into two parts, one for the summer, and the other for the winter half of the year[s], and sometimes it was divided into four parts; so that it was more portable and convenient for the use of those clergy and monks who were accustomed to recite the offices for the canonical hours at some

[q] See Zaccaria, as quoted above.

[r] Micrologus, A D 1080, is supposed to have been the first writer who takes notice of the Breviarium, lib. de Eccl Observ c. 28. A MS containing the whole of the offices with rubrics, &c. and written about A.D. 1100. for the monastery of Casino, bears the title of Breviarium See Ducange, voce Breviarium, Zaccaria, Bibliotheca Ritualis, lib. i. c 4. art 4 p. 107.

[s] This is the case with the Breviaries of the churches of Sarum, York, and Hereford, which were formerly used in England.

time in the day. From this cause also it was sometimes entitled *Portiforium*.

With regard to the canonical hours and offices of the church of Constantinople, and of the oriental churches of the Jacobites, &c. which differed in some respects from those I have noticed, it is sufficient to refer the reader to Bona, de Divina Psalmodia, c. 18. §. 13, &c.; Zaccaria, Bibliotheca Ritualis, liber i. c. 4. art. 1 and 2; and Cave, *Dissertatio de Libris et Officiis ecclesiasticis Græcorum*, at the end of his *Historia Literaria*, where abundant information on this subject will be found.

SECTION I.

OF MORNING PRAYER.

The office of Matins, or Morning Prayer, according to the English ritual, may be divided into three principal parts. First the Introduction, which extends from the beginning of the office to the end of the Lord's Prayer. Secondly, the Psalmody and reading, which extends to the end of the Apostles' Creed: and, thirdly, the prayers and collects, which occupy the remainder of the service. It is not, however, my intention to consider the Morning Prayer solely under these heads, which would be too few; but we shall find them useful in assisting the memory to retain distinct ideas of the antiquity and importance of each part of the office. The Introduction of the Morning Prayer consists of the sentences of Scripture, the Address, Confession, Absolution, and Lord's Prayer. On each of these subjects I shall speak as briefly as is consistent with a detail of its antiquity or a defence of its use.

SECTION II.

THE SENTENCES OR VERSES.

The introduction commences with one or more verses of Scripture. Whoever is familiar with the ancient offices of the western churches, will admit that nothing has been more common for many ages, than the use of verses or small portions of Scripture in various parts of the public service of the church. Whether in the form of antiphonæ, verses, responsories, or capitula, we meet them continually in all the ancient offices. According to the rites of many western churches, a verse or capitulum was read before the office of compline, or the latest evening service; a custom which is at least as ancient as the time of Amalarius, A.D. 820, for he mentions it[t]. The nocturnal office in the ancient Gallican church also began with a lesson[u], and the matins and nocturns have for many ages been accounted one office. These things are sufficient to shew that the commencement of Morning Prayer does not merit the reproof of Schultingius, who says that such a mode of beginning the prayers is novel, and unknown to the ancient ecclesiastical writers[v]. In

---

[t] "Solent religiosi viri ante præsens officium (*Completorium*) lectionem legere." Amalarius de Eccl. Offic lib iv c. 8.

[u] "Evenit autem ut ea nocte, cum lector *secundum morem* inciperet lectionem a Moyse, incidit in illa verba Domini, *Sed ego indurabo cor ejus*, &c. Deinde cum post Psalmos decantatos recitaret ex Prophetis, occurrerunt verba, &c.—Cumque adhuc Psalmi fuissent decantati et legeret ex Evangelio, &c." Collatio Episcoporum, A D 499 Mabillon, Liturgia Gall. p 399.

[v] "Novus hic modus exordiendi preces a sententiis, incognitus est Scriptoribus Ecclesiasticis veteribus, olim enim ut et hodie ab oratione Dominica, *Domine labia*, &c *Deus in adjutorium*, semper incipiebant, ut notatum est in Flori-

this he is evidently mistaken, as he is also in saying that the office always began with the Lord's Prayer; for it is now generally agreed, that the Roman Introduction, consisting of the Lord's Prayer, Ave Maria, and Apostles' Creed, is itself very modern; that there is no trace of it before the thirteenth century, and that it was not used by public authority in the Roman church until the revision of their Breviary in the time of Pius the Fifth, bishop of Rome, A.D. 1568.[w]

SECTION III

THE ADDRESS OR EXHORTATION

It does not appear that an address was repeated before the office of Morning Prayer in early times. Neither in the ancient offices of the English church, nor in those of any other western church, have I been able to discover such a form in this place. Omitting, however, all consideration of the utility of this exhortation, of its judicious position immediately before the Confession, and of the right which the church of England possessed to establish any such formulary, even if no other church had ever done the same, we can shew that an address to the people at the beginning of the offices, is by no means unwarranted by the ancient customs of the church.

The liturgies of the churches of Gaul and Spain always prescribed an address to the people after the

bus ex Durando collectis, et recte quoque in hoc libro precum iste modus postea observatur" Schultingii Bibliothec Ecclesiast tom. iv pars 2. p. 132.

[w] Gavanti Thesaurus a Merati, tom ii p 103, 104

catechumens had been dismissed, and before the more important part of the Communion-service[x]: and we have placed this address in the same relative position in our offices, namely, before the Psalmody and reading of Scripture. The earlier part of the exhortation bears a considerable resemblance to a passage in a sermon of Avitus, bishop of Vienne in Gaul in the fifth century. Avitus was speaking of the solemn season of Rogation, instituted by Mamertus; and amongst other things spoke as follows:

If we say that we have no sin, we deceive ourselves, &c. Dearly beloved brethren, the Scripture moveth us in sundry places to acknowledge and confess our manifold sins and wickedness—And although we ought at all times humbly to acknowledge our sins before God; yet ought we most chiefly so to do when we assemble and meet together, to render thanks, &c.

Si dixerimus inquit Apostolus, *quia peccatum non habemus, nos ipsos seducimus.* Et si confiteri debemus assidue nos peccare, opus est confitendi officio, humilitate poenitendi, præsertim cum plebis adunatæ compunctio sic ad incitamentum boni operis possit aptari, ut rebellis magis convenientius erubescat, si cunctæ multitudini propriæ mentis solitudine contradicens, peccata—non defleat, &c.[y]

SECTION IV.

CONFESSION.

A Confession was formerly recited in the office for the first hour of the morning, according to the rites of the English churches[z]. It occurred in the course

---

[x] Le Brun, Explication, &c. vol. iii. p. 255. Isidorus Hispalensis, de Officiis, c. 15

[y] Avitus, Sermo de Rogationibus, p. 138. tom. ii. Oper. Sirmondi, A D 1696

[z] Breviarium Sarisburiense, Psalter. fol xiii. et lvii. Breviar. Eboracense, fol. 252 et fol. 3. Breviar. Herefordens. Dominica ad primam.

of prayers which came at the end of the service: and had this arrangement been regarded by the reformers of the offices for Matins, or the Morning Prayer, the Confession and Absolution would now be placed immediately before the Collect for the day. There were, however, good reasons for placing the Confession at the beginning of the office. Christian humility would naturally induce us to approach the infinitely holy God with a confession of our sinfulness and unworthiness; and this position of the Confession is justified by the practice of the eastern church in the time of Basil, who observes that the people all confessed their sins with great contrition, at the beginning of the nocturnal service, and before the Psalmody and Lessons commenced[a]. We find also that some churches of the west recited a Confession after the short Lesson, or Capitulum of Compline, which custom appears as old as the tenth century[b]. Formerly also the liturgies of the English church prescribed a Confession at the beginning of the Communion-service[c], and the same custom prevails in many western churches to the present day.

I have observed that the English offices for prime, or the first hour of the morning, contained a confession. I cannot, however, assign to it any very great antiquity in the west. Benedict, who lived in the sixth century, gives no hint of any Confession

---

[a] Ἐκ νυκτὸς γὰρ ὀρθρίζει παρ' ἡμῖν ὁ λαὸς ἐπὶ τὸν οἶκον τῆς προσευχῆς, καὶ ἐν πόνῳ, καὶ θλίψει, καὶ συνοχῇ δακρύων, ἐξομολογούμενοι τῷ Θεῷ, τελευταῖον ἐξαναστάντες τῶν προσευχῶν, εἰς τὴν ψαλμῳδίαν καθίστανται, κ.τ.λ. S. Basil. Epist. 207. ad Clericos Neocæsarienses, (alias 63) tom. iii. Operum, p. 311. ed. Benedict.

[b] Martene de Antiq. Discipl. in Div Officiis, &c c. viii p. 54.

[c] Missale Sarisbur. fol. lxxi. Miss. Eboracens. Modus præparandi ad Missam. Miss. Hereford. ibid.

and Absolution in the daily offices, although he minutely detailed the service for the direction of those Cœnobites who adopted his discipline[d]. Amalarius, who wrote in the ninth century, is also silent on the subject, though he describes accurately the prayers at prime, which were evidently the same as those used by the church of England in after-times[e]. The first mention of a Confession in this place occurs in the book of Honorius, entitled, *Gemma Animæ*, and written in the eleventh century, and it is there spoken of, as following the Creed in the prayers at prime[f]. Durandus, in the thirteenth century, also mentioned it[g]. A Confession in the morning prayers, though of great antiquity in the East, is probably not more ancient in the West than the time when it was first placed at the beginning of the Liturgy or Communion-service, according to the Roman rite; and that was not much prior to the time of Micrologus, who lived in the eleventh and twelfth centuries[h].

SECTION V.

ABSOLUTION.

An Absolution followed the Confession formerly in the offices of the English churches, for prime, or

[d] S. Benedict Regula, c. 17.
[e] Amalarius de Eccles. Offic lib. iv. c 2
[f] Honorius, Gemma Animæ, lib. ii. c. 61.
[g] Durandi Rationale, lib. v. c 5. fol. 242. de prima.
[h] Micrologus, de Eccl. Observat. c. 23, appears to be the first person who speaks of this confession made at the beginning of the liturgy Although a confession was very customary in the western churches during the most primitive ages, yet it appears to have been made after the dismissal of the catechumens, and before the oblations of the faithful were received. See Dissertation on primitive Liturgies, sections vi. and vii. p. 122, 129 where this subject is more particularly considered.

the first hour of the day[1]. We may perhaps assign to the Absolution thus placed an antiquity equal to that of the Confession, though *Gemma Animæ* and Durandus do not appear expressly to mention it. The sacerdotal benediction of penitents was in the earliest times conveyed in the form of a prayer to God for their absolution; but in after-ages different forms of benediction were used, both in the East and West. With regard to these varieties of *form*, it does not appear that they were formerly considered of any importance. A benediction seems to have been regarded as equally valid, whether it was conveyed in the form of a petition or a declaration, whether in the optative or the indicative mood, whether in the active or the passive voice, whether in the first, second, or third person[j]. It is true that a direct prayer to God is a most ancient form of blessing; but the use of a precatory, or an optative form, by no means warrants the inference, that the person who uses it is devoid of any divinely instituted authority to bless and absolve in the congregation of God. Neither does the use of a direct indicative form of blessing or absolution imply any thing but the exercise of an authority which God has given, to such an extent, and under such limitations, as Divine Revelation has declared.

SECTION VI.

THE LORD'S PRAYER.

The Lord's Prayer was used in the English

[1] See Breviar. Sarisb. Ebor. Hereford. as referred to at the beginning of last section.

[j] For much information connected with this subject, see Bingham's Antiquities, book xix. c. 2 and letter ii. to the bishop of Winchester. Morinus de Pœnitentia, lib. viii c 16. 21, &c. Smith's Account of the Greek Church, p. 180.

church at the beginning of matins, and the other canonical hours, some time before the reign of Edward the Sixth, when the offices were brought to their present form[k]. In the primitive ages, however, it is totally improbable that the Lord's Prayer was ever repeated at the beginning of any public office; for it was a part of ecclesiastical discipline to keep this prayer from the knowledge of all who were not baptized[l]; and during the earlier part of divine service, the heathen were commonly permitted to be present. Tertullian has been often cited to prove that the primitive Christians prefixed the Lord's Prayer to their offices[m], but there is not the least proof that, in the place cited, he is speaking of *public* devotions. That Tertullian does not speak of public service in that place, is satisfactorily proved to me by the subsequent practice of all churches, who never recited the Lord's Prayer while the heathen were present; and still further by the silence of all the contemporary and subsequent Fathers, who never allude to the repetition of the Lord's Prayer at the beginning of the canonical hours, or of any other public service. It is not mentioned by Isidore Hispalensis, by Benedict, by Amalarius, or by any other writer on ecclesiastical offices who lived before the thirteenth century. In fact, the custom of prefixing the Lord's Prayer to the offices of the day and night, seems to have commenced amongst the monastic orders of the West. It would appear that the first allusion to the Lord's Prayer,

[k] Breviar. Sarisb. fol. 2.
[l] Bingham's Antiquities, book x. c. 5. § 9.
[m] "Præmissa legitima et ordinaria oratione, quasi fundamento, accidentium jus est desideriorum, jus est superstruendi extrinsecus petitiones." Tertullian. de Oratione, c ix p. 133 ed. Rigalt.

as used at the beginning of the hours, is found in the Book of the Customs of the Cistercian Order, where it is prescribed, that after the sign for beginning the office was given, the brethren should all pray upon the *Misericordiæ* (seats), repeating the Lord's Prayer and Creed, before they began to chant the commencement of the service, " O Lord, make " speed to save us[n]." Durandus, who wrote at the end of the thirteenth century, says, that the Lord's Prayer was repeated three times on entering the church before matins, and once before the other hours[o]. So that formerly the Lord's Prayer was not considered part of the office, but was preparatory to it; and accordingly we find in the Breviary of the church of Salisbury, that after the Lord's Prayer was repeated, the priest was to *begin* the service, " Postea sacerdos *incipiat* servitium hoc " modo, *Domine labia mea aperies*[p]," &c. Various monastic orders imitated the Cistercian after that time, and the clergy of the west in many places gradually adopted the same custom. The churches of England generally used the Lord's Prayer before the offices, as we may see by the breviaries of Salisbury, York, Hereford, &c. It does not seem to have been used in the Roman church until the publication of the Roman breviary revised by cardinal Quignon, A. D. 1536; and it was not received by public authority into that breviary until the revision made by Pius the Fifth of Rome, A. D. 1568[q].

[n] "Dimisso officii signo, orationem super misericordias faciunt, id est, Pater Noster, et Credo in Deum, antequam versum *Deus in adjutorium* decantent" Liber Consuetudin. Cisterciensis, c. 68.

[o] Durandi Rationale, lib v. c. 3. fol. 226.

[p] Breviar. Sarisbur. fol. 2.

[q] Gavanti Thesaurus a Merati, tom. ii. p 104.

At the same time that the Lord's Prayer began to be used before the offices, the Creed was repeated after it. In later ages the *Ave Maria* was inserted between them, and thus the introduction to the hours, according to the Roman breviary, was formed. The form beginning *Ave Maria* was not used before the hours until the sixteenth century, in the Roman offices. It was then first introduced into the breviary by cardinal Quignon[r]. Cardinal Bona admits that it is modern[s].

SECTION VII

THE VERSICLES, GLORIA PATRI, &c

I have been considering thus far the Introduction to Morning Prayer; and it appears that no part of it can be justly said to be inconsistent with the customs of the Christian church before the reform of our offices. I now proceed to the second part of this office, namely, the Psalmody and Lessons of Scripture, which is generally of much greater antiquity; and in the present section I will notice the Versicles, *Gloria Patri*, &c. which may be regarded as the ancient introduction to the psalms.

The first versicle, and response, "O Lord, open "thou our lips," &c. are spoken of by Benedict in the sixth century[t], by Amalarius A. D. 820[u], and by Walafridus Strabo, who lived in the same century[v],

[r] Gavanti, ibid.
[s] Bona, de Div. Psalmodia, c. xvi §. 2. p. 417.
[t] "Præmisso in primis versu *Deus in adjutorium*, &c. in secundo dicendum est, *Domine labia mea*," &c. S Benedict. Regula, c. 9. *Quot Psalmi dicendi sint in nocturnis horis*.

[u] " In nocturnali officio dicimus primo, *Domine labia mea aperies, et os meum annunciabit laudem tuam*, deinde sequitur *Gloria*." Amalar. de Eccl. Off lib. iv. c. 9 de Nocturnali Officio
[v] Walafridus Strabo de Rebus Eccl c. 25

as occurring at the beginning of the matins and other offices: and they have been thus used from time immemorial by the English church[w].

The second versicle, and response, "O God, make "speed," &c. are mentioned by Benedict, and have also been long used by the church of England, since they appear in the Anglo-Saxon offices[x]. Though Benedict only appoints the versicle and response which we use, yet it appears that other persons repeated not only these, which form the first verse of the 70th psalm, but the whole psalm after them, with *Gloria Patri*. An anonymous rule for the use of regular canons written after the year 816, directed the clergy, when they awoke in order to perform the office of matins, to repeat immediately *Domine labia mea*, ("O Lord, open thou our lips," &c.) and then the whole psalm, *Deus in adjutorium*, ("O God, make speed," &c.) ending with *Gloria Patri*; and then to go to the church[y]. From this it appears, that these versicles were not, perhaps, originally repeated in church, but at home, as a preparation for divine service.

The primitive and apostolical hymn, *Gloria Patri*, was probably first used in this place as a

[w] Breviar. Sarisbur. fol. 2.

[x] See Benedict, quoted above, and Anglo-Saxon Office of Prime, in the Appendix to Dr. Hickes's Letters to a Popish Priest.

[y] "Nocturnis horis cum ad opus divinum de lecto surrexerit clericus, primum signum sibi S. crucis imprimat per invocationem S Trinitatis, deinde dicat versum *Domine labia mea aperies, et os meum annunciabit laudem tuam.* Deinde psalmum, *Deus in adjutorium meum intende,* totum cum *Gloria*. Et tunc provideat sibi corpoream necessitatem naturæ, et sic ad oratorium festinet, psallendo psalmum, *Ad te levavi animam meam,* cum summa reverentia et cautela intrans, ut aliis orantibus non impediat. Et tunc prostratus in loco congruo effundat preces in conspectu Domini magis corde quam ore." Canonicorum Regula, &c. Labbe, Concilia, tom. vii p. 1465

proper termination for the psalm *Deus in adjutorium*, or some other introductory psalm. Benedict, in his Rule, speaks of the *Gloria Patri*, as used at the beginning of the offices[z]. Amalarius, and Walafridus, who lived in the ninth century, also refer to it[a], and we find it prescribed in the Anglo-Saxon offices[b]. We may probably conjecture that the *Gloria Patri* began to be used here at some time before the age of Benedict, as a termination to some introductory psalms, which were then repeated entirely. The versicle, " Praise ye the Lord," is a translation of the Hebrew word *Alleluia*, which was from a very remote period much used by the Christian churches in divine service ; and more especially during the season of Easter[c].

Durandus in the thirteenth century mentions Alleluia as occurring in this place[d], and Ivo Carnotensis also probably alludes to it[e]. The churches of England formerly used Alleluia here, except for a certain part of the year[f]. We may perhaps refer the introduction of Alleluia into this part of the offices to the same cause which placed the *Gloria Patri* here.

The response of the people, " The Lord's name

[z] " In primis semper diurnis horis dicantur versus. *Deus in adjutorium*, &c. *Domine ad adjuvandum*, &c. et *Gloria*." S. Benedict. Regula, c. 18

[a] Amalar. de Eccl. Off. lib iv. cap. 9. Walafrid. Strabo, de Reb. Eccl. c. 25

[b] Appendix to Hickes's Letters.

[c] Benedict Regula, c 15. Bona, Divina Psalmodia, cap. 16. §. 7.

[d] Durandi Rationale, lib. vi. c. 24. no. 19. fol. 292

[e] Ivo Carnotensis Sermo de Sacramentis dedicationis, inter Sermones de Rebus Eccl p. 786. 787. apud Melchior. Hittorp.

[f] " Dominica in Septuagesima ad vesperas, et abhinc usque ad Miss. in vigilia Paschæ non dicitur Alleluia, scilicet in principio vesperarum et horarum loco Alleluia dicitur hoc modo, *Laus tibi Domine, Rex æternæ gloriæ*." Breviarium Sarisb. fol. lvii

" be praised," did not originally occur in the offices of the church of England, having been first placed here in A.D. 1661; however, it had been introduced many years before, into those of the church of Scotland.

¶ *Then likewise he shall say,*

O Lord open thou our lips.
Answer. And our mouth shall shew forth thy praise.
Priest. O God, make speed to save us.
Answer. O Lord make haste to help us.
¶ *Here all standing up, the priest shall say,*
Glory be to the Father, and to the Son, and to the Holy Ghost
Answer. As it was in the beginning, is now, and ever shall be, world without end Amen.
Priest. Praise ye the Lord.
Answer. The Lord's name be praised.

Postea sacerdos incipiat servitium hoc modo :
Domine labia mea aperies
Chorus. Et os meum annuntiabit laudem tuam.
Sacerdos statim. Deus in adjutorium meum intende.
Respons. Domine ad adjuvandum me festina.

Sacerdos. Gloria Patri, et Filio, et Spiritui Sancto

Respons. Sicut erat in principio, et nunc, et semper, et in sæcula sæculorum [g]. Amen.

Alleluia [h]

SECTION VIII.

THE NINETY-FIFTH PSALM.

This psalm has from a very remote period been placed before the psalms of the nocturn, in the western churches. It is probable that the custom of prefixing one or two psalms to the nocturnal office, arose from a desire to allow some little time for the clergy and people to collect, before the office

[g] Breviarium, Sarisb. fol. 2.
[h] Breviar. Sarisb. fol. lvii. ut supra

began. In the time of Cassian, or early in the fifth century, it was lawful for the brethren to enter the church at any time before the end of the second psalm[1]. In the following century, this custom was probably thought inconvenient, so that Benedict appointed two psalms to be chanted before the nocturns began, in order to afford sufficient time for the brethren to assemble[j]: and of these two Psalms, the second was the 95th, or *Venite exultemus*. Amalarius also speaks of this psalm as occurring at the beginning of nocturns[k], and he says that it was only sung on Sundays in his time, (A. D. 820,) because the people, who were engaged in labour, did not ordinarily attend this service on the week-days, but only on Sundays; and therefore there was no need of singing the invitatory psalm to call them to church[l].

In the ancient offices of the English churches this was generally termed the invitatory psalm; it followed the versicles, which were the subject of the last section, and preceded psalms of the nocturn or matins, which will be the subject of the next[m]. An anthem called invitatory was prefixed to this, and was repeated in part, or entirely, after each verse.

---

[1] Cassian. Instit. Cœnob. lib. iii c. 7. "In nocturnis vero conventiculis usque ad secundum Psalmum præbetur tardanti dilatio, ita dumtaxat, ut antequam finito eodem Psalmo fratres in oratione procumbant, semetipsum congregationi inserere atque admiscere festinet"

[j] Benedict Regula, c. 9.

[k] "Dein sequitur invitatorium in eo communis cœtus fratrum convocat omnes degentes undique ut excitentur et veniant ad confitendum Domino." Amalar. de Eccl Off. lib. 4. c 9

[l] In Supplemento, c 4, cited by Merati in Gavanti Thesaur. p 110

[m] Breviar Sarisb. fol 2, 3 Breviar. Eborac fol. 3

SECTION IX.

THE PSALMS

In the position of the psalms we follow the ancient order of matins according to the English church; in which the psalms of the day followed the invitatory psalm[n]. In the breviaries or common prayers of the churches of Sarum, York, and Hereford, the psalms at matins, together with the lessons which followed, were called nocturn. I have already spoken of the nocturn or nocturnal office of the primitive Christians, and observed that the persecutions which they suffered, obliged them to meet for public worship in the night-time; and that this custom was afterwards continued from choice, especially by the ancient ascetics and monks. I have also remarked that there was much variety in the service for the nocturnal assembly in different churches. Thus in Egypt, at first, in some places they read sixty psalms, in others fifty, and afterwards all agreed to recite twelve only[o]. According to Cassian, other churches were accustomed to repeat twenty or thirty psalms, some still more, and some only eighteen[p]; so that he says there were as many rules and appointments as there were monasteries[q]. Again, Columbanus in his rule appointed the number of psalms to vary according to the seasons of the year, and the length of the nights; so

---

[n] Breviar. Sarisb. fol. 3. Breviar. Eborac fol. 3.

[o] Cassian. Institut. Cœnob. lib. ii c. 5 "Cum—alii quinquagenos, alii sexagenos psalmos, nonnulli vero ne hoc quidem numero contenti, excedi eum debere censerent"

[p] Cassian. lib. ii. c. 2.

[q] "Totque propemodum typos et regulas vidimus usurpatas, quot etiam monasteria cellasque conspeximus." Cassian. lib. ii. c. 2.

that sometimes seventy-five were sung[r]. In the monasteries of Armenia they repeat ninety-nine psalms at the present day[s]. On the other hand, in Spain, according to Isidore, three psalms only were sung in the nocturnal office[t], a number which is still preserved in the Mosarabic or Spanish breviary[u]. Previously to the reform of our offices, the English church prescribed twelve psalms for the nocturn; but at that period the number was reduced on an average to three, by the division of the 119th, and by reckoning some other long psalms as each more than one[v]. This number of three is independent of the responsorial psalms and canticles, which follow the lessons; and, as I have observed, the same number is mentioned by Isidore Hispalensis; and cardinal Quignon, in his revision of the Roman

[r] " Ita ut totum Psalterium inter duas supradictas noctes—cantent " Columbani Regula, c 7

[s] Bona, de Div Psalmodia, c 18 § 15 p 649, 650

[t] " In quotidianis officiis Vigiliarum, primum tres psalmi canonici recitandi sunt." Regula S Isidori Hispalensis, c 7.

[u] Bona, de Div. Psalmod. c. xviii. §. 11. p. 635. Schultingius in vain objects to the English office, that sometimes five psalms are recited at matins and vespers, sometimes two, sometimes only one, and at other times four; which he says is new and unheard of, tom iv. pars 2. p. 128. For it appears that every church, and even monastery, arranged all things relating to the number of Psalms, as it pleased. Schultingius also blames us because we do not regulate the office according to the decree of Gregory the seventh, bishop of Rome , but this decree, except it be confirmed by the British church, neither is, nor ever was, binding on us, since the Roman patriarchate did not extend to these countries, and whatever authority was at any time conceded to the Roman patriarch by the church of England, might at any time have been resumed again, as in fact it was. The decree is null and void in these countries, another constitution having been made by the catholic church within this realm.

[v] The same method of dividing long Psalms is prescribed in Regula S. Benedicti, c. 18

breviary, also reduced the number of Psalms at matins from twelve to three.

SECTION X.

THE FIRST LESSON

The council of Laodicea in Phrygia, held in the fourth century, directed the Psalms and lessons to be read alternately[w]; and we find that the psalms of the nocturnal vigils were interspersed with lessons in the Gallican church[x]. It does not appear certain that lessons were read in the nocturns, by the Roman church, before the time of Gregory the Great[y]. In Egypt, after the twelve psalms of the nocturn, two lessons, one from the Old Testament, the other from the New, were read[z]; and this rule has been adopted by the church of England. Benedict appointed only one lesson at the nocturnal office during the summer[a]; but for the rest of the year several lessons were recited. In after-times, many churches of the West read sometimes three, some-

[w] Ἐν ταῖς συνάξεσιν ἀναγνώσεις τοὺς ψαλμοὺς περικοπτέτωσαν. Concil. Laodicen. can. 17.

[x] See Collatio Episcoporum, A D. 499. referred to in section ii. p. 210.

[y] "Necdum eo tempore (sc. S. Benedicti) in Romana ecclesia, sicut nunc leguntur, Sacras Scripturas legi mos fuit: sed post aliquot tempora hoc institutum sive a beato papa Gregorio, sive, ut ab aliis affirmatur, ab Honorio." Epist. Theodemari Abbatis ad Carolum M. Imperat. cited by Mabillon, Liturgia Gall p 385.

[z] Cassian. Inst Cœnob. lib. ii. c. 6.

[a] Benedict. Regula, c. 10. Schultingius objects to the English office thus · " Præter consuetudinem, praxin et traditionem omnium veterum auctorum de divinis officiis est, quod in Dominicis diebus tantum una legatur lectio, vel saltem addatur secunda; cum ecclesia catholica, a mille annis et amplius, novem lectiones semper ad minimum, et raro tres in Dominicis adhibuerit," Tom. iv. pars 2 p. 129. This objection is sufficiently met by the practice of the catholic church of Egypt, and the Rule of Benedict, just cited.

times five, seven, or nine lessons[b]. So it was formerly in the church of England, were there were either three or nine lessons at nocturns or matins; but these lessons were generally so short, that one chapter of Scripture often contained more than nine of them. For instance, the three first lessons for the first Sunday in Advent contained altogether six verses of the first chapter of Isaiah[c]. Besides this, the lessons were followed by anthems and responsories, which greatly interrupted the reading of Scripture; for which reason they were removed by us, as they had been some time before by cardinal Quignon[d], whose edition of the Roman breviary has been much applauded by learned men, and was recommended by Paul the third, patriarch of Rome.

The ancient English offices, and Benedict, prescribed the same position for this lesson as we do, namely, after the psalms of the nocturn or matins, and before *Te Deum.*

SECTION XI.

THE HYMN TE DEUM.

This sublime composition has been referred to several different authors. Some have ascribed it to Ambrose and Augustine, others to Ambrose alone; others again to Abondius, Nicetius, bishop of Triers, or Hilary of Poictiers. In truth, it seems that there

---

[b] Merati in Gavanti Thesaur. tom. ii. p. 141.
[c] Breviarium Sarisbur. fol. 3.
[d] "Versiculos, Responsoria, et capitula, omittere idcirco visum est, non quod hæc supervacanea aut inutilia viderentur —sed quoniam cum introducta sint ad cantus potissimum modulandos et legentes sæpe morentur cum molestia quæritandi; locum relinqui voluimus continenti lectioni Scripturæ Sacræ." Præf. ad Breviar. p. 3. edit. Lugduni, 1546.

is no way of determining exactly who was the author of this hymn. Archbishop Usher found it ascribed to Nicetius in a very ancient Gallican Psalter, and the Benedictine editors of the works of Hilary of Poictiers cite a fragment of a manuscript epistle of Abbo Floriacensis, in which Hilary is unhesitatingly spoken of as its author[e]; but Abbo lived five or six centuries after that prelate, and therefore such a tradition is most doubtful. Some reasons, however, appear to justify the opinion, that *Te Deum* was composed in the Gallican church, from which source we also derive the inestimable Creed bearing the name of Athanasius. The most ancient allusions to its existence are found in the Rule of Cæsarius, bishop of Arles, who lived in the fifth century[f], and in that of his successor Aurelian[g]. It has been judged from this, that the *Te Deum* may probably have been composed by some member of the celebrated monastery of Lerins, which was not far from Arles; or perhaps by Hilary of Arles, who seems to have composed the Athanasian Creed in the fifth century. Another presumption in favour of the same notion is deducible from the wording or this hymn. The verse, " Vouchsafe, O Lord, to " keep us *this day* without sin," *Dignare Domine die isto sine peccato nos custodire*, gives reason to

[e] Num. 22. p. vii.

[f] "Perfectis Missis (*lectionibus*) dicite Matutinos, directaneo; *Exaltabo te Deus meus et Rex meus.* Deinde, *Confitemini.* Inde, *Cantemus Domino. Lauda anima mea Dominum.* Benedictionem, *Laudate Dominum de cœlis Te Deum laudamus, Gloria in excelsis Deo* et *Capitellum.* Omni Dominica sic dicatur." Regula S. Cæsarii c. xxi p. 56 pars 2. Codex Regularum.

[g] " Omni Sabbato Matutinos, *Cantemus Domino:* et *Te Deum laudamus.*" Regula S. Aureliani juxta finem, p. 68. Codex Regular.

think that it was originally composed for the matin, and not for the nocturnal office, for it appears that the day is supposed to have actually commenced. Now Cæsarius and Aurelian both appoint *Te Deum* to be sung in the morning, while Benedict directed it to be sung in the nocturnal office on Sundays[h], and thence we may observe that the former appear to have adhered closer to the intentions of the author of this hymn than the latter; that therefore they were better acquainted with the author's design than Benedict, and therefore the hymn was probably not composed in Italy, but in Gaul.

In the office of matins this hymn occupies the same place as it always has done, namely, after the reading of Scripture[1]. The ancient offices of the English church gave this hymn the title of the " Psalm *Te Deum*," or the " Song of Ambrose and " Augustine" indifferently. As used in this place, it may be considered as a responsory psalm, since it follows a lesson; and here the practice of the church of England resembles that directed by the council of Laodicea, which decreed that the psalms and lessons should be read alternately. The following original Latin of *Te Deum* is transcribed from the breviary of Sarum, Psalter, folio vii.

We praise thee, O God: we acknowledge thee to be the Lord.	Te Deum laudamus te Dominum confitemur.
All the earth doth worship thee: the Father everlasting.	Te æternum Patrem: omnis terra veneratur.
To thee all angels cry aloud · the Heavens, and all the Powers therein.	Tibi omnes Angeli: tibi cœli et universæ potestates,

---

[h] Regula S. Benedicti, c. 11.
[1] Breviar. Sarisbur. fol. 4. 22. Breviar. Eboracens. fol. 5

Te Deum.

To thee Cherubin and Seraphin : continually do cry,

Holy, Holy, Holy . Lord God of Sabaoth ;

Heaven and Earth are full of the Majesty of thy Glory.

The glorious company of the Apostles : praise thee

The goodly fellowship of the Prophets · praise thee.

The noble army of Martyrs : praise thee.

The holy Church throughout all the world . doth acknowledge thee ;

The Father . of an infinite Majesty ;

Thine honourable, true . and only Son ;

Also the Holy Ghost the Comforter

Thou art the King of Glory · O Christ.

Thou art the everlasting Son of the Father.

Tibi Cherubin et Seraphin: incessabili voce proclamant,

Sanctus, Sanctus, Sanctus . Dominus Deus Sabaoth ;

Pleni sunt cœli et terra : majestatis gloriæ tuæ.

Te gloriosus Apostolorum chorus,

Te Prophetarum laudabilis numerus,

Te Martyrum candidatus . laudat exercitus J.

Te per orbem terrarum : sancta confitetur Ecclesia,

Patrem immensæ majestatis ;

Venerandum tuum verum · et unicum Filium ;

Sanctum quoque Paracletum Spiritum.

Tu Rex gloriæ Christe.

Tu Patris sempiternus es Filius

J This will remind the reader of that eloquent passage of Cyprian, where he exhorts us to fix our affections and desires on heaven : " Magnus illic nos carorum numerus expectat, parentum, fratrum, filiorum, frequens nos et copiosa turba desiderat, jam de sua immortalitate secura, et adhuc de nostra salute solicita. Ad horum conspectum et complexum venire, quanta et illis et nobis in commune lætitia est ! Qualis illic cœlestium regnorum voluptas, sine timore moriendi, et cum æternitate vivendi ! Quam summa et perpetua felicitas ! *Illic Apostolorum gloriosus chorus: illic Prophetarum exultantium numerus: illic Martyrum innumerabilis populus, ob certaminis et passionis victoriam coronatus* · triumphantes illic virgines, quæ concupiscentiam carnis et corporis continentiæ robore subegerunt · remunerati misericordes, qui alimentis et largitionibus pauperum justitiæ opera fecerunt qui Dominica præcepta servantes, ad cœlestes thesauros terrena patrimonia transtulerunt." Cyprianus de Mortalitate, p. 166. edit. Fell.

When thou tookest upon thee to deliver man . thou didst not abhor the Virgin's womb.

When thou hadst overcome the sharpness of death : thou didst open the Kingdom of Heaven to all believers.

Thou sittest at the right hand of God · in the Glory of the Father.

We believe that thou shalt come : to be our Judge.

We therefore pray thee, help thy servants : whom thou hast redeemed with thy precious blood.

Make them to be numbered with thy Saints : in glory everlasting.

O Lord, save thy people and bless thine heritage.

Govern them : and lift them up for ever.

Day by day · we magnify thee ;

And we worship thy name : ever world without end.

Vouchsafe, O Lord : to keep us this day without sin.

O Lord, have mercy upon us : have mercy upon us.

O Lord, let thy mercy lighten upon us : as our trust is in thee.

O Lord, in thee have I trusted : let me never be confounded.

Tu ad liberandum suscepturus hominem : non horruisti Virginis uterum.

Tu devicto mortis aculeo · aperuisti credentibus regna cœlorum.

Tu ad dexteram Dei : sedes in gloria Patris.

Judex crederis esse venturus.

Te ergo quæsumus, famulis tuis subveni : quos pretioso sanguine redemisti.

Æterna fac cum sanctis tuis : in gloria numerari.

Salvum fac populum tuum Domine . et benedic hæreditati tuæ.

Et rege illos : et extolle illos usque in æternum.

Per singulos dies : benedicimus te.

Et laudamus nomen tuum : in sæculum et in sæculum sæculi.

Dignare Domine die isto sine peccato nos custodire.

Miserere nostri Domine : miserere nostri.

Fiat misericordia tua Domine super nos : quemadmodum speravimus in te.

In te Domine speravi : non confundar in æternum.

SECT. XII.   *Benedicite—The Second Lesson.*   231

BENEDICITE.

In the ancient English offices the matins (nocturns) terminated with *Te Deum,* and were immediately followed by lauds (ancient matins). This office began with several psalms, of which one was the " psalm *Benedicite,*" or " the Song of the Three " Children," as it was variously called[k]. This canticle was retained in the position it now occupies, and is appointed to follow the first lesson, in place of *Te Deum,* at the pleasure of the officiating minister. In the Mosarabic, or ancient Spanish office, *Benedicite* is also used at lauds[l]. The ancient liturgies of the Gallican and Spanish churches prescribed the Song of the Three Children to be sung between the lessons[m], and we adopt the same rule in the office of Morning Prayer. Benedict and Amalarius both speak of *Benedicite* as used at matins (lauds[n]); and Athanasius appointed it to be said at the same time[o]. When used as appointed by the English office, it may be regarded in the light of a responsory psalm.

SECTION XII.

THE SECOND LESSON.

After the psalms of lauds, amongst which *Benedicite* occurred, the ancient English offices prescribed

[k] Brev. Sar. fol. 5. et Psalt. ibid. fol. 8 Brev Ebor. fol. 5.
[l] Bona, de Div. Psalmod. p. 636 c. 18. §. 11.
[m] Mabillon. de Lit. Gall. p. 108.
[n] S Benedict. Regula, c. 11, 12. Amalarius de Eccl. Off. lib. iv. c. 10. de Matutinali Officio.

[o] Πρὸς ὄρθρον δὲ τὸν ψαλμὸν τοῦτον λέγετε· ὁ Θεὸς ὁ Θεός μου πρὸς σὲ ὀρθρίζω. ἐδίψησέ σε ἡ ψυχή μου. (διάφαυμα δέ·) εὐλογεῖτε πάντα τὰ ἔργα κυρίου τὸν κύριον. δόξα ἐν ὑψίστοις Θεῷ κ. τ λ. Athanasius de Virginitate, c. 20. p. 122. tom. ii. Oper. ed. Benedict.

a short lesson from scripture[p]. Benedict, in the sixth century, and Amalarius, A. D. 820, both speak of the lesson in this place[q]. The reformers of our offices enlarged this short lesson, appointing it always to be taken from the New Testament, according to the ancient rule of the Egyptian church in the fifth century; for, according to Cassian, only two lessons were read in their nocturnal or matutinal assembly, of which the second was always taken from the New Testament[r].

SECTION XIII

BENEDICTUS.

The lesson at lauds, in the ancient English offices, was followed by the canticle which is the subject of the present section, and which was indifferently called the "psalm *Benedictus*," and the "Song of "the Prophet Zacharias[s]." It occupies at present the same relative position as it has always done in the English offices. Benedict speaks of a *Canticum de Evangelio* as occurring in this place, but whether he refers especially to this Song of Zacharias or not, I cannot determine[t]; however, Amalarius, A. D. 820, speaks of this position of Benedictus[u].

---

[p] Breviar Sarisb. fol 5 et Psalt. fol. 8. 22. Brev. Ebor. fol. 5. Brev. Hereford.

[q] S. Benedict. Regula, c. 12, 13 Amalar. de Eccl. Off. lib iv. c. 10. "Dein sequitur lectio quæ pro admonitione fraterna recitatur in choro, quæ semper placita erit quamdiu in præ-senti sæculo deget ecclesia."

[r] Cassian Institut. Cœnob. lib. ii. c. 6.

[s] Brev. Sarisb. fol. 5. Brev. Ebor. fol. 6. Brev. Hereford. Psalt. in Dominica die.

[t] S. Benedict. Regula, c. 13.

[u] Amalar. de Eccl. Off. lib. iv. c. 12

PSALM JUBILATE DEO.

This was read amongst the Psalms of lauds in the office of Salisbury, and other English churches[v]; and the only difference between its present and former position is, that it was formerly read before the lesson, and is now read after it. Amalarius, A. D. 820, speaks of this psalm as used in lauds[w]. *Benedictus* and *Jubilate Deo*, either of which may be used in this place, are to be regarded in the light of responsories to the second lesson, according to the ancient custom of the Christian church, by which psalms and lessons were appointed to be said alternately.

SECTION XIV.

THE CREED OF S. ATHANASIUS.

The office of lauds was succeeded by that of prime, or the first hour, according to the ancient English offices. In the office of prime, after several psalms, which have not been retained, the Athanasian Creed, termed " Psalmus *Quicunque vult*," was sung on Sundays[x]. According to the English ritual at present, this psalm, or creed, is still repeated or sung on certain feasts in the same position relatively to the *Benedictus,* and the following prayers, as it has always occupied.

Dr. Waterland says, that we cannot assign a later period than the year 880, for the introduction of this creed into the office of prime by the English

---

[v] Brev. Sar. fol. 5. et Psalt. ibid fol. 7 Brev. Ebor. fol. 5.
[w] Amalar. de Eccl. Off. lib. iv. c 10. de Matutinali Officio.
[x] Brev. Sar. fol. 5. Psalt. ibid fol. 11. Brev. Eborac. fol. 250. Brev. Hereford. ad primam.

churches; but we have no reason to think that it may not have been used long before that date. It is found in MS. psalters of the seventh and eighth centuries, where no doubt it was placed for the purpose of being sung at prime[y]. Space does not permit me to do more than refer to the excellent work of Dr. Waterland, as affording a most satisfactory account of this inestimable creed, which, with much ingenuity and reason, he refers to the composition of Hilary, archbishop of Arles, about A.D. 430.

The Athanasian Creed was only recited on Sundays, according to the offices of Sarum and other English churches, and on other days nothing was appointed instead of it. To supply its place on the days when it does not occur, the revisers of our offices appointed the Apostles' Creed to be repeated. The same rule had also been adopted by cardinal Quignon, in his revision of the Roman breviary, A.D. 1536[z].

The Athanasian Creed was sung like the psalms in the English offices, and it was even designated by the title of the psalm *Quicunque*. These circumstances account for the custom of repeating and singing this creed in the same manner as the psalms, which still prevails in the Christian churches of England.

SYMBOLUM ATHANASII[a].

| Whosoever will be saved before all things it is necessary that he hold the catholic faith. | Quicunque vult salvus esse: ante omnia opus est ut teneat catholicam fidem. |

---

[y] Waterland's Critical History of the Athanasian Creed, p. 84, 85. ch. iv. p. 46, &c

[z] Breviar. fol. 3. 9

[a] Breviarium Sarisbur. Psalt. fol. 11, 12. Dominicis diebus ad primam.

Athanasian Creed.

Which faith except every one do keep whole and undefiled : without doubt he shall perish everlastingly.

And the catholic faith is this : that we worship one God in Trinity, and Trinity in Unity.

Neither confounding the persons : nor dividing the substance.

For there is one person of the Father, another of the Son : and another of the Holy Ghost.

But the Godhead of the Father, of the Son, and of the Holy Ghost is all one : the glory equal, the majesty coeternal.

Such as the Father is, such is the Son : and such is the Holy Ghost.

The Father uncreate, the Son uncreate : and the Holy Ghost uncreate.

The Father incomprehensible, the Son incomprehensible and the Holy Ghost incomprehensible.

The Father eternal, the Son eternal : and the Holy Ghost eternal.

And yet they are not three eternals : but one eternal.

As also there are not three incomprehensibles . nor three uncreated : but one uncreated, and one incomprehensible.

So likewise the Father is almighty, the Son almighty : and the Holy Ghost almighty.

Quam nisi quisque integram, inviolatamque servaverit · absque dubio in æternum peribit.

Fides autem catholica hæc est, ut unum Deum in Trinitate : et Trinitatem in Unitate veneremur.

Neque confundentes personas : neque substantiam separantes.

Alia est enim persona Patris, alia Filii : alia Spiritus Sancti.

Sed Patris, et Filii, et Spiritus Sancti, una est Divinitas : æqualis gloria, coæterna majestas.

Qualis Pater, talis Filius : talis Spiritus Sanctus.

Increatus Pater, increatus Filius . increatus Spiritus Sanctus.

Immensus Pater, immensus Filius : immensus Spiritus Sanctus.

Æternus Pater, æternus Filius : æternus Spiritus Sanctus.

Et tamen non tres æterni : sed unus æternus.

Sicut non tres increati, nec tres immensi : sed unus increatus, et unus immensus.

Similiter omnipotens Pater, omnipotens Filius : omnipotens Spiritus Sanctus.

And yet they are not three almighties : but one almighty.

So the Father is God, the Son is God : and the Holy Ghost is God.

And yet they are not three Gods . but one God.

So likewise the Father is Lord, the Son Lord : and the Holy Ghost Lord.

And yet not three Lords : but one Lord.

For like as we are compelled by the Christian verity : to acknowledge every person by himself to be God and Lord ;

So are we forbidden by the catholic religion : to say, there be three Gods, and three Lords.

The Father is made of none . neither created nor begotten.

The Son is of the Father alone : not made, nor created, but begotten.

The Holy Ghost is of the Father and of the Son : neither made, nor created, nor begotten, but proceeding.

So there is one Father, not three Fathers, one Son, not three Sons : one Holy Ghost, not three Holy Ghosts.

And in this Trinity none is afore or after other : none is greater or less than another.

But the whole three persons are coeternal together · and coequal.

So that in all things, as is aforesaid the Unity in Tri-

Et tamen non tres omnipotentes : sed unus omnipotens.

Ita Deus Pater, Deus Filius : Deus Spiritus Sanctus.

Et tamen non tres Dii . sed unus est Deus.

Ita Dominus Pater, Dominus Filius : Dominus Spiritus Sanctus.

Et tamen non tres Domini . sed unus est Dominus.

Quia sicut singillatim unamquamque Personam, Deum et Dominum confiteri Christiana veritate compellimur ;

Ita tres Deos aut Dominos dicere : catholica religione prohibemur.

Pater a nullo est factus · nec creatus, nec genitus.

Filius a Patre solo est . non factus, nec creatus, sed genitus.

Spiritus Sanctus a Patre et Filio · non factus, nec creatus, nec genitus, sed procedens.

Unus ergo Pater, non tres Patres ; unus Filius, non tres Filii : unus Spiritus Sanctus, non tres Spiritus Sancti.

Et in hac Trinitate nihil prius aut posterius . nihil majus aut minus.

Sed totæ tres personæ : coæternæ sibi sunt et coæquales.

Ita ut per omnia (sicut jam supra dictum est) et Unitas in

nity, and the Trinity in Unity, is to be worshipped.

He therefore that will be saved . must thus think of the Trinity.

Furthermore it is necessary to everlasting salvation : that he also believe rightly the incarnation of our Lord Jesus Christ.

For the right faith is, that we believe and confess : that our Lord Jesus Christ, the Son of God, is God and man.

God of the substance of the Father, begotten before the worlds : and man of the substance of his mother, born in the world.

Perfect God, and perfect man : of a reasonable soul, and human flesh subsisting.

Equal to the Father as touching his Godhead : and inferior to the Father as touching his manhood.

Who although he be God and man . yet he is not two, but one Christ.

One, not by conversion of the Godhead into flesh · but by taking of the manhood into God.

One altogether, not by confusion of substance : but by unity of person.

For as the reasonable soul and flesh is one man : so God and man is one Christ.

Trinitate . et Trinitas in Unitate veneranda sit.

Qui vult ergo salvus esse : ita de Trinitate sentiat.

Sed necessarium est ad æternam salutem . ut incarnationem quoque Domini nostri Jesu Christi fideliter credat.

Est ergo fides recta, ut credamus et confiteamur · quia Dominus noster Jesus Christus, Dei Filius, Deus et homo est.

Deus est ex substantia Patris ante sæcula genitus : et homo est ex substantia matris in sæculo natus.

Perfectus Deus, perfectus homo . ex anima rationali et humana carne subsistens.

Æqualis Patri secundum Divinitatem : minor Patre secundum humanitatem.

Qui licet Deus sit et homo · non duo tamen, sed unus est Christus.

Unus autem, non conversione Divinitatis in carnem : sed assumptione humanitatis in Deum.

Unus omnino, non confusione substantiæ : sed unitate personæ.

Nam sicut anima rationalis et caro unus est homo ita Deus et homo unus est Christus.

Who suffered for our salvation : descended into hell, rose again the third day from the dead.	Qui passus est pro salute nostra, descendit ad inferos : tertia die resurrexit a mortuis.
He ascended into heaven, he sitteth on the right hand of the Father, God Almighty : from whence he shall come to judge the quick and the dead.	Ascendit ad cœlos, sedet ad dexteram Dei Patris Omnipotentis : inde venturus est judicare vivos et mortuos.
At whose coming all men shall rise again with their bodies : and shall give account for their own works.	Ad cujus adventum omnes homines resurgere habent cum corporibus suis : et reddituri sunt de factis propriis rationem.
And they that have done good shall go into life everlasting : and they that have done evil into everlasting fire.	Et qui bona egerunt ibunt in vitam æternam : qui vero mala in ignem æternum.
This is the catholic faith : which except a man believe faithfully he cannot be saved.	Hæc est fides catholica, quam nisi quisque fideliter firmiterque crediderit : salvus esse non poterit.
Glory be to the Father, and to the Son : and to the Holy Ghost.	Gloria Patri, et Filio : et Spiritui Sancto.
As it was in the beginning, is now, and ever shall be : world without end. Amen.	Sicut erat in principio, et nunc, et semper : et in sæcula sæculorum.

THE APOSTLES' CREED.

This primitive Creed of the Italian and Roman churches has long been used by the church of England in nearly the same position which it occupies at present. Until the reform of the English offices in the reign of Edward the Sixth, it followed the Lord's Prayer, amongst those prayers which it now precedes[d]. This position of the Apostles' Creed had

---

[d] Breviar. Sarisb. Psalt. fol. 13. Breviar Eborac. fol. 251

been customary in the ages preceding the Norman conquest, as we may see by the Anglo-Saxon offices[e]. Amalarius also, A. D. 820, speaks of the Creed as following the Lord's Prayer amongst the prayers of Prime[f].

SECTION XV.

THE PRAYERS.

These prayers, including the lesser Litany, the Lord's Prayer, and the versicles and responses, came at the end of the office, according to the ancient English rites[g], and they still preserve the same position. Formerly, however, the Apostles' Creed occurred in this part of the service, from whence it was transferred to its present position. From these prayers also the Confession and Absolution were removed, and replaced by superior formularies at the commencement of the whole office. All this part of the service is very ancient in the morning offices of the western churches. Amalarius, A. D. 820. and Benedict, A. D. 530. both speak of the lesser Litany, "Lord have mercy upon us," &c. and the Lord's Prayer, as occurring in this place[h]; the councils of Girone, A. D. 517. and Toledo, A. D. 633. prescribed the latter[i]; both also are found in the monuments of the Anglo-Saxon church[j]. The versicles

---

[e] Appendix to Hickes's Letters, ad primam.
[f] Amalar. de Eccl. Off. lib. iv. c. 2.
[g] Brev. Sarisb. Pselt. fol 13. Breviar. Eborac. fol. 251 Breviar. Herefordens. ad primam.
[h] S. Benedict. Regula, c. 17. c. 13. Amalarius de Eccl. Off. lib. iv c. 2

[i] Concil. Toletan. iv. c. 9. Concil. Gerundens. can. 10. "Item nobis semper placuit observari, ut omnibus diebus post Matutina, et Vesperas Oratio Dominica a sacerdote proferatur."
[j] Appendix to Hickes's Letters, ad primam.

which follow the Lord's Prayer are described by Amalarius, who wrote in A. D. 820[k]; and they are found in the Anglo-Saxon offices[l]: they varied, however, in different churches of the West, even where the same prayers in general were used; but all our versicles and responses are found in the ancient ritual of the English churches, both before and after the Norman conquest; and they occurred in the same place which they occupy at present.

¶ *And after that, these Prayers following, all devoutly kneeling; the Minister first pronouncing with a loud voice,*
The Lord be with you
Answer. And with thy spirit.
Minister Let us pray
Lord, have mercy upon us
Christ, have mercy upon us.
Lord, have mercy upon us

Tunc fiant preces cum prostratione ad omnes horas[m].

Dominus vobiscum.
Et cum spiritu tuo.
Oremus[n].
Kyrie eleeson
Christe eleeson.
Kyrie eleeson[o].

Our Father, which art in heaven, Hallowed be thy Name. Thy kingdom come. Thy will be done in earth, As it is in heaven. Give us this day our daily bread. And forgive us our trespasses, As we forgive them that trespass against us. And lead us not

Pater noster qui es in cœlis, sanctificetur nomen tuum. Adveniat regnum tuum. Fiat voluntas tua sicut in cœlo et in terra. Panem nostrum quotidianum da nobis hodie. Et dimitte nobis debita nostra, sicut et nos dimittimus debitoribus nostris. Et ne nos indu-

---

[k] Amalar. de Eccl. Off. lib. iv. c 4.
[l] Appendix, &c. ut supra
[m] Brev. Sar. Psalt. fol. 12
[n] Brev. Sar. Psalt. fol. 13. These three forms were placed before the Collects in the ancient offices of the English churches, but their present position is very good, at the commencement of the prayers.
[o] Brev. Sar. Psalt. fol. 13. Brev. Eboracens. fol. 251. Brev Herefordens. ad primam.

SECT. XV.   *The Prayers.*   241

into temptation; But deliver us from evil: For thine is the kingdom, and the power, and the glory, for ever and ever. Amen.

¶ *Then the priest standing up shall say,*

O Lord, shew thy mercy upon us.

Answer. And grant us thy salvation.

Priest. O Lord, save the king.

Answer. And mercifully hear us when we call upon thee.

Priest. Endue thy ministers with righteousness.

Answer. And make thy chosen people joyful.

Priest. O Lord, save thy people.

Answer. And bless thine inheritance.

Priest. Give peace in our time, O Lord.

Answer. Because there is none other that fighteth for us, but only thou, O God.

cas in tentationem. Sed libera nos a malo. Amen [p].

Erigat se sacerdos solus sic dicens [q].

Ostende nobis, Domine, misericordiam tuam.

Et salutare tuum da nobis [r].

Domine, salvum fac regem.

Et exaudi nos in die qua invocaverimus te [s].

Sacerdotes tui induantur justitiam.

Et sancti tui exultent [t].

Salvum fac populum tuum, Domine.

Et benedic hæreditati tuæ [u].

Da pacem, Domine, in diebus nostris.

Quia non est alius qui pugnet pro nobis nisi tu Deus noster [v].

---

[p] Brev. Sar. Psalt. fol. 13. Brev. Ebor. fol. 251.

[q] Brev. Sar. Psalt. fol. 57. p. 2. fol. 22. p. 2. This rubric appears to be derived from those I have referred to, for in both the priest alone stood up after a certain part of the prayers had been said.

[r] Brev. Sar. Psalt. fol. 13.

[s] Brev. Sar. Psalt. fol. 22. Brev. Hereford. ad primam. Offic. Anglo-Sax. ad prim. Appendix to Hickes's Letters.

[t] Brev. Sar. Psalt. fol. 22. Brev. Hereford. ad prim. preces feriales.

[u] Brev. Sar. Psalt. fol. 22. Brev. Hereford. ad prim. Offic. Anglo-Sax. ad primam.

[v] Brev. Eboracens. fol. 264. Brev. Sarisb. fol. 85. Bishop Lloyd remarks on this verse and response as follows: "I do not know what Burnet means by stating that this response

Priest O God, make clean our hearts within us.	Cor mundum crea in me, Domine
Answer. And take not thy holy Spirit from us.	Et Spiritum sanctum tuum ne auferas a me [w].

SECTION XVI

THE COLLECTS.

The position of the collects (*orationes*) in the English offices is precisely the same as in the ancient offices of the churches of Sarum, York, &c.; namely, after the prayers (*preces*)[x]. It is not very easy to trace the antiquity of this custom of repeating collects at the end of the service. It has certainly, however, prevailed in these churches, even during the period preceding the Norman Conquest [y]. Amalarius, A. D. 820, speaks of the " oratio consueta," or customary collect after the office of matins [z]; and he also speaks of a prayer, or collect, and benediction, which always were repeated at the end of the offices [a]. John Bona endeavours to prove that the collect is mentioned by Benedict, when he directs that the Gospel should be read at the end of nocturns, and the Benediction being given, they should begin matins. Bona explains this benediction to mean a prayer; for Amalarius in one place says that the prayer of the priest is called by two names,

was made in the year 1549, on the occasion of political occurrences—for this answer is found in all the foreign breviaries, in the Salisbury primer, and in the primer of Hen VIII. See Burnet's Hist Ref. p. ii. b. 1. anno 1549."

[w] Brev. Sar. Psalt. fol. 13 Brev. Eborac fol 251 Offic Anglo-Sax. ad primam.

[x] Brev. Sar. fol. 9. 13. 22. Brev. Eboracens. fol. 252.

[y] Officium Anglo-Sax. ad primam. Appendix to Hickes's Letters.

[z] Amalar. de Eccl. Off. lib. iv c 12.

[a] Amalar lib iv. c. 45.

either a benediction or a prayer[b]. This shews indeed that the word *benediction* may sometimes mean *prayer*, but it does not prove that it is to be taken in this sense in the present instance; and in another part of the works of Amalarius we find that the offices terminated not only with a prayer, but with a benediction also[c]: and it is most simple and reasonable to refer the word in the present instance directly to the benediction, which we find actually to have existed. The council of Agde, A.D. 1517, appointed collects to be repeated after the antiphonæ or anthems, at the end of morning and evening prayer[d]. We also find that the office of morning prayer in the eastern church terminated with a collect or prayer by the priest or bishop, in the third or fourth century[e]. In Egypt, each psalm was followed by a silent prayer of the congregation, and a collect by the priest[f]. This custom prevailed in the time of Cassian, and the same appears to have existed even in the time of Athanasius; for when Syrianus, at the instigation of the Arians, proceeded to seize Athanasius, it is related that the people were keeping their vigil or nocturn, and Athanasius desired the deacon to read a psalm, and the people to respond; after which it seems that they prayed in silence by the direction of the

[b] Bona, Divina Psalmodia, c. xvi. §. 17. N°. 2

[c] "Oratio et benedictio semper in fine sunt, antequam disjungantur fratres singuli ad propria" Amalar. de Eccl Off. lib. iv c. 45.

[d] "Sicut, ubique fit, et post antiphonas collectiones per ordinem ab episcopis vel presbyteris dicantur——plebs collecta oratione ad vesperam ab episcopo cum benedictione dimittatur." Concil Agathens. can. 30 Concil. Labbe, tom. iv. p. 1388.

[e] Apost. Const. lib. viii. c. 37.

[f] Cassian Inst Cœnobit. lib. ii. c. 7.

bishop[g]. Athanasius also, in his Treatise on Virginity, enjoins the alternate repetition of psalms and prayers[h]. Here we have precisely that alternation of which Cassian speaks. Collects to be said at matins and evensong are found in the sacramentary books of Gregory the Great, A. D. 590, and Gelasius, 494, patriarchs of Rome[i]. It would appear that only one collect was said at the end of the offices, according to the Roman order[j]. Amalarius speaks of the prayer in the singular number[k]. Fulbertus Carnotensis, A. D. 1010, in his epistle to Hildegarius, dean of the church of St. Hilary, says, that "the prayer" which is read from the book of sacraments should follow the Lord's Prayer and versicles[l]. This probably meant the proper prayer for the time of the day, of which (as I have observed) many are found in the sacramentaries of Gregory and Gelasius. On the other hand, in the Gallican church several collects were said, as appears by the council of Agde, referred to above. The church of

[g] Athanasii Apologia pro Fuga, p. 334. tom. i. ed. Benedict. Historia Arianorum ad Monachos, ibid. p. 394.

[h] τοσούτους δὲ ψαλμοὺς εἰπέ, ὅσους δύνῃ στήκουσα εἰπεῖν· καὶ κατὰ ψαλμὸν, εὐχὴ καὶ γονυκλισία ἐπιτελείσθω. Athan. de Virginitate, p 122. tom. ii ed. Benedict. The γονυκλισία after the εὐχὴ mentioned here, is also spoken of by Cassian, Inst. lib. ii. c. 7. "Apud illos (Ægyptios) ergo non ita est, sed antequam flectant genua, paulisper orant, et stantes in supplicatione majorem temporis partem expendunt. Itaque post hæc puncto brevissimo procidentes humi, velut adorantes tantum divinam clementiam, summa velocitate consurgunt," &c.

[i] Sacramentar. Gregorii a Menard. p. 212. Gelasii Sacramentar. Muratori, Liturg. Vet. Rom. tom. i. p. 743.

[j] Gavanti Thesaurus a Merati, tom. ii. p. 152, 153.

[k] Amalar. de Eccl. Off. lib. iv. c 12 "Oratio consueta."

[l] Fulbertus Carnotensis, Ep. 79. "Finitis autem capitulis post orationem Dominicam, ubi dicitur *Domine exaudi orationem meam*, statim esset subdenda oratio, quæ ex libro Sacramentario recitatur."

Milan also repeated several collects at the close of the offices [m].

COLLECT FOR THE DAY.

The collect for the day, the collect for peace, and the collect for grace, all occurred in the ancient offices of the English churches, and are placed in the same position relatively to each other, as they formerly occupied. The collect of the day was read at the end of matin lauds [n]; after this the " memo- " ria de pace," with the present collect for peace, was read [o]; and subsequently, nearly at the end of Prime, the collect for grace occurred [p]. The collects of the day are considered specially in the third chapter of this work, where it appears that, with some exceptions, they are as ancient as the time of Gelasius, patriarch of Rome A. D. 494; and that many of them are much older.

COLLECT FOR PEACE.

Although I cannot exactly fix the period at which the collect for peace was introduced into this part of the English offices, yet the composition itself is probably as old as the fifth century, and has been used in some way by the English church for above twelve hundred years.

| O God, who art the author of peace and lover of concord, in knowledge of whom standeth our eternal life, whose service is perfect freedom; De- | Deus auctor pacis et amator, quem nosse vivere; cui servire regnare est; protege ab omnibus impugnationibus supplices tuos; ut qui in defen- |

---

[m] Bona, de Div. Psalmod. c. xviii. §. 10. p. 631.
[n] Brev. Sar. fol. 5. and 8. Brev. Eborac. fol. 7. and 221.
[o] Brev. Sar. fol. 83.
[p] Brev. Sar. fol. 13. Brev. Heref. ad primam. Brev. Ebor. fol. 252.

fend us thy humble servants in all assaults of our enemies, that we, surely trusting in thy defence, may not fear the power of any adversaries, through the might of Jesus Christ our Lord. Amen.

sione tua confidemus, nullius hostilitatis arma timeamus. Per &c.^q

COLLECT FOR GRACE.

With regard to the antiquity of this prayer, I might repeat what has been said of the collect for peace; but it may be added, that this collect was especially appointed, in the sacramentaries of Gregory and Gelasius, to be repeated in matins. In the time of Gelasius, this form was both a thanksgiving for being brought to the beginning of the day, and a prayer for grace[r].

O Lord, our heavenly Father, Almighty and everlasting God, who hast safely brought us to the beginning of this day; Defend us in the same with thy mighty power, and

Domine sancte, Pater omnipotens, æterne Deus, qui nos ad principium hujus diei pervenire fecisti; tua nos hodie salva virtute, et concede ut in hac die ad nullum declinemus

---

[q] Miss. Sarisb. Commune, fol. 19 MS. Leofric. Missa pro Pace, fol. 223. Gelasii Sacramentarium, Muratori Lit. Vet Rom. tom. 1. p. 727. Gregorii Sacr. Menard p. 216. A passage in S. Augustin's Meditations (c. 32) seems to have suggested a part of this collect "Deus, cujus nos fides excitat, spes erigit, charitas jungit; Deus, qui pati te jubes, et inveniri te facis, et pulsanti aperis, Deus a quo averti, cadere est, ad quem converti, surgere est, in quo manere, consistere est; Deus, quem nemo amittit, nisi deceptus, nemo quærit, nisi admonitus,

nemo invenit, nisi purgatus, *Deus, quem nosse, vivere est; cui servire, regnare est,* quem laudare, salus et gaudium animæ est; te labiis et corde, omnique, qua valeo virtute, laudo, benedico, atque adoro."

[r] "Gratias agimus, Domine sancte, Pater omnipotens, æterne Deus, qui nos transacto noctis spatio, ad matutinas horas perducere dignatus es : quæsumus ut dones nobis diem hunc sine peccato transire; quatenus ad vesperum gratias referamus. Per." Gelasii Sacr. Murat. tom. i. p 743. Orationes ad Matutinas.

grant that this day we fall into no sin, neither run into any kind of danger. but that all our doings may be ordered by thy governance, to do always that is righteous in thy sight; through Jesus Christ our Lord. Amen.

peccatum; nec ullum incurramus periculum, sed semper ad tuam justitiam faciendam omnis nostra actio tuo moderamine dirigatur. Per &c [s]

COLLECTS FOR THE KING AND ROYAL FAMILY.

Although the following prayers have long been used by the church of England, yet they were not placed in their present position until the year 1661, having been previously repeated at the end of the Litany. The appellation of "prayers," which is given to these collects, in itself marks their introduction into the office of morning prayer at a different period from the "collects." The rubric before the collect for the day says, "Then shall follow "three *collects.*" That before the collect for the king, "Then these five *prayers* following." Had all these prayers been introduced at the same time, they would all have been called "collects," or "prayers."

---

[s] Gregorii Sacramentar. a Menard p. 212. Breviar. Sarisb. fol 13. Psalter. Offic. Anglo-Sax. in Appendix to Hickes's Letters, ad primam. Bishop Lloyd remarks on this prayer as follows: "In the Brev. Rom. this prayer is as follows · ' Domine Deus omnipotens, qui ad principium hujus diei nos pervenire fecisti; tua nos hodie salva virtute, ut in hac die ad nullum declinemus peccatum, sed semper ad tuam justitiam faciendam nostra procedant eloquia, dirigantur cogitationes et opera per Dominum.' That in Brev. Sarisb is somewhat different ·" (Then follows the collect which I have given above in the text.) " It is clear that our collect was taken from Brev. Sarisb., and this is one instance, among many, that the reformers of our liturgy did not use the Brev. Rom. It is to be observed, that the collect is the same in the Roman breviaries both before and after the reformation of Pius V." *MS. Annotations on Book of C. P.*

In fact, there are now six collects after the collect for the day, besides the benediction. According to the ancient English offices, these collects would be termed *Memoriæ*, or commemorations, *de Pace, de Gratia, pro Rege,*&c.[t] The collects for the king, &c. are placed in precisely the situation they would have occupied, had they been repeated at morning prayer by the English church in ancient times. On the days when these prayers are omitted, the litany is said at the end of the office of morning prayer. This is according to the rites of the church of Constantinople, where, at the office of matin lauds every morning, the service is terminated by a litany, and prayer or benediction[u]; and the eastern church, in the third or fourth century, also adopted the same custom exactly, as may be seen in the Apostolic Constitutions[v]. The two prayers for the king and royal family, although they do not appear to have been actually translated from any very ancient offices, are yet, both in expressions and substance, perfectly conformable to the many prayers for kings, &c. which are found in the liturgies and offices of the primitive church[w].

---

[t] Brev. Sarisb. fol. 22. Psa. Memoriæ Communes ad Laudes.

[u] Goar, Rituale Græcum, p. 54, 55. The English church also from ancient times has been accustomed to recite the Litany in the morning, during Quadragesima, or Lent. See Brev. Sarisb. Pars hiemalis, fol. 68.

[v] Apost. Const. lib. viii. c. 38.

[w] Liturgia Basilii, Goar, Rit. Græc. p. 171. 178. Liturgia Marci, Renaudot, Liturg. Oriental. tom. i. p. 133. Miss. Sarisb. fol. 19. Commune. Missa pro Rege, &c. In the Gothic or Gallican liturgy, we find the same ideas as those which occur in the first part of our prayer for the king. "*Dominum dominantium et Regem regnantium*—deprecemur ut nobis populo suo pacem tribueredignetur." Mabillon, Lit. Gall. p. 246. Μνήσθητι Κύριε

SECT. XVI. *Collects for Clergy, &c.—of S. Chrysostom.* 249

COLLECT FOR THE CLERGY AND PEOPLE.

This collect is as old as the fifth century, being found in the sacramentary of Gelasius, A. D. 494. We can have no reasonable doubt that it has been used by the English church for above twelve hundred years.

Almighty and everlasting God, who alone workest great marvels; Send down upon our Bishops and Curates, and all Congregations committed to their charge, the healthful Spirit of thy grace; and that they may truly please thee, pour upon them the continual dew of thy blessing. Grant this, O Lord, for the honour of our Advocate and Mediator, Jesus Christ *Amen*.	Omnipotens sempiterne Deus, qui facis mirabilia magna solus; prætende super famulos tuos Pontifices, et super cunctas Congregationes illis commissas, Spiritum gratiæ salutaris; et ut in veritate tibi complaceant, perpetuum eis rorem tuæ benedictionis infunde[x].

PRAYER OF S. CHRYSOSTOM.

This prayer occurs in the liturgy of the church of Constantinople, which bears the name of Chrysostom. It must be confessed, however, that it is not found in the most ancient manuscripts of that liturgy, but in those of the liturgy of Basil, where it is recited as the prayer preceding the third anthem at the beginning of the Communion-service.

τῶν εὐσεβεστάτων καὶ πιστοτάτων ἡμῶν βασιλέων .... ὑπόταξον αὐτοῖς πάντα τὰ βάρβαρα ἔθνη, τὰ τοὺς πολέμους θέλοντα. *Lit. Basilii ut supra.* " Quæsumus, omnipotens et misericors Deus, ut rex noster—qui tua miseratione regni suscepit gubernacula, *virtutum omnium percipiat incrementa.*" Miss. Sar. Com. fol. 19. MS. Leofric Missa cotidiana pro Rege.

[x] Gelasii Sacramentar. Muratori, tom. i. p. 719. Sacr. Gregorii, Menard. p. 254. Miss. Sarisb. Commune, fol. 24. Brev. Sarisb. post Letaniam, fol. 60. Psalt.

It occurs in a MS. of Basil's liturgy, which has been referred by Goar and others to the ninth century. Whether this prayer be as old as the time of either Basil or Chrysostom, is very doubtful to me, because all the commencement of those liturgies which bear their names (except the lessons) appears to be more recent than the time of Chrysostom: however, this prayer has certainly been very anciently used in the exarchate of Cæsarea, and the patriarchate of Constantinople.

Almighty God, who hast given us grace at this time with one accord to make our common supplications unto thee; and dost promise, that when two or three are gathered together in thy Name, thou wilt grant their requests Fulfil now, O Lord, the desires and petitions of thy servants, as may be most expedient for them; granting us in this world knowledge of thy truth, and in the world to come life everlasting. *Amen.*

Ὁ τὰς κοινὰς ταύτας καὶ συμφώνους ἡμῖν χαρισάμενος προσευχὰς, ὁ καὶ δύο καὶ τρισὶ συμφωνοῦσιν ἐπὶ τῷ ὀνόματί σου, τὰς αἰτήσεις παρέχειν ἐπαγγειλάμενος· αὐτὸς καὶ νῦν τῶν δούλων σου τὰ αἰτήματα πρὸς τὸ συμφέρον πλήρωσον, χωρηγῶν ἡμῖν ἐν τῷ παρόντι αἰῶνι τὴν ἐπίγνωσιν τῆς σῆς ἀληθείας, καὶ ἐν τῷ μέλλοντι ζωὴν αἰώνιον χαριζόμενος [y].

THE BENEDICTION.

The office of matins terminated with a benediction, according to Benedict, A.D. 530, Amalarius,

[y] Liturgia Chrysostomi, Goar Rituale Græc. p. 66. Basilii, ibid. p. 160. Goar refers this prayer, not to Chrysostom, but to Basil. See Rituale Græc. not. 106 in Chrysostomi Liturg. But although the absence of the form in question in the ancient MSS. of Chrysostom's liturgy affords sufficient reason for thinking that it was not composed by him, yet the mere existence of the prayer in the MSS. of Basil's liturgy is no proof that it is to be attributed to him.

A.D. 820[z], and the offices of the Anglo-Saxon church[a]. We find also by the Apostolical Constitutions, that the conclusion of the office of matins in the eastern church, in the third or fourth century, was a benediction given by the bishop[b]. The benediction we use is derived from the liturgies of the eastern churches. This form occurred in the liturgies of Antioch, Cæsarea, Constantinople, and Jerusalem. It is spoken of by Chrysostom (A.D. 380), Theodoret (A.D. 420), and many others; and had probably been used in those oriental churches from the most primitive times.

The grace of our Lord Jesus Christ, and the love of God, and the fellowship of the Holy Ghost, be with us all evermore. *Amen.*	Ἡ χάρις τοῦ Κυρίου ἡμῶν Ἰησοῦ Χριστοῦ, καὶ ἡ ἀγάπη τοῦ Θεοῦ καὶ Πατρὸς, καὶ ἡ κοινωνία τοῦ ἁγίου Πνεύματος εἴη μετὰ πάντων ὑμῶν[c].

---

[z] Benedict Regula, c. 11. Amalar. de Off. Eccl. lib iv. c. 45.

[a] Off. Anglo-Sax. ad primam. Appendix to Hickes's Letters.

[b] Apost. Const. lib. viii. c. 38.

[c] Liturgia Basilii, Goar, p. 165 Chrysostomi, ibid. p. 75. Jacobi Græcè, Assemani, Codex Liturg. tom. v. p. 32. Jacobi Syriacè, Renaudot, Liturg. Oriental. tom. ii. p 30.

CHAPTER I.—PART II.

EVENING PRAYER.

SECTION I.

INTRODUCTION.

WHAT has been already said with regard to the sentences of morning prayer is even more applicable to those of evening prayer; for if a verse or capitulum was read before the last evening service, or compline, in the time of Amalarius, A.D. 820[a], there could be no impropriety in placing one before the earlier evening service of vespers or evensong.

The idea of placing an address to the people at the commencement of the office is derived from the primitive Gallican and Spanish liturgies, where an exhortation, called *Præfatio*, was recited at the beginning of the communion office[b].

A confession and absolution formerly occurred at the end of the office of compline, according to the offices of the English churches[c]; but it also appears that they were sometimes repeated at the

---

[a] "Solent religiosi viri ante præsens officium (completorii) lectionem legere." Amalar. de Eccl. Off. lib. iv. c. 8.

[b] It was repeated after the catechumens were dismissed, and before the oblations of the people were received. See Dissertation on primitive Liturgies, p. 160. and 174.

[c] Brev. Sarisb. Psalt. fol. 57. Brev. Ebor. fol. 3.

beginning of that office, and immediately after the Sentence, or short Lesson[d].

The forms of confession and benediction, which are inserted in this place, are not to be found in the more ancient offices of England, but they are much superior to those that occur there. The Lord's Prayer was recited before the office of evensong, according to the English breviaries; and I have already remarked, that this prayer was first used at the beginning of the canonical hours about the thirteenth century. The office of evensong, or evening prayer, is (as I have before observed) a judicious abridgment of the offices of evensong and compline, as formerly used by the English church; and it appears that the revisers of our offices formed the introduction to evening prayer from those parts of both vespers and compline, which seemed best suited to this place, and which preserved uniformity with the introduction of morning prayer.

SECTION II.

VERSICLES, GLORIA PATRI, &c.

Of these versicles, the two former do not appear originally to have been used before the evening offices in England, but they have been used before the morning prayer since the time of Benedict, 530[e]. The two latter versicles were appointed to precede evening prayer, by the offices of Sarum, York, &c. and by the Anglo-Saxon offices[f]. In the same services we find the *Gloria Patri* appointed to succeed these latter versicles[g].

[d] Martene, de Antiq. Eccl. in celebr. Off. c. viii. p. 54.
[e] Benedict. Regula, c. 9.
[f] Brev. Sarisb. fol. 2. Off.

Anglo-Sax ad Vesperas, Appendix to Hickes's Letters.
[g] Offic. Anglo-Sax. ut supra. Brev. Sar. fol. 2

SECTION III.

THE PSALMS.

We here follow the order of evensong which was anciently used in the English churches. After the versicles and *Gloria Patri* which I have just been considering, the psalms of the evening were sung[h]. Very different rules prevailed in different places anciently with regard to the number of psalms sung at evening prayer. The Egyptian churches recited twelve psalms always at the evening service[i]. Benedict appointed four[j]. The church of Rome used five[k]. In the evening service of the eastern church, contained in the Apostolical Constitutions, we find only one psalm for vespers[l]: and in the Mosarabic breviary there is no psalm at vespers[m]. In the patriarchate of Constantinople they repeat six psalms, besides the *cathisma*, or twentieth portion of the psalter, which on an average makes more than seven in addition[n]. It appears therefore that the church of England was perfectly at liberty to make what

---

[h] Breviar. Sarisb. fol. 47, 48. Psalt.

[i] Cassian lib. ii. Inst Cœnob. c. 4. " Igitur per universam, ut diximus, Ægyptum et Thebaidem duodenarius psalmorum numerus tam in vespertinis, quam in nocturnis solemnitatibus custoditur, ita dumtaxat ut post hunc duæ lectiones, Veteris scilicet ac Novi Testamenti singulæ, subsequantur." It is singular, that after the lapse of fourteen centuries the same number of psalms should still be used in the Egyptian churches. See Bona, Divina Psalmodia, c xviii. §. 18. p. 660.

[j] " Vespertina autem synaxis quatuor psalmis cum antiphonis terminetur, post quos psalmos Apostoli lectio recitanda est." Benedict. Regula, c 17.

[k] Bona, Divina Psalmodia, c. 18 §. 2. p 608.

[l] Apost. Const. lib. viii. c. 35.

[m] Bona, Divina Psalmodia, c. 18. §. 11. p. 637. " Ad vesperas nullos concinunt psalmos."

[n] Bona, Divina Psalmodia, c. 18. §. 13. p. 643.

regulation she pleased relative to the number of psalms at evensong.

SECTION IV.

THE FIRST LESSON.

After the psalms of evening prayer, the English churches formerly appointed a short lesson of scripture; and this order is still continued. Amalarius, A. D. 820, speaks of the lesson of vespers as following the psalms, and he adds, that he had heard that responsories (or psalms) were formerly sung after this lesson, but that in his time the hymn of the Virgin (*Magnificat*) followed it[o]. Benedict also, A. D. 530, appointed a lesson after the psalms of vespers, which he directed to be taken from the Epistles[p]. This lesson is now always taken from the Old Testament, according to the custom of the Egyptian churches described by John Cassian in the beginning of the fifth century.

SECTION V.

MAGNIFICAT.

The lesson of vespers was followed by the hymn of the holy Virgin in the offices of the churches of Salisbury, York, and Hereford[q]. In the last section we have seen this position of *Magnificat* recognised by Amalarius, A. D. 820. The same is found in the

[o] "Post hoc sequitur lectio a pastore prolata . . . Audivi olim responsorios cantari apud quosdam post lectionem vespertinalem . . . occurrit mihi ut sicut hymnus Zachariæ excludit responsorium post matutinalem lectionem, ita excludat responsorium hymnus Sanctæ Mariæ post vespertinalem lectionem." Amalar. de Eccl. Off. lib. iv. c. 7.

[p] "Post quos psalmos Apostoli lectio recitanda est." S. Benedict. Regula, c. 17.

[q] Brev. Sarisb. fol. 2. et Psalt. 54. Brev. Ebor. fol. 2.

offices of the English church before the Norman Conquest[r]. And Benedict, A. D. 530, probably refers to it, when he appoints a canticle from the Gospel, to be repeated after the lesson[s].

CANTATE DOMINO. PSALM XCVIII.

Though Amalarius speaks of the *Magnificat* as following the lesson of vespers, yet he observes, that it was formerly customary in some places to sing a responsory or psalm after this lesson. The psalm *Cantate Domino*, when used here, is to be considered as a responsory psalm, since it immediately follows a lesson; and this is in accordance with the seventeenth canon of the council of Laodicea, which appointed lessons and psalms to be read alternately.

SECTION VI.

THE SECOND LESSON.

The office of compline followed that of vespers in the ancient English offices, and after some psalms, contained a short lesson[t], which may have contributed to the establishment of that which we now consider; and the same also occurs in the Anglo-Saxon offices[u]. But the use of a second lesson at the evening service is of a much more ancient date than can be assigned to the English offices referred to. The Egyptian church in the time of Cassian, or the beginning of the fifth century, had from time immemorial used two lessons at the evening office,

---

[r] Offic. Anglo-Sax. Appendix to Hickes's Letters, ad Vesperas.
[s] Benedict. Regula, c. 17.
[t] Brev. Sarisb. fol. 2. et Psalt. fol. 54. Brev. Eborac. fol. 3.
[u] Appendix to Hickes's Letters, in nocte.

of which the second was always taken from the New Testament[v]; and the church of England has adopted precisely the same rule.

SECTION VII

NUNC DIMITTIS.

The song of Simeon followed the lesson of compline, which I have noticed in the last section[w]. However, though *Nunc dimittis* was contained in the office of compline at the period when our offices were to be revised, yet in the most ancient times this hymn had been sung at vespers. Thus in the Apostolical Constitutions we find *Nunc dimittis* appointed for the evening prayer, though this may probably have been designed for an office of private devotion[x]; but even at the present day this hymn is repeated at the end of evening prayer in the patriarchate of Constantinople[y]. Benedict does not speak of the *Nunc dimittis* as used at compline, but Amalarius, A.D. 820, mentions it[z].

DEUS MISEREATUR. PSALM LXVII

When this psalm is used in the place of *Nunc dimittis*, it is as a responsory psalm, according to the practice of many churches, and more especially to that of the churches of Asia and Phrygia, regu-

[v] Cassian. lib. ii Inst. Cœnobit. c 4. quoted in note¹, p. 254 Schultingius objects to the English office of evensong thus: "Apud veteres scriptores divinorum officiorum et in praxi ecclesiæ *inauditum*, assignari vesperis *duas* lectiones."tom iv. pars 2 p 130

[w] Brev Sar fol. 2. et Psalt. fol. 55.

[x] Apost. Const. lib. vii c. 48.

[y] Goar, Rituale Græc p. 43. Bona, Div. Psalmod. c. 18. § 13. p. 648.

[z] Amalar. lib. iv c. 8.

lated by the council of Laodicea, of which I have spoken already.

SECTION VIII.

THE CREED.

The creed occurred amongst the prayers of compline, according to the ancient English offices; and it appears to have occupied this position even in Anglo-Saxon times. It followed the song of Simeon, or *Nunc dimittis*, as it does at present[a]. This creed is now placed before the prayers and collects, in order to preserve uniformity with the office of morning prayer.

SECTION IX.

THE PRAYERS.

These prayers, including the lesser litany, the Lord's Prayer, and the versicles and responses which follow, have long been used in the English and other western churches, at the end of the evening service. They occur not only in the offices of the churches of Salisbury, York, Hereford, &c. but in those of the Anglo-Saxon ages. Benedict, A. D. 530, speaks of the lesser litany and the Lord's Prayer as used at the end of evening prayer[b]. The council of Girone, A.D. 517, appointed that every day after vespers the Lord's Prayer should be said by the priest[c].

---

[a] Brev. Sar. Psalt fol. 57. Brev. Eborac. fol. 3

[b] "Canticum de evangelio, litania, et oratio Dominica, et fiant missæ." Benedict. Regula, c 17

[c] Concil. Gerundense, canon x. "Placuit observari, ut omnibus diebus post matutinas et vesperas oratio Dominica a sacerdote proferatur.

SECT. IX — The Prayers

¶ *And after that, these prayers following, all devoutly kneeling, the Minister first pronouncing with a loud voice,*
The Lord be with you
Answer. And with thy spirit.
Minister. Let us pray.
Lord, have mercy upon us
Christ, have mercy upon us.
Lord, have mercy upon us.
Our Father, which art in heaven, hallowed be &c.
¶ *Then the priest standing up shall say,*
O Lord, shew thy mercy upon us.
Answer. And grant us thy salvation.
Priest. O Lord, save the king.
Answer. And mercifully hear us when we call upon thee.
Priest. Endue thy ministers with righteousness.
Answer. And make thy chosen people joyful
Priest. O Lord, save thy people.

Tunc omnia fiant in prostratione ab inceptione I. Kyrie Eleison[d].

Dominus vobiscum.
Et cum spiritu tuo.
Oremus[e].
Kyrie eleison.
Christe eleison
Kyrie eleison[f].
Pater noster qui es in cœlis, sanctificetur &c[g].
Erigat se Sacerdos solus sic dicens[h].
Ostende nobis Domine misericordiam tuam.
Et salutare tuum da nobis[i]

Domine salvum fac regem
Et exaudi nos in die qua invocaverimus te[j].
Sacerdotes tui induant justitiam.
Et sancti tui exultent[k].

Salvum fac populum tuum, Domine.

---

[d] Breviar. Sarisb fol. 57 Psalt ad completorium.
[e] Breviar Sar fol. 57. Psalt. These three forms are not placed before the lesser litany in any of the ancient offices, as far as I am aware. Their former position was immediately before the collect, and in that place their antiquity is very great, however, they are well placed at present at the very commencement of the prayers.
[f] Brev. Sar. fol. 57. ad completor. Offic. Anglo-Sax ad Vesper et in nocte. Appendix to Hickes's Letters. Brev Ebor. fol. 3.
[g] Breviar Sar fol. 57 Offic. Anglo-Sax. ad Vesper. et in nocte. Brev. Ebor. fol. 3.
[h] Breviar. Sar. fol. 57. ad completorium.
[i] Brev. Sar. fol. 57. ad completorium.
[j] Brev. Sar. fol. 22. Psalt. ad Vesperas.
[k] Brev. Sar. fol. 22. Psalt. ad Vesperas.

Answer. And bless thine inheritance.	Et benedic hæreditati tuæ[1].
Priest. Give peace in our time, O Lord	Da pacem Domine in diebus nostris.
Answer. Because there is none other that fighteth for us, but only thou, O God.	Quia non est alius qui pugnet pro nobis nisi tu Deus noster[m].
Priest. O God, make clean our hearts within us.	Cor mundum crea in me Domine
Answer. And take not thy holy Spirit from us.	Et Spiritum sanctum tuum ne auferas a me[n]

SECTION X.

THE COLLECTS.

The collects are placed in the same position relatively to the prayers as they have always occupied in the offices of the English churches. The collects of the day, for peace, and for aid against perils, are also in the same order, in relation to each other, as in the ancient English offices. Here the collect of the day followed *Magnificat* at vespers, the collect for peace was recited after vespers, and the collect for aid against perils succeeded the prayers at the end of compline. Collects were repeated at the end of evening prayer according to the Anglo-Saxon offices[o]; and Amalarius, A. D. 820, refers to the same custom[p].

We find in the sacramentaries of Gregory, A. D. 590, and Gelasius, A. D. 494, collects appointed peculiarly to be said at evening prayer[q]; and the

---

[l] Brev. Sar. fol. 22. ad Vesperas.
[m] Brev Ebor. fol. 264. p. ii. Suffragia ad Vesperas.
[n] Brev. Sar. fol. 13
[o] Offic Anglo-Sax. ad Vesperas et in Nocte. Appendix to Hickes's Letters.
[p] Amalar de. Eccl. Officiis, lib. iv c. 7
[q] Gregorii Sacramentar. a Menard. p. 209, 210 Gelasii. Sacr. Muratori, tom. i p 745.

council of Agde, A. D. 517, ordained that the people should be dismissed with a benediction in the evening, after the prayer had been collected; that is, after the collect had been said[r]. The office of vespers, according to the eastern church in the third or fourth century, also terminated with a collect, and a benediction by the bishop, as we may perceive in the Apostolical Constitutions[s]; and the same order is visible in the most ancient monuments of the office of vespers, according to the rites used in the patriarchate of Constantinople[t].

THE COLLECT FOR PEACE.

This collect is found in all the ancient monuments of the English church, where it has been used for above twelve hundred years. It is, without any reasonable doubt, as old as the fifth century, since it occurs in the sacramentary of Gelasius, A. D. 494.

O God, from whom all holy desires, all good counsels, and all just works do proceed, Give unto thy servants that peace which the world cannot give; that both our hearts may be set to obey thy commandments, and also that by thee we being defended from the fear of our enemies may pass our time in rest and quietness, through the merits of Jesus Christ our Saviour. *Amen.*

Deus, a quo sancta desideria, recta consilia, et justa sunt opera; da servis tuis illam, quam mundus dare non potest, pacem; ut et corda nostra mandatis tuis dedita, et hostium sublata formidine, tempora sint tua protectione tranquilla. Per &c [u]

---

[r] Concil. Agathense, can. 30. "Plebs collecta oratione ad vesperam ab episcopo cum benedictione dimittatur" Concilia, Labbe, tom iv. p. 1388.

[s] Apost. Const. lib. viii c. 36.
[t] Goar, Rituale Græcum, p. 46.
[u] Brev. Sarisb. fol. 83. Brev.

THE COLLECT FOR AID AGAINST PERILS.

This collect is also found in the most ancient monuments of the English church, and likewise occurs in the sacramentaries of Gregory the Great and Gelasius. In this last it is expressly appointed to be used at evening service; so that this collect has been appropriated to evening prayer for nearly fourteen hundred years.

Lighten our darkness, we beseech thee, O Lord, and by thy great mercy defend us from all perils and dangers of this night, for the love of thy only Son, our Saviour, Jesus Christ Amen.	Illumina, quæsumus Domine Deus, tenebras nostras, et totius hujus noctis insidias tu a nobis repelle propitius Per Dominum &c.[v]

CONCLUDING COLLECTS AND BENEDICTION.

With regard to the collects for the king, royal family, clergy and people, and the prayer of S. Chrysostom, I have nothing to say, which has not already been said at the end of the remarks on morning prayer. It may, however, be observed, that there is nothing whatsoever inconsistent with the ancient practice of the English churches in placing these collects in the place they occupy; since they are to be regarded in the light of *memoriæ*, or commemorations, which were very common after the collects of the canonical hours.

I have also spoken of the benediction at the close

Ebor. fol. 264. Miss. Sar Commune, fol. 19 MS Leofric. fol 27. Gregorii Sacramentar. a Menard. p. 216. Gelasii Sacr. Muratori Lit. Rom. Vet. tom. 1. p. 690.

[v] Breviar. Sarisb. fol. 57 Brev Ebor. fol. 3 Gregorii Sacr a Menard. p. 210. Gelasii Sacram. Muratori, tom. 1. p. 745. MS. Leofric fol 329.

of morning prayer; and have now only to add, that the evening office terminated with a benediction in the eastern church, about the fourth century[w]; and also in the patriarchate of Constantinople, then, or not long after[x]. The council of Agde, Benedict, and Amalarius speak of the same in the west[y]; and it appears in the offices of the church of England during the period antecedent to the Norman Conquest[z].

[w] Apost. Const. lib. viii. c. 36.
[x] Goar, Rituale Græc. p. 46.
[y] Concil Agath. can. 30. ut supra. S. Benedict. Regula, c. 17. Amalarius de Eccl. Off. lib. iv. c. 45. "Oratio et benedictio semper in fine fiunt."
[z] Officium Anglo-Sax. in nocte, ad finem completorii; see Appendix to Hickes's Letters, &c.

CHAPTER II.

THE LITANY.

SECTION I.

ANCIENT USE OF THE TERM.

THE word *litany* has been used in so many different senses by ancient writers, that persons who were not sufficiently aware of this variety of application have fallen into great errors in attempting to trace the antiquity of various things which have all borne the same name. At first, this term was applied in general to all prayers and supplications, whether public or private. Thus Eusebius speaks of Constantine's custom of retiring to his tent before a battle, and there propitiating God with supplications and litanies[a]; and he also says, that shortly before his death, Constantine entered the church of the martyrs at Helenopolis, and there, for a long time, offered supplicatory prayers and litanies to God[b]. In the fourth century, the word *litany* became more especially applied to solemn offices which were performed with processions of the clergy and people.

Basil observes to the clergy of Neocæsarea, that

[a] Τὸν Θεὸν ἱκετηρίαις καὶ λιταῖς ἱλεούμενος Eusebii Vita Constantini, lib II c. 14. p. 450 ed. Valesii.

[b] Κἀνταῦθα τῷ τῶν μαρτύρων εὐκτηρίῳ ἐνδιατρίψας οἴκῳ, ἱκετηρίους εὐχάς τε καὶ λιτανείας ἀνέπεμπε τῷ Θεῷ Euseb. Vit. Const lib IV. c 61. p. 557. ed. Valesii

litanies which they then used had been introduced after the time of Gregory Thaumaturgus[c]. The term here seems to mean processional supplications, which could only have come into use after the season of persecution had passed by, and therefore not until after the time of Gregory. On the other hand, we have reason to think that supplications in the church without public processions were more ancient. I think it is therefore not unreasonable to interpret the litanies spoken of by Basil to mean processional litanies. It appears that very shortly after litanies of this kind came into use at Constantinople. Socrates relates, that in the time of John Chrysostom, the Arians of Constantinople, being obliged to perform divine service outside the walls, were accustomed to assemble themselves within the gates of the city, and sing anthems and hymns suited to the Arian heresy for great part of the night. And early in the morning, singing anthems of the same sort through the middle of the city, they went out of the gates, and proceeded to the places where they celebrated their worship[d].

Chrysostom, fearful that his people might be induced to join the Arians by these processions, established them on a greater and more splendid scale in his own church. By the liberality of the empress Eudoxia, the people were furnished with silver crosses, bearing wax lights, which were carried

[c] 'Αλλ' οὐκ ἦν φησὶ ταῦτα ἐπὶ τοῦ μεγάλου Γρηγορίου ἀλλ' οὐδὲ αἱ λιτανεῖαι, ἃς ὑμεῖς νῦν ἐπιτηδεύετε Basil. Epist 207. ad Cler. Neocæs (olim 63)p 311. tom. iii. ed. Benedict

[d] Αὐτοὶ ἐντὸς τῶν τῆς πόλεως πυλῶν περὶ τὰς στοὰς ἀθροιζόμενοι, καὶ ᾠδὰς ἀντιφώνους πρὸς τὴν 'Αρειανὴν δόξαν συντιθέντες ᾖδον καὶ τοῦτο ἐποίουν κατὰ τὸ πλεῖστον μέρος τῆς νυκτός ὑπὸ δὲ ὄρθρον, τὰ τοιαῦτα ἀντίφωνα λέγοντες διὰ μέσης τῆς πόλεως, ἐξῄεσαν τῶν πυλῶν Socrat. Hist Eccl lib. vi. c 8. p. 312 ed Valesii.

before them[e]. Such processional offices were called *litanies*, as appears from the life of Chrysostom, by Palladius, where it is said, that the people celebrated their litany in the fields, carrying the cross on their shoulders[f]. The emperor Arcadius shortly afterwards forbad by an edict[g] the heretics to make their litany within the city.

As the word *litany* was applied to the complex idea of a species of worship connected with public processions; so it was sometimes given to the persons who went in procession: thus Gregory the Great directs seven litanies to proceed fron seven different churches[h]. The service performed on these occasions was also called by the same name. Thus in ancient manuscripts we find the whole office termed *litany*. Walafridus Strabo says that we are not to call merely the part in which the saints are invocated, the litany, but likewise all the rest of the service[i]. Again, we find parts of the office thus termed. For instance, in the sacramentary of Gregory, the prayers which anciently followed *Kyrie eleëson* are spoken of as the litany[j]; and Benedict

[e] Socrates Hist Eccl lib. vi. c. 8. p. 313 Sozomen lib viii. c 8. p 768 ed Valesii

[f] Palladius Vita S. Joannis Chrysostomi, p 58. tom xiii Oper. Chrysost ed. Benedict. Montfaucon.

[g] Codex Theodosian lib xvi. Tit. 5.

[h] "Litania clericorum exeat ab ecclesia sancti Joannis Baptistæ, litania virorum ab ecclesia sancti martyris Marcelli," &c. Joannes Diaconus Vita S Gregorii, lib 1. c 42 p. 37 Oper. Gregorii, tom iv ed. Benedict.

[i] "Notandum autem, litanias non tantum dici illam recitationem nominum, qua sancti in adjutorium vocantur infirmitatis humanæ; sed etiam cuncta quæ supplicationibus fiunt, rogationes appellari." Walafrid. Strabo. de Reb. Eccl. c 28

[j] Sacramentar. Gregorii, a Menard. p 1 "Quando vero litania agitur neque *Gloria in excelsis Deo*, neque *Alleluia* canitur" Compare Bona, Rer Liturg. lib. ii. c. 4 No. 3 p. 337, &c

and others speak of the *Kyrie eleëson* alone, as a litany[k]. In later times, when the invocation of saints occupied a large portion of the office of the western litanies, the part that contained this invocation came to be spoken of as the litany. Amidst so many different meanings for this word, it is not easy to preserve the present subject from confusion. I will, however, attempt to elucidate it, by considering, first, the antiquity of special public supplications in the Christian church, and secondly, the nature and rites of those supplications after they became a distinct office.

SECTION II.

ANTIQUITY OF SPECIAL SUPPLICATIONS.

It is difficult to determine the period, when the custom of public supplication to God, under circumstances of peculiar urgency and importance, was introduced into the Christian church. We are indeed well aware that from the beginning, it has not only been the habit, but the duty of Christians, to apply specially to the throne of grace, when calamities are to be deprecated, or benefits implored, for themselves or for their neighbours. During the captivity of the holy apostle Peter, prayer was made to God for him by the church; and as he found them all assembled together, and praying on his delivery from prison, it is not improbable that they may at that very time have been met together to offer up

---

[k] S Benedict. Regula "Post hos—supplicatio litaniæ, id est *Kyrie eleison*," c 9. In an ancient MS. cited by Martene, describing the rites of baptism, it is said; " Procedit pontifex de ecclesia cum omni ordine sacerdotum, *letania* cantentes, hoc est, *Kyrie eleison*, usque dum perveniant ad fontes." Martene de Antiq. Eccl. Rit lib i c 1 art. 18. p. 175.

prayers for him. Tertullian says that drought was removed by the prayers and fastings of the Christians[1]. Cyprian said that they continually made prayers and supplications for the repelling of enemies, for rain, for the removal or moderation of calamities[m]. We find by the testimony of Sidonius, that supplications for rain and fine weather were customary in Gaul, before the middle of the fifth century[n]. We read of the emperor Theodosius, in the fourth century, preparing for battle with his enemies, by fasting and prayer to God during the whole night, and by going with the priests and people, and praying in sackcloth in all the churches[o]. Basil, in a homily delivered during a season of famine and drought, complains that the people did not attend the church to make their litany[p]. And we read that a solemn litany, or supplication, on account of a great earthquake, was celebrated at Constantinople in the time of the emperor Theodosius the younger, and the patriarch Proclus, about A. D. 430[q]. It appears from all these circumstances, that

---

[1] " Quando non geniculationibus et jejunationibus nostris etiam siccitates sunt depulsæ." Tertull ad Scapulam, p 71. ed. Rigalt " Denique cum ab imbribus æstiva hiberna suspendunt et annus in cura est, vos quidem balneis et cauponis et lupanaribus operantibus aquilicia Jovi immolatis—nos vero jejuniis aridi et omni continentia expressi, ab omni vitæ fruge dilati, in sacco et cinere volutantes, invidia cœlum tundimus," &c Apologet c. 40. p 33

[m] " Pro arcendis hostibus, et imbribus impetrandis, et vel auferendis vel temperandis adversis, rogamus semper et preces fundimus." Cypr ad Demetrian p 193 ed Fell.

[n] Sidonius Arvernens. Epistola ad Apium " Erant quidem prius (ante tempora Mamerti, sc) vagæ, tepentes, infrequentesque, atque (sic dixeris) oscitabundæ supplicationes," &c.

[o] Ruffinus, Historia, lib 11. c. 33

[p] Basil. Homilia in famem et siccitatem, tom ii. p. 64. Oper. Ed Benedict.

[q] Nicephor. Hist. lib. xiv. c 46.

public supplications and prayers to God, on occasions of especial urgency, were certainly prevalent in the church during the fourth and fifth centuries. It also is manifest, that supplications were made by the church on the same occasions, from the earliest ages: and there is no improbability that these supplications may always have been made in public assemblies of the church. We know that such supplications were accompanied by fastings; and when we reflect that in the second and third centuries, the Christians were accustomed to meet in church for the purpose of divine worship, on the ordinary fasts of the fourth and sixth days of the week[r], we may see good reason for thinking that they also met together to celebrate the fasts, which were enjoined on occasions of great moment. They certainly did assemble for this purpose in the fourth century, both in the eastern and western churches; as we may perceive by the instances above cited from Basil, and the life of Theodosius the Great; and therefore they probably had done so long before.

These supplications were called litanies in the eastern churches, from whence the name passed to the west. Here they were called rogations or supplications, until the name of litany became more prevalent than any other. It is probable that the prevalence of the name of litany in the west, may have arisen from the derivation of processional supplications from the eastern to the western churches. I have already observed that processions could only have commenced in the fourth century, when the

[r] See Bingham's Antiquities of the Christian Church, book xxi c 3 § 4.

persecutions had terminated; and in fact there is no notice of any such custom until that century.

Rogations, or litanies, were customary in Gaul in the fifth century, as we learn from Sidonius, who observes that they were principally for the purpose of praying for rain or fine weather[s]; but it appears that they were not celebrated at that time with the regularity, solemnity, and devotion which afterwards attended on them. Mamertus, bishop of Vienna in Gaul, on occasion of several dreadful calamities, which about the year 460 fell on the people of that diocese, instituted solemn litanies, or rogations, on the three days immediately preceding the feast of Ascension[t]. These three days acquired shortly the appellation of rogation days, because they were the only days of the year which were annually set apart for the purpose of celebrating litanies or rogations. The rogation days of Mamertus were before long received throughout Gaul; and they were also received in the English church at an early period, as the council of Cloveshoe appointed that these three days should be kept holy, after the manner of former times[u]. In Spain they were received at a later period; and at Milan the three rogation days were not celebrated before Ascension, but in the week after[v]. However, though these three days were set apart for supplications or litanies every year, litanies were also celebrated whenever any particular circumstance rendered it desirable; as,

[s] Sidonius Epist. ad Aprum, cited above, p 268
[t] Gregorius Turon Hist. lib. ii. c 34.
[u] Concil Cloveshoviense, 2. can 16
[v] Martene de Antiq Eccl discipl. in div. offic. c. 27. p. 514.

for instance, during drought, or continual rain, &c. In the next century after that in which Mamertus lived, another annual litany or rogation was established in the diocese of Auvergne, or Clermont, by Gallus, A.D. 545, who, on occasion of a plague in the city, directed an annual procession from Clermont to the church of St. Julian the Martyr[w].

At Rome, no doubt, litanies were in use at an early period, since we find that in the time of Gregory the Great, A.D. 590, the appellation of litany had been so long given to processional supplications, that it was then familiarly applied to those persons who formed the procession. Hence when this patriarch gave directions for the celebration of a sevenfold litany, on occasion of a great pestilence, he spoke thus: "Let the litany of clergy depart from "the church of St. John Baptist, the litany of men "from the church of St. Marcellus, the litany of "monks from the church of St. John and St. Paul, "the litany of virgins from the church of Cosmas "and Damian, the litany of married women from "the church of St. Stephen, the litany of widows "from the church of St. Vitalis, the litany of the "poor and the children from the church of St. Ce-"cilia—[x]." These different litanies were all to go in procession to some one principal church, where a solemn service was performed. Thus commenced the *Litania Septena* in the Roman church, which was entitled *Litania Major*, and was celebrated on the twenty-fifth of March. This litany or rogation does not appear to have been adopted soon by the

[w] Gregor. Turon. Hist. lib. iv. c 5.
[x] Vita Gregorii a Joanne Diacono, lib. i. c. 42. p 37. tom iv. Oper. Gregor. edit. Benedict

Gallican church, which preferred the season of rogations appointed by Mamertus; and though formerly received in England, it has long been abolished amongst us. These annual litanies of the western churches appear never to have been received by the oriental churches. Though we frequently read of litanies and processions in the monuments of the east, yet it does not seem that they have ever adopted the seasons of rogation which Mamertus and Gregory appointed. However, they had annual supplications also. Thus we read that an annual litany was celebrated in commemoration of the great earthquake in the reign of the emperor Justinian[y]. But the litanies of the patriarchate of Constantinople seem only to be celebrated now on occasions of some peculiar urgency, as, for instance, in the time of drought, peril of earthquake, pestilence, storms[z], &c. And these certainly appear to have been originally the proper seasons for litanies.

SECTION III.

THE SERVICE PERFORMED IN SUPPLICATIONS

We have no distinct account of the nature of the service which was used on occasions of peculiar supplications during the earliest ages. That the people fasted and prayed on such occasions we learn from Tertullian; and it may be considered highly probable, that during the first three centuries the service at such times differed but little from that of ordinary fast days. On the weekly fast days the church in some places assembled at the sixth hour, or twelve o'clock, and the service consisted of psal-

[y] Cedrenus, cited by Goar, Rituale Græc. p. 770.

[z] See Goar, Rituale Græc. p 766 770, &c.

mody and lessons of scripture, which were continued till the ninth hour, or three o'clock, at which time the sacrament was celebrated[a]. Something of the same sort appears in the western supplications or rogations of later times, where the service began at the third hour, or nine o'clock in the morning, in order to allow time for the procession; and in the latter part of the day the sacrament was also administered[b]. Psalmody and lessons of scripture were the ordinary exercises of devotion in Christian assemblies, and therefore it is highly probable that they were used in the public offices of supplication for any especial occasion. To this, no doubt, we may add prayers made by the bishop or priest at a proper part of the service. In the fourth century, however, we have a distinct reference to the use of psalmody on such occasions. Basil, in a discourse delivered during a season of dry weather and famine, speaks of the public service of a litany as terminating with psalmody. He complains of the small number of persons who attended the office, and of their inattention; and observes, that they watched when the singer should conclude the verses of the psalms, that being delivered from the church, as if from a prison, they might be relieved from the necessity of praying[c]. In the same place he speaks

[a] Bingham, Antiquities, b xiii. c 9. §. 2. Book xxi. c. 3. §. 4.

[b] This appears in the ancient MS litany of the church of Lyons, published by Martene, p. 520—524 De Antiq. Eccl. Discipl in Div Off. In the last station, which was held at the church of St. Justus, after the litany and the office for the ninth hour were sung, the liturgy was performed. "Hic nonam cantabis cum missa." We find the same custom in the church of Milan. The office for the ninth hour was sung in the seventh station, and the liturgy in the eighth. See Martene ut supra, p. 533.

[c] καὶ ἐπιτηροῦντες πότε τοὺς στίχους ὁ ψαλμῳδὸς συμπληρώσει,

of this service as a supplication and prayer, and he observes, that the infants who were sent instead of their parents, could not pray as was customary[d].

In the nocturnal and processional litanies of the Arians of Constantinople, in the time of Chrysostom, we find that they sung psalms, to which they added certain terminations, composed to suit their own heresy[e]; and the catholics, by the direction of Chrysostom, adopted this custom of nocturnal and processional psalmody. And from that period to the present, these nocturnal psalms and processions have borne the name of litany in the patriarchate of Constantinople; for even now the litany of that church is chiefly, if not entirely, celebrated in the night, and consists principally of psalmody. as it did in the days of Chrysostom[f]. The offices performed in the rogations instituted by Mamertus appear chiefly to have consisted of psalmody and prayers, as we learn from Sidonius and Avitus[g]; but besides this, we find that very long lessons of scripture were read,

ποτέ ὡς δεσμωτηρίου, τῆς ἐκκλησίας, καὶ τῆς ἀνάγκης τῆς προσευχῆς ἀφαιρεθήσονται Basil Hom. in Famem et Siccitatem, tom. ii. p. 64 ed. Benedict

[d] Οἷα δὲ ἡμῶν ἡ προσευχὴ καὶ ἡ δέησις; ibid. ὀλίγοι λοιπὸν μετ᾽ ἐμοῦ καὶ τῆς προσευχῆς ibid. Βρέφη—οὔτε τοῦ συνήθως προσεύξασθαι γνῶσιν ἢ δύναμιν ἔχοντα ibid.

[e] Sozomen Hist. Eccl lib viii. c. 8 p 767, 768. ed. Valesii.

[f] See Goar, Rituale Græcum, p. 766, &c.

[g] "In his autem (rogationibus) quas suprafatus sacerdos et protulit pariter, et contulit, jejunatur, oratur, psallitur, fletur." Sidonius Epistola ad Aprum.

"Sanctus Mamertus sacerdos—totas in ea quam supradiximus vigiliarum nocte, sancto paschæ, concepit animo rogationes; atque ibi cum Deo tacitus definivit, quidquid hodie psalmis ac precibus mundus inclamat" Avitus de rogationibus. "Nec porro magni intererat quod triduum eligeretur, dummodo psalmorum officia, lachrymarum functionibus cernuis persolverentur." Ibid

SECT. III.   *Service performed in Litanies.*   275

as appears by the ancient Gallican lectionary[h]. The service during the procession consisted of psalmody; for we read in the history of Gregory of Tours, that St. Gallus appointed the people to go in procession with psalmody from Clermont to the church of St. Julian[i]. We also find in the ancient Gallican liturgy, offices for the three rogation days, and collects to be said at different churches in the procession[j]. It seems that the liturgy was celebrated early in the morning. It is said that a certain blind woman, in the time of Germanus, bishop of Paris, hearing the chorus of singers passing by in the time of the litanies, implored with tears the assistance of Germanus, and having recovered her sight on the third day, went early in the morning to the liturgy in procession with the people[k]. After the liturgy was over, they probably went in procession to different churches, singing psalms and anthems on the road; and in the churches they recited some prayers, and the collects and lessons, which we find in the Gallican missal and lectionary. Very nearly the same

---

[h] See Mabillon de Liturgia Gallicana, p 149, &c.

[i] " Rogationes illas instituit, ut media quadragesima psallendo, ad Basilicam beati Juliani Martyris itinere pedestri venirent." Gregor. Turonens. Hist. Franc. lib. iv. c. 5. "Erant autem quadragesimæ dies, et Cautinus episcopus in Brivatensem diœcesim psallendo adire disposuerat, juxta institutionem Sancti Galli, sicut supra scripsimus—ascenso equo, relicto psallentio, solus usque in porticum Basilicæ S. Juliani ambobus urgens calcaneis cornipedem, pænè exanimis percurrit " Gregorius Turon lib. iv. c 13.

[j] Missale Gothicum ap. Mabillon. Lit. Gall. p. 263—268.

[k] "Quædam mulier—dum tempore litaniarum præcæcatis oculis non posset ire cum populo, audiens chorum psallentium, cum lachrymis domini Germani implorat auxilium— clarescente quoque die, ad missam cum populo progreditur mulier in processu " Fortunatus vita S Germani ap. Surium, tom. iii. p. 416.

custom prevails to the present time in the church of Milan. On the days of litanies or rogations, the clergy and people go in procession to several churches, at each of which they recite a litany like ours, a collect, and two lessons. Anthems or psalms are sung all the way from one church to another[1]. In the church of Rome the procession is celebrated in a different manner. There the invocation of saints, &c. and most of the prayers, are sung in procession, and at each of the churches which is visited only a collect is repeated. The remainder of the prayers and collects are recited in the principal church at the close of the rogation[m]. The office for the litany, according to the church of Constantinople, consists chiefly of psalmody and precatory anthems, which are either selected from the psalms, or composed in the same style. Besides these, there are prayers by the deacon and people, collects, and lessons. And there are various precatory anthems and lessons for the different occasions which call for the celebration of the litany[n].

Before I conclude this section, it may be considered proper for me to notice one peculiarity of the offices for litanies according to certain western churches. I allude to those long invocations of saints which occur at the beginning of the Roman litany. None of the eastern churches have ever used this sort of prayers in their litanies. On this subject let Renaudot, a most learned ritualist, be heard. "Litanies, in our manner of speaking, there are

---

[1] See Martene de Ant. Eccl. Discipl. in Div. Off. c. 27. p. 532, 533
[m] Rituale Romanum. Ordo in Processione, &c. p 325—327. ed. Antwerp. 1652
[n] Goar, Rituale Græc p. 766, &c.

SECT. III.   *Invocations of Saints examined.*   277

none in the oriental churches, although **Kyrie eleëson**, with which our litanies begin and end, is frequently repeated. Neither do the Greeks know them[o]."

It is in fact certain, that none of the eastern churches use the invocations of saints which appear in the Roman litanies; and if so, the eastern litanies never could have contained such invocations; for no reason can be assigned why those churches should ever have omitted them, if they had been once introduced. Invocations of saints are then the peculiar characteristic of western litanies. Let me attempt to trace the antiquity of these invocations in the western churches, premising, however, that I make this inquiry solely with the object of ascertaining an historical fact: for there is no occasion whatsoever to prove that such invocations are not of the greatest antiquity in the western churches, in order to justify the church of England for removing them from her litany.

There can be no doubt that these invocations of

---

[o] "Litaniæ nostro more loquendo, nullæ in ritu orientali sunt, etiamsi *Kyrie eleison* pluries repetatur, a qua formula litaniæ nostræ incipiunt, et eadem concluduntur. Sed neque Græci illas noverunt. Hanc opinionem habuit Josephus Scaliger, litanias esse illas orationes ubi *Kyrie eleison* sæpius repetitur, et existimavit a diptychis manasse · ingeniose, sed non vere. Diptycha adhuc conservantur in ritu Alexandrino, ut etiam ipsa vox · neque commune quidquam habent cum ista oratione, quam litaniam vocavit hujus liturgiæ interpres Sacerdos orat pro omnibus et de omnibus. Diaconus initio cujusque orationis, quarum aliquam et majorem partem sacerdos secreto dicit, alta voce monet circumstantes, ut orent secundum sacerdotis intentionem. *Orate pro pace, pro papa, pro ecclesia,* &c. Populus acclamat *Kyrie eleison,* ter ut plurimum, aliquando pluries *Nulla sanctorum, ut in litaniis nostris, commemoratio.*" Renaudot, Liturg. Oriental. tom. i. p. 356.

T 3

saints were customary in the ninth century, for they are mentioned by Walafridus Strabo and Amalarius. The former remarks, that "litanies mean not "only that recitation of names in which the saints "are invoked for the assistance of human infirmity, "but all things which are done in supplications are "to be called rogations[p]." From this we may infer, that these invocations must then have been for some time in use, since it was necessary to remark that the name of litany was not to be applied to them alone. Accordingly manuscript litanies, containing invocations, have been discovered by learned men, which appear from internal evidence to be as old as the eighth century[q]. Beyond this point there appears to be no tangible evidence for the use of invocations in litanies. It is true that innumerable passages have been cited from more ancient writers, to shew that the invocation of saints is more ancient than the eighth century[r]. But independently of the fact, that most of those passages do not refer to the

[p] "Notandum autem, litanias non tantum dici illam recitationem hominum, qua sancti in adjutorium vocantur infirmitatis humanæ sed etiam cuncta quæ supplicationibus fiunt, rogationes appellari" Walafrid. Strabo. de Reb. Eccles. c. 28. *de Litaniis agendis.* " Litaniæ quæ fiunt circa baptisterii consecrationem, intercessiones sanctorum designant pro renascentibus" Amalarius de Eccl Officiis, lib i. c. 28

[q] It seems that one of the most ancient litanies containing the invocation of saints is that printed by Mabillon, in the third volume of his Analecta. This litany does not contain the names of any saints who flourished after the end of the seventh, or beginning of the eighth, century. From whence Mabillon conjectures that it may have been used about that time. See Analecta, tom. iii. p 669, &c. The Irish litanies alluded to by O'Conor, "Appendix to vol. i. of Catalogue of MSS. in Stowe Library," p 41, 49, seem to be equally ancient.

[r] For instance, by Serarius, in his "Litaneutici seu de Litaniis," &c

invocation of saints, but to prayers made *to God* for the intercession of saints; it is to be observed, that these quotations do not affect the question, which is not concerning the invocation of saints in general, but their invocation in the litany. It appears then that there is no evidence for the use of such invocations in the western churches before the eighth century, even on the most liberal allowance. In this case we must conclude that the invocations of saints were only introduced into the litany about the seventh or eighth century. This conclusion is rendered stronger by the fact, that authors who mention the psalmody and prayers, and lessons of the litany, do not allude to the invocations. Even the form of *Kyrie eleëson* is mentioned, but the invocations are not. If the invocation of saints had been practised in the litany during the fifth and sixth centuries, we should assuredly have found some allusion to it in the writings of Gregory of Tours, of Avitus, or Sidonius, or Gregory the Great, who all speak repeatedly of litanies. But this silence of the Fathers of those ages is well accounted for by the actual production of several most ancient western litanies, in which there is no invocation of saints. Such a one is that used in the church of Milan during Lent, at the beginning of the Liturgy, and immediately before the collect of the day[s].

[s] Missale, Ambrosian. Dominica prima quadragesimæ. "Finita ingressa sacerdos dicat Dominus vobiscum, et Diaconus dicat sequentes preces choro respondente." The prayers are cited by Bingham, Antiquities, b. xv. ch. 1. §. 2; and Bona, Rer. Lit. b. ii. c. 4. n 3, and it is therefore needless to copy them here. After these prayers comes the collect of the day. See Miss. Ambros. fol. 63, 64. In the same missal, on the second Sunday of Lent, another litany prayer,

According to cardinal Bona, the same sort of prayers used to follow *Kyrie eleëson* at the beginning of the Roman liturgy, until the ninth century[t]. Now Gregory the Great, in his sacramentary, gives the prayers used at that place the name of *litany*; and therefore we may infer, that in his time the prayers of the litany resembled those of the Ambrosian liturgy[u]. Another ancient litany, from a MS. of the monastery of Fulda, contains no invocations of saints[v]. And a third occurs in a book of offices ascribed to Alcuin[w]. It is there entitled, "A Deprecation which pope "Gelasius appointed to be sung for the universal "Church:" and though there is no reasonable ground for denying that Alcuin compiled this book, yet if any person should choose to do so, it will hardly be

still more like the Greek litanies, occurs in exactly the same part of the liturgy. See fol. 70

[t] " Post *Kyrie eleison* sequitur hymnus *Gloria in excelsis Deo*, si dicendus sit, alioquin præmissa populi salutatione *Dominus vobiscum* dicitur oratio sive collecta, de quibus sigillatim agendum erit, si prius notavero olim diebus, quibus omittitur *Gloria in excelsis*, immediate post *Kyrie*, prolixas preces pro omni statu hominum recitari consuevisse, iis prorsus similes, quas Irenicas sive diaconicas Græci vocant, et initio liturgiæ diacono præcinente, choro respondente decantant Permansit hic ritus in ecclesia Latina usque ad sæculum ix. ut observat Goar in notis ad missam Chrysostomi, n. 62, et nunc etiam permanet in ecclesia Mediolanensi diebus Dominicis quadragesimæ." Bona, Rer. Lit. lib. ii c 4 N°. 2. p 337

[u] " Quando vero litania agitur, neque *Gloria in excelsis Deo*, neque Alleluia canitur." Sacr Gregorii a Menard. p. 1.

[v] Tom. iii. Antiq. Liturgicarum, p 307 "Cujusmodi sunt illa, quæ ex litania vetustissima bibliothecæ Fuldensis transcripsit Wicelius. . atque hæc Wicelius transcribit, ut partem litaniarum in quibus explicandis nunc versamur, quamvis mihi magis probetur hanc litaniam esse litaniam missalem . cujusmodi sunt nonnullæ in quadragesima in officio Ambrosiano, et plurimæ in omnibus missis Græcorum." This litany is also transcribed by Bingham and Bona, as above

[w] Alcuini Abbatis Officia per Ferias, p. 241. oper Paris 1617.

denied that the Deprecation is a most ancient document, and that it is not improbable that it is as old as the time of Gelasius. In this formulary there is no invocation of saints, and yet we cannot consider it to be any thing else than the prayer used in a litany or supplication, which, in fact, is the meaning of the title prefixed to it.

Whether the knowledge of such facts as these had any influence on the mind of Walafridus Strabo, who wrote in the ninth century, or not; it is certain that he virtually affirms, that in his time the invocations of saints were believed *not* to have been originally in the litany. For he says, " the litany of " the holy names *is believed* to have come into use " *after* Jerome composed the martyrology[x]." With the correctness of this chronology we have nothing to do; but the passage shews, that the opinion in the time of Walafridus was, that the invocations did not *originally* form part of the litany.

The form in which the prayers of the litany are conveyed, according to which the minister precents or repeats the beginning of each prayer, which the people conclude or respond to, is plainly derived from oriental models. From the earliest period such forms appear to have prevailed in the east, and we find them not merely in the litanies, but in the liturgies and all the other offices of the oriental churches. In the western churches such forms do not seem to have prevailed till a much later period; and we may therefore very fairly conclude, that, when the word

---

[x] " Litania autem sanctorum nominum, postea creditur in usum assumpta, quam Hieronymus martyrologium, secutus Eusebium Cæsareensem, composuit " Walafrid. Strabo. de Reb. Eccl c 28

litany was imported from the east to the west, and when the ***Kyrie eleëson,*** which formed the commencement of the eastern litanies, was likewise conveyed to the west, the form of the oriental prayers, and great part of their substance accompanied them.

It appears probable, that, at first, the place at the beginning of the litany, afterwards occupied by the long invocations of saints, was filled up by a frequent repetition of the form ***Kyrie eleëson.*** We learn from Gregory of Tours, that on occasion of a litany at Rome in the time of Gregory the Great, the choirs of singers came to the church, crying through the streets of the city, ***Kyrie eleëson***[y]. From this it appears, that in the time of Gregory this form was continually repeated in the procession. And the council of Vaison in Gaul, A. D. 529, appears to recognise this custom: "Because, as well in the "Apostolical see, as in all the provinces of the east "and of Italy, an agreeable and very salutary cus- "tom has been introduced, namely, to use a *frequent* "*repetition* of ***Kyrie eleëson,*** with great earnestness "and contrition; therefore," &c.[z] It must have been this continual repetition of ***Kyrie eleëson*** in the litany, that gave this form itself the name of *litany,* which

---

[y] "Hæc eo dicente, congregatis clericorum, catervis, psallere jussit per triduum, ac deprecari Domini misericordiam. De hora quoque tertia veniebant utrique chori psallentium ad ecclesiam clamantes per plateas urbis, *Kyrie eleison.*" Gregor. Turon. Hist. lib. x. c. 1 p 483

[z] "Et quia tam in sede Apostolica, quam etiam per totas orientales atque Italiæ provincias, dulcis et nimium salutaris consuetudo est intromissa, ut *Kyrie eleison* frequentius cum grandi affectu et compunctione dicatur, placuit etiam nobis, ut in omnibus ecclesiis nostris ista tam sancta consuetudo et ad matutinum, et ad missas, et ad vesperum Deo propitio intromittatur." Concil. Vasens, 2. can. 3. p. 1680. tom. iv. concil. Labbe

it bears in the rule of St. Benedict[a]. And we find a trace of the ancient custom of the Roman church in a manuscript ritual, referred to by Mabillon, where, in a litany on the vigil of the Assumption, the people repeated, with tears and prayers, *Kyrie eleëson* a hundred times, *Christe eleëson* a hundred times, and *Kyrie eleëson* again a hundred times[b]. That the service performed in the procession according to the Roman church is much altered from what it formerly was, will appear by comparing the Roman ritual with the Antiphonary of Gregory the Great[c]. In this last there are only a great number of anthems appointed to be sung during the procession; in the former there is but one anthem and a psalm, which are followed by the invocations and prayers and penitential psalms. These anthems were certainly sung in the procession formerly; for venerable Bede relates, that Augustine and his brethren, approaching for the first time the city of Canterbury, sang with one voice this litany; "We implore thee, "O Lord, in thy great mercy, to remove thy wrath "and anger from this city, and from thy holy "dwelling, for we have sinned. Alleluia[d]." This

---

[a] S. Benedict. Regula, c. 9. "Supplicatio litaniæ, id est, *Kyrie eleison*"—c. 11. "Canticum de evangelio, litania, et completum est."

[b] Mabillon, Musæum Italicum, tom. ii. p. xxxiv. In an ancient MS. cited by Martene it appears that *Kyrie eleeson* was called *litany:* "Procedit pontifex de ecclesia cum omni ordine sacerdotum, *lætania* cantentes, *hoc est Kyrie eleison*, usque dum perveniant ad fontes." Martene de Antiq Eccl.

Rit. lib i. c. 1 art. 18 p. 175.

[c] Antiphonarius Gregorii ap. Pamel. Liturgic tom. ii. p. 124 Rituale Romanum, p. 326, &c

[d] "Fertur autem quia adpropinquantes civitati, more suo, cum cruce sancta, et imagine magni regis Domini nostri JESU CHRISTI, hanc lætaniam consona voce modularentur: ' Deprecamur te Domine, in omni misericordia tua, ut auferatur furor tuus et ira tua a civitate ista, et de domo sancta

anthem occurs in the Antiphonary of Gregory, above referred to, and is there appointed to be used in the procession[e]. We also find in the Ordo Romanus that anthems were sung in procession, when relics were carried on the days of litany; and for those anthems it refers us to the Antiphonary[f]. It is to be noted, however, that the Ordo Romanus speaks as if the repetition of *Kyrie eleëson* formed a great part of the service: " Let no one then presume to " ride, but let all walk with bare feet. Let not women " lead the choirs, but let all together sing *Kyrie eleë-* " *son*, and with contrition of heart implore the mercy " of God for pardon of their sins, for peace, for deli- " verance from plague, for preserving the fruits of the " earth, and for other necessities[g]." It appears from

tua, quoniam peccavimus. Alleluia.' ' Beda, Hist. Eccl lib. 1 c. 25. p 61. ed. Smith.

[e] Antiphonarius Gregorii ap Pamelii Liturgic tom ii. p. 124 See also Martene de Antiq. Eccl. Discip in Div. Off p. 525.

[f] " Antiphonæ vero ad reliquias deducendas, in libro gradali vel Antiphonario quærentibus occurrent per singulos tres dies." Ordo Romanus de Litania minore Rogationum apud Hittorp p 89

[g] " Nemo ibi equitare præsumat, sed discalceatis pedibus omnes incedant Nequaquam mulierculæ ducant choros, sed omnes in commune *Kyrie eleison* decantent, et cum contritione cordis Dei misericordiam exorent pro peccatis, pro pace, pro peste, pro conservatione frugum, et pro cæteris necessitatibus " *Ordo Romanus ibid*

It would seem that the words of this passage confirm the antiquity of those litanies already noticed, which do not contain the invocation of saints. The petitions of these litanies are not exactly in the form of the more recent litanies, thus, " *Ut* fructus terræ dare et conservare digneris—*Resp. Te rogamus audi nos*." but thus; " *Pro* aeris temperie ac fructu et fœcunditate terrarum precamur te—*Resp. Domine miserere* " Bona, Rer. Lit. lib ii. c 4 §. 3. or thus; " *Pro* jucunditate et serenitate pluviæ, atque aurarum vitalium blandimentis, ac prospero diversorum operum cursu, rectorem mundi Dominum deprecamur —*Resp. Domine exaudi et miserere*." Deprecatio Gelasii Papæ. ap. Alcuin. Officia Opera, p. 241 Paris. 1617.

this that the Roman office for procession formerly consisted of many anthems, of a very frequent repetition of *Kyrie eleëson*, (for which the invocation of saints was afterwards substituted,) and of the obsecrations, deprecations, and intercessions, which are still found in the latter part of the litany in the Roman offices. After the procession, no doubt, they repeated in station appropriate collects or prayers; but we have no account, I believe, of the reading of any lessons during the Roman litany; though the church of Milan and the churches of Gaul and of Constantinople certainly had lessons in their station, or that part of the office which was performed in the church.

SECTION IV.

LITANIES OF THE CHURCH OF ENGLAND.

The church of England appears to have received the stated rogation or litany days of the Gallican church at an early period, and from that time to the present, she has reckoned them amongst her days of fasting. Formerly in this church there were processions on all these days, but in the course of time this ancient custom has been confined to one day, on which the people still perambulate the bounds of their parishes. According to the injunctions or advertisements of queen Elizabeth, the office for these days was to consist of the two psalms, beginning "Benedic anima mea," of the litany and suffrages, and a homily especially appointed for the occasion. This office was recited in church, on the return of the people from the procession, and in the course of the procession the curate was to admonish the people to give thanks to God, with the saying of the hundred and third psalm; and at the same time he should inculcate these, or such sentences, "Cursed be he which translateth the bounds " or dolles of his neighbour[h]," &c. The repetition of psalms and verses of Scripture in the procession was perfectly accordant with the practice of the church during the fifth century, and afterwards.

Let us however pass from the consideration of this ancient litany or rogation, which appears indeed to bear some of the marks of time; and consider the extraordinary supplications of the church, which are made for rain, for fair weather, in time of rain, dearth, and famine, in times of war, or of pestilence. On these occasions, according to the English ritual, there is no procession, but as in primitive ages, the whole office is performed in the church; and the peculiarity of the offices for these occasions consists in the addition of an appropriate collect to the morning prayer, or litany, according to the day of the week. When these offices comprise the litany, they certainly approach nearest to the practice of primitive ages, at least to that of the eastern churches in early times.

Considering the litany simply as a certain assemblage of prayers ordinarily used in divine service, it may be regarded in three points of view. First, as a termination of the office of morning prayer; in which case we may refer for a confirmation of its antiquity and propriety, to the ancient office of matins, according to the church of Constantinople, when a form of prayer resembling our litany occurs

---

[h] See Injunctions of Edward VI. in Sparrow's Collection of Articles, p. 8, and of Elizabeth, p. 7?

near the conclusion[1]: and a similar form of prayer is visible in the morning office of the Apostolical Constitutions, which were written in the east, about the end of the third, or beginning of the fourth century[j]. Secondly, we may consider the litany as a distinct service, said after the morning prayer: and in this case we find a confirmation of our practice in the ancient rites of the English church, where the litany was appointed to be said in the same manner during the greatest part of Lent[k].

Thirdly, we may consider the litany as an introduction to the liturgy or communion service: and to prove the antiquity and propriety of this position, we refer to the ancient liturgies of the patriarchate of Constantinople, and of the church of Milan[l], and to the liturgy of the Roman church in *ancient* times; for since the ninth century the litany has not been repeated after *Kyrie eleëson* in the Roman liturgy[m].

The form of prayer in our litany, according to which the minister or priest precents, or repeats the beginning of each petition, and the people respond, has been used in the western churches from a remote period; but we cannot with justice ascribe its origination to these churches. The most ancient western formularies of this kind are too evidently

[i] Goar, Rituale Græc p. 54.
[j] Apost. Const. lib. viii. c. 37. The prayers for the faithful there referred to are contained in c 10 of the same book.
[k] Breviar. Sarisb. pars hyemalis fol. 68. The litany was said with the gradual psalms, after the office for the third hour, from Monday in the first week of Lent, to Wednesday before Easter, whenever there was no proper service of Sundays or holy-days.
[l] Liturgia Basilii Goar, p. 159. Chrysostomi ibid. p. 64. Missale Ambros apud Pamelii Liturgic. tom. 1. p. 328, 329.
[m] Bona, Rer. Lit. lib. ii. c 4. Nº. 2 p. 337.

copied from Greek or oriental models, to leave any doubt as to the source from whence they were derived. In fact, we have memorials in the writings of primitive antiquity, which trace back this sort of prayer to the third century in the eastern churches; while it does not appear that there are any notices of a similar practice in the west, until after the introduction of processions, in imitation of the eastern church, which probably took place early in the fifth century. Besides this, the litaneutical form of praying is visible in all the offices of the eastern churches, in the liturgies, the canonical hours, the administration of all rites. In the west it has always been very sparingly used. Of the petitions which are comprised in our litany, it may be observed, that they are generally of remote antiquity in the English church. Mabillon has printed a litany of the church of England, written probably in the eighth century, which contains a large portion of that which we repeat at the present day, and which preserves exactly the same form of petition and response which is still retained. The still more ancient litanies of the abbey of Fulda, of the Ambrosian missal, and of Gelasius, patriarch of Rome; together with the Diaconica or Irenica of the liturgies and offices of the churches of Constantinople, Cæsarea, Antioch, Jerusalem, &c. which all preserve the form of the litany; all these ancient formularies contain very much the same petitions as the English litany. This is in fact so manifest, even to the most superficial observer, that Schultingius could find nothing to blame in the English litany, except the omission of the invocations of saints. "It is not " pleasing to him," he says, " that the suffrages and

SECT. VI. *Invocation of Saints rightly discontinued.* 289

"intercessions of the saints are omitted, contrary to
"the practice of the primitive church, and the cus-
"tom of ancient litanies[n]." In reply to this objection, I may remark, first, that the litanies of the eastern apostolical churches have never contained the invocations which appear in many of the western litanies; therefore those invocations are not essential in the litany. Secondly, the most ancient western litanies do not contain any invocations of saints, and there is no proof that these invocations were introduced into them before the eighth century. Therefore the western churches in early times did not use those invocations which now appear at the beginning of their litanies.

If then the church of England had only wished to assimilate her rites to those of the catholic church during the first seven centuries, she would have been obliged to omit the invocations of saints which had for a considerable time been placed at the beginning of her litany. And who will venture to blame the church of England for assimilating her rites to those of the primitive catholic church? The church of England, however, is justified on other grounds for removing the invocation of saints from the litany.

First, it is *unnecessary* to invoke the saints, by the admission of all parties; and it is so for two reasons; because, first, while we are not commanded by the word of God to invoke the saints, we are

[n] "De hac litania idem judico quod de litaniis Lutheranorum antea dixi, nempe mihi non placere quod sanctorum suffragia et intercessiones contra praxin priscæ ecclesiæ, et morem antiquarum litaniarum, de quibus antea copiose et iterato dixi, prætermittantur." Schultingii Biblioth Eccl. tom iv. pars 2. p. 133.

invited to "call on the Lord in the day of trouble," to "ask" and "receive;" and we have the repeated assurance of Christ, that "if we ask any thing in "his name he will do it." Secondly, the Fathers of the church affirm, that the saints departed pray for their brethren in this world: therefore it is not necessary to invoke their prayers, because they are given spontaneously.

Secondly, it is *imprudent* to invoke the saints, because, as cardinal Cajetan has observed, we have no certain way of knowing whether they can hear our invocations. The catholic church has not taught us that the saints certainly hear any address made to them. Those Fathers who invoked the saints expressed some doubts whether they knew any thing of what passed on earth. But we are certain that God hears every prayer that is addressed to him, and that he is ready to succour to the utmost those that come to him. If, then, we fly from such prayers to invocations of the saints, we exchange a certain means of grace for an uncertainty, and therefore act imprudently.

Thirdly, it was the duty of the church of England to remove all invocations of saints from her litany and other offices, in order to rescue her children effectually from the peril of heresy and blasphemy. The custom of invoking the saints in the offices of the church, or on other occasions, produces at length a conviction in the minds of men, that the saints hear all invocations addressed to them. They who hear the church continually repeating the words "Saint Mary pray for us," must be led to believe that the saint hears this address. Now if it be firmly believed and taught, that the saints always

SECT. IV. *Invocation of Saints rightly discontinued.* 291

hear invocations, a wide field is opened for the spread of error and superstition. The refinements of schoolmen, as to the mode by which a knowledge of our prayers is said to be communicated to the saints, cannot be intelligible to the capacities of the ignorant and unlearned, nor will they be communicated to them. The majority of Christians are therefore, by the custom of invoking the saints, placed in peril of ascribing a natural intrinsic power, little less than divine, to beings who, though invisible to mankind, can hear all prayers addressed to them in all parts of the world. This sentiment, admitted by all to be erroneous and perilous in itself, gives encouragement and impulse to evils which follow from another species of invocation addressed to the saints. Bellarmine, a Romanist, affirms that it is lawful to say, " St. Peter, have mercy upon me, " save me, open to me the way to heaven; grant " me health of body, grant me patience, fortitude[o]," &c. If we take such prayers in a literal sense, they are heretical and blasphemous; and as many of the unlearned must necessarily take them in a literal sense, the use of such prayers must lead many persons into heresy and blasphemy.

Now, before the Reformation many prayers of this kind were not only recited in private, but even in the public offices of some churches; and it would

---

[o] " Est tamen notandum, cum dicimus, non debere peti a Sanctis, nisi ut orent pro nobis, nos non agere de verbis, sed de sensu verborum. nam quantum ad verba, licet dicere: S. Petre miserere mei, salva me, aperi mihi aditum cœli · item da mihi sanitatem corporis, da patientiam, da mihi fortitudinem, &c. *dummodo intelligamus,* salva me, et miserere mei orando pro me, da mihi hoc et illud tuis precibus et meritis." Bellarminus de Sanct. Beatit. lib i c. 17.

not have been sufficient to abolish these prayers, if the invocation of saints to pray for us had been retained. For when erroneous notions of the power of saints had been engrafted on the mind of any person, it would have been impossible to eradicate them while the church continually supplied a ready and popular argument in favour of the ubiquity and universal intelligence of the saints by invoking them. The church of England was therefore justified in omitting the invocation of saints in her litany. First, because the litanies of all churches were devoid of them for seven centuries. Secondly, because they were unnecessary. Thirdly, because they were imprudent. And, fourthly, because they originated and promoted the danger of heresy and blasphemy. And on the same grounds we affirm, that it is the duty of all other churches to follow her example. Those catholic fathers, who in the fourth century invoked the saints, were too well instructed in the Christian faith, either to believe positively that the saints heard our prayers, or that they could aid us in any way except by their own; and they never contemplated the dangers of heresy and blasphemy into which this practice, originally intended for the promotion of piety, has led many of the simple and unlearned.

SECTION V.

THE LITANY.

O God the Father, of heaven : have mercy upon us miserable sinners.	Pater de cœlis Deus, miserere nobis.
O God the Son, Redeemer of the world : have mercy upon us miserable sinners.	Fili redemptor mundi Deus, miserere nobis.

O God the Holy Ghost, proceeding from the Father and the Son : have mercy upon us miserable sinners.

O holy, blessed, and glorious Trinity, three persons and one God have mercy upon us miserable sinners.

Remember not, Lord, our offences, nor the offences of our forefathers; neither take thou vengeance of our sins : spare us good Lord, spare thy people, whom thou hast redeemed with thy most precious blood, and be not angry with us for ever

Spare us, good Lord.

From all evil and mischief, from sin, from the crafts and assaults of the Devil : from thy

Spiritus Sancte Deus, miserere nobis.

Sancta Trinitas unus Deus, miserere nobis[p].

Ne reminiscaris Domine delicta nostra vel parentum nostrorum; neque vindictum sumas de peccatis nostris. Parce Domine, parce populo tuo quem redemisti precioso sanguine tuo, ne in æternum irascaris nobis[q].

Parce nobis Domine[r].

Ab omni malo[s]—A peccatis nostris[t]—Ab infestationibus dæmonum[u]—a ventura ira[v].—

---

[p] Breviar. Sarisb. fol. 59. pars hiemalis. These four invocations have been used for many centuries in the western litanies, they do not, however, occur in the eastern They may be considered as a paraphrase of the Kyrie eleeson, Christe eleëson, Kyrie eleeson, which have from the fifth or sixth century being recited at the beginning of the litany in the west. In the east, the form of Kyrie eleeson is much more ancient. The oldest litany in which I have found the words used in the text, is that of the Codex Chisii, printed by Bona, Rer. Lit. Appendix, p. 558. Martene de Antiq. Eccl Rit lib. i c. 4 art. 12 p 551 This MS. was written in the tenth century Bona, lib. i. c. 12. N°. 4.

[q] Breviar. Sarisb fol. 59. It was formerly used as an anthem at the end of the penitential psalms, which were frequently repeated before the litany. But I have seen ancient litanies, in which very nearly this form was placed at the beginning of the litany

[r] Breviar. Sarisb. fol. 60.

[s] Brev Sar. 60. Litania Anglica Octavi Sæculi ap. Mabillon, Anal tom. iii. p. 674.

[t] Brev. Trajectens, fol. 72.

[u] Brev. Sar. 60.

[v] Brev Eboracens, fol. 263

wrath, and from everlasting damnation,

Good Lord, deliver us.

From all blindness of heart; from pride, vain-glory, and hypocrisy; from envy, hatred, and malice, and all uncharitableness,—

From fornication, and all other deadly sin; and from all the deceits of the world, the flesh, and the devil,—

From lightning and tempest; from plague, pestilence, and famine; from battle and murder, and from sudden death,—

From all sedition, privy conspiracy, and rebellion; from all false doctrine, heresy, and schism; from hardness of heart, and contempt of thy Word and Commandment,—

By the mystery of thy holy Incarnation; by thy holy Nativity and Circumcision; by thy Baptism, Fasting, and Temptation,—

By thine agony and bloody Sweat; by thy Cross and Passion; by thy precious Death and Burial; by thy glorious Resurrection and Ascension, and by the coming of the Holy Ghost,—

a damnatione perpetua[w],

Libera nos Domine[x].

A cæcitate cordis[y]; a peste superbiæ[z]; ab appetitu inanis gloriæ[a]; ab ira et odio et omni mala voluntate.

A spiritu fornicationis[b]; a carnalibus desideriis[c]; ab insidiis diaboli.

A fulgure et tempestate[d]; ἀπὸ λοιμοῦ, λιμοῦ,—μαχαίρας[e]; a subitanea et improvisa morte[f].

Per mysterium sanctæ Incarnationis tuæ; per Nativitatem tuam, per sanctam Circumcisionem tuam; per Baptismum tuum; per jejunium tuum.

Per Crucem et Passionem tuam; per preciosam Mortem tuam; per gloriosam Resurrectionem tuam; per admirabilem Ascensionem tuam; per gratiam Spiritus Sancti.

---

[w] Brev. Sarisb. 60. Mabillon, p. 674.
[x] Brev. Sar. 60. Mabillon, 674. Brev. Ebor. 263.
[y] Ibid
[z] Brev. Ebor. fol. 263
[a] Brev. Sar. fol. 60
[b] Ibid.
[c] Brev. Ebor. fol. 263.
[d] Brev. Sar. fol. 60.
[e] Orationes Lucernarii apud Goar, Rit. Græc p. 42.
[f] Brev. Sar. fol. 60.

SECT. V. *Originals of the English Litany.* 295

In all time of our tribulation; in all time of our wealth; in the hour of death, and in the day of judgment,
  Good Lord, deliver us.

We sinners do beseech thee to hear us, O Lord God; and that it may please thee to rule and govern thy holy Church universal in the right way;
  We beseech thee to hear us, good Lord.

That it may please thee to keep and strengthen in the true worshipping of thee, in righteousness and holiness of life, thy Servant N, our most gracious King and Governor;

That it may please thee to rule his heart in thy faith, fear, and love, and that he may evermore have affiance in thee, and ever seek thy honour and glory,

That it may please thee to be his defender and keeper, giving him the victory over all his enemies;

That it may please thee to bless and preserve our gracious Queen N., and all the Royal Family;

In hora mortis succurre nobis Domine; in die judicii,

Libera nos Domine[g].

Peccatores te rogamus audi nos; ut Ecclesiam tuam regere et defensare digneris,

Te rogamus audi nos.

Ut Regi nostro et principibus nostris pacem et veram concordiam atque victoriam donare digneris[h]; ut Regem et Episcopum nostrum conservare digneris; ut vitam et sanitatem eis dones[i]

Ut Regi nostro .... victoriam donare digneris[k]—ὑπὲρ τῶν εὐσεβεστάτων καὶ Θεοφυλάκτων βασιλέων, κράτους, νίκης ... αὐτῶν[l].

Pro ... famula tua N. Imperatrice[m]—Ut ... principibus nostris pacem et veram concordiam ... donare digneris[n].

---

[g] Brev. Sar. fol. 60.
[h] Ibid.
[i] Litania Anglicanæ Ecclesiæ apud Mabillon. Analecta, tom. iii. p. 675.
[k] Brev Sar fol. 60.

[l] Goar, Rit. Græc. Orationes Lucernaris, p. 41.
[m] Missale Ambrosian apud Pamelii. Liturgic. tom. i. p. 331.
[n] Brev. Sar. fol. 60.

That it may please thee to illuminate all Bishops, Priests, and Deacons, with true knowledge and understanding of thy Word ; and that both by their preaching and living they may set it forth, and shew it accordingly ;

That it may please thee to endue the Lords of the Council, and all the Nobility, with grace, wisdom, and understanding ;

That it may please thee to bless and keep the Magistrates, giving them grace to execute justice, and to maintain truth ;

That it may please thee to bless and keep all thy people ;

That it may please thee to give to all nations unity, peace, and concord ,

That it may please thee to give us an heart to love and dread thee, and diligently to live after thy commandments ;

That it may please thee to give to all thy people increase of grace to hear meekly thy Word, and to receive it with pure affection, and to bring forth the fruits of the Spirit ,

Ut Episcopum nostrum et Prælatos nostros, et nos congregationes illis commissas, in tuo sancto servitio conservare digneris [o]—ὑπὲρ τῶν πρεσβυτέρων ἡμῶν δεηθῶμεν—ὑπὲρ πάσης τῆς ἐν Χριστῷ διακονίας [p].

Ὑπὲρ τῶν εὐσεβεστάτων καὶ Θεοφυλάκτων βασιλέων ἡμῶν, παντὸς τοῦ παλατίου, καὶ τοῦ στρατοπέδου αὐτῶν, τοῦ Κυρίου δεηθῶμεν [q].

Omnibus judicibus et cuncto exercitui . . vita et victoria [r].

Ut cunctum populum Christianum precioso sanguine tuo redemptum conservare digneris [s].

Ut populo Christiano pacem et unitatem largiri digneris [t]— ὑπὲρ τῆς εἰρηνῆς καὶ τῆς εὐσταθείας τοῦ κόσμου . . . δεηθῶμεν [u].

Ut gratiam Sancti Spiritus cordibus nostris clementer infundere digneris [v].

---

[o] Brev. Herefordens
[p] Apost. Const. lib. viii. c. 11.
[q] Goar, Rituale Græc p 65.
[r] Laudes Ecclesiæ Suessionensis, from a MS. seven hundred years old. Martene de Antiq. Eccl. Rit. tom. i. p. 365.
[s] Brev. Sar. fol. 60.
[t] Litania Anglica Mabillon. Analecta, p 675.
[u] Apost. Const. lib. viii. c. 11
[v] Menard. notæ in Sacr. Gre-

That it may please thee to bring into the way of truth all such as have erred, and are deceived;

That it may please thee to strengthen such as do stand; and to comfort and help the weak-hearted; and to raise up them that fall; and finally to beat down Satan under our feet;

That it may please thee to succour, help, and comfort, all that are in danger, necessity, and tribulation,

That it may please thee to preserve all that travel by land or by water, all women labouring of child, all sick persons, and young children; and to shew thy pity upon all prisoners and captives;

That it may please thee to defend, and provide for, the fatherless children, and widows, and all that are desolate and oppressed;

That it may please thee to have mercy upon all men;

That it may please thee to forgive our enemies, persecutors, and slanderers, and to turn their hearts;

Ut errantes ad viam salutis reducas[w].

Stantes confirma—conforta pusillanimes—lapsos erige[x]— τὸν Σατανᾶν καὶ πᾶσαν αὐτοῦ τὴν ἐνέργειαν καὶ πονηρίαν σύντριψον ὑπὸ τοὺς πόδας ἡμῶν[y].

Ἐξέλου τοὺς ἐν ἀνάγκαις[z].

Ὑπὲρ πλεόντων καὶ ὁδοιπορούντων δεηθῶμεν—ὑπὲρ τῶν ἐν ἀρρωστίᾳ ἐξεταζομένων ἀδελφῶν ἡμῶν δεηθῶμεν—τῶν νηπίων τῆς ἐκκλησίας μνημονεύσωμεν[a]—Ut miserias pauperum et captivorum intueri et relevare digneris[b].

Ὑπὲρ χηρῶν τε καὶ ὀρφανῶν δεηθῶμεν[c]—.

Ὑπὲρ ἐχθρῶν καὶ μισούντων ἡμᾶς δεηθῶμεν· ὑπὲρ τῶν διωκόντων ἡμᾶς διὰ τὸ ὄνομα τοῦ Κυρίου δεηθῶμεν· ὅπως ὁ Κύριος πραΰνας

---

gorii, p. 157. from a litany a thousand years old.

[w] Litania Lugdunensis Ecclesiæ, from a MS. six hundred years old. Martene de Antiq. Eccl. Discipl. in Div. Officiis, p. 521.

[x] Liturgia Cyrilli Renaudot

Liturg. Oriental tom. i. p 45. Marci, p. 153.

[y] Liturgia Marci Renaudot, p. 152.

[z] Ibid. p. 153.

[a] Apost Const. lib. viii. c 11.

[b] Brev Sar. fol. 60.

[c] Apost. Const. as before.

That it may please thee to give and preserve to our use the kindly fruits of the earth, so as in due time we may enjoy them;

That it may please thee to give us true repentance; to forgive us all our sins, negligences, and ignorances; and to endue us with the grace of thy Holy Spirit, to amend our lives according to thy holy Word;

We beseech thee to hear us, good Lord.

Son of God, we beseech thee to hear us.

O Lamb of God, that takest away the sins of the world;

Grant us thy peace.

O Lamb of God, that takest away the sins of the world;

Have mercy upon us.

O Christ, hear us.

Lord, have mercy upon us.

Christ, have mercy upon us.

Lord, have mercy upon us.

Our Father, which art in heaven, &c.

τὸν θυμὸν αὐτῶν διασκεδάσῃ τὸν καθ' ἡμῶν ὀργήν [d].

Ut fructus terræ dare et conservare digneris [e].

Ut nobis veram pœnitentiam concedas agere [f]—Ut remissionem omnium peccatorum nostrorum nobis donare digneris [g]—Ut gratiam Sancti Spiritus cordibus nostris infundere digneris—ut locum pœnitentiæ nobis concedas [h],

Te rogamus audi nos [i].

Fili Dei te rogamus audi nos [j].

Agnus Dei qui tollis peccata mundi, exaudi nos Domine.

Agnus Dei qui tollis peccata mundi miserere nobis.

Christe audi nos.
Kyrie eleison.
Christe eleison.
Kyrie eleison [k].

Pater noster, qui es in cœlis, &c. [l]

---

[d] Apost. Const. as before.
[e] Brev. Sar. fol. 60.
[f] Litan. Angl. Mabillon, p. 676.
[g] Brev. Ebor. fol. 263.
[h] Bona, Rer. Lit. p. 564. from the Codex Chisii of the tenth century.
[i] Brev. Sar. 60. Brev. Ebor.

Herefordens, &c. &c. Menard conjectures, that the words "audi nos" did not form part of the response originally; see notæ in Gregor. Sacr. p. 157, 158.

[j] Brev. Sar. fol. 60. Mabillon, p. 676.
[k] Ibid.   [l] Ibid.

O Lord, deal not with us after our sins

Neither reward us after our iniquities.

O God, merciful Father, that despisest not the sighing of a contrite heart, nor the desire of such as be sorrowful; Mercifully assist our prayers that we make before thee in all our troubles and adversities, whensoever they oppress us; and graciously hear us, that those evils, which the craft and subtilty of the Devil or man worketh against us, be brought to nought; and by the providence of thy goodness they may be dispersed; that we thy servants, being hurt by no persecutions, may evermore give thanks unto thee in thy holy Church; through Jesus Christ our Lord.

O Lord, arise, help us, and deliver us for thy Name's sake.

O God, we have heard with our ears, and our Fathers have declared unto us, the noble works that thou didst in their days, and in the old time before them.

O Lord, arise, help us, and deliver us for thine honour.

Domine non secundum peccata nostra facias nobis.

Neque secundum iniquitates nostras retribuas nobis[m].

Deus qui contritorum non despicis gemitum, et mœrentium non spernis affectum; adesto precibus nostris quas pietati tuæ pro tribulatione nostra offerimus, implorantes ut nos clementer respicies, et solito pietatis tuæ intuitu tribuas, ut quicquid contra nos diabolicæ fraudes atque humanæ moliuntur adversitates, ad nihilum redigas, et consilio misericordiæ tuæ allidas, quatenus nullis adversitatibus læsi, sed ab omni tribulatione et angustia liberati, gratias tibi in Ecclesia referamus consolati. Per[n].

Exurge Domine adjuva nos et libera nos propter nomen tuum. Alleluia.

Deus auribus nostris audivimus patresque nostri annunciaverunt nobis, opus quod operatus es in diebus eorum, et in diebus antiquis.

Exurge Domine adjuva nos et libera nos propter nomen tuum. Alleluia.

---

[m] Brev. Sar. fol. 60. Brev. Ebor. fol. 263.

[n] Miss. Sarisb. Commune, fol. xxi. Missa de tribulatione cordis. Miss. Leofr. Exon. Episcopi. Missa Illyrici Bona, Rer. Lit. p. 538.

Glory be to the Father, and to the Son and to the Holy Ghost;

As it was in the beginning, is now, and ever shall be world without end. Amen.

From our enemies defend us, O Christ.

Graciously look upon our afflictions.

Pitifully behold the sorrows of our hearts.

Mercifully forgive the sins of thy people.

Favourably with mercy hear our prayers.

O Son of David, have mercy upon us.

Both now and ever vouchsafe to hear us, O Christ.

Graciously hear us, O Christ; graciously hear us, O Lord Christ

O Lord, let thy mercy be shewed upon us;

As we do put our trust in thee.

We humbly beseech thee, O Father, mercifully to look upon our infirmities; and for the Glory of thy Name turn from us all those evils that we most righteously have deserved; and grant, that in all our

Gloria Patri, et Filio, et Spiritui Sancto.

Sicut erat in principio, et nunc, et semper, et in sæcula sæculorum. Amen[o].

Ab inimicis nostris defende nos Christe.

Afflictionem nostram benignus vide.

Dolorem cordis nostri respice clemens.

Peccata populi tui pius indulge.

Orationes nostras pius exaudi.

Fili Dei vivi miserere nobis.

Hic et in perpetuum nos custodire digneris Christe.

Exaudi nos Christe, exaudi exaudi nos Christe[p].

Fiat misericordia tua Domine super nos.

Quemadmodum speravimus in te[q].

Infirmitatem nostram quæsumus Domine propitius respice, et mala omnia quæ juste meremur, omnium Sanctorum tuorum intercessionibus averte. Per Christum Dominum[r].

---

[o] This was chanted at the beginning of the litany, on the second day of rogations, in the church of Salisbury. See Processionale Sarisb fol. 99. Antwerp 1525.

[p] Processionale Sarisb. fol.

113. This was said in the litany on St. Mark's day.

[q] Anglo-Saxon Office for prime, in Hickes's Letters.

[r] Processionale Sarisb. fol. 114.

troubles we may put our whole trust and confidence in thy mercy, and evermore serve thee in holiness and pureness of living, to thy honour and glory; through our only Mediator and Advocate, Jesus Christ our Lord. *Amen.*

Almighty God, who hast given us grace at this time with one accord, &c.

The grace of our Lord Jesus Christ, and the love of God, &c.[s]

SECTION VI.

PRAYERS AND THANKSGIVINGS UPON SEVERAL OCCASIONS.

In speaking of the litany, I have already noticed the antiquity and propriety of making special prayers and supplications, and of returning due thanks to God on occasions of peculiar importance. The prayers which I proceed to consider, are those which the church of this empire appoints for several occasions, and which are directed to be said before the two final prayers of the litany, or of morning and evening prayer. When processions were customary in this church, such collects as those which we use were repeated, as now, at the end of the litany[t]; this position is therefore of considerable antiquity. The church of Constantinople has from time immemorial adopted a similar custom, as we may see in the Greek Euchologium, where the precatory anthems and prayers for particular occasions

---

[s] See the end of morning and evening prayer.

[t] Processionale Sarisb fol 168. "Cum Letania et Collecta."

are directed to be repeated after the general office for the litany[u]. I now proceed to notice the different formularies of this nature which occur in the English ritual.

For Rain.

This prayer, (with the exception of its introduction,) and the next also, bear some resemblance to those which occur in Gregory's sacramentary on similar occasions, and which had been used in England from a period of remote antiquity.

O God, heavenly Father, who by thy Son Jesus Christ hast promised to all them that seek thy kingdom, and the righteousness thereof, all things necessary to their bodily sustenance; Send us, we beseech thee, in this our necessity, such moderate rain and showers, that we may receive the fruits of the earth to our comfort, and to thy honour; through Jesus Christ our Lord. *Amen.*

Deus in quo vivimus movemur et sumus, pluviam nobis tribue congruentem, ut præsentibus subsidiis sufficienter adjuti, sempiterna fiducialius appetamus. Per Dominum[v],

For Fair Weather.

O Almighty Lord God—— We humbly beseech thee, that although we for our iniquities have worthily deserved a plague of rain and waters, yet upon our true repentance thou wilt send us such weather, as that

Ad te nos Domine clamantes exaudi, et aeris serenitatem nobis tribue supplicantibus, ut qui juste pro peccatis nostris affligimur, misericordia tua præveniente clementiam sentiamus. Per Dominum[w].

---

[u] Goar, Rituale Græcum, p. 766, 771, &c.

[v] Menard. Sacramentar. Gregorii, p. 221. Missale Sarisb. fol. 22 Commune. Missale

MS. Leofric. fol. 229.

[w] Sacr. Gregorii, p. 222. Miss. Sar. fol. 22. MS. Leofr. 229.

we may receive the fruits of the earth in due season; and learn both by thy punishment to amend our lives, and for thy clemency to give thee praise and glory, through Jesus Christ our Lord, Amen.

In the time of Dearth and Famine.

These prayers are not unlike those used in the church of Constantinople on occasions of drought and famine.

O God, heavenly Father, whose gift it is, that the rain doth fall, the earth is fruitful, beasts increase, and fishes do multiply; Behold, we beseech thee, the afflictions of thy people; and grant that the scarcity and dearth, which we do now most justly suffer for our iniquity, may through thy goodness be mercifully turned into cheapness and plenty; for the love of Jesus Christ our Lord, to whom with thee and the Holy Ghost be all honour and glory, now and for ever. Amen.

Κύριε ὁ Θεὸς ὁ παντοκράτωρ ὁ ἀνάγων νεφέλας ἐξ ἐσχάτου τῆς γῆς, ὁ ἀστραπὰς εἰς ὑετὸν πεποιηκὼς—σου δεόμεθα καὶ σὲ ἱκετεύομεν ἐξομολογούμενοι τὰς ἁμαρτίας ἡμῶν, καὶ αἰτούμενοι τὸ παρά σου πλούσιον ἔλεος—ἐξάγαγε ἡμῖν ἄρτον εἰς βρῶσιν, καὶ χλόην τοῖς κτήνεσι. πρόσδεξαι τὰς δεήσεις παντὸς τοῦ λαοῦ σου, καὶ μὴ ἀπώσῃ τοὺς στηναγμοὺς τῶν πενήτων, μὴ τῷ θυμῷ σου ἐλέγξῃς ἡμᾶς, μηδὲ τῇ ὀργῇ σου παιδεύσῃς ἡμᾶς· μηδὲ διαφθείρῃς λιμῷ καὶ δίψει τὸν λαόν σου—καὶ σοὶ τὴν δόξαν ἀναπέμπομεν, τῷ Πατρὶ, καὶ τῷ Υἱῷ, καὶ τῷ Ἁγίῳ Πνεύματι· νῦν καὶ ἀεὶ, καὶ εἰς τοὺς αἰῶνας τῶν αἰώνων. Ἀμήν[x].

O God, merciful Father, who, in the time of Elisha the prophet, didst suddenly in Samaria turn great scarcity and dearth into plenty and cheapness, Have mercy upon us,

Δέσποτα Κύριε ὁ Θεὸς ἡμῶν, ὁ διὰ τὸν πρὸς σὲ ζῆλον ἐπακούσας Ἠλίου τοῦ Θεσβίτου, καὶ τὸν κατὰ καιρὸν τῇ γῇ πεμπόμενον ὑετὸν ἐπισχεθῆναι κελεύσας, εἶτα πάλιν διὰ τῆς αὐτοῦ ἱκεσίας ὄμβρον καρ-

---

[x] Goar, Rituale Græc. p 777

that we, who are now for our sins punished with like adversity, may likewise find a seasonable relief; Increase the fruits of the earth by thy heavenly benediction — through Jesus Christ our Lord. *Amen.*

ποφόρον αὐτῇ χαρισάμενος· αὐτὸς δέσποτα—τὰ πεπλημμελημένα ἡμῖν παριδῶν—εὔφρανον τὸ πρόσωπον τῆς γῆς διὰ τοὺς πτωχοὺς τοῦ λαοῦ σου,—καὶ τὰ ἄλλα πάντα κ τ.λ [y]

In time of War and Tumults.

This collect seems to resemble one which occurs in the ancient English offices and in the sacramentary of Gregory.

O Almighty God, King of kings, and Governor of all things, whose power no creature is able to resist, to whom it belongeth justly to punish sinners, and to be merciful to them that repent; Save and deliver us, we humbly beseech thee, from the hands of our enemies;—that we, being armed with thy defence, may be preserved evermore from all perils, to glorify thee, who art the only giver of all victory; through the merits of thy only Son, Jesus Christ our Lord. *Amen.*

Deus, regnorum omnium, regumque dominator, qui nos et percutiendo sanas, et ignoscendo conservas, prætende nobis misericordiam tuam, ut tranquillitate pacis, tua potestate firmata, ad remedia correctionis utamur. Per [z]

In time of Plague or Sickness.

This collect does not resemble in its allusions any that I have met in the offices of the Greek or Latin churches, though many prayers on a similar occasion are to be found[a].

---

[y] Goar, Rituale Græc. p 776
[z] Sacr. Gregorii, p. 214
Miss Sar. fol 23.
[a] Sacr. Gregorii, p. 218, &c.
Goar, Rit Græc. p 792, &c.

For Ember Weeks.

These collects are, I apprehend, peculiar to the English ritual.

A Prayer that may be said after any of the former.

This collect occurs in the sacramentary of Gregory, and in the most ancient monuments of the English offices.

O God, whose nature and property is ever to have mercy and to forgive, receive our humble petitions; and though we be tied and bound with the chain of our sins, yet let the pitifulness of thy great mercy loose us; for the honour of Jesus Christ, our Mediator and Advocate. *Amen*	Deus cui proprium est misereri semper et parcere, suscipe deprecationem nostram. et quos delictorum catena constringit, miseratio tuæ pietatis absolvat. Per Dominum nostrum[b].

A Prayer for the High Court of Parliament, to be read during their Session.

Such a prayer as this of course cannot be expected to have occurred in any of the primitive offices, but it is perfectly consistent with the practice of the catholic church, which has ever obeyed the apostolic precept of praying for kings, and for all that are in authority. The appellation of "most religious and "gracious king" corresponds with those high titles of respect and veneration which the primitive church gave to the Christian emperors and kings; thus in the liturgy of Basil it is said, Μνήσθητι κύριε τῶν εὐσεβεστάτων, καὶ πιστοτάτων ἡμῶν βασιλέων—Μνήσθητι κύριε πάσης ἀρχῆς καὶ ἐξουσίας, καὶ τῶν ἐν παλατίῳ ἀδελφῶν ἡμῶν, καὶ παντὸς τοῦ στρατοπέδου[c].

[b] Sacr. Greg. p. 204. MS. Leofric. fol. 325. Brev. Sarisb. fol 61.
[c] Liturgia Basilii Goar, Rituale Græc. p. 171.

A Prayer for all Conditions of Men, to be used at such times when the Litany is not appointed to be said.

This excellent prayer is not unlike the "Orationes "generales" which are found in the ancient monuments of the English church[d], and which, like this, comprise petitions for all estates of men. The likeness is not however sufficiently strong to induce me to occupy space by transcribing the formularies alluded to.

THANKSGIVINGS.

A General Thanksgiving.

This excellent prayer does not seem to have been derived in any way from the ancient offices of the English church, nor from any other western formularies. A prayer however, at the beginning of the very ancient Coptic liturgy of Basil, seems to bear some resemblance to it.

Almighty God, Father of all mercies, we thine unworthy servants do give thee most humble and hearty thanks for all thy goodness and lovingkindness to us, and to all men. We bless thee for our creation, preservation, and all the blessings of this life; but above all, for thine inestimable love in the redemption of the world by our Lord Jesus Christ; for the means of grace, and for the hope of glory. And, we beseech thee, give us that due sense of all thy mercies,

Domine Deus omnipotens, Pater Domini Dei et Salvatoris nostri Jesu Christi, gratias agimus de omnibus et propter omnia, et in omnibus, quia protexisti nos, adjuvasti nos, conservasti nos, suscepisti nos ad te, et misertus es nostri; auxilium dedisti nobis, et ad hanc horam perduxisti. Ea propter petimus et obsecramus bonitatem tuam, ô amator hominum, ut concedas nobis hunc diem sanctum, et omnes dies vitæ nostræ in pace cum timore tuo transigere—per gra-

---

[d] Miss. Sar. Commune, fol. 34, &c. MS. Leofric. fol. 236, 262.

that our hearts may be unfeignedly thankful, and that we may shew forth thy praise, not only with our lips, but in our lives; by giving up ourselves to thy service, and by walking before thee in holiness and righteousness all our days; through Jesus Christ our Lord, to whom with thee and the Holy Ghost be all honour and glory, world without end. *Amen.*

tiam et misericordiam, amoremque erga homines Filii tui unigeniti, Domini Dei et Salvatoris nostri Jesu Christi, per quem tibi debetur honor, gloria, et imperium, cum ipso et Spiritu Sancto vivificante, tibique consubstantiali, nunc et semper et in omnia sæcula sæculorum Amen[e].

Occasional Thanksgivings.

The English ritual, I believe, is the only one which contains special thanksgivings for the mercies of God, others having confined themselves to general expressions of gratitude on all such occasions. It has therefore, in the present case, improved on the ancient customs of the Christian church, instead of being in any way inconsistent with them.

[e] Liturgia Basilii Coptice Renaudot, Liturg. Oriental. tom. i p 2.

CHAPTER III.

COLLECTS, EPISTLES, AND GOSPELS.

BEFORE I proceed to ascertain the antiquity of this portion of our ritual, I would observe, that the collects, and the lessons which we now call Epistles and Gospels, were originally recited from two books, the former entitled the Sacramentary, the latter the Lectionary. These two books, with a third called Antiphonary, contained the whole service for the Eucharist. The *Sacramentary* comprised the collects and the canon or prayers that never varied[a]. The *Lectionary* consisted of lessons from the Old and New Testaments, corresponding to our Law, Epistles, and Gospels[b]: and the *Antiphonary* supplied the anthems or verses for the beginning of the communion, the offertory, &c.[c] About the eleventh or twelfth century it was found convenient generally to unite these three books, and the volume obtained the name of the Complete or Plenary Missal, or Book of Missæ[d]. Of this description were almost all

---

[a] See Zaccaria, Bibliotheca Ritualis, tom. 1. p. 39, &c.

[b] The *Lectionary*, sometimes called "Comes," or "Liber Comitis," often contained the Gospels as well as the other lessons; but generally the Gospels were read from a separate volume, entitled, "Evangelistarium," or "Evangeliarium." See Zaccaria, p. 35--39.

[c] The *Antiphonary* was often called "Graduale," because some of the anthems were chanted on the steps (*gradus*) of the ambon, or pulpit. Zaccaria, p. 28, &c.

[d] Zaccaria, p. 49, 50.

the liturgical books of the western churches, and the arrangement is still preserved in our own.

The eastern churches have no sacramentaries, because they do not employ different prefaces and collects for different days, but make use of several liturgies, each of which is appropriated to a particular season of the year. The lessons and anthems are by them recited from distinct lectionaries and anthem books[e].

COLLECTS.

The origin of collects, or prayers read before or between the lessons during the celebration of the liturgy, is involved in obscurity. Such prayers have certainly been used in all the western churches from a remote period; for we not only find them in the earliest monuments of the Roman liturgy, and of all which adopted that rite, but even in those of Gaul and Spain. None such occur in the ancient liturgies of Jerusalem, Antioch, Cæsarea, or Constantinople; but they appear in the same position as in the western liturgies in that of the Monophysites of Alexandria[f]; and we conclude that they must have been used in the Alexandrian liturgy prior to the council of Chalcedon, A. D. 451. because the liturgy of the orthodox of that church gives plain signs of having been altered from one resembling in this respect that of the Monophysites[g]; and such resemblance must have been caused by the derivation of both from a common original, before their total

[e] See Zaccaria, p. 17, 18. Cave's second Dissertation, at the end of his "Historia Literaria," contains an account of all the ritual books of the Greek church, in alphabetical order.

[f] Liturgia Basilii Copt. Renaudot, Liturg. Oriental. tom. i. p. 2—8.

[g] Liturgia Marci, *ibid*. p. 131—137.

separation at that time. We have also Cassian's testimony that collects were recited in his time, amongst the psalms and lessons of morning and evening prayer, by the Egyptians [h]: and Athanasius, in more than one place, seems plainly to allude to the existence of the same practice in his time, or early in the fourth century[i]. There is therefore a high degree of probability that the collects of the Alexandrian liturgy are of great antiquity. The use of collects is certainly very ancient in the west, but they probably cannot be traced so far as those of Alexandria. The latter indeed look much as if they were the models on which those of Rome and other western churches were formed; and if I were to hazard a conjecture on the origin of collects, I should say that they were introduced from Alexandria. We know certainly that the eastern Christians at an early period devised many improvements in the mode of celebrating divine service, which did not occur to the less lively and inventive imaginations of their brethren in the west; and that the latter were accustomed to imitate the former in their rites and ceremonies[j]. A time came, however, when

[h] Cassian. Instit lib ii c. 5, 6, &c.

[i] See the passages quoted above in chap. i part 1. §. 16.

[j] Thus the custom of alternate chanting, according to which the choir were divided into two parts, who sang alternately, was brought from the east by Ambrose, according to Paulinus and Augustine. The council of Toledo, A D. 589, introduced the Constantinopolitan Creed into the liturgy, in accordance with the eastern churches. "Constituit synodus ut per omnes ecclesias Hispaniæ et Galliciæ, secundum formam orientalium ecclesiarum, concilii Constantinopolitani, hoc est 150 episcoporum, symbolum fidei decantetur." Concil. iii. Toletan. can. 2. This custom was followed afterwards at Rome. Bona, Rer. Lit. lib. ii. c 8. p. 387. The form *Kyrie eleeson* was evidently derived from the east, and the council of Vaison, directing it to be used,

the tide of invention turned, and innumerable additions and alterations began to be originated in the west, while the eastern rites continued with little variation from age to age.

It has been thought that the collects originally did not vary with each celebration of the liturgy, but were always the same; and the office for Good Friday, or Parasceve in the ancient Roman sacramentary, where there are several collects for the clergy, people, heretics, Jews, infidels[k], &c. has been pointed out as a relic of the primitive custom. Augustine seems to allude to some such custom in his epistle to Vitalis of Carthage, who affirmed that we ought not to pray for unbelievers. " Employ thy
" disputations against the prayers of the church ; and
" when thou hearest the priest of God at the altar
" exhorting the people to pray for the unbelieving,
" that God may convert them to the faith ; and for
" the catechumens, that he may breathe into them a
" desire for regeneration ; and for the faithful, that
" by his grace they may persevere in that which they
" have begun to be, then ridicule the pious words[1]."

refers to the custom of the east. Concil. ii. Vasens. can. 3. Litanies and processions were also introduced from the east. Gregory the Great certainly imitated the liturgy of Constantinople in placing the Lord's Prayer immediately after the Roman canon ; and the circumstance gave great offence to some who were zealous for the superiority of the see of Rome above that of Constantinople Gregorii Mag. Epist. lib. ix. Epist. 12. p. 940. tom. ii. oper. edit. Benedictin.

[k] Menard Sacram. Gregorii p. 61, &c

[1] " Exerce contra orationes ecclesiæ disputationes tuas, et quando audis sacerdotem Dei ad altare exhortantem populum Dei orare pro incredulis, ut eos Deus convertat ad fidem ; et pro catechumenis, ut eis desiderium regenerationis inspiret; et pro fidelibus, ut in eo quod esse cœperunt, ejus munere perseverent, subsanna pias voces." August. Epist. ad Vitalem Carthag.

Cœlestinus of Rome, about the same time, speaks of prayers resembling those mentioned by Augustine[m]. The ancient Leonian sacramentary, used in the Roman church in the fifth century, contains several collects for each feast, sometimes four or five; and the Irish sacramentary, originally derived from the Roman, contained several collects for different estates of men, which did not vary[n]. It is so difficult, however, to reconcile the idea of the invariableness of collects with the directions of the African church in the fourth and fifth centuries, which prohibited the use of collects, &c. that were not approved by competent authority[o], evidently permitting any new collects that should be so approved; and with the variety of collects seen in the most ancient sacramentaries of Rome, Milan, &c. that I am inclined to think the variation of collects has been customary in the west from a most remote period; and the words of Augustine and Cœlestinus probably relate to some peculiar offices.

I now proceed to consider the antiquity of those individual collects which are found in the English

---

[m] Cœlestinus in Epistola ad Galliar. episcopos de gratia Dei pro Prospero et Hilario, c. 11.

[n] See Dissertation on Liturgies, section xi.

[o] *De precibus ad altare dicendis* canon ciii. "Placuit etiam hoc, ut preces quæ probatæ fuerint in concilio, sive præfationes, sive commendationes, seu manus impositiones, ab omnibus celebrentur, nec aliæ omnino contra fidem præferantur, sed quæcumque a prudentioribus fuerint collectæ dicantur." Labbe, Concilia, tom. ii. p. 1117. See also Concil. African. can. 70. Labbe, tom. ii. p. 1662. "Preces" here mean collects, "præfationes" prefaces; "commendationes" refer to the part after "hanc igitur," in the canon of the ancient Roman liturgy, which was often varied on special occasions, Bona, Rer. Lit. p. 438. "Manus impositiones" signified the long benedictions before communion. See Bona, Rer. Lit. p. 465, &c.

ritual. The majority of these occur in the Latin language, in the ancient missals of Salisbury, York, Hereford, &c. and they are also in the sacramentaries of the English church, written before the Norman Conquest. We meet them in all the ancient MSS. of Gregory's sacramentary, as used in the Roman, Italian, and other western churches, and thence shew that they formed part of that sacramentary when it was introduced into England by Augustine, first archbishop of Canterbury; and in consequence, that they have been used by the church in this country for above twelve hundred years. Many of the collects, however, are much more ancient than the time of Gregory, A. D. 590; they occur in the sacramentary of Gelasius, patriarch of Rome A.D. 494, and some may be traced to the Leonian sacramentary, used in the Roman church about A. D. 483. In the following pages I have placed in parallel columns the English text of our collects, and the Latin, extracted from the ancient liturgical offices of the church of Salisbury, with which those of York and Hereford almost always agree[p]. I have also cited a manuscript sacramentary of the Anglo-Saxon church, written probably about the ninth or tenth century, and given by Leofric, bishop of Exeter, to his church before the Norman Conquest[q]. I have likewise referred to the sacramentary of Gregory, as published by Menard. When references to the above three monuments are appended to any collect, we may fairly consider it to have formed part of the sacramentary of Gregory

[p] For notices of these ancient English rites, see Dissertation, section xi

[q] Now in the Bodleian Library.

A. D. 590, and may conclude that it has been used in the English church for above twelve hundred years. When to these references I have subjoined another to the sacramentary of Gelasius, the collect to which it is appended may be considered as old as the year 494. Those collects which I have traced to the sacramentary of Leo are much more ancient than the time of Gelasius, and may be referred to the end of the fourth, or the earlier part of the fifth century[r]. I have also occasionally quoted the sacramentary or missal of Ambrose, or more properly of the church of Milan. This sacramentary has been different from that of Rome from a most remote period, and though the liturgy of Milan was originally derived from Rome[s], yet the latter church may afterwards have borrowed from the sacramentary of the former some of those collects which are found in both, and have been so long used in the church of England. I have also had occasion to refer to the sacramentaries of the ancient Gallican church, which were in use before the emperor Charlemagne introduced the Roman liturgy into France[t].

THE EPISTLES AND GOSPELS.

In another part of this work the reader will find some remarks on the antiquity of the custom of reading lessons from scripture in the Christian liturgy[u]. I have there remarked on the custom of the English church, of continually reading the same portion of the Law, containing the Decalogue, be-

---

[r] For an account of the sacramentaries of Gelasius and Leo, see Dissertation, section vi.

[s] See Dissertation, sect. vii.
[t] See Dissertation, section ix.
[u] Chap. iv. sect. ii. iv. v.

CHAP. III. *Antiquity of English Epistles and Gospels.* 315

fore the other lessons[v]. In addition to this lesson from the Law, two others are taken from the Prophets, the Epistles of Paul, the catholic Epistles, the Acts of the holy Apostles, and the Gospels. The first being frequently taken from St. Paul's Epistles, and the second always from the Gospels, they have long currently obtained the names of "the "Epistle and the Gospel."

Almost all our Epistles and Gospels have been appropriated to their present situations for a great length of time. They are appointed for the same occasions in the most ancient monuments of the English church. In the succeeding pages I have traced the Epistles and Gospels now used by the church of England to her ancient liturgies. I have thought it sufficient to refer to the missal or sacramentary of the church of Sarum, because it generally agrees with those of Hereford and York, and was commonly used in England. I have traced these lessons to a period antecedent to the Norman Conquest, by means of the manuscript of Leofric before referred to[w]: and, finally, by means of the ancient Lectionarium or Comes of the Roman church, published by Pamelius[x], I have shewn that they

---

[v] Chapter iv. sect. ii

[w] The beginning words of each epistle and gospel are inserted in the margin of this manuscript by some later hand than that which wrote the text: but the character of these annotations is so ancient, that we are justified in referring them to a period long prior to the Norman Conquest.

[x] Pamelii Liturgicon, tom. ii. I have referred to this lectionary, which bears the name of "Comes Hieronymi" in the work of Pamelius, because it seems to be at least as old as any other ancient Roman lectionary that has been published. Jerome is said to have arranged the lectionary of the Roman church, but as this only rests on the authority of writers of the eleventh or twelfth century, it is not worthy of attention

were brought to this country by Augustine, archbishop of Canterbury, and consequently have been used in the church of England, as at present, for more than twelve hundred years.

Before I conclude these introductory remarks, I wish to explain the manner in which the Epistles and Gospels are referred to in the following pages. I have only thought it necessary to insert the chapter and verse which mark the commencement of those lessons in the English ritual, because any one may immediately refer to them in the Prayer Book. In like manner I have only extracted the title, and the beginning and concluding words of the corresponding passage in the ancient lectionaries, &c. because any one with a Latin Bible can easily find the original.

CHAP. III.   *Originals of the English Collects, &c.*   317

COLLECTS, EPISTLES, AND GOSPELS.

THE FIRST SUNDAY IN ADVENT[a].

THE EPISTLE. Rom. xiii. 8. Lectio Epistolæ beati Pauli Apostoli   Ad Romanos xiii. Fratres scientes quia hora est . sed induemini Dominum Jesum Christum[b].

THE GOSPEL. St. Matthew xxi. 1. Evangelium secundum Mattheum xxi. In illo tempore cum appropinquasset ...... benedictus qui venit in nomine Domini[c].

THE SECOND SUNDAY IN ADVENT[d].

THE EPISTLE. Romans xv. 4. Ad Romanos xv. Quæcumque enim scripta   .. et virtute Spiritus Sancti[e].

---

[a] A post-communion prayer for Advent, in the sacramentary of Gelasius, seems to resemble the collect. "Preces populi tui, quæsumus Domine, clementer exaudi: ut qui de adventu Unigeniti tui secundum carnem lætantur; in secundo cum venerit in majestate sua, præmium æternæ vitæ percipiant. Per." Gelasii Sacr. Muratori, Liturg Rom. Vet. tom. i. p. 683. Ambros Sacr. ap. Pamel. Liturgic. tom. i. p 441. MS. Leofr. fol. 154. The introduction of this collect is evidently derived from the Epistle.

[b] Miss. Sarisb. Dom. 1 Adv. fol. x.

[c] Miss. Sarisb. fol. xi.

[d] The collect is founded on the epistle. In the liturgy of S. James, there is a good collect after the reading of the scriptures, which may be thought to merit transcription. Ὁ ἐνηχήσας ἡμᾶς Θεὸς τὰ θεῖα σου λόγια καὶ σωτήρια, φώτισον τὰς ψυχὰς ἡμῶν τῶν ἁμαρτωλῶν εἰς τὴν τῶν προλεχθέντων κατάληψιν, ὡς μὴ μόνον ἀκροατὰς ὀφθῆναι τῶν πνευματικῶν ᾀσμάτων, ἀλλὰ καὶ ποιητὰς πράξεων ἀγαθῶν, πίστιν μετερχομένους ἀνύπουλον, βίον ἄμεμπτον, πολιτείαν ἀνέγκλητον. In the very next prayer part of our collect is embodied. Δέσποτα ζωοποιὲ, καὶ τῶν ἀγαθῶν χορηγὲ, ὁ δοὺς τοῖς ἀνθρώποις τὴν μακαρίαν ἐλπίδα τῆς αἰωνίου ζωῆς, τὸν κύριον ἡμῶν Ἰησοῦν Χριστὸν, κ. τ. λ. Lit. Jacobi Assemani Cod Lit. tom. v. p. 14, 15.

[e] Miss Sarisb fol. xii. Dom. 2. Adventus.

THE GOSPEL. St. Luke xxi. 25. Secundum Lucam xxi. Erunt signa in sole .. verba autem mea non transibunt[f].

THE THIRD SUNDAY IN ADVENT[g].

THE EPISTLE. 1 Cor. iv. 1. Ad Corinthios 1. iv. Sic nos existimet homo ut ministros Christi . laus erit unicuique à Deo[h].

THE GOSPEL. St. Matt. xi. 2. Secundum Matthæum xi. Cum audisset Joannes . qui præparabit viam tuam ante te[i].

THE FOURTH SUNDAY IN ADVENT.

THE COLLECT. O Lord, raise up we pray thee thy power, and come among us, and with great might succour us; that whereas, through our sins and wickedness, we are sore let and hindered in running the race that is set before us, thy bountiful grace and mercy may speedily help and deliver us; through the satisfaction of thy Son our Lord, to whom with thee and the Holy Ghost be honour and glory, world without end. *Amen.*

Excita, quæsumus, Domine potentiam tuam et veni, et magna nobis virtute succurre; ut per auxilium gratiæ tuæ quod nostra peccata præpediunt, indulgentia tuæ propitiationis acceleret. Qui vivis et regnas cum Deo Patre[j].

---

[f] Miss. Sar. fol. xii.

[g] This collect resembles some very ancient prayers for Advent. "Excita Domine *corda* nostra ad *præparandas* Unigeniti tui *vias*, ut per ejus adventum purificatis tibi mentibus servire mereamur Qui tecum vivit et regnat," &c. Miss Sar. Dom. 2. Advent. fol. xii MS. Leofr. 150. "Conscientias nostras quæsumus, Omnipotens Deus, cotidie visitando purifica; ut *veniente Domino Filio tuo,* paratam sibi in nobis inveniat mansionem" Gelas Sacr. Murat. tom. i. p. 681. Gregorii Sacr. Menard. p. 202. Ambros. Sacr. Pamel. tom. 1. p. 443. MS. Sacrament. Leofr. fol. 154.

[h] Miss. Sar. Dom. 3 Adv. fol. xiii.

[i] Miss. Sar. Dom. 3. Adv. fol. xiii.

[j] Miss. Sar. Dom. 4. Adventus, fol. xv, MS. Leofr. fol. 153; Sacr. Gelasii, Murat. tom. i p. 680; Gregorii, Menard. p. 201, Ambrosii, Pamel. tom i. p. 445.

CHAP. III. *Originals of the English Collects, &c.* 319

THE EPISTLE. Phil. iv. 4. Ad Philippenses iv. Gaudete in Domino... et intelligentias vestras in Christo Jesu Domino nostro[k].

THE GOSPEL. St. John i. 19. Secundum Johannem primo. Miserunt Judæi... ubi erat Joannes baptizans[l].

THE NATIVITY OF OUR LORD[m].

THE EPISTLE. Hebrews i. 1. Ad Hebræos primo. Multifarie multisque modis.... et anni tui non deficient[n].

THE GOSPEL. St. John i. 1. Initium sancti evangelii secundum Joannem primo. In principio erat Verbum... plenum gratiæ et veritatis[o].

SAINT STEPHEN'S DAY.

THE COLLECT. Grant, O Lord, that in all our sufferings here upon earth for the testi-

Da nobis, quæsumus, Domine, imitari quod colimus, ut discamus et inimicos diligere,

---

[k] Miss. Sarisb. Dom. 4. Adv. fol. xv.

[l] Miss. Sarisb. Dom. 4. Adv fol. xv.

[m] Though the collect for this day is not directly translated from the ancient offices of the church; yet we may trace a similarity of ideas between it and two collects in the sacramentary of Gregory and the liturgy of Sarum. "Almighty God, who hast given us thus thine only begotten Son to take our nature upon him, and as at this time to be born of a pure virgin: Grant that we being regenerate, and made thy children by adoption and grace, may daily be renewed by thy Holy Spirit; through the same our Lord Jesus Christ," &c "Præsta quæsumus, Omnipotens Deus, ut natus hodie Salvator mundi, sicut divinæ nobis ge-

nerationis est auctor, ita et immortalitatis sit ipse largitor. Qui tecum vivit, et regnat Deus." Miss. Sarisb. fol. xviii. Sacramentar. Gregorii Menard. p. 7. "Omnipotens sempiterne Deus, qui hunc diem per incarnationem Verbi tui, et partum beatæ Mariæ Virginis consecrasti, da populis tuis in hac celebritate consortium, *ut qui, tua gratia sunt redempti, tua sint adoptione securi.* Per eundem." Sacr. Gregor. Menard. p. 7

[n] Miss. Sarisb. 3. Missa in die Nativit. Domini fol. xviii. Miss. Mosarabic Mabillon, de Lit. Gall. p. 107. Comes vel Lectionarius Pamel. Liturg. tom. ii p 2.

[o] Miss. Sarisb. 3. Missa in die Nat. Dom. fol. xviii. Capitula ap Marten. tom. v. Anecdot. p. 65.

mony of thy truth, we may steadfastly look up to heaven, and by faith behold the glory that shall be revealed; and being filled with the Holy Ghost, may learn to love and bless our persecutors by the example of thy first martyr St. Stephen, who prayed for his murderers to thee, O blessed Jesus, who standest at the right hand of God to succour all those that suffer for thee our only Mediator and Advocate. *Amen*

quia ejus natalitia celebramus, qui novit etiam pro persecutoribus exorare Dominum nostrum Jesum Christum Filium tuum qui tecum vivit et regnat [p].

For the Epistle   Acts vii. 55. ... obdormivit in Domino [q].

Epistola. Lectio Actuum Apostolorum vi. et vii. Stephanus plenus gratia et fortitudine

The Gospel.   St. Matth xxiii. 34. Ecce ego mitto ad vos in nomine Domini [r].

Secundum Mattheum xxiii. . dicatis, Benedictus qui venit

SAINT JOHN THE EVANGELIST'S DAY.

The Collect. Merciful Lord, we beseech thee to cast thy bright beams of light upon thy church, that it being enlightened by the doctrine of thy blessed apostle and evangelist St. John, may so walk in the light of thy truth, that

Ecclesiam tuam quæsumus Domine benignus illustra: ut beati Joannis apostoli tui et evangelistæ illuminata doctrinis, ad dona perveniat sempiterna. Per Dominum [s].

---

[p] Miss. Sarisb. in die Sancti Stephani, fol. xviii. Gregorii Liber Sacrament. Menard p. 8. MS Sacrament. Leofric. Exon. fol. 158. "It is ordered in the missal and breviary, that every day till the circumcision, ' fiat commemoratio de Nativitate.' " *MS. Annotations of bishop Lloyd on B. of C. P.*

[q] Miss. Sarisb. fol. xix MS. Leofric. 158. Comes Pamel. tom. ii. p. 2.

[r] Miss. Sarisb. fol. xix. MS. Leofric. 158. Capitula Marten. p. 66. Comes Pamel. tom. ii. p. 2.

[s] Miss. Sarisb In die sancti

CHAP. III. *Originals of the English Collects, &c.* 321

it may at length attain to the light of everlasting life; through Jesus Christ our Lord. *Amen.*

THE GOSPEL. St. John xxi. 19. Dixit Jesus Petro . . . . timonium ejus [t].

Evangelium secundum Joannem xxi. . et scimus quia verum est testimonium ejus [t].

THE INNOCENTS' DAY.

THE COLLECT. O Almighty God, who out of the mouths of babes and sucklings hast ordained strength, and madest infants to glorify thee by their deaths; Mortify and kill all vices in us, and so strengthen us by thy grace, that by the innocency of our lives, and constancy of our faith, even unto death, we may glorify thy holy name; through Jesus Christ our Lord. *Amen.*

Deus cujus hodierna die præconium innocentes martyres, non loquendo sed moriendo, confessi sunt; omnia in nobis vitiorum mala mortifica, ut fidem tuam, quam lingua nostra loquitur, etiam moribus vita fateatur Per [u].

FOR THE EPISTLE. Rev. xiv 1. Lectio libri Apocalypsis beati Joannis Apostoli xiv. In diebus illis vidi . . . . sine macula enim sunt ante thronum Dei [v].

THE GOSPEL. St. Matth. ii. 13. Secundum Mattheum ii Angelus Domini apparuit in somnis Joseph . . . . et noluit consolari quia non sunt [w].

Joannis evangelistæ. fol. xix. MS. Leofric. 159 Gregorii Liber Sacr. Menard. p. 10.

[t] Miss. Sarisb. in die S. Joannis evangelistæ, fol. xix. MS. Leofric. 159. Capitula Martene, p 66. tom v Comes Pamel. Lit. tom. ii. p 3.

[u] Miss Sarisb. in die Sanctorum Innocentium martyrum, fol. xix. MS. Sacramentar.

Leofr. 160. Sacramentar. Gregorii Menard, p. 11. Sacr. Gelasii Muratori Lit. Rom. tom. i. p. 499.

[v] Miss Sarisb fol. xix. MS Sacr. Leofr. fol. 160. Comes Pamel. tom. ii. p. 3.

[w] Miss. Sar. fol. xx. MS. Leofr. 160. Capitula Martene Anec. tom. v. p. 66. Comes Pamel. tom. ii. p. 3.

THE SUNDAY AFTER CHRISTMAS-DAY[x]

THE EPISTLE. Gal. iv. 1. Ad Galathas iv Quanto tempore heres . . . . quod si filius et heres per Deum[y].

THE GOSPEL. St. Matthew i 18. Secundum Mattheum primo. Cum esset desponsata . . . salvum faciet populum suum a peccatis eorum[z].

THE CIRCUMCISION OF CHRIST.

THE COLLECT. Almighty God, who madest thy blessed Son to be circumcised, and obedient to the law for man; Grant us the true circumcision of the Spirit; that our hearts, and all our members, being mortified from all worldly and carnal lusts, we may in all things obey thy blessed will, through the same thy Son Jesus Christ our Lord. *Amen.*

Omnipotens Deus, cujus unigenitus hodierna die, ne legem solveret, quam adimplere venerat, corporalem suscepit circumcisionem; spirituali circumcisione mentes vestras ab omnibus vitiorum incentivis expurget; et suam in vos infundet benedictionem. Amen[a].

THE GOSPEL St. Luke ii. 15. Secundum Lucam ii. Postquam consummati sunt . . . . priusquam in utero conciperetur[b].

THE EPIPHANY

THE COLLECT. O God, who by the leading of a star didst manifest thy only begotten Son to the Gentiles; Mercifully grant, that we, which know thee now by faith, may

Deus, qui hodierna die unigenitum tuum Gentibus, stella duce, revelasti; concede propitius, ut qui jam te ex fide cognovimus, usque ad contemplandum speciem tuæ cel-

---

[x] The same collect as that for Christmas-day.

[y] Miss. Sarisb 6 die a Nativ. Dom. fol. xx. MS. Leofr. 69. Comes Pamel. tom. ii. p. 3

[z] Miss. Sarisb. in Vigil Nativ. Dom. fol. xvi. Capitula ap Martene Anecdota, tom. v. p.

65. Comes Pamel. Lit. tom. ii. p. 1.

[a] Benedictio in octavis Domini Gregor. Sacr. Menard. p. 13. MS. Leofr. Sacr. fol. 70.

[b] Miss. Sarisb. fol. xxi. MS. Leofr fol 69.

after this life have the fruition of thy glorious Godhead; through Jesus Christ our Lord. Amen.

situdinis perducamur. Per eumdem [c]

THE GOSPEL. St Matthew ii. 1. Secundum Mattheum ii Cum natus esset .... reversi sunt in regionem suam [d]

THE FIRST SUNDAY AFTER THE EPIPHANY.

THE COLLECT. O Lord, we beseech thee mercifully to receive the prayers of thy people which call upon thee, and grant that they may both perceive and know what things they ought to do, and also may have grace and power faithfully to fulfil the same, through Jesus Christ our Lord. Amen.

Vota, quæsumus, Domine, supplicantis populi cœlesti pietate prosequere; ut et quæ agenda sunt, videant; et ad implenda quæ viderint, convalescant Per [e].

THE EPISTLE. Rom xii. 1 Epistola ad Romanos xii. Fratres, obsecro vos per misericordias Dei . alterius membra in Christo Jesu Domino nostro [f].

THE GOSPEL. St. Luke ii. 41. Secundum Lucam ii. Cum factus esset Jesus annorum duodecim . proficiebat sapientia ætate et gratia apud Deum et hominem [g].

THE SECOND SUNDAY AFTER THE EPIPHANY.

THE COLLECT. Almighty and everlasting God, who dost govern all things in heaven and

Omnipotens sempiterne Deus, qui cœlestia simul et terrena moderaris, supplicationes po-

---

[c] Miss. Sarisb. in die Epiphaniæ, fol. xxii. MS. Leofric fol. 71. Gregorii Liber Sacramentorum Menard p. 15.

[d] Miss. Sarisb. fol. xxii. MS Leofr fol. 71. Comes Pamel. tom. ii. p. 4.

[e] Miss Sarisb fol. xxiii. Dominica prima post octavas Epiphaniæ. MS Sacr. Leofr. fol

73. Gregor. Liber Sacr. Menard. p. 17 Ambrosii Liturgia Pamel. Liturg. tom. i. p. 316.

[f] Miss. Sar. fol. xxiii. MS Leofr. 73. Comes Pamel tom. ii. p. 4.

[g] Miss. Sar. fol. xxiii. MS. Leofr. 73. Comes Pamel tom. ii. p 4

earth; Mercifully hear the supplications of thy people, and grant us thy peace all the days of our life; through Jesus Christ our Lord. *Amen.*

puli tui clementer exaudi, et pacem tuam nostris concede temporibus. Per Dominum [h].

THE EPISTLE. Romans xii. 6. Ad Romanos xii. Habentes donationes . sed humilibus consentientes [i].

THE GOSPEL. St. John ii. 1. Evangelium secundum Joannem ii. Nuptiæ factæ sunt .et crediderunt in eum discipuli ejus [j].

THE THIRD SUNDAY AFTER THE EPIPHANY.

THE COLLECT. Almighty and everlasting God, mercifully look upon our infirmities, and in all our dangers and necessities stretch forth thy right hand to help and defend us; through Jesus Christ our Lord. *Amen.*

Omnipotens sempiterne Deus, infirmitatem nostram propitius respice, atque ad protegendum nos dexteram tuæ majestatis extende. Per Dominum [k].

THE EPISTLE. Romans xii. 16. Ad Romanos xii. Nolite esse prudentes apud vosmetipsos.... noli vinci a malo, sed vince in bono malum [l].

THE GOSPEL. St. Matthew viii. 1. Secundum Mattheum viii. Cum descendisset Jesus de monte.... et sanatus est puer in illa hora [m].

THE FOURTH SUNDAY AFTER THE EPIPHANY.

THE COLLECT. O God, who knowest us to be set in the midst of so many and great

Deus qui nos in tantis periculis constitutos, pro humana scis fragilitate non posse sub-

---

[h] Miss. Sarisb. Dom. secunda post octavas Epiphaniæ, fol. xxiv. MS. Leofr. 73. Gregorii Liber Sacr. Menard. p. 18. Ambros. Miss. Pamel. Liturg. tom. i. p. 316.

[i] Miss. Sarisb. fol. xxiv. MS. Leofr. fol. 74. Comes Pamel tom. ii. p. 5.

[j] Miss. Sar. fol. xxiv MS. Sacr. Leofr. fol. 74. Comes Pamel. tom. ii. p. 6.

[k] Dominica tertia post oct. Epiph. Miss. Sar. fol. xxv. Ambros. Miss. ap. Pamel. Liturg. tom. i. p. 317. Gregorii Liber Sacr. Menard. p. 25. MS. Sacr. Leofric. fol. 73.

[l] Miss. Sarisb. fol. xxv. MS. Leofr. fol. 75. Comes Pamel. tom. ii. p. 6.

[m] Miss. Sar. fol xxv. MS. Leofr. fol. 75. Comes Pamel. tom. ii. p. 6

CHAP. III. *Originals of the English Collects, &c.* 325

dangers, that by reason of the frailty of our nature we cannot always stand upright; Grant to us such strength and protection, as may support us in all dangers, and carry us through all temptations, through Jesus Christ our Lord. *Amen.*

sistere; da nobis salutem mentis et corporis, ut ea quæ pro peccatis nostris patimur, te adjuvante vincamus. Per[n].

THE EPISTLE. Romans xiii. 1. Ad Romanos xiii. Omnis anima potestatibus sublimioribus subdita sit .... ministri enim Dei sunt, in hoc ipsum servientes[o].

THE GOSPEL. St. Matth. viii. 23. Secundum Mattheum viii. Ascendente Jesu in naviculam .... quia venti et mare obediunt ei[p].

THE FIFTH SUNDAY AFTER THE EPIPHANY.

THE COLLECT. O Lord, we beseech thee to keep thy church and household continually in thy true religion; that they who do lean only upon the hope of thy heavenly grace, may evermore be defended by thy mighty power; through Jesus Christ our Lord. *Amen.*

Familiam tuam, quæsumus, Domine, continua pietate custodi; ut quæ in sola spe gratiæ cœlestis innititur, tua semper protectione muniatur. Per Dominum[q].

THE EPISTLE. Coloss. iii. 2. Ad Colossenses iii. Induite vos sicut electi .... gratias agentes Deo et Patri Per Jesum Christum Dominum nostrum[r].

THE GOSPEL. St. Matthew xiii. 24. Secundum Mattheum xiii.

---

[n] Miss. Sar. Dominica quarta post octav. Epiph. fol. xxv. MS. Leofr. fol. 74. Gregorii Liber Sacr. Menard. p. 26.

[o] Miss. Sar. feria vi. post Dom. 1. post octav. Epiph. fol. xxiv. The Epistle for this Sunday is taken from the same chapter, a little further on.

[p] Miss. Sar. fol. xxv. Comes Pamel. tom. ii. p. 7.

[q] Miss. Sarisb. Dominica v. post octav. Epiph. fol. xxvi. Ambros. Miss. Pamel. Liturg. tom i. p. 325. Gregorii Liber Sacr. Menard. p 26. MS. Leofr. fol. 75.

[r] Miss. Sar. Dom. v. post. octav Epiph fol. xxvi. Comes Pamel. tom. ii. p. 8

Simile factum est regnum cœlorum homini ... triticum autem congregate in horreum meum[s].

SEPTUAGESIMA.

THE COLLECT. O Lord, we beseech thee favourably to hear the prayers of thy people; that we who are justly punished for our offences, may be mercifully delivered by thy goodness, for the glory of thy name, through Jesus Christ our Saviour, who liveth and reigneth with thee and the Holy Ghost, ever one God, world without end. *Amen.*

Preces populi tui, quæsumus Domine, clementer exaudi, ut qui juste pro peccatis nostris affligimur, pro tui nominis gloria misericorditer liberemur. Per Dominum[t].

THE EPISTLE. 1 Cor. ix. 24. Ad Corinthios 1 ix. Nescitis quia hi qui in stadio currunt... Petra autem erat Christus[u].

THE GOSPEL. St. Matth. xx. 1. Secundum Mattheum xx. Simile est regnum cœlorum homini patrifamilias. multi enim sunt vocati, pauci vero electi[v].

SEXAGESIMA.

THE COLLECT. O Lord God, who seest that we put not our trust in any thing that we do; Mercifully grant that by thy power we may be defended against all adversity, through Jesus Christ our Lord. *Amen.*

Deus qui conspicis quia ex nulla nostra actione confidimus, concede propitius, ut contra omnia adversa Doctoris gentium protectione muniamur[w].

---

[s] Miss. Sar. fol. xxvi. Comes Pamel. tom ii p. 8.

[t] Miss. Sarisb. Dominica in Septuagesima fol. xxvi Ambros. Miss. Pamel. Liturg. tom. i. p. 324. Gregorii Sacram. Menard. p. 32. MS Leofr. fol 78.

[u] Miss. Sar. fol. xxvi. MS. Leofr f. 78. Comes Pamel tom. ii. p 9.

[v] Miss Sar fol xxvi. MS Leofr f 78. Comes Pamel. tom. ii. p 9

[w] Miss. Sarisb. Dominica in Sexagesima fol. xxvii Gregorii Sacramentar. Menard. p 32. MS Leofr. f 78

CHAP. III. *Originals of the English Collects, &c.*

THE EPISTLE. 2 Cor. xi. 19. Ad Corinthios 2 xi. Libenter suffertis insipientes... libenter igitur gloriabor in infirmitatibus meis ut inhabitet in me virtus Christi[x].

THE GOSPEL. St Luke viii. 4. Secundum Lucam viii. Cum turba plurima conveniret... et fructum afferunt in patientia[y].

QUINQUAGESIMA[z].

THE EPISTLE. 1 Cor. xiii. 1. Ad Corinthios 1 xiii. Si linguis hominum loquar et angelorum.. major autem horum est caritas[a].

THE GOSPEL. St. Luke xviii. 31. Secundum Lucam xviii. Assumpsit Jesus duodecim ... et omnis plebs ut vidit dedit laudem Deo[b]

ASH-WEDNESDAY[c].

FOR THE EPISTLE. Joel ii. 12 Lectio Johelis Prophetæ ii. Hæc dicit Dominus convertimini ad me.. opprobrium in gentibus. Dicit Dominus omnipotens[d].

THE GOSPEL St. Matthew vi. 16. Secundum Mattheum vi. Cum jejunetis nolite... ubi enim est thesaurus tuus ibi est cor tuum[e].

---

[x] Miss. Sar. fol. xxvii MS Leofr 79 Comes Pamel. tom. ii. p 10.

[y] Miss. Sar. fol. xxvii. MS Leofr fol. 79. Comes Pamel. tom. ii. p. 10.

[z] The collect in Miss. Sar. fol xxviii. and in MS. Leofr. fol. 79. is different from ours, which is beautifully formed from the ancient epistle.

[a] Miss Sar. fol xxvii. MS Leofr. fol 79 Comes Pamel. tom. ii. p. 10.

[b] Miss. Sar. fol xxviii. MS. Leofr. fol 79 Comes Pamel. tom. ii. p. 10.

[c] The collect for Ash-Wednesday is not amongst the ancient English offices, though there is a great similarity between the topics of this collect, and of those appointed for Ash-Wednesday in the missal of Sarum, fol xxx. However, the Introduction of our prayer appears to have been derived from that source. "Almighty and everlasting God, who hatest nothing that thou hast made, and dost forgive the sins of all them that are penitent:" "Omnipotens sempiterne Deus qui misereris omnium et nihil odisti eorum quæ fecisti, dissimulans peccata hominum propter pœnitentiam." Miss. Sar. fol. xxx.

[d] Miss. Sar. fol. xxxi. MS. Leofr. fol. 81. Comes Pamel. tom. ii p. 11

[e] Miss. Sar. fol. xxxi. MS. Leofr. fol. 81. Comes Pamel. tom. ii p. 11.

THE FIRST SUNDAY IN LENT.

The Collect. O Lord, who for our sakes didst fast forty days and forty nights; Give us grace to use such abstinence, that, our flesh being subdued to the Spirit, we may ever obey thy godly motions in righteousness, and true holiness, to thy honour and glory, who livest and reignest with the Father and the Holy Ghost, one God, world without end. *Amen*

Da nobis quæsumus Domine, per gratiam Spiritus sancti novam tui Paracliti spiritalis observantiæ disciplinam, ut mentes nostræ sacro purgatæ jejunio, cunctis reddantur ejus muneribus aptiores. Per Dominum [f].

The Epistle. 2 Cor. vi. 1. Ad Corinthios 2 vi. Hortamur vos ne in vacuum gratiam Dei recipiatis.... tanquam nihil habentes, et omnia possidentes [g].

The Gospel. St. Matthew iv. 1. Secundum Mattheum iv. In illo tempore ductus est Jesus in desertum . . et ecce Angeli accesserunt et ministrabant ei [h].

THE SECOND SUNDAY IN LENT.

The Collect. Almighty God, who seest that we have no power of ourselves to help ourselves, Keep us both outwardly in our bodies, and inwardly in our souls; that we may be defended from all adversities which may happen to the body, and from all evil thoughts which may assault and hurt the soul, through Jesus Christ our Lord. Amen.

Deus, qui conspicis omni nos virtute destitui, interius exteriusque custodi: ut ab omnibus adversitatibus muniamur in corpore, et a pravis cogitationibus mundemur in mente. Per Dominum [1].

The Epistle. 1 Thess. iv. 1. Ad Thessalonienses 1 iv.

---

[f] Miss. Ambros Pamel. Liturg. tom. i. p. 378.

[g] Miss. Sar. Dominica prima xl. fol. xxxii. MS. Leofr. fol. 82. Comes Pamel. tom. i. p. 12.

[h] Miss. Sar. fol. xxxiii. MS. Leofr. fol. 82. Comes Pamel. tom. ii. p. 12.

[1] Miss. Sar. Dom. 2. Quadragesimæ, fol. xxxvii. Gregor. Sacr. Menard. p. 42. MS. Leofr fol. 87.

CHAP. III.   *Originals of the English Collects, &c.*   329

Fratres rogamus vos et obsecramus in Domino Jesu .. ... sed in sanctificationem in Christo Jesu Domino nostro J.

THE GOSPEL. St. Matthew xv. 21. Secundum Mattheum xv. Egressus Jesus secessit in partes Tyri .. et sanata est filia ejus ex illa hora[k].

THE THIRD SUNDAY IN LENT.

THE COLLECT. We beseech thee, Almighty God, look upon the hearty desires of thy humble servants, and stretch forth the right hand of thy Majesty, to be our defence against all our enemies; through Jesus Christ our Lord. *Amen*

Quæsumus, omnipotens Deus, vota humilium respice; atque ad defensionem nostram dexteram tuæ majestatis extende. Per Dominum[l].

THE EPISTLE. Ephes. v. 1. Ad Ephesios v. Estote imitatores Dei sicut filii carissimi.... fructus enim lucis est in omni bonitate et justitia et veritate[m].

THE GOSPEL. St. Luke xi. 14. Secundum Lucam xi. Erat Jesus ejiciens dæmonium... beati qui audiunt verbum Dei et custodiunt illud[n].

THE FOURTH SUNDAY IN LENT.

THE COLLECT. Grant we beseech thee, Almighty God, that we, who for our evil deeds do worthily deserve to be punished, by the comfort of thy grace may mercifully be relieved; through our Lord and Saviour Jesus Christ. *Amen.*

Concede quæsumus, omnipotens Deus, ut qui ex merito nostræ actionis affligimur, tuæ gratiæ consolatione respiremus. Per Dominum[o].

---

[j] Miss. Sar. fol. xxxvii. MS. Leofr. 87. Comes Pamel. tom. ii. p. 14.

[k] Miss. Sar. fol. xxxvii. MS. Leofr. 87 Comes Pamel. tom. ii. p. 14.

[l] Miss. Sar. Dom tertia xl. fol. xl. Gregor. Liber Sacrament. Menard. p 46 MS. Leofr. fol. 90

[m] Miss. Sar. fol. xl. MS. Leofr. fol. 91. Comes Pamel. tom. ii. p. 16.

[n] Miss. Sar. fol xl. MS. Leofr. fol 91. Comes Pamel. tom. ii p. 16

[o] Miss. Sar. Dominica media xl. fol xliii. MS. Leofr fol. 94. Gregorii Liber Sacr. Menard p. 50.

THE EPISTLE. Gal. iv 21. Ad Galathas iv. Scriptum est quoniam Abraham duos filios habuit. . . . qua libertate Christus nos liberavit P.

THE GOSPEL St John vi. 1. Secundum Joannem vi. Abiit Jesus trans mare . . . quia hic est vere Propheta qui venturus est in mundum q.

THE FIFTH SUNDAY IN LENT

THE COLLECT. We beseech thee, Almighty God, mercifully to look upon thy people; that by thy great goodness they may be governed and preserved evermore, both in body and soul; through Jesus Christ our Lord. *Amen.*

Quæsumus, omnipotens Deus, familiam tuam propitius respice; ut te largiente regatur in corpore, et te servante custodiatur in mente. Per Dominum r

THE EPISTLE. Hebrews ix. 11. Ad Hebræos ix. Christus assistens Pontifex futurorum bonorum . . . . repromissionem accipiunt qui vocati sunt æternæ hereditatis in Christo Jesu Domino nostro s

THE GOSPEL. St. John viii 46 Secundum Joannem viii Quis ex vobis arguet me de peccato . abscondit se, et exivit de templo t.

THE SUNDAY NEXT BEFORE EASTER.

THE COLLECT. Almighty and everlasting God, who, of thy tender love towards mankind, hast sent thy Son, our Saviour Jesus Christ, to take upon him our flesh, and to suffer death upon the cross, that all mankind should follow the example

Omnipotens sempiterne Deus, qui humano generi ad imitandum humilitatis exemplum, Salvatorem nostrum carnem sumere, et crucem subire fecisti concede propitius, ut et patientiæ ipsius habere documenta, et resurrectionis consortia me-

---

p Miss. Sar. fol. xliv. MS. Leofr fol. 94. Comes Pamel. tom. ii. p. 18.

q Miss. Sar. fol. xlv. MS. Leofr. fol 94. Comes Pamel. tom. ii. p. 18.

r Miss Sar. fol. xlix. MS. Leofr. fol. 98. Gregorii Liber Sacr. Menard p. 55.

s Miss. Sar fol. xlix. MS. Leofr. 98 Comes Pamel tom ii p. 19.

t Miss. Sar. fol. xlix. MS. Leofr. 98. Comes Pamel. tom. ii. p. 19.

CHAP. III.   *Originals of the English Collects, &c.*   331

of his great humility ; Mercifully grant, that we may both follow the example of his patience, and also be made partakers of his resurrection ; through the same Jesus Christ our Lord. *Amen.* reamur. Per eumdem Christum Dominum[u].

THE EPISTLE. Phil. ii. 5. Ad Philippenses ii. Fratres hoc etiam sentite in vobis quod et in Christo Jesu ..... in gloria est Dei Patris[v].

THE GOSPEL. St. Matthew xxvi. 2. is included in the Passio Domini nostri Jesu Christi secundum Mattheum xxvi. Scitis quia post biduum Pascha fiet.... erant autem ibi Maria Magdalene et altera Maria sedentes contra sepulchrum[w].

MONDAY BEFORE EASTER[x].

FOR THE EPISTLE. Isaiah lxiii. 1. is included in the lesson for "feria IV ebdomadæ sanctæ." Lectio Isaiæ Prophetæ lxii. et lxiii. Hæc dicit Dominus Deus, dicite filiæ Syon ecce Salvator tuus venit ..... laudem Domini annunciabo super omnibus quæ reddidit nobis Dominus Deus noster[y].

THE GOSPEL. St Mark xiv. 1. Included in the "Passio Domini nostri Jesu Christi secundum Marcum xiv." In illo tempore erat Pascha et azyma post biduum.... et aliæ multæ quæ simul cum eo ascenderant Hierosolymam[z].

TUESDAY BEFORE EASTER

FOR THE EPISTLE. Isaiah l. 5. Lectio Isaiæ Prophetæ l. Dominus Deus meus aperuit mihi aurem... speret in nomine Domini et innitatur super Dominum Deum suum[a].

---

[u] Miss Sar. Dominica in ramis palmarum, fol. liii. Gelasii Sacramentar. Muratori Liturg. Rom. tom 1 p. 546. Gregorii Sacr. Menard. p 59 MS Leofr. fol. 102. See one like it, Mabillon. Liturg. Gallican p. 295.

[v] Miss Sar. fol liii MS. Leofr. 102. Comes Pamel tom. ii. p. 21.

[w] Miss. Sar fol liv MS. Leofr. 102. Comes Pamel. tom ii p. 21.

[x] The collects for this and the following days are the same with that of the preceding Sunday.

[y] Miss. Sar. fol. lvii. MS. Leofr. 104. Comes Pamel. tom. ii p. 22

[z] Miss. Sar fol. lvi. MS. Leofr 104. Comes Pamel. tom. ii. p. 22.

[a] Miss. Sar. fol. lv. MS.

THE GOSPEL. St. Mark xv. 1. Included in the " Passio Domini nostri Jesu Christi secundum Marcum xiv." In feria tertia ebdomadæ sanctæ [b].

WEDNESDAY BEFORE EASTER.

THE GOSPEL St. Luke xxii. 1. Included in the " Passio Domini nostri Jesu Christi secundum Lucam xxii." In illo tempore appropinquabat autem dies festus azymorum . . . . et mulieres quæ secutæ erant eum a Galilæa hæc videntes [c].

THURSDAY BEFORE EASTER.

THE EPISTLE. 1 Cor. xi. 17. Ad Corinthios 1 xi. Convenientibus vobis in unum jam non est Dominicam cœnam manducare . . . . ut non cum hoc mundo damnemur [d].

THE GOSPEL. St. Luke xxiii. 1. Included in the " Passio Domini nostri Jesu Christi secundum Lucam xxii." In illo tempore appropinquabat autem dies festus azymorum . . . . et mulieres quæ secutæ erant eum a Galilæa hæc videntes [e].

GOOD FRIDAY.

THE COLLECTS. Almighty God, we beseech thee graciously to behold this thy family, for which our Lord Jesus Christ was contented to be betrayed, and given up into the hands of wicked men, and to suffer death upon the cross, who now liveth and reigneth with thee and the Holy Ghost,

Respice, Domine, quæsumus, super hanc familiam tuam, pro qua Dominus noster Jesus Christus non dubitavit manibus tradi nocentium, et crucis subire tormentum. Qui tecum vivit [f].

Leofr. 103. Comes Pamel. tom. ii. p. 21.

[b] Miss. Sar fol. lvii. MS. Leofr. 104. Comes Pamel. tom. ii. p. 22.

[c] Miss. Sar. fol. lviii. MS. Leofr. 104. Comes Pamel. tom. ii. p 22.

[d] Miss. Sar. Feria v. Ebdomadæ sanctæ in cœna Domini, fol. lx. MS. Leofr. fol. 106. Comes Pamel. tom. ii. p. 22.

[e] Miss. Sar. fol. lix. Comes Pamel. tom. ii. p. 22.

[f] Miss. Sar. fol. lix. Gregorii Sacr. Menard. p. 64. MS. Leofr. fol. 104. Missale Gothicum Mabillon Liturg. Gall. p. 239. Miss. Gall. Vet. Id. p. 352.

ever one God, world without end. *Amen.*

Almighty and everlasting God, by whose Spirit the whole body of the church is governed and sanctified; Receive our supplications and prayers, which we offer before thee for all estates of men in thy holy church, that every member of the same, in his vocation and ministry, may truly and godly serve thee; through our Lord and Saviour Jesus Christ. *Amen.*

O merciful God, who hast made all men, and hatest nothing that thou hast made, nor wouldest the death of a sinner, but rather that he should be converted and live; Have mercy upon all Jews, Turks, Infidels, and Heretics, and take from them all ignorance, hardness of heart, and contempt of thy word; and so fetch them home, blessed Lord, to thy flock, that they may be saved among the remnant of the true Israelites, and be made one fold under one Shepherd, Jesus Christ our

Omnipotens sempiterne Deus, cujus spiritu totum corpus ecclesiæ sanctificatur et regitur; exaudi nos pro universis ordinibus supplicantes. ut gratiæ tuæ munere ab omnibus tibi gradibus fideliter serviatur. Per [g].

Omnipotens sempiterne Deus, qui salvas omnes homines, et neminem vis perire; respice ad animas diabolica fraude deceptas, ut omni hæretica pravitate deposita, errantium corda resipiscant, et ad veritatis tuæ redeant unitatem. Per [h].

Omnipotens sempiterne Deus, qui etiam Judaicam perfidiam a tua misericordia non repellis; exaudi preces nostras quas pro illius populi obcæcatione deferimus; ut agnita veritatis tuæ luce quæ Christus est, a suis tenebris eruatur. Per eumdem Dominum[1].

---

[g] Miss. Sar. in die Parasceves, fol. lxiv. Gelasii Sacram. Muratori Liturg. Rom. tom. i. p. 560. Gregorii Sacr. Menard. p 62. MS. Leofr. fol. 108. Miss. Vet. Gall. Mabillon Liturg. Gall. p. 351.

[h] Miss. Sar. fol. lxiv. Sacr. Gregorii Menard. p. 62. MS. Leofr. 109. Sacr. Gelasii. Murat. Lit. Rom. tom. i. p. 562. Miss. Gall. Vet. Mabill. Liturg. Gall. p. 352.

[1] Miss. Sar. fol. lxv. Sacr.

Lord, who liveth and reigneth with thee and the Holy Spirit, one God, world without end. *Amen*

Omnipotens sempiterne Deus, qui non vis mortem peccatorum, sed vitam semper inquiris; suscipe propitius orationem nostram; et libera eos (paganos) ab idolorum cultura; et aggrega ecclesiæ tuæ sanctæ ad laudem et gloriam nominis tui. Per Dominum[j].

THE GOSPEL. St. John xix. 1 cap." Included in the "Passio Joannis xviii cap." Egressus est Jesus cum discipulis suis trans torrentem Cedron . . . . et iterum alia scriptura dicit, videbant in quem transfixerant[k].

EASTER EVEN

THE COLLECT. Grant, O Lord, that as we are baptized into the death of thy blessed Son our Saviour Jesus Christ, so by continually mortifying our corrupt affections we may be buried with him; and that through the grave, and gate of death, we may pass to our joyful resurrection, for his merits who died, and was buried, and rose again for us, thy Son Jesus Christ our Lord. *Amen.*

Christe, fave desideriis et precibus nostris, et præsta prosperam hanc supervenientem sanctæ paschæ noctem, in qua tecum resurgentes de morte, transire mereamur ad vitam; Salvator mundi qui vivis &c.[1]

THE GOSPEL. St. Matthew xxviii. 57. Secundum Mattheum xxviii. Vespere autem sabbati, quando lucescit in prima sabbati . . . ibi eum videbitis, ecce prædixi vobis[m].

Gregorii Menard. p. 63 MS. Leofr. 110. Sacr. Gelasii Murat. Lit. Rom. tom i p 562. Miss. Gall. Vet Mabill. Liturg Gall. p. 352.

[j] Miss. Sar fol. lxv. Sacr. Gregorii Menard. p 63. MS. Leofr. 110. Sacr. Gelasii Murat. Lit. Rom. tom i. p. 562

Miss Gall. Vet. Mabill. Liturg. Gall. p 352.

[k] Miss. Sar. in die Parasceve, fol. lxiii. Comes Pamel. tom. ii p. 23.

[l] Miss. Gall. Vet. in Sabbato Sancto. Mabill. Liturg. Gallican. p 356.

[m] Miss Sar in Vigil Pas-

CHAP. III.   *Originals of the English Collects, &c.*   335

EASTER DAY.

ANTHEMS AT MATINS Christ our Passover is sacrificed for us : therefore let us keep the feast ;

Not with the old leaven, nor with the leaven of malice and wickedness · but with the unleavened bread of sincerity and truth

Christ being raised from the dead dieth no more   death hath no more dominion over him.

THE COLLECT AlmightyGod, who through thine only-begotten Son Jesus Christ hast overcome death, and opened unto us the gate of everlasting life, We humbly beseech thee, that as by thy special grace preventing us thou dost put into our minds good desires, so by thy continual help we may bring the same to good effect, through Jesus Christ our Lord, who liveth and reigneth with thee and the Holy Ghost, ever one God, world without end. *Amen.*

Pascha nostrum immolatus est Christus . itaque epulemur,

In azymis sinceritatis et veritatis[n].

Christus resurgens ex mortuis, jam non moritur; Alleluia. mors illi ultra non dominabitur[o]

Deus, qui hodierna die per Unigenitum tuum æternitatis nobis aditum, devicta morte, reserasti ; vota nostra, quæ præveniendo aspiras, etiam adjuvando prosequere Per eumdem Dominum nostrum[p]

---

chæ, fol. lxx   MS. Leofr. fol. 114.   Comes Pamel tom. ii. p. 25.

[n] One of the proper anthems for Easter in Antiphonar. Gregorii Pamel. tom. ii. p. 112.

[o] Anthem ad communionem Antiphonar. Gregorii feria 4. post Pascha   Pamel tom. ii. p 113

[p] Miss, Sar. in die Paschæ, fol. lxxxv. Miss. Ambros Pamel. Liturg. tom. i. p. 354. Sacramentar. Gelasii Muratori Lit Rom. tom. i. p. 574. Gregorii Sacr. Menard. p 75. Muratori Liturg. Rom. tom. ii. p. 67 Miss. Gall. Vet. Mabillon Lit Gall. p. 366. MS. Leofr. fol. 115

THE GOSPEL. St John xx. 1. Secundum Joannem xx. In illo tempore una sabbathi Maria Magdalene venit . . . . quia oportebat eum a mortuis resurgere [q].

MONDAY IN EASTER WEEK [r]

FOR THE EPISTLE. Acts x 34 Lectio Actuum Apostolorum x. Stans Petrus in medio plebis dixit, Viri fratres, vos scitis quod factum est verbum per universam Judæam . . . . per nomen ejus omnes qui credunt in eum [s].

THE GOSPEL St. Luke xxiv. 13. Secundum Lucam xxiiii. Exeuntes duo ex discipulis Jesu . . . cognoverunt eum in fractione panis [t].

TUESDAY IN EASTER WEEK.

FOR THE EPISTLE. Acts xiii 26. Lectio Actuum Apostolorum xiii. Surgens Paulus et manu silentium indicens, ait, Viri fratres, ... resuscitans Jesum Christum Dominum nostrum [u].

THE GOSPEL. St. Luke xxiv. 36 Secundum Lucam xxiiii. Stetit Jesus in medio discipulorum suorum . . . . et remissionem peccatorum in omnes gentes [v].

THE FIRST SUNDAY AFTER EASTER [w].

THE EPISTLE. 1 St. John v. 4. Lectio Epistolæ beati Joannis Apostoli 1 v. Omne quod natum est ex Deo vicit mundum . . . . qui credit in Filium Dei habet testimonium Dei in se [x].

THE GOSPEL St. John xx 19 Evangelium secundum Joannem xx Cum esset sero die illo una sabbatorum . . . . et ut credentes vitam habeatis in nomine ejus [y].

---

[q] Miss. Sar. in sabbato post Pascha, fol. lxxxviii. MS. Leofr. fol. 115.

[r] The same collect for this day and the next as for Easter Sunday.

[s] Miss. Sar. Fer. 2 post Pascha, fol. lxxxv. MS. Leofr. fol. 117. Comes Pamel. tom. ii. p 25.

[t] Miss. Sarisb. fol. lxxxvi. MS. Leofr. fol. 117. Comes Pamel tom ii. p 25.

[u] Miss. Sar. Fer 3 post Pascha, fol. lxxxvi. MS. Leofr. fol. 117. Comes Pamel. tom. ii. p. 25.

[v] Miss. Sar. fol lxxxvi. MS. Leofr. 117 Comes Pamel. tom. ii p. 25

[w] I have not found any original of the collect

[x] Miss. Sar. Dominica prima post Pascha, fol lxxxix. Comes Pamel. tom. ii. p. 27.

[y] Miss. Sar. fol. lxxxix. Comes Pamel. tom. ii. p 27.

CHAP. III.   *Originals of the English Collects, &c.*   337

THE SECOND SUNDAY AFTER EASTER[z].

THE EPISTLE. 1 St. Peter ii. 19. Lectio Epistolæ beati Petri Apostoli 1 ii. Christus passus est pro vobis relinquens exemplum... sed conversi estis nunc ad Pastorem et Episcopum animarum vestrarum[a].

THE GOSPEL. St. John x. 11. Secundum Joannem x. Dixit Jesus discipulis suis, Ego sum Pastor bonus   . et fiet unum ovile et unus Pastor[b]

THE THIRD SUNDAY AFTER EASTER.

THE COLLECT. Almighty God, who shewest to them that be in error the light of thy truth, to the intent that they may return into the way of righteousness; Grant unto all them that are admitted into the fellowship of Christ's religion, that they may eschew those things that are contrary to their profession, and follow all such things as are agreeable to the same; through our Lord Jesus Christ. *Amen.*

Deus, qui errantibus, ut in viam possint redire justitiæ, veritatis tuæ lumen ostendis; da cunctis qui Christiana professione censentur, et illa respuere, quæ huic inimica sunt nomini, et ea quæ sunt apta, sectari. Per Dominum[c].

THE EPISTLE. 1 St. Peter ii. 11. Lectio Epistolæ beati Petri Apostoli 1 ii. Carissimi, obsecro vos tanquam advenas et peregrinos abstinere vos a carnalibus desideriis.. non tantum bonis et modestis sed etiam dyscolis, hæc est enim gratia in Christo Jesu Domino nostro[d].

THE GOSPEL. St. John xvi. 16. Secundum Joannem xvi.

---

[z] I have not yet found any original of the collect.
[a] Miss. Sar. Dom. 2. post Pascha, fol. xc. Comes Pamel. tom. ii. p. 27.
[b] Miss. Sar. fol xc Comes Pam. tom. ii. p. 27.
[c] Miss. Sar. fol. xci. Dominica tertia post Pascha. Ambros. Miss. Pamel. tom. i. p.

369. Leon. Sacram. Muratori Liturg. Rom. tom. i. p. 301. Gelasii Sacr. ibid. tom. i. p. 584. Gregorii Liber Sacrament. Menard. p. 89. MS. Leofr. fol. 124.
[d] Miss. Sarisb. fol. xci. MS. Leofr. 124. Comes Pamel. tom. ii. p. 28.

VOL. I.   Z

Dixit Jesus discipulis suis, Modicum et jam non videbitis me et gaudium vestrum nemo tollet a vobis[e].

THE FOURTH SUNDAY AFTER EASTER.

THE COLLECT. O Almighty God, who alone canst order the unruly wills and affections of sinful men, Grant unto thy people, that they may love the thing which thou commandest, and desire that which thou dost promise; that so, among the sundry and manifold changes of the world, our hearts may surely there be fixed, where true joys are to be found; through Jesus Christ our Lord. *Amen.*

Deus, qui fidelium mentes unius efficis voluntatis, da populis tuis id amare quod præcipis, id desiderare quod promittis, ut inter mundanas varietates ibi nostra fixa sint corda ubi vera sunt gaudia. Per[f].

THE EPISTLE. St. James i 17 Lectio Epistolæ beati Jacobi Apostoli i. Omne datum optimum et omne donum perfectum . quod potest salvare animas vestras[g].

THE FIFTH SUNDAY AFTER EASTER.

THE COLLECT. O Lord, from whom all good things do come, Grant to us thy humble servants, that by thy holy inspiration we may think those things that be good, and by thy merciful guiding may perform the same; through our Lord Jesus Christ. *Amen.*

Deus, a quo bona cuncta procedunt; largire supplicibus tuis ut cogitemus te inspirante quæ recta sunt, et te gubernante eadem faciamus. Per[h].

---

[e] Miss. Sar. fol. xci. MS. Leofr. 124. Comes Pamel. tom. ii. p. 28.

[f] Miss. Sar. Dominica iv. post Pascha, fol. xcii. Ambros. Miss. Pamel. Liturg. tom. i. p. 368 Gelasii Sacramentar. Muratori tom. 1. p. 585 Gregorii Sacram. Menard. p. 90. MS. Leofr. fol. 124.

[g] Miss. Sarisb. fol xcii. MS. Leofr. fol. 125. Comes Pamel. tom. ii. p. 29.

[h] Miss. Sar. Dom. v. post Pascha, fol. xcii. Gelasii Sacramentar. Muratori Lit. Rom.

THE EPISTLE. St. James i. 22. Lectio Epistolæ beati Jacobi Apostoli i. Estote factores verbi et non auditores tantum . . . et immaculatum se custodire ab hoc sæculo¹

THE GOSPEL. St. John xvi. 23 Secundum Joannem xvi. Amen, Amen, dico vobis . . . in hoc credimus quia a Deo existiJ.

THE ASCENSION DAY.

THE COLLECT. Grant we beseech thee, Almighty God, that like as we do believe thy only begotten Son our Lord Jesus Christ to have ascended into the heavens; so we may also in heart and mind thither ascend, and with him continually dwell, who liveth and reigneth with thee and the Holy Ghost, one God, world without end. *Amen.*

Concede quæsumus omnipotens Deus, ut qui hodierna die unigenitum tuum Redemptorem nostrum ad cœlos ascendisse credimus, ipsi quoque mente in cœlestibus habitemus. Per eundem ᵏ.

FOR THE EPISTLE. Acts i. 1. Lectio Actuum Apostolorum i. Primam quidem sermonem feci de omnibus Theophile . . . . sic veniet quemadmodum vidistis eum euntem in cœlum¹.

THE GOSPEL. St. Mark xvi. 14. Secundum Marcum xvi. Recumbentibus undecim discipulis . . . . Domino cooperante et sermonem confirmante sequentibus signis ᵐ.

SUNDAY AFTER ASCENSION DAY.

O God the King of Glory who hast exalted thine only

" O rex Gloriæ, Domine virtutum, qui triumphator hodie

---

tom. i. p. 585. Gregorii Liber Sacram. Menard p. 91. MS. Leofr. fol. 125.
¹ Miss. Sar. fol. xcii. MS. Leofr. fol. 125. Comes Pamel. tom. ii. p. 29.
J Miss Sar. fol. xcii. MS Leofr. fol. 125.
ᵏ Miss. Sarisb. in die Ascensionis Domini, fol. xciii Gregorii Sacr. Menard. p. 95. Muratori tom. ii. p 85 MS.

Leofr. fol. 128. derived from Gelasii Sacramentar. Muratori Lit Rom. tom. i. p. 587.
¹ Miss. Sarisb. fol. xciii. Lectionar. Gallic. in Ascensione Domini nostri Jesu Christi Mabillon. Liturg Gall. p. 155. Comes Pamel. tom. ii. p 31.
ᵐ Miss. Sar. fol. xciv. Comes Pamel. tom. ii. p. 31.

Son Jesus Christ with great triumph unto thy kingdom in heaven; we beseech thee leave us not comfortless, but send to us thy Holy Ghost to comfort us, and exalt us unto the same place whither our Saviour Christ is gone before, who liveth and reigneth with thee, and the Holy Ghost, one God, world without end. *Amen.*

super omnes cœlos ascendisti, ne derelinquas nos orphanos, sed mitte promissum Patris in nos Spiritum Veritatis[m]."

THE EPISTLE. 1 St. Peter iv. 7. Lectio Epistolæ beati Petri Apostoli iv. Estote prudentes et vigilate in orationibus.... ut in omnibus honorificetur Deus per Jesum Christum Dominum nostrum[n].

THE GOSPEL. St. John xv. 26. and part of chap. xvi. Secundum Joannem xv. et xvi. Cum venerit Paraclitus.... et cum venerit hora, eorum reminiscamini, quia ego dixi vobis[o].

WHITSUNDAY.

THE COLLECT. God, who as at this time didst teach the hearts of thy faithful people, by the sending to them the light of thy Holy Spirit; Grant us by the same Spirit to have a right judgment in all things, and evermore to rejoice in his

Deus, qui hodierna die corda fidelium Sancti Spiritus illustratione docuisti; da nobis in eodem Spiritu, recta sapere, et de ejus semper consolatione gaudere. Per Dominum, in unitate ejusdem[p].

---

[m] The collect for this Sunday, "appears to have been made altogether new, by the original compilers of our liturgy. The whole of the beginning, however, is taken from the anthem for vespers on Ascension-day; which anthem (antiphona) was also sung on this day" For the above quotation and remarks I am indebted to the MS. annotations of bishop Lloyd on the Book of Common Prayer.

[n] Miss. Sar. Dominica infra octav. Ascensionis fol. xciv. MS. Leofr. fol. 129. Comes Pamel tom ii. p. 31.

[o] Miss. Sar. fol. xciiii. MS. Leofr fol. 129. Comes Pamel. tom. ii. p. 31.

[p] Miss Sar. in die Pentecostes, fol. xcvi. Gregorii Sacram. Menard. p. 98. MS. Leofr. fol. 131.

CHAP. III. *Originals of the English Collects, &c.* 341

holy comfort: through the merits of Jesus Christ our Saviour, who liveth and reigneth with thee in the unity of the same spirit, one God, world without end. *Amen.*

FOR THE EPISTLE. Acts ii. 1. Lectio Actuum Apostolorum ii. Dum complerentur dies Pentecostes.... audivimus eos loquentes nostris linguis magnalia Dei [q].

THE GOSPEL. St. John xiv. 15. Secundum Joannem xiv. Dixit Jesus discipulis suis, Si quis diligit me ... et sicut mandatum dedit mihi Pater sic facio [r].

MONDAY IN WHITSUN-WEEK.

FOR THE EPISTLE. Acts x. 34 Lectio Actuum Apostolorum x. In diebus illis aperiens Petrus os suum dixit.... et jussit eos baptizari in nomine Domini nostri Jesu Christi [s].

THE GOSPEL. St. John iii. 16. Secundum Joannem. iii. Sic Deus dilexit mundum ut Filium suum unigenitum daret. . ut manifestentur ejus opera quia in Deo sunt facta [t].

TUESDAY IN WHITSUN-WEEK.

FOR THE EPISTLE. Acts viii. 14. Lectio Actuum Apostolorum viii. Cum audissent Apostoli qui erant Hierosolymis.... et accipiebant Spiritum Sanctum [u].

THE GOSPEL. St. John x. 1. Secundum Joannem x. Amen, Amen, dico vobis, qui non intrat. .. et abundantius habeant [v].

TRINITY SUNDAY.

THE COLLECT. Almighty and everlasting God, who hast given unto thy servants grace, by the confession of a true

Omnipotens sempiterne Deus, qui dedisti famulis tuis, in confessione veræ fidei æternæ Trinitatis gloriam agnoscere, et

---

[q] Miss. Sar. fol. xcvi. MS. Leofr. fol. 132. Lectionar. Gall. Mabillon. de Liturg. Gall. p. 155. Comes Pamel. tom. ii. p. 32.

[r] Miss. Sar. fol. xcvi. MS. Leofr. 132. Comes Pam. tom. ii. p. 32

[s] Miss. Sar. fol. xcvi. Feria 2 post Pentecost. MS. Leofr. 132. Comes Pamel. tom. ii. p. 32.

[t] Miss. Sar. fol. xcvii. MS. Leofr. fol. 132. Comes Pamel. tom. ii. p. 33.

[u] Miss. Sar. Fer. 3 post Pentecost. fol. xcvii. MS. Leofr. 133. Comes Pam. tom. ii. p. 33.

[v] Miss. Sar. fol. xcvii. MS. Leofr. 133. Comes Pamel. tom ii. p. 33.

faith, to acknowledge the glory of the eternal Trinity, and in the power of the Divine Majesty to worship the Unity; We beseech thee that thou wouldst keep us steadfast in this faith, and evermore defend us from all adversities, who livest and reignest, one God, world without end. *Amen.*

in potentia Majestatis adorare Unitatem; quæsumus, ut ejusdem fidei firmitate ab omnibus semper muniemur adversis. Per Dominum nostrum[w].

FOR THE EPISTLE. Rev. iv. 1. Lectio libri Apocalypsis beati Joannis Apostoli iv. Vidi ostium apertum in cœlo.... procedebant viginti quatuor seniores ante sedentem in throno, et adorabant viventem in sæcula sæculorum[x].

THE GOSPEL. St. John iii. 1. Secundum Joannem iii. Erat homo ex Pharisæis Nicodemus nomine... ut omnis qui credit in ipso non pereat sed habeat vitam æternam[y].

FIRST SUNDAY AFTER TRINITY.

THE COLLECT. O God, the strength of all them that put their trust in thee, mercifully accept our prayers; and because through the weakness of our mortal nature we can do no good thing without thee, grant us the help of thy grace; that in keeping thy commandments we may please thee, both in will and deed, through Jesus Christ our Lord. *Amen.*

Deus, in te sperantium fortitudo, adesto propitius invocationibus nostris; et quia sine te nihil potest mortalis infirmitas; præsta auxilium gratiæ tuæ; ut in exequendis mandatis tuis; et voluntate tibi et actione placeamus. Per Dominum[z].

THE EPISTLE. 1 St. John iv. 7 Lectio Epistolæ beati Joannis

---

[w] Miss. Sar in die sanctæ Trinitatis, fol. c. Gregorii Liber Sacr. Menard. p 105 MS. Leofr. Missa de sancta Trinitate, fol. 212.

[x] Miss Sar. fol c Comes Pamel. tom. ii. p 34.

[y] Miss. Sar. fol. c. Comes Pamel. tom ii p 34.

[z] Miss. Sar. Dominica prima post festum sanctæ Trinitatis fol. xci. MS Leofr. 136. Ambros Miss. Pamel. Liturg. tom. i. p 369. Gelasii Sacram. Muratori Liturg. Rom. tom. 1. p. 587. Gregorii Sacramentar. Menard. p 175.

CHAP. III. *Originals of the English Collects, &c.* 343

Apostoli I iv. Deus caritas est In hoc apparuit caritas Dei . . et hoc mandatum habemus a Deo, ut qui diligit Deum, diligat et fratrem suum [a].

THE GOSPEL. St Luke xvi. 19. Secundum Lucam xvi. Homo quidam erat dives, et induebatur purpura... neque si quis ex mortuis resurrexerit credent [b].

THE SECOND SUNDAY AFTER TRINITY.

THE COLLECT. O Lord, who never failest to help and govern them whom thou dost bring up in thy steadfast fear and love; Keep us, we beseech thee, under the protection of thy good providence, and make us to have a perpetual fear and love of thy holy name, through Jesus Christ our Lord. *Amen.*

Sancti nominis tui, Domine, timorem pariter et amorem fac nos habere perpetuum; quia nunquam tua gubernatione destituis, quos in soliditate tuæ dilectionis instituis. Per Dominum [c].

THE EPISTLE. 1 St. John iii. 13. Lectio Epistolæ beati Joannis Apostoli I iii. Carissimi, nolite mirare si odit vos mundus . . non diligamus verbo neque lingua, sed opere et veritate [d]

THE GOSPEL. St. Luke xiv. 16. Secundum Lucam xiv. Homo quidam fecit cœnam magnam . nemo virorum illorum qui locuti sunt gustabit cœnam meam [e].

THE THIRD SUNDAY AFTER TRINITY.

THE COLLECT. O Lord, we beseech thee mercifully to hear us; and grant that we, to whom thou hast given an hearty desire to pray, may by thy mighty aid be defended and comforted

Deprecationem nostram, quæsumus Domine, benignus exaudi, et quibus supplicandi præstas affectum, tribue defensionis auxilium. Per Dominum [f].

---

[a] Miss. Sar fol. ci MS Leofr. fol 136. Comes Pamel. tom ii. p. 35.

[b] Miss. Sar. fol cii MS Leofr fol. 136. Comes Pamel. tom. ii. p. 35

[c] Miss Sar Dominica ii. post Trinitatem, fol. cii. MS Leofr. 136 Gelasii Sacram. Muratori tom. i p 590. Gregorii Sacram. Menard. p. 176.

[d] Miss. Sar. fol. cii. MS. Leofr. 136. Comes Pamel tom. ii p. 35.

[e] Miss Sar. fol cii. MS. Leofr. 136. Comes Pam. tom ii. p. 35.

[f] Miss Sarisb Dominica tertia post Trinitat. fol. ciii. MS.

in all dangers and adversities, through Jesus Christ our Lord. *Amen.*

THE EPISTLE. 1 St. Peter v. 5. Lectio Epistolæ beati Petri Apostoli 1 ultimo. Humiliamini sub potenti manu Dei. ipsi gloria et imperium in sæcula sæculorum [g].

THE GOSPEL. St. Luke xv. 1. Secundum Lucam xv. Erant appropinquantes ad Jesum publicani et peccatores.... gaudium erit in cœlo coram angelis Dei super uno peccatore pœnitentiam agente [h].

THE FOURTH SUNDAY AFTER TRINITY.

THE COLLECT. O God, the protector of all that trust in thee, without whom nothing is strong, nothing is holy; Increase and multiply upon us thy mercy; that, thou being our Ruler and Guide, we may so pass through things temporal, that we finally lose not the things eternal: Grant this, O heavenly Father, for Jesus Christ's sake, our Lord. *Amen.*

Protector in te sperantium Deus, sine quo nihil est validum, nihil sanctum; multiplica super nos misericordiam tuam, ut te Rectore, te Duce, sic transeamus per bona temporalia, ut non amittamus æterna. Per Dominum nostrum [i].

THE EPISTLE. Rom. viii. 18. Ad Romanos viii. Existimo enim quia non sint condignæ passiones hujus temporis.... expectantes redemptionem corporis nostri in Christo Jesu Domino nostro [j]

THE GOSPEL. St. Luke vi. 36. Secundum Lucam vi. Estote misericordes sicut et Pater vester .. et tunc perspicies ut educas festucam de oculo fratris tui [k].

Leofr. fol. 137. Gregorii Sacram. Menard. p. 177.
[g] Miss. Sar. fol. ciii. MS. Leofr. fol. 137. Comes Pamel. tom. ii. p. 37.
[h] Miss. Sar. fol ciii. MS. Leofr. 137. Comes Pamel. ibid.
[i] Miss. Sar. Dominica quarta post Trinitat. fol. ciii Gregorii Sacram. Menard. p. 178. MS. Leofr. 137. Miss. Franc. Mabillon Lit. Gall. p. 322.
[j] Miss. Sar. fol. ciii. MS. Leofr. 137. Comes Pamel. tom. ii. p 37.
[k] Miss. Sar. fol. ciii. MS. Leofr. 137. Comes Pamel. ibid. p. 38

THE FIFTH SUNDAY AFTER TRINITY.

THE COLLECT. Grant, O Lord, we beseech thee, that the course of this world may be so peaceably ordered by thy governance, that thy Church may joyfully serve thee in all godly quietness; through Jesus Christ our Lord. *Amen.*

Da nobis quæsumus Domine, ut et mundi cursus pacifice nobis tuo ordine dirigatu, et Ecclesia tua tranquilla devotione lætetur. Per Dominum nostrum[l].

THE EPISTLE. 1 St. Peter iii. 8. Lectio Epistolæ beati Petri Apostoli 1 iii. Omnes unanimes in oratione estote, compatientes.... Dominum autem Christum sanctificate in cordibus vestris[m].

THE GOSPEL. St. Luke v. 1. Secundum Lucam v. Cum turbæ irruerent ad Jesum ut audirent verbum Dei.... et subductis in terram navibus, relictis omnibus, secuti sunt eum[n].

THE SIXTH SUNDAY AFTER TRINITY.

THE COLLECT. O God, who hast prepared for them that love thee such good things as pass man's understanding; Pour into our hearts such love toward thee, that we, loving thee above all things, may obtain thy promises, which exceed all that we can desire; through Jesus Christ our Lord. *Amen.*

Deus qui diligentibus te bona invisibilia præparasti; infunde cordibus nostris, tui amoris affectum; ut te in omnibus et super omnia diligentes, promissiones tuas, quæ omne desiderium superant, consequamur. Per Dominum nostrum[o].

---

[l] Miss. Sar. fol. cvi. Dominica v. post Trinitatem. MS. Leofr. fol. 138. Gregorii Sacramentar. Menard. p. 179.

[m] Miss. Sar. fol. ciii. MS. Leofr. 138. Comes Pamel. tom. ii. p. 38.

[n] Miss. Sar. fol. civ. MS. Leofr. 138. Comes Pamel. ibid.

[o] Miss. Sar. Dominica sexta post Trinitatem, fol. civ. Ambros. Miss. Pamel. Liturg .tom. i. p. 387. Gelasii Sacramentar Muratori, tom. i. p. 687. Gregorii Sacram. Menard. p. 179. MS. Leofr. fol. 138. Miss. Franc. sæc. 7. vel 8. Mab. Lit. Gall. p. 322.

THE EPISTLE Rom. vi. 3. Ad Romanos vi. Quicunque baptizati sumus in Christo Jesu, in morte ipsius baptizati sumus .... viventes autem Deo in Christo Jesu Domino nostro P.

THE GOSPEL. St. Matth. v. 20. Secundum Mattheum v. Dixit Jesus discipulis suis. Amen, dico vobis, quia nisi abundaverit justitia vestra   et tunc veniens offeres munus tuum q.

THE SEVENTH SUNDAY AFTER TRINITY.

THE COLLECT Lord of all power and might, who art the author and giver of all good things; Graft in our hearts the love of thy Name, increase in us true religion, nourish us with all goodness, and of thy great mercy keep us in the same; through Jesus Christ our Lord. *Amen.*

Deus virtutum, cujus est totum quod est optimum; insere pectoribus nostris amorem tui nominis, et præsta in nobis religionis augmentum; ut quæ sunt bona nutrias, ac pietatis studio quæ sunt nutrita custodias. Per r.

THE EPISTLE. Rom. vi. 19. Ad Romanos vi. Humanum dico propter infirmitatem carnis vestræ .. gratia autem Dei, vita æterna in Christo Jesu Domino nostro s.

THE GOSPEL. St. Mark viii. 1. Secundum Marcum viii In illo tempore cum turba multa esset cum Jesu.... erant autem qui manducaverunt quasi quatuor millia, et dimisit eos t.

THE EIGHTH SUNDAY AFTER TRINITY

THE COLLECT. O God, whose never-failing providence ordereth all things both in heaven

Deus, cujus providentia in sui dispositione non fallitur; te supplices exoramus, ut noxia

---

p Miss. Sar fol. civ. MS. Leofr. 138. Comes Pamel. tom. ii p. 40.

q Miss. Sar. fol. civ. MS. Leofr. 138. Comes Pamel. ibid.

r Miss. Sar. Dominica vii. post Trinitatem, fol. cv. Ambros. Miss. Pamel tom i p. 380. Gelasii Sacr Muratori, tom. i. p 687 Gregorii Sacr.

Menard. p. 180. MS Leofr fol. 139. Miss. Franc. Mabill. Lit. Gall p. 322.

s Miss Sar. fol. cv. MS. Leofr 139 Comes Pamel. tom. ii. p. 41.

t Miss. Sar fol. cv. MS. Leofr. fol. 139. Comes Pamel ibid.

CHAP. III.   *Originals of the English Collects, &c.*   347

and earth; We humbly beseech thee to put away from us all hurtful things, and to give us those things which be profitable for us; through Jesus Christ our Lord. *Amen.*

cuncta submoveas, et omnia nobis profutura concedas. Per[u].

THE EPISTLE. Rom. viii. 12. Ad Romanos viii. Fratres debitores sumus, non carnis .... hæredes quidem Dei, cohæredes autem Christi[v].

THE GOSPEL. St. Matthew vii. 15. Secundum Mattheum vii. Attendite a falsis prophetis .... sed qui facit voluntatem Patris mei qui in cœlis est, ipse intrabit in regnum cœlorum[w].

THE NINTH SUNDAY AFTER TRINITY.

THE COLLECT. Grant to us, Lord, we beseech thee, the spirit to think and do always such things as be rightful; that we, who cannot do any thing that is good without thee, may by thee be enabled to live according to thy will; through Jesus Christ our Lord. *Amen*

Largire nobis Domine, quæsumus, semper spiritum cogitandi quæ recta sunt, propitius, et agendi, ut qui sine te esse non possumus, secundum te vivere valeamus. Per[x]

THE EPISTLE 1 Cor. x. 1. Ad Corinthios 1 x. Non simus concupiscentes malorum sicut et illi .... sed faciet cum temptatione etiam proventum ut possitis sustinere[y].

THE GOSPEL. St. Luke xvi. 1. Secundum Lucam xvi. Homo quidam erat dives .... ut cum defeceritis recipiant vos in æterna tabernacula[z].

---

[u] Miss. Sar. Dominica viii. post Trinitatem, fol cv. Gelasii Sacramentar. Muratori Lit. Rom tom. i. p. 688. Gregorii Sacrament. Menard. p. 181. MS. Leofr. fol. 139
[v] Miss. Sar. fol. cv. MS. Leofr. 139. Comes Pamel. tom. ii. p. 42.
[w] Miss. Sar. fol. cv MS. Leofr. 139. Comes Pamel. ibid.
[x] Miss. Sar Dom. ix. post Trinitatem, fol. cvi. Leon. Sacramentar. Muratori, tom. i. p. 379. Gelasii Sacram ibid. p. 689. Gregorii Liber Sacr. Menard. p. 182. MS. Leofr. fol. 140.
[y] Miss. Sar. fol. cvi. MS. Leofr. 140. Comes Pamel. tom ii. p 42.
[z] Miss Sar. fol. cvi. MS. Leofr. 140. Comes Pamel. ibid.

THE TENTH SUNDAY AFTER TRINITY.

THE COLLECT. Let thy merciful ears, O Lord, be open to the prayers of thy humble servants; and that they may obtain their petitions, make them to ask such things as shall please thee; through Jesus Christ our Lord. *Amen*.

Pateant aures misericordiæ tuæ, Domine, precibus supplicantium; et ut petentibus desiderata concedas, fac eos quæ tibi placita sunt postulare. Per Dominum [a].

THE EPISTLE. 1 Cor. xii. 1. Ad Corinthios I xii. Scitis quoniam cum gentes essetis .... dividens singulis prout vult [b].

THE GOSPEL. St. Luke xix. 41. Secundum Lucam xix. Cum appropinquaret Jesus Hierusalem .... et erat docens quotidie in templo [c].

THE ELEVENTH SUNDAY AFTER TRINITY.

THE COLLECT. O God, who declarest thy almighty power most chiefly in shewing mercy and pity; Mercifully grant unto us such a measure of thy grace, that we, running the way of thy commandments, may obtain thy gracious promises, and be made partakers of thy heavenly treasure; through Jesus Christ our Lord. *Amen*.

Deus, qui omnipotentiam tuam parcendo maxime et miserando manifestas; multiplica super nos gratiam tuam, ut ad tua promissa currentes, cœlestium bonorum facias esse consortes. Per [d].

THE EPISTLE. 1 Cor. xv. 1. Ad Corinthios I xv. Fratres notum vobis facio evangelium .... et gratia ejus in me vacua non fuit [e].

---

[a] Miss. Sar. Dominica x. post Trinitatem, fol. cvi. Miss. Ambros. Pamel. tom. i. p. 310. Leon. Sacramentar. Muratori Lit. Rom. tom. i. p. 381. Gelasii Sacr. ibid. p 689 MS. Leofr. 140. Miss. Franc. Mabillon Lit. Gall p 325.

[b] Miss. Sar fol. cvi MS. Leofr. 140. Comes Pamel. tom. ii. p. 43.

[c] Miss Sar. fol. cvi. MS. Leofr 140. Comes Pamel. ibid.

[d] Miss. Sar. Dom. xi. post Trinitatem, fol. cvii. Gelasii Sacramentar. Muratori, tom. i. p. 690 Gregorii Sacr. Menard p. 183. MS. Leofr. 141. Miss. Gothicum Mabillon. Lit. Gall. p. 292. Miss. Franc. ibid. p. 324.

[e] Miss. Sar. fol. cvii. MS.

THE GOSPEL. St. Luke xviii. 9. Secundum Lucam xviii. Dixit Jesus ad quosdam qui in se confidebant tanquam justi .... et qui se humiliat exaltabitur f.

THE TWELFTH SUNDAY AFTER TRINITY.

THE COLLECT. Almighty and everlasting God, who art always more ready to hear than we to pray, and art wont to give more than either we desire or deserve; Pour down upon us the abundance of thy mercy; forgiving us those things whereof our conscience is afraid, and giving us those good things which we are not worthy to ask, but through the merits and mediation of Jesus Christ, thy Son, our Lord. Amen.

Omnipotens sempiterne Deus, qui abundantia pietatis tuæ et merita supplicum excedis et vota; effunde super nos misericordiam tuam; ut dimittas quæ conscientia metuit, et adjicias quæ oratio non præsumit. Per g.

THE EPISTLE. 2 Cor. iii. 4. Ad Corinthios 2 iii. Fiduciam talem habemus per Christum ad Deum .... multo magis abundat ministerium justitiæ in gloria h.

THE GOSPEL. St. Mark vii 31. Secundum Marcum vii. Exiens Jesus de finibus Tyri venit ad Sidonem .... et surdos fecit audire, et mutos loqui i.

THE THIRTEENTH SUNDAY AFTER TRINITY.

THE COLLECT. Almighty and merciful God, of whose only gift it cometh that thy faithful people do unto thee true and

Omnipotens et misericors Deus, de cujus munere venit, ut tibi a fidelibus tuis digne et laudabiliter serviatur: tribue

---

Leofr. 141. Comes Pamel. tom. ii. p. 44.

f Miss. Sar. fol. cvii. MS. Leofr. 141. Comes Pamel. ibid.

g Miss. Sar. Dominica xii. post Trinitatem, fol. cvii. Leon. Sacram. Muratori, tom. i. p. 418. Gelasii Sacr. ibid. p. 690. Gregorii Sacr. Menard. p. 184.

MS. Leofr. 141. Miss. Franc. Mabill. Lit. Gall. p. 324.

h Miss. Sar. Dom. xii. post Trinitatem, fol cvii. MS. Leofr. 141. Comes Pamel. tom. ii. p. 45.

i Miss. Sar. fol. cvii. MS. Leofr. fol. 141. Comes Pamel. ibid.

laudable service; Grant, we beseech thee, that we may so faithfully serve thee in this life, that we fail not finally to attain thy heavenly promises; through the merits of Jesus Christ our Lord. *Amen.*

nobis quæsumus ut ad promissiones tuas sine offensione curramus. Per[j].

THE EPISTLE. Gal. iii. 16. Ad Galathas iii. Abrahæ dictæ sunt promissiones .... ut promissio ex fide Jesu Christi daretur credentibus[k].

THE GOSPEL. St. Luke x. 23. Secundum Lucam x. Beati oculi qui vident .... vade et tu fac similiter[l].

THE FOURTEENTH SUNDAY AFTER TRINITY.

THE COLLECT. Almighty and everlasting God, give unto us the increase of faith, hope, and charity; and that we may obtain that which thou dost promise, make us to love that which thou dost command: through Jesus Christ our Lord. *Amen.*

Omnipotens sempiterne Deus, da nobis fidei, spei, et charitatis augmentum; et ut mereamur adsequi quod promittis; fac nos amare quod præcipis. Per[m].

THE EPISTLE. Gal v 16. Ad Galathas v. Spiritu ambulate .... carnem suam crucifixerunt cum vitiis et concupiscentiis[n].

THE GOSPEL. St. Luke xvii. 11. Secundum Lucam xvii. Cum iret Jesus in Hierusalem transibat per mediam Samariam .... surge et vade, quia fides tua te salvum fecit[o].

---

[j] Miss. Sar. Dominica xiii. post Trinitatem, fol. cviii. Leon. Sacram. Muratori Lit. Rom. tom. i. p. 371. Gelasii Sacr. ibid. p. 691. MS. Leofr. fol. 142.

[k] Miss. Sar fol. cviii MS. Leofr. fol. 142. Comes Pamel tom. ii.p. 46.

[l] Ibid.

[m] Miss. Sar. fol. cviii Dominica xiv. post Trinitatem. Miss. Ambros. Pamel. Liturg. tom. i. p. 432. Leon. Sacram. Muratori tom. i p. 374. Gelasii Sacr. ibid. p. 691. Gregorii Sacr. Menard. p. 186. MS. Leofr. 142.

[n] Miss. Sar. fol. cviii. MS. Leofr fol. 142. Comes Pamel. tom. ii. p. 46.

[o] Ibid.

THE FIFTEENTH SUNDAY AFTER TRINITY

THE COLLECT. Keep, we beseech thee, O Lord, thy church with thy perpetual mercy: and, because the frailty of man without thee cannot but fall, keep us ever by thy help from all things hurtful, and lead us to all things profitable to our salvation, through Jesus Christ our Lord. *Amen.*

Custodi, Domine, quæsumus, ecclesiam tuam propitiatione perpetua; et quia sine te labitur humana mortalitas; tuis semper auxiliis et abstrahatur a noxiis, et ad salutaria dirigatur. Per p.

THE GOSPEL. St Matth. vi. 24. Secundum Mattheum vi. Nemo potest duobus dominis servire.... et hæc omnia adjicientur vobis q.

THE SIXTEENTH SUNDAY AFTER TRINITY

THE COLLECT. O Lord, we beseech thee, let thy continual pity cleanse and defend thy church; and, because it cannot continue in safety without thy succour, preserve it evermore by thy help and goodness, through Jesus Christ our Lord. *Amen.*

Ecclesiam tuam, Domine quæsumus, miseratio continuata mundet et muniat; et quia sine te non potest salva consistere; tuo semper munere gubernetur. Per r.

THE EPISTLE. Ephes. iii. 13. Ad Ephesios iii. Obsecro vos ne deficiatis in tribulationibus meis.... ipsi gloria in ecclesia et in Christo Jesu in omnes generationes sæculi sæculorum. Amen s.

THE GOSPEL. St. Luke vii 11. Secundum Lucam vii Ibat

---

p Miss. Sarisb. Dominica xv. post Trinitatem, fol. cix. Gelasii Sacramentar. Muratori tom. i. p 692. Gregorii Sacr. p. 186. Menard. MS. Leofr. fol. 143. The Epistle for this Sunday is taken from the same chapter as our own, in the missal of Sarum, fol. cix.

q Miss. Sarisb. fol. cix. MS.

Leofr. 143. Comes Pamel. tom. ii. p. 47.

r Miss. Sar. Dominica xvi. post Trinitatem, fol. cix. Gelasii Sacr. Muratori, tom. i. p. 692. Gregorii Sacr. Menard. p. 187. MS. Leofr. fol. 143.

s Miss. Sar. fol. cix. MS. Leofr. fol. 143. Comes Pamel. tom. ii. p. 48

Jesus in civitatem quæ vocatur Naim. ... et quia Deus visitavit plebem suam [t].

THE SEVENTEENTH SUNDAY AFTER TRINITY.

THE COLLECT. Lord, we pray thee that thy grace may always prevent and follow us, and make us continually to be given to all good works; through Jesus Christ our Lord. *Amen.*

Tua nos Domine, quæsumus, gratia semper et præveniat et sequatur; ac bonis operibus jugiter præstet esse intentos. Per Dominum [u].

THE EPISTLE. Ephes. iv. 1. Ad Ephesios iv. Obsecro itaque vos ego vinctus in Domino.... qui est benedictus in sæcula sæculorum [v].

THE GOSPEL. St. Luke xiv. 1. Secundum Lucam xiv. Cum intraret in domum cujusdam principis Pharisæorum ... et qui se humiliat exaltabitur [w].

THE EIGHTEENTH SUNDAY AFTER TRINITY.

THE COLLECT. Lord, we beseech thee, grant thy people grace to withstand the temptations of the world, the flesh, and the Devil, and with pure hearts and minds to follow thee the only God; through Jesus Christ our Lord. *Amen.*

Da, quæsumus Domine, populo tuo diabolica vitare contagia; et te solum Deum puro corde sectari. Per [x].

THE EPISTLE. 1 Cor. i. 4. Ad Corinthios primæ i. Gratias Deo meo semper pro vobis .. in die adventus Domini nostri Jesu Christi [y].

THE GOSPEL. St. Matth. xxii. 34. Secundum Mattheum xxii.

---

[t] Miss. Sar. fol. cix. MS. Leofr. fol. 143. Comes Pamel. ibid.

[u] Miss. Sar. Dom. xvii. post Trinitatem, fol. cx. Gregorii Sacr. Menard. p. 208.

[v] Miss. Sarisb. fol. cx. MS. Leofr. 144. Comes Pamel. tom. ii. p. 48.

[w] Ibid.

[x] Miss. Sar. Dom. xviii. post Trinitatem, fol. cx. Gelasii Sacramentar. Muratori, tom. i. p. 693. Gregorii Sacr. Menard. p. 190. MS. Leofr. 147.

[y] Miss. Sarisb. fol. cx. MS. Leofr. 146. Comes Pamel. tom. ii. p. 50.

Accederunt ad Jesum Pharisæi . . . neque ausus fuit quisquis ex illa die eum amplius interrogare [z].

THE NINETEENTH SUNDAY AFTER TRINITY.

THE COLLECT. O God, forasmuch as without thee we are not able to please thee; Mercifully grant, that thy holy Spirit may in all things direct and rule our hearts; through Jesus Christ our Lord. *Amen.*

Dirigat corda nostra, quæsumus Domine, tuæ miserationis operatio; quia tibi sine te placere non possumus. Per Dominum [a]

THE EPISTLE. Ephes. iv. 17. Ad Ephesios iiii. Renovamini spiritu mentis vestræ et induite novum hominem . . . ut habeat unde tribuat necessitatem patienti [b]

THE GOSPEL. St. Matth. ix. 1. Secundum Mattheum ix. Ascendens Jesus in naviculam . . . . et glorificaverunt Deum qui dedit potestatem talem hominibus [c].

THE TWENTIETH SUNDAY AFTER TRINITY

THE COLLECT O Almighty and most merciful God, of thy bountiful goodness, keep us, we beseech thee, from all things that may hurt us, that we, being ready both in body and soul, may cheerfully accomplish those things that thou wouldest have done; through Jesus Christ our Lord. *Amen.*

Omnipotens et misericors Deus, universa nobis adversantia propitiatus exclude; ut mente et corpore pariter expediti, quæ tua sunt liberis mentibus exequamur. Per Dominum [d].

THE EPISTLE. Ephes v. 15   Ad Ephesios v Videte quomodo

---

[z] Miss. Sar. fol. cx. MS. Leofr. 146. Comes Pamel. tom. ii. p. 50.
[a] Miss. Sar. Dom. xix. post Trinitatem, fol. cxi. Gelasii Sacr. Muratori, tom. i. p. 693. Sacr. Gregorii Menard. p. 191. MS. Leofr. Exon. episcopi, fol. 147.

[b] Miss. Sarisb. fol. cxi. MS Leofr. 146. Comes Pamel. tom ii. p. 51.
[c] Ibid.
[d] Miss. Sar. Dom xx. post Trinitatem, fol. cxi. Gelasii Sacr. Muratori, tom. i. p. 694. Gregorii Sacr. Menard. p 192. MS Leofr. fol 147.

caute ambuletis non quasi insipientes.... subjecti invicem in timore Christi[e].

THE GOSPEL. St. Matth. xxii. 1. Secundum Mattheum xxii. Simile factum est regnum cœlorum homini regi qui fecit nuptias ... multi enim sunt vocati pauci vero electi[f].

THE ONE AND TWENTIETH SUNDAY AFTER TRINITY.

THE COLLECT. Grant, we beseech thee, merciful Lord, to thy faithful people pardon and peace; that they may be cleansed from all their sins, and serve thee with a quiet mind; through Jesus Christ our Lord. *Amen.*

Largire, quæsumus Domine, fidelibus tuis indulgentiam placatus et pacem; ut pariter ab omnibus mundentur offensis, et secura tibi mente deserviant. Per[g].

THE EPISTLE. Ephes vi. 10. Ad Ephesios vi. Confortamini in Domino, et in potentia virtutis ejus.... et gladium spiritus quod est verbum Dei[h].

THE GOSPEL. St. John iv. 16. Secundum Joannem iiii. Erat quidam regulus cujus filius infirmabatur Capharnaum.... et credidit ipse et domus ejus tota[i].

THE TWO AND TWENTIETH SUNDAY AFTER TRINITY.

THE COLLECT. Lord, we beseech thee to keep thy household the church in continual godliness; that through thy protection it may be free from all adversities, and devoutly given to serve thee in good works, to the glory of thy

Familiam tuam, quæsumus Domine, continua pietate custodi; ut a cunctis adversitatibus te protegente sit libera, et in bonis actibus tuo nomini sit devota. Per Dominum[j].

---

[e] Miss. Sarisb. fol. cxi. MS. Leofr. fol. 147. Comes Pamel. tom. ii. p. 52.

[f] Ibid.

[g] Miss. Sarisb. Domin. xxi. post Trinit. fol. cxii. Gelasii Sacr. Muratori, tom. i. p. 694. Gregorii Sacr. Menard. p. 193.

MS. Leofr. fol. 148.

[h] Miss. Sarisb. fol. cxii. Comes Pamel. tom. ii. p. 52.

[i] Ibid.

[j] Miss. Sar. Dom. xxii. post Trin. fol. cxii. MS. Leofr. fol. 148.

CHAP. III.   *Originals of the English Collects, &c.*   355

name; through Jesus Christ our Lord. *Amen.*

THE EPISTLE. Phil. i. 3. Ad Philippenses i. Confidimus in Domino Jesu quia qui cœpit in vobis opus bonum perficiet.... in gloriam et laudem Dei [k].

THE GOSPEL. St. Matth. xviii 21. Secundum Mattheum xviii. Simile est regnum cœlorum homini regi qui voluit rationem ponere cum servis suis . . si non remiseritis unusquisque fratri suo de cordibus vestris [1].

THE THREE AND TWENTIETH SUNDAY AFTER TRINITY.

THE COLLECT. O God, our refuge and strength, who art the author of all godliness; Be ready, we beseech thee, to hear the devout prayers of thy Church, and grant that those things which we ask faithfully, we may obtain effectually; through Jesus Christ our Lord. *Amen.*

Deus, refugium nostrum et virtus, adesto piis Ecclesiæ tuæ precibus, auctor ipse pietatis; et præsta, ut quod fideliter petimus, efficaciter consequamur. Per [m].

THE EPISTLE. Phil. iii. 17. Ad Philippenses iii. Fratres imitatores mei estote .... secundum operationem qua possit etiam subjicere sibi omnia in Christo Jesu Domino nostro [n].

THE GOSPEL. St. Matthew xxii. 15. Secundum Mattheum xxii. Abeuntes Pharisæi consilium inierunt ut caperent Jesum in sermone .... et quæ sunt Dei Deo [o].

THE FOUR AND TWENTIETH SUNDAY AFTER TRINITY.

THE COLLECT. O Lord, we beseech thee, absolve thy people from their offences; that

Absolvere, quæsumus Domine, tuorum delicta populorum; ut a peccatorum nostro-

---

[k] Miss. Sarisb. fol. cxii. Comes Pamel. tom. ii. p. 53.
[l] Ibid.
[m] Miss. Sar. Dom. xxiii. post Trin. fol. cxiii. Gregorii Sacr.

Menard. p. 194. MS Leofr. 149
[n] Miss. Sarisb. Dom. xxiii. post Trin. fol cxiii. MS. Leofr. fol. 148. Comes Pamel. tom. ii. p. 54.   [o] Ibid.

through thy bountiful goodness we may all be delivered from the bands of those sins, which by our frailty we have committed; Grant this, O heavenly Father, for Jesus Christ's sake, our blessed Lord and Saviour. *Amen.*

rum nexibus, quæ pro nostra fragilitate contraximus, tua benignitate liberemur. Per Dominum [p].

THE EPISTLE. Col. i. 3. Ad Colossenses i. Non cessamus pro vobis orantes .... in omni patientia et longanimitate cum gaudio in Christo Jesu Domino nostro [q].

THE GOSPEL. St. Matthew ix. 18. Secundum Mattheum ix. Loquente Jesu ad turbas ecce princeps unus accessit ... et salva facta est mulier ex illa hora [r].

THE FIVE AND TWENTIETH SUNDAY AFTER TRINITY.

THE COLLECT. Stir up, we beseech thee, O Lord, the wills of thy faithful people; that they plenteously bringing forth the fruit of good works, may of thee be plenteously rewarded; through Jesus Christ our Lord. *Amen.*

Excita, quæsumus Domine, tuorum fidelium voluntates; ut divini operis fructum propensius exequentes, pietatis tuæ remedia majora percipiant. Per Dominum [s].

FOR THE EPISTLE. Jer. xxiii. 5. Lectio Hieremiæ Prophetæ xxiii. Ecce dies veniunt, dicit Dominus .... et habitabunt in terra sua. Dicit Dominus omnipotens [t].

THE GOSPEL St. John vi. 5. Secundum Joannem vi. Cum sublevasset oculos Jesus .... quia hic est vere Propheta qui venturus est in mundum [u].

---

[p] Miss. Sar. Dom. xxiiii. post Trin. fol. cxiii. Gregorii Sacr. Menard. p. 188. MS. Leofr. fol. 144.

[q] Miss. Sar. fol. cxiii. Comes Pamel. tom. ii. p. 55.

[r] Ibid.

[s] Miss. Sarisb. Dom. proxima ante Adventum, fol. cxiiii. Gregorii Sacr. Menard. p. 195. MS.

Leofr. 149. The rubric of Sarum, like ours, always appointed this collect, epistle, and gospel for the last Sunday before the season of Advent began. See Miss. Sar. fol. cxiiii.

[t] Miss. Sarisb. fol. cxiiii. Comes Pamel. tom. ii. p. 56.

[u] Ibid.

SAINT ANDREW'S DAY.

THE EPISTLE. Rom. x. 9. Ad Romanos x. Corde creditur ad justitiam.... et in fines orbis terræ verbum eorum [v]

THE GOSPEL. St. Matth. iv. 18. Secundum Mattheum iiii. Ambulans Jesus juxta mare Galileæ .... relictis retibus et patre secuti sunt eum [w].

SAINT THOMAS THE APOSTLE.

THE EPISTLE. Ephes. ii. 19. Ad Ephesios ii. Jam non estis hospites et advenæ .... et vos coædificamini in tabernaculum Dei in Spiritu Sancto [x].

THE GOSPEL. St. John xx. 24. Secundum Joannem xx. Thomas unus ex duodecim qui dicitur Didymus .... beati qui non viderunt, et crediderunt [y].

THE CONVERSION OF SAINT PAUL.

THE COLLECT. O God, who through the preaching of the blessed Apostle Saint Paul, hast caused the light of the Gospel to shine throughout

Deus, qui universum mundum beati Pauli Apostoli tui prædicatione docuisti; da nobis, quæsumus, ut qui ejus hodie conversionem colimus, per

---

[v] Miss. Sar. in die Sancti Andreæ Sanctorale, fol. i. MS. Leofr. fol. 202. Comes Pamel. tom. ii. p. 56. The collect for this day does not occur in the old English formularies. In the liturgy of the ancient Gallican church, a passage in the Contestatio for St. Andrew's day somewhat resembles our collect. "Almighty God, who didst give such grace unto thy holy apostle St. Andrew, that he readily obeyed the calling of thy Son Jesus Christ, and followed him without delay."
"Per Christum Dominum nostrum qui beato Andreæ in prima vocatione dedit fidem, et in passione dedit victoriam." Miss. Gothicum, Mabillon de Lit. Gal. p. 221.

[w] Miss Sar. Sanctor. fol. 2 MS. Leofr 202. Comes Pamel. p. 56.

[x] This epistle, according to the Sarum rubric, was taken from the "commune unius Apostoli;" and the rule was adopted by the revisers and translators of our liturgy. Miss. Sar. in die Sancti Thomæ Apostoli Sanctorale, fol. iii. and Commune, fol. i.

[y] Miss. Sar. in die Sancti Thomæ Sanctorale, fol. iiii.

the world; Grant, we beseech thee, that we, having his wonderful conversion in remembrance, may shew forth our thankfulness unto thee for the same, by following the holy doctrine which he taught; through Jesus Christ our Lord. *Amen.*

ejus ad te exempla gradiamus. Per[z].

FOR THE EPISTLE. Acts ix. 1. Lectio Actuum Apostolorum ix. Saulus adhuc spirans minarum et cædis .... affirmans quoniam hic est Christus[a].

THE GOSPEL. St. Matthew xix. 27. Secundum Mattheum xix. Dixit Symon Petrus ad Jesum ecce nos relinquimus omnia .... et vitam æternam possidebit[b].

THE PURIFICATION OF ST. MARY THE VIRGIN.

THE COLLECT. Almighty and everliving God, we humbly beseech thy Majesty, that as thy only begotten Son was this day presented in the temple in substance of our flesh, so we may be presented unto thee with pure and clean hearts, by the same thy Son Jesus Christ our Lord. *Amen.*

Omnipotens sempiterne Deus, Majestatem tuam supplices exoramus, ut sicut unigenitus Filius tuus hodierna die cum nostræ carnis substantia in templo est præsentatus, ita nos facias purificatis tibi mentibus præsentari. Per eundem Dominum[c].

---

[z] Miss. Sar. in Conversione Sancti Pauli Sanctor. fol. vi. Miss. Ambros. Pamel. tom. i. p. 322. Greg. Sacr. Menard p. 22. MS. Leofr. 164. See a very ancient collect in the Alexandrian liturgy, entitled, "Oratio post Apostoli seu Paulinæ Epistolæ lectionem," which recognises several of the same circumstances as our collect does. Renaudot, Liturg. Oriental. tom. i. Liturgia S. Basilii, p. 6.

[a] Miss. Sar. fol. vi. Sanctor. MS. Leofr. 164. Comes Pamel. p. 40.

[b] Ibid.

[c] Miss. Sar. Sanctorale, fol. ix. Purificatio beatæ Mariæ. Gregorii Sacr. Menard. p. 24. MS. Leofr. fol. 76. The original form, before the improvements of Gregory, is to be seen in Gelasii Sacram. Muratori, tom. i. p. 639.

CHAP. III. *Originals of the English Collects, &c.* 359

FOR THE EPISTLE. Mal. iii. 1. Lectio Malachiæ Prophetæ iii. Ecce mitto Angelum meum . . . sicut dies sæculi et sicut anni antiqui[d].

THE GOSPEL. St. Luke ii. 22. Secundum Lucam ii. Postquam impleti sunt dies purgationis Mariæ . . . . et gloria plebis tuæ Israel[e].

SAINT MATTHIAS'S DAY.

FOR THE EPISTLE. Acts i. 15. Lectio Actuum Apostolorum, primo. Exurgens Petrus in medio fratrum dixit . . . . et annumeratus est cum undecim Apostolis[f].

THE GOSPEL. St. Matth. xi. 25. Secundum Mattheum xi. In illo tempore respondens Jesus dixit, Confitebor tibi Pater, Domine cœli et terræ . . . . et onus meum leve[g].

ANNUNCIATION OF THE BLESSED VIRGIN MARY.

THE COLLECT. We beseech thee, O Lord, pour thy grace into our hearts; that, as we have known the incarnation of thy Son Jesus Christ by the message of an angel, so by his cross and passion we may be brought unto the glory of his resurrection; through the same Jesus Christ our Lord. *Amen.*

Gratiam tuam, quæsumus Domine mentibus nostris infunde; ut qui angelo nuntiante Christi Filii tui incarnationem cognovimus, per passionem ejus et crucem ad resurrectionis gloriam perducamur Qui tecum vivit et regnat Deus[h].

FOR THE EPISTLE. Isaiah vii. 10. Lectio Isaiæ Prophetæ vii. Locutus est Dominus ad Achaz dicens, Pete sibi signum . . . . ut sciat reprobare malum et eligere bonum[1]

THE GOSPEL. St. Luke i. 26. Secundum Lucam, primo. Missus est angelus Gabriel a Deo in civitatem Galileæ . . . . fiat mihi secundum verbum tuum[j].

---

[d] Miss. Sar. Sanctorale, fol. ix. Comes Pamel. p. 8.
[e] Ibid.
[f] Miss. Sar. Sancti Matthæi Apostoli Sanctor. fol. xi.
[g] Miss. Sar. Sanctor. fol. xi

[h] Miss. Sar. Annunciatio Mariæ. Post Communion. Sanctor. fol. xiii. Gregorii Sacr. p. 31. Menard. MS. Leofr. fol. 77.
[1] Miss. Sar. fol. xiii. Sanctor.
[j] Ibid

SAINT MARK'S DAY.

THE EPISTLE. Ephes. iv. 7. Ad Ephesios iiii. Unicuique nostrum data est gratia . . . . in mensuram ætatis plenitudinis Christi [k].

THE GOSPEL. St. John xv. 1. Secundum Joannem xv. Ego sum vitis vera . . . quodcunque volueritis petetis et fiet vobis [l].

SAINT PHILIP AND SAINT JAMES'S DAY.

THE GOSPEL. St. John xiv. 1. Secundum Joannem xiv. Dixit Jesus discipulis suis. Non turbetur cor vestrum . . . . et quodcunque petieritis Patrem in nomine meo hoc faciam [m].

SAINT BARNABAS THE APOSTLE.

THE GOSPEL. St. John xv. 12. Secundum Joannem xv. Hoc est præceptum meum ut diligatis invicem . . . et quodcunque petieritis Patrem in nomine meo, det vobis [n].

SAINT JOHN BAPTIST'S DAY.

FOR THE EPISTLE. Isaiah xl. 1. Lectio Isaiæ Prophetæ xl. Consolamini, consolamini, populus meus, dicit Deus vester . . . et opus illius coram eo [o].

THE GOSPEL. St. Luke i. 57. Secundum Lucam primo. Elizabeth impletum est tempus pariendi . . . . quia visitavit et fecit redemptionem plebis suæ [p].

SAINT PETER'S DAY.

FOR THE EPISTLE. Acts xii. 1. Lectio Actuum Apostolorum xii. In diebus illis misit Herodes . . . . et de omni expectatione plebis Judæorum [q].

---

[k] Miss. Sar. in die Sancti Marci Evangelistæ Sanctor. fol. xv.

[l] By Sarum rubric, this gospel was taken from the "Vigilia unius Apostoli vel Evangelistæ," in the "Commune Sanctorum." Miss. Sar. in S. Marci Evang. Sanctor. fol. xv. et Commune, fol. 1.

[m] Miss. Sar. in die Apostolorum Philippi et Jacobi Sanctorale, fol. xv. MS. Leofr. 169.

[n] Miss. Sar. in die S. Barnabæ Apostoli Sanctor. fol. xix.

[o] Lectionarium Gallicum, in festivitate Joannis Baptistæ, Mabill. Lit. Gall. p. 158.

[p] Miss. Sar. in die S Joannis Baptistæ, fol. xxii. Sanctorale. MS. Leofr. 175. Comes Pamel. p. 38.

[q] Miss. Sar. in die SS Apost. Petri et Pauli Sanctorale, fol

CHAP. III. *Originals of the English Collects, &c.* 361

THE GOSPEL. St. Matthew xvi. 13. Secundum Mattheum xvi. Venit Jesus in partes Cæsareæ .... erit solutum et in cœlis[r].

SAINT JAMES THE APOSTLE.

THE GOSPEL. St. Matthew xx. 20. Secundum Mattheum xx. Accessit ad Jesum mater filiorum Zebedæi .... sed quibus paratum est a Patre meo[s].

SAINT BARTHOLOMEW THE APOSTLE.

THE COLLECT. O Almighty and everlasting God, who didst give to thine Apostle Bartholomew grace truly to believe and to preach thy Word; Grant, we beseech thee, unto thy Church, to love that Word which he believed, and both to preach and receive the same; through Jesus Christ our Lord. Amen.

Omnipotens sempiterne Deus, qui hujus diei venerandam sanctamque lætitiam in beati Bartholomæi Apostoli tui festivitate tribuisti; Da Ecclesiæ tuæ quæsumus et amare quod credidit, et prædicare quod docuit. Per Dominum nostrum[t].

FOR THE EPISTLE. Acts v. 12. Lectio Actuum Apostolorum v. Per manus Apostolorum fiebant signa .... afferentes ægros et vexatos a spiritibus immundis, qui curabantur omnes[u].

THE GOSPEL. St. Luke xxii. 24. Secundum Lucam xxii. Facta est contentio inter discipulos Jesu .... judicantes duodecim tribus Israel[v].

SAINT MATTHEW THE APOSTLE

THE GOSPEL. St. Matthew ix. 9 Secundum Mattheum ix. Cum transiret Jesus videt hominum sedentem .... non enim veni vocare justos sed peccatores[w]

---

xxiii. MS. Leofr. 178. Comes Pamel. tom ii. p. 40.

[r] Miss. Sar. Sanctorale, fol. xxiii. et Commune, fol. ii. MS. Leofr. 178. Comes Pamel. p. 40.

[s] Miss Sar. in die S. Jacobi Apostoli Sanctor. fol. xxix.

[t] Miss. Sar. in die Sancti Bartholomei Apstoli Sanctor. fol. xxxvi. Gregorii Sacr. Me-

nard. p. 125. MS. Leofr. fol 187.

[u] Miss. Sar. Sanctorale, fol. xxxvi. et Commune unius Apostoli, fol. 1.

[v] Miss. Sar. ibid. et Commune, fol. 2.

[w] Miss. Sar. in die Sanct Matthæi Apostoli, fol. xliiii Sanctor. Comes Pamel. p. 49.

SAINT MICHAEL AND ALL ANGELS.

The Collect. O everlasting God, who hast ordained and constituted the services of Angels and men in a wonderful order; Mercifully grant, that as thy holy Angels always do thee service in heaven, so by thy appointment they may succour and defend us on earth; through Jesus Christ our Lord. *Amen.*

Deus, qui miro ordine Angelorum ministeria hominumque dispensas; concede propitius, ut quibus tibi ministrantibus in cœlo semper assistitur, ab his in terra vita nostra muniatur[x].

The Gospel. St Matthew xviii. 1. Secundum Mattheum xviii. In illo tempore accederunt discipuli ad Jesum dicentes, Quis putas major est in regno cœli . . . . semper vident faciem Patris mei qui in cœlis est[y].

SAINT LUKE THE EVANGELIST.

The Gospel. St. Luke x. 1. Secundum Lucam x. Designavit Dominus et alios septuaginta duos . . . . dignus est enim operarius mercede sua[z].

SAINT SIMON AND SAINT JUDE, APOSTLES.

The Gospel. St. John xv. 17. Secundum Joannem xv. Hæc mando vobis ut diligatis invicem . . . . sed ut adimpleatur sermo qui in lege eorum scriptus est, quia odio habuerunt me gratis[a].

ALL SAINTS' DAY.

For the Epistle. Rev. vii. 2. Lectio libri Apocalypsis beati Joannis Apostoli vii. Ecce ego Joannes vidi alterum Angelum

---

[x] Miss. Sar. in festo Sancti Michaelis Archangeli Sanctor fol. xliii. Gregorii Sacr Menard. p. 135. MS Leofr. fol. 194.

[y] Miss. Sar. Sanctorale, fol xliii. Comes Pamel. p. 47.

[z] Miss. Sar Sancti Lucæ Evangelistæ Sanctorale, fol. xlvii. et Commune "in Natali unius Evangelistæ," fol. 2

[a] Miss. Sar. in die Apostolorum Symon et Judæ Sanctorale, fol xlviii. et Commune unius Apostoli, fol 1. Comes Pamel. p. 54.

ascendentem ab ortu solis . . . . et fortitudo Deo nostro in sæcula sæculorum. Amen [b].

THE GOSPEL. St. Matthew v. 1. Secundum Mattheum v. Videns turbas Jesus ascendit in montem et cum sedisset . . . . quoniam merces vestra copiosa est in cœlis [c].

---

[b] Miss. Sar. in die Omnium Sanctorum, fol. xlix Sanctor
[c] Miss. Sar. fol. xlix. in die Omnium Sanctorum, et Commune plurimorum Martyrum, fol. vi

END OF VOL. I.

www.ingramcontent.com/pod-product-compliance
Lightning Source LLC
Chambersburg PA
CBHW072132220426
43664CB00013B/2220